You Know Me

Published in 2010 by Ebury Press, an imprint of Ebury Publishing • A Random House Group Company
• Text copyright © You're Not Famous LLP 2010 • Robert P. Williams and Chris Heath have asserted their
right to be identified as the authors of this Work in accordance with the Copyright,
Designs and Patents Act 1988

Addresses for companies within the Random House Group can be found at www.randomhouse.co.uk
• A CIP catalogue record for this book is available from the British Library

The Random House Group Limited supports The Forest Stewardship Council (FSC), the leading
international forest certification organisation. All our titles that are printed on Greenpeace approved
FSC certified paper carry the FSC logo. Our paper procurement policy can be found at www.rbooks.co.uk/
environment • To buy books by your favourite authors and register for offers visit www.rbooks.co.uk

Design by Two Associates • Project editing by Emma Marriott • Colour origination by XY Digital •
Cover photograph by Julian Broad

Printed and bound by Firmengruppe APPL, aprinta druck, Wemding, Germany • ISBN 9780091939014

1 3 5 7 9 10 8 6 4 2

© Mixed Sources
Product group from well-managed
forests, controlled sources and
recycled wood or fibre
www.fsc.org   Cert no. SGS-COC-004238
FSC   © 1996 Forest Stewardship Council

You Know Me

Robbie Williams
Chris Heath

EBURY
PRESS

Contents |

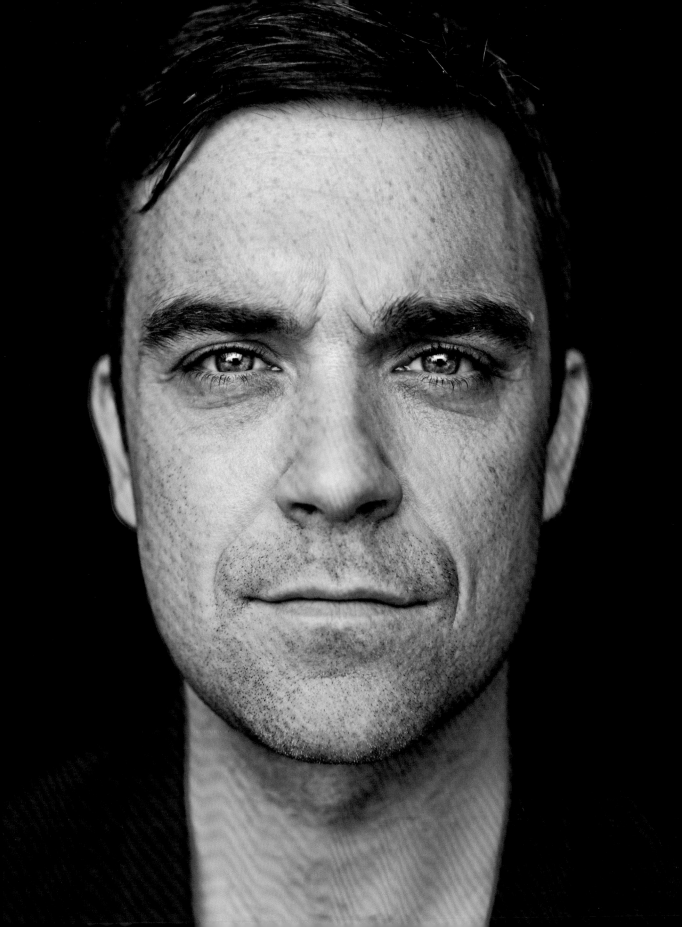

FOREWORD

For the last twenty years – ever since a sixteen-year-old boy called Robert Peter Williams, fresh from a short and disastrous double-glazing apprenticeship, joined a boy band and was told his new name – he has been Robbie Williams. And here, laid out in front of him in his Los Angeles home, is the photographic evidence.

Twenty years of singing, songwriting and performing. Twenty years of adventure and mischief, hiding and self-exposure, triumph and mishap, uncertainty and irrepressibility, all staring back at him. To be honest, for him it's a little odd. He is not the kind of man who surrounds himself with photographs that remind him who he is and what he has done. He is baffled when he visits someone else's house to discover that they have decorated it with multiple images of themselves. So he finds it strange, and surprising, to do what he is now doing. To spend weeks looking at photographs of Robbie Williams, and remembering who he has been.

We are all separated from who we once were. By time. By our own best or worst efforts. By biology. By fate – or, if you prefer, the random aggregation of events that impact each one of us differently. But for the famous, there are other kinds of separation. There are all the ways in which who you are – and so who you were – is distorted as it is reflected back at you by the world. There are also the ways – through performance, acting, self-mythologising, self-protection and so on – in which you do your very best to distort who you are. (To succeed as an entertainer, and to be beloved, seems to require a delicate, curious and individual balancing act between the parallel skills of being who you are and being who you are not.)

To look back across everything that has separated us from our former selves can be unnerving for any of us, but for the famous maybe more so. Especially as, for the famous, photographs have so many more uses and misuses. They are not just visual memos – they are part of how you invent yourself, they are part of how you sell yourself, they are part of how you are harassed, and they are part of how you are judged.

So when he takes the time to look back over the twenty years he has been photographed as Robbie Williams, there is occasionally the fond rush that comes when a buried happy memory is triggered and exhumed, but as a rule his reactions are more complicated – the kind of reactions that feed this book's content, but also to some extent form its subject.

After one particularly long day reflecting on the escapades, glories and missteps of someone who looks exactly like him, but younger, he notes this:

'It's like it happened to someone else.'

He knows very well that it didn't. But I also think he needs to remind us, and himself, that it did.

* * *

This February, Robbie Williams appeared as the closing act at the 2010 Brit Awards. He was there to receive the Outstanding Contribution to Music Award (his fifteenth Brit Award) and to perform a medley of songs that have lit his path. Earlier that day, a man came up to him. The man was about the same age as he was – Rob had turned 36 three days earlier. Rob didn't recognise him until the man explained where and when they had last met. It was twenty years ago, in the Manchester offices of the manager, Nigel Martin-Smith, who was putting together the teen band that became Take That. Rob and this other man had both applied and been granted interviews. Rob had travelled up from Stoke. This meeting would determine whether he – and the other hopefuls – would be invited to audition.

Rob's application letter was mostly written by his mother, but the sentiment expressed at its end had been his own:

I only have one ambition, which is: TO BE FAMOUS.

He points out that in 1990 this wasn't quite as gauche, grasping and empty as it might seem nowadays. 'In the last decade or so, it's become so sinister wanting to be famous. There was a time when being famous meant that you were good at something.' After consideration, he adds, 'Or you'd killed someone.'

Still, he doesn't pretend that the dreams of his sixteen-year-old self were more sophisticated than they were: 'He just wanted a white Porsche. To be able to pick his mate up in a white Porsche. It didn't go beyond that really. Why wouldn't you want that? When the map before you doesn't seem that inspiring? I'd been told by my careers teacher to join the army. That wasn't something that I wanted.'

All of Rob's most obvious skills were in entertainment, and he had been working hard on them: 'It meant a great deal to me when

I was a kid. I spent a lot of time fashioning some kind of talent, being in the amateur operatic society, auditioning and singing when I could. I was reasonably good at it. I did *The King and I*, *Chitty Chitty Bang Bang*, and *Fiddler on the Roof*.' A version of the showbusiness dream had instilled itself within him from early on: 'My dad was my hero, and he found showbiz intoxicating. He'd talk about Frank Sinatra like he was a deity. And I think somewhere in your subconscious that rubs off on you – that these people live in a very special place. You know, how impressive they all are. The way my dad still talks about them: as legends of our time. They are his modern deities. And they kind of became mine.'

While waiting to hear whether he had the audition, Rob joined his father where he was working in a Carmarthen holiday camp. In the evenings he remembers dancing at the club on the camp grounds to New Kids on the Block's 'Tonight'. 'I'd think, "I'm going to be a New Kid on the Block!"' he reminisces, 'the endorphins kicking in, being lost in the fantasy that I might be part of that world.' He sings to me now the lines he'd sing to himself back then as he'd pretend to live their dream and imagine it as his own.

The man Rob met at the Brits never got the call. He was never asked to the Take That audition. (He now works in radio.)

Rob did.

This is a book about the consequences of that call.

* * *

At the beginning of chapter one is a photograph of Rob on the very day he received that call. On the day it all started. There are all kinds of ways to look at this photograph – and of all the photographs that follow, as each new improbable episode plays out. Each is now locked into the history of what did happen, but only in retrospect. There is

another way of looking at any photo in this book. You can stare at
that first shot, for instance, and at the pre-pop star confidence the
teenager in it seems to be oozing, and wonder this: was that sixteen-
year-old on the beach always destined to become Robbie Williams
with all that has come to mean? Was it already all inside him, and
– even if that particular call had never come – would he always have
somehow, somewhere found a way to let it out?

And if not then, was there a moment later on when that path
was set? Linger for a moment over any photo of Take That and ask
yourself: was, by this point, all the rest of this inevitable? Or was it
never inevitable, not until the final photo in this book was taken?
Photographs draw their power from what they show, but also
from what they cannot. They enchant us by seeming to offer pure
witness to what actually happened, but also by showing us a frozen
moment; a moment that prompts us to consider what happened to
the photograph's subject after the photograph was taken – not just
in the moment after, but the weeks and months and years. They
goad us to think about what happens when the photograph's subject
unfreezes and steps out of the frame into the unknown. By stopping
time, they remind us that a story of someone's life is also a reminder
of all its dodged disasters and missed opportunities, of the other
lives not lived.

One way to consider this book is as a book of around 250
pictures of Robbie Williams captured on film. But there is another
way to see it too: as around 250 pictures of Robbie Williams, just as
he is on the verge of escaping.

* * *

'Everything in this book is done,' he reflects. 'Literally is done.' More
than that. There are moments in life that release us, moments when

our future opens up. 'I know it's my past and it's done anyway, but it does feel as though it is the end of something.'

Twenty years: twenty years of progress and setbacks, highways and loops and cul-de-sacs, frustration and resolution, innovation and repetition, celebrity and drudgery and glory and calumny, self-destruction and deliverance, overreaction and forbearance, peacockery and laying low, dead-ends and epiphanies. Of searching for the right balance between growing up and gloriously refusing to grow up. Twenty years since he announced his quest to find fame above all. The shape our past makes as it stretches backwards from each of us changes all of the time, largely dependent on where we are as we look back, and by what we see coming in our future. Rob talks as though his recent years have been ones of uncertainty. He often mentions the damage he still feels from his long, record-breaking 2006 tour. He likes to tell how, in the years that followed, he became a hermit, though – as chapter seven will show – it was more complicated and colourful than that, and these would also be the years when he formed by far the longest attachment of his adult life.

By the time he released a new record, *Reality Killed The Video Star*, in the autumn of 2009, it was greeted as a comeback, a narrative he at first resisted, then embraced and triumphantly rode its wave home. As a collection of songs, he was deeply proud of that album, but as far as indicating a way forward he seemed less sure. But now he once more sees a shape, a direction, a momentum, a path onwards. That first ambition – to be famous – was quickly satisfied and moved beyond. Now what he wants sounds simpler, though the answers life provides rarely match the simplicity of the largest questions we ask.

'If I was writing that letter now, it would be: my ambition is to be fulfilled,' he says. 'And my ambitions are being fulfilled.'

1

'... the ones where we all laugh...'

When I arrive today, he is in the basement gym with his girlfriend, Ayda, and his trainer. His iPod, plugged into the gym speakers, is playing his favourite Pet Shop Boys album *Behaviour*. 'Being Boring' has just started. Its first line rings out:

I came across a cache of old photos...

It seems appropriate.

A short while later, I spread out a sheaf of images from his boy band youth. The beginning. Sometimes he pauses to tell me that he can remember more or less nothing, and perhaps it feels like that to him, but it seems to me that when it comes to the things that matter he can remember everything.

More than that, it often seems as if he remembers things as though they have only just happened and he is reacting to them still.

* * *

Eight years ago, this particular conversation would have been very different. While there were always occasional flickers of warm nostalgia when he thought back to Take That, these were usually dwarfed by his negative memories, and by the shadow of the enduring estrangement that had resulted.

At times the scars showed. Whenever I heard him giving advice to anyone younger in the music world, he would usually focus on the same point: superficially his message to them would be about not allowing themselves to be driven too hard, but its implication was that they shouldn't get in a position where their views, needs, feelings and wellbeing were ignored. What he really seemed to be saying was: *don't let them do to you what they did to me*.

If things have changed, it is not so much that he feels differently about his Take That years, but that he certainly feels differently about his former band members. The first time the five of them got together after many years, at the Chelsea Harbour Hotel in 2006, a few bridges were mended, but only somewhat.

'It was weird, and lovely,' he recalls. All that history. 'I'd got a lot of unresolved stuff with Gary that stopped me from really enjoying the moment, although I did really, really enjoy being with the boys and laughing, and being in a hotel room with them and kicking back.'

The real sea change came in 2008. The revitalised four-piece Take That were in Los Angeles, recording what would become their album *The Circus*. 'We had a great meeting at their hotel,' Rob remembers, 'and then they came up to mine the next night. Gaz and I sat down and I said, "This is why I've said what I said, and this is why I've thought what I thought," and it seemed that we were both mature enough to be in the right place to hear it.'

For years before, Rob had taunted Gary Barlow relentlessly in public. 'There was a long period of really, really not liking him because of the person that I thought he was when he was younger. And even when the anger died down, it became part of my schtick. It became something that I did without even thinking about it. I'm not a monk. I'm a human, and forgiveness doesn't come that naturally to people. To anybody. And I found it very difficult to forgive. He was part of some broken teenage years, and he was the figurehead for a lot of it.'

But after that meeting, and whatever private words and feelings were shared, something had been almost magically mended.

'I couldn't fucking believe it,' says Rob. 'I felt with Gaz like I'd never felt in Take That: I got him, and he got me. It was fucking lovely. There's me from Stoke and him from Frodsham and we got to a very, very happy medium very quickly. And it was beautiful. I didn't realise how much of a weight it was on my shoulders – all the things that had been left unsaid from a major part of my life. It's fantastic not to have that now. I'm so glad that we sorted it out, because I could still be going around pontificating about a man who doesn't exist any more. You know, he's just a different Gary Barlow now.'

*　*　*

Rob reads to me from a series of emails he has been exchanging with Jason Orange, recreating a long telephone call he and Jason had in 2006. It was a discussion about whether Rob might consider even momentarily rejoining his band mates onstage, which had then spiralled into a fairly heavy debate about the different ways in which they saw the world, and in particular the career of Robbie Williams. At one point Rob has written this:

> *I wish I could be the person you thought I was. I wish I had no vulnerabilities. I wish that my sense of self was impervious to silly baseless judgements from outside sources, but I'm not. I've spent many years in therapy trying, and lots of medication to help... but at the end of the day I'm just a sensitive soul. My sensitivity has also been the driving force behind what's made me so successful. It's the yin and yang of life. What helps me hurts me, and what hurts me helps me.*

'Jay's a great sounding board,' says Rob, 'and he makes you look at things differently, more so than anybody I've ever met. He's a hippie, basically.'

He adds that now all five of them talk again, he realises that in their own ways they each have their issues, their own uncertainties. 'We all think we're shit,' he says, 'apart from Gaz, who doesn't think he's ace, but he's quite happy in his own shoes. Gaz is so black and white: "Gaz, I hurt when things are said..." "Who cares?... It makes me feel sorry for them when they say that... Why would you even take it on board?" He can swat things away.'

* * *

The day after their Los Angeles summit – or, as Rob puts it, 'me and Gary having an epiphany' – Rob went to a tattoo parlour. He wanted a new tattoo: the Take That symbol, two mirror-image 'T's inside a circle, on the outer part of his right wrist. 'I was thinking that it's a part of my life that had great sadness attached to it that had done a 180 and become something different and something beautiful and something really lovely, and the hidden part of me that was immensely proud of what we achieved came to the forefront now that everything was alright. You know, it's a demon slayed, as far as I'm concerned. Putting it right. Anger and aggression serves no purpose really other than self-destruction, and it was self-destructive to think and feel the way I did about my time there.'

That evening, at his house, he proudly showed his former band mates what he had done. I have heard him tell several versions of their response:

'They all just went, "What've you done that for?", and then didn't mention it again.'

'They looked at me like I was a dick.'

'And they all just went, "You're mental."'

What he says to me is this:

'I'm sure they thought it was a mixture of brilliant and daft. As I do, too.'

* * *

What was once unthinkable is now possible.

In the autumn of 2009 Gary Barlow was holidaying in Malibu. Rob invited him up for a quiz night at his house, and at the end of the evening suggested they get together to write something. ('Get your ballad fingers on, Gaz, let's do a song,' is how Rob remembers pitching it.) They agreed to meet in Malibu. A writer from British *GQ*, Alex Bilmes, who had been writing about Rob ahead of the release of *Reality Killed The Video Star*, was also at the quiz night. 'Alex from *GQ* was leaving at the same time as him,' says Rob, 'and asked Gaz, "What did you think of that?", and Gaz was like, "I don't even bloody know if he'll turn up – you never know with him."'

But Rob did. Gary already had some music prepared; by the time Ayda and Gary's wife Dawn had returned from a Malibu shopping trip, the song was finished. 'Shame', a duet. They sung it on a microphone plugged into the computer.

'It became the story of us,' says Rob. 'It's two people spending a lot of time together, falling out outrageously, spending a lot of time not liking each other, and then realising through the folly and the hubris of youth that maybe we'd got it wrong. It was one of those songs that come every now and again that kind of make you cry as you're writing it.'

It is planned as his next single. And if that could happen, who knows what else might follow?

'It has that lovely symmetry,' says Rob, 'as the song is about healing and it is the healing.'

* * *

Tell me a story where we all change...

That is how Rob began 'No Regrets', his sad, bitter, ironic, heartbroken, spiteful, loving song about his boy band years, written at a time when he surely imagined the story he was requesting was one that he would never come to hear. Let alone that new chapters might begin to unfold.

Remember this when he talks about the hurt. If he needs to be honest about the hurt, and honest in a way that is sometimes still harsh and raw nearly two decades on, perhaps it's because the hurt still feels fresh too. And if he is not honest about the hurt that was there at the start, even as he remembers all that was joyous, too, then how could anyone else begin to make sense of all that has happened in its wake? Never mind Rob.

The healing is a part of the same story – a happy part of the story, but not a part that cancels out all that has gone before it. For the point of healing is to heal the hurt, not to hide it.

Carmarthen | 1990

'On the beach in Wales, at Kidwelly, the holiday camp Dad was working at. I'm doing a good model impression there. I borrowed the glasses off one of the bluecoats. That's the orange Naf Naf top I used to have with Naf Naf in felt down the side. A good mate of mine, Richard Kirkham, who I was at school with and share the same birthday with, his sister wanted that Naf Naf top off me at the time, and I promised I'd give it to her but I've since lost it, so I apologise. This was the day I found out that I'd got the audition for the band. My mum had called and I was about to leave the holiday early. At the auditions there were only six of us – the sixth person that didn't make it had Dr Martens on and was into Morrissey. He didn't stay very long. It was scary. Tense. Nervous. I didn't find anybody too friendly, apart from Mark. I got on with Mark because we were roughly the same age. But the beginning bits were really tough, really scary. I used to get a lot of bollockings because I wasn't learning the routines quick enough. My God was I made to feel like I was letting people down. I wanted to learn them but I just wasn't as quick as the other lads. And the first few months I was told that I needed to lose two stone. I used to come home and cry a lot. A few months in, I wanted to leave. I just wasn't getting on with anybody apart from Mark. I found it really unfriendly, and I found myself being an outsider which I'd never been before. I was singled out an awful lot and it really affected me. So I went to see my dad to get me a job as a bluecoat. He said, "I could do that... but you're not being on a camp with me – you have to do your own ironing, your own washing, you work twelve hours a day, you get paid fuck all..." And he also said, "When they're number one you'll really regret that decision." So I thought I'd stay and stick it out. The right decision? Oh yeah. Just a bit.'

Manchester | 1990

'I remember that suit. Phil Black Luomo. My mum bought me that suit for my Christmas present. For the first eighteen months of Take That, all we did was gay clubs, all the way round Britain. I assume that's what our manager, Nigel Martin-Smith, thought our market was, because when we did our first 'under 18s' gig in Hull, where they went fucking mental, I remember that he was a bit reluctant to push it that way. I enjoyed the gay clubs. All of a sudden you're in a world of men being nice to other men, and you don't have to worry about your head being kicked in. Gay people also know how to go out. So it's a very hedonistic, happy world for those few hours the nightclub's open. For our performances, I would wear a unitard with big black pit boots. There used to be this gay club in Manchester, and downstairs was this place called the Mineshaft. It was very dark down there and I didn't dare go down, but I thought, "We must wear what people who go down there wear."'

Photo session | 1991

'The three old ones have got silver studs, the two young ones haven't. When the three big boys aren't letting you in, it's hard. Jay thought I was a geek, he's since told me. He was very flippant towards me. Howard was very quiet. And Gary couldn't understand why there were four other people with him. Gary was single-minded back then, and bloody-minded. He wasn't a very sensitive soul, Gaz: he's very black and white, there's no sort of grey areas. And I didn't like him for it. If somebody resents you being there, you resent them for that. But he did save me once. We were in a van going up to Scotland to do the *Disney Club*, after Nigel had been away for a couple of weeks. Nigel said something and from nowhere I just went, "Oh, fuck off, Nigel." And as it left my mouth, I thought: "I just really fucked up... oh my God, I just said that." I was really scared. And Gaz went, "Oh, since you went away, Rob's developed a sense of humour, Nige," and it defused the situation. He saved me that day. He really did. He could have just left me out to die, but he didn't.'

'Do What U Like' video | 1991

'Our first video shoot. It wasn't until I was going out with Ayda when I showed her this for the first time that she pointed out that there was something wrong about a naked sixteen-year-old on film with his arse out, writhing naked on the floor with four other boys. Great day, though. Really good day. Good fun. I think it appealed to my naturist self. I just enjoyed being naked in front of a lot of people. This was the video where Nigel charged us a tenner each to buy a copy of it. And we did. I can remember getting the videotape and playing it to family and then I remember friends coming round and me not playing it to them. To family, it was: "I've got a video!" But to people who could judge me, I was thinking: "Fuck no, I'm naked and there's jelly and it's weird..."'

Photo session | 1991

'For the *Sun*, I think. It's the stage of: yeah, we'll do that. We wouldn't question it. We'd probably done another two photo sessions that morning for *My Guy* and *No 1* magazine. It's the classic thing that boy bands do: try to look hard when something silly is set up around them. I was designated "the cheeky one" early on because I was. Those characters were forming anyway, and then Nigel decided that it was his idea. Before interviews, he'd go: "Right, Jason, you be the studious one. Gary, you be the one that talks about music. Robbie, you be the cheeky one..." And one day in a meeting he told Gary and Mark that they'd met at a recording studio where Mark was doing the tea and they'd formed a band called The Cutest Rush; he told Howard and Jason that they had been in the same dance group; and he told me that I'd had a role on *Brookside* and that I was brought into the group as an afterthought. That was to be our story. It was a brainwashing of a sort, I suppose. And he told me that my name was being changed from Rob to Robbie.'

How did you feel about being told you were now Robbie?

'I hated that name. I thought it was twee, and I wanted to be hard and cool. I didn't want to be soft and girlie. I'd rather him have given me a new name completely. At the time I probably would have said "Maximilian". Though I think Robbie was a wiser choice.'

Had people ever called you Robbie before that?

'Just one girl, Kelly, who was a year older than me, and who I did a show or two with, and who I really fancied. I think we kissed and had a snog and all that business, but I think that ultimately she called me Robbie because she saw me as being way younger than her: "little Robbie".'

So did you always associate the name with being slightly patronised?

'Yes. Which I suppose means that I've been slightly patronised for the last twenty years.'

But have you come to accept that that is what the person who makes the records is called?

'Not really. For some reason it still irks me when people call me Robbie – not all the time, but every now and again it will cause a twinge.'

So when you see it on the cover of each new album, what do you think?

'I think: "That's not my name." But I think it's definitely better than "Rob" or "Robert" as a pop name.'

Rehearsals | 1992

'Bollockings were continuing. We'd all get a bollocking as a group, and then there'd
be a singled-out bollocking for me, all the fucking time. You know, we were all really
desperate, we all really wanted it to work. Nobody was taking the piss. Or being sloppy.
If any sloppiness came from me at this point, it wasn't because I was unprofessional,
it was because I was just finding it difficult to take things on board. And giving me a
bollocking wasn't going to change it. It affected me for a long time. Still, there was a
point where we'd been around the country so many times and everywhere we went
girls went mental and you got the feeling that we were onto something. We did in-store
signings, and thousands were turning up, and that was pretty incredible. It was just
very, very, very exciting – being taken out of record signings by the police and put into
the back of a police van for our safety and everybody else's safety. And these in-store
signings did the trick. We got "It Only Takes A Minute" to number six. A momentous
day. And then we were away.'

On tour | 1992

'What an extremely silly hat. I look like a crusty. Or a fire-eater. I also had a gold-plated dummy then. Ravers were wearing dummies at the time and I adopted it as my thing, naughty because it had connections with ecstasy and acid. The tabloids hadn't moved up in temperature towards celebrities at that point, so you could get away with an awful lot more then. And I subsequently did for years. During the five years of being in Take That, nothing came out or was said, but I was quite obviously off my head in an awful lot of public places. But if it wasn't in London you weren't going to get found out. That was an incredibly exciting and euphoric time, but at the same time incredibly sad. When I went back home, I discovered that I'd become an alien to a lot of people I knew at school and grown up with. There used to be a hundred kids outside the house all the time – the curtains at the front were shut and were never opened again until we left the house years later.'

New York | 1993

'Howard Johnson's diner in Times Square. We couldn't afford the food at our hotel so we went across the road. New York was a pointless exercise. The record company just didn't know what to do with us. They sent us to urban schools and Nirvana were massive and everybody was wearing plaid shirts and being grungy, and turning their back on anything to do with pop and boy bands. And here we were: "You've got me hooked on a string!" It was just embarrassing really.'

'Sure' video | **1994**

'I'd just shaved my hair off, which I was excited about. I was rebelling, man. I'd got a scar down the front of my head and I quite liked it – I got it from Howard pushing me into a fountain in the reception of a hotel in Switzerland when I was drunk. I had to get stitches and then I went back out to a nightclub with blood down my face. I thought I was Terry Butcher. Loved it. I can remember Jay saying to me: "You know, Rob, it wasn't till you cut your hair off that I realised how pretty your face is." At the time, I really thought it was a compliment, but now I think the intention was to go: here he is, thinks he's being all hard and controversial, but he just looks pretty.'

London | 1994

'I look cool as fuck there. Love it.
That's when I was having it the
largest, and that's how I'd go out
raving. I loved my rave kilt. I wore
it when I went to Ibiza for a lost
week. Well, three days, and on the
third night I wasn't going to take
any drugs because I had to be back
at Gary's house the next day to do
backing vocals. But I drank these
drinks called Poco Locos, 30 quid
a glass, which had mescaline, acid
and ecstasy in them. I had to catch
a plane early in the morning, totally
and utterly off my head. I got to Gary
Barlow's house and everybody was
waiting for me. I went in and I put
my hands up and went, "I've found
God!" And then I collapsed and
went to sleep for 48 hours in
his bed.'

Italy | 1994

'The Versace shoot. Loved that photo shoot. I'm wearing a silver vest made out of chain link, and I am sexy as fuck there. That's as thin as I'd like to be. I'm all sinew because I've been caning it. I think that vest's in my mum's attic now. Great photos (*See also overleaf*). Howard looks incredible. We were taken to Gianni Versace's house, a very different world than we were used to. Billionaires who lived in billionaire houses with billionaire cars. I'd never seen so many cars before. We were being invited into this uber-uber-glamorous world, and the king of this world was Gianni Versace. He came over at dinner and whispered to me, "You are my favourite." I didn't tell anyone. It felt really good, though.'

Rehearsals | 1995

'Apparently, they had to shoot this again when I had gone. I can't even remember it. The problem at the end was that I just wasn't brave enough to leave by myself. I should have left before then, under my own steam, because I was just a problem for them and for me. Really bad time. I just couldn't stop drinking. Really, really sad time, too – I wasn't fit enough to rehearse because I'd get that wasted the night before. In the end, they were, "We think we're best off as a four-piece and proving that we can do it without you – what do you think?" And I was, "I think you're right, bye..." I went home and I told my mum, and she gave me a bollocking. But being in Take That gave me the best ever springboard that you could have for the solo career I've had. It also gave me an enforced work ethic – one that I've since tried to shed. And then there's what it's still to give me, which I think will be more beneficial than what it's given me already.'

2

'...live to relive the days gone by...'

In his bedroom he reclines on a lounger that sits between the balcony and where the TV rises up from the foot of his bed. He plays songs from his computer. First, something new that will probably be on this year's greatest hits album. The song starts. He's always excited to share new songs...

You've been bending so long now you feel it's standing up

As they line up behind you to build you up buttercup

... though he rarely allows them to finish before he moves onto something else. (It's a common theme in his life, a tendency to be more excited about the next thing than the current thing.)

He plays other songs – grand, sweeping, elegant ones – from what seems likely to be the project after the greatest hits:

Standing on the edge of forever

At the start of whatever

Shouting love at the world...

Some of these are nearly finished, some are rough and some don't even have vocals. When they don't have vocals, he simply sings them himself from where he is resting. Ayda lies on the bed behind, sticking her legs in the air. For one of these newer songs, he stands up and steps onto his balcony. The Los Angeles valley stretches before him, the mountains in the hazy distance behind. He dances, a water bottle in his left hand, his right arm raised. Then he walks back inside and finds a further small cluster of tunes, ones he sees as having a place even further in his future, carrying with them other new possibilities. Often, in recent years, his future plans have involved other people – he has sometimes talked about wanting to be in a group over the years, and has made various abortive attempts to make that happen – but the impulse now seems stronger than ever.

'It's been a little bit lonely,' he says. 'You do Knebworth and you've pretty much done it. Since then I've wanted to be in a band really.' The camaraderie appeals to him, and he has long been attracted by the notion of a responsibility shared. 'Doing all these colossal tours and it all being on your shoulders...' he says. 'I kind of want a bit where you're just playing the tambourine.'

And so he likes to imagine what he sees as tambourine days ahead. But today – prompted by all these images, all this looking back – he also reaches into his past. The beginning of his solo career was full of false starts when it came to songwriting. If he hadn't instinctively picked out Guy Chambers from a long list of potential collaborators presented to him then perhaps he might never have discovered how to set free what was within him.

'So easily,' he says. 'So easily... Just which side of the knife it fell on...'

Still, thinking about this inspires him to search through his iTunes for one of these false starts – maybe the first song he wrote as a solo artist, or, at the very least, the earliest song he cares enough about to have a copy of, though it has never been released. It was written with Oasis's producer, Owen Morris.

'We wrote in Wales in this cowshed,' he remembers. 'Literally – there was a desk in one bit and cows in the other bit. We thought we'd written the best songs ever. Total cocaine thinking. We'd do these songs and then we'd play them in the car on the way back and we'd be looking at each other, mouths open wide, going "Fucking hell! We're amazing! These are the best songs that have ever been written, *ever*..." And they were a pile of shit.'

Apart from one – this one: 'Go Now'.

'I'm quite fond of it,' he says, and presses play. The music is clearly influenced by New Order. Maybe the Pet Shop Boys, too. Frantic but melodic, the words cleverly tripping over each other:

> *It's obviously evident*
> *You're definitely decadent*
> *And I should know better but I don't*

* * *

'I'd lived a whole life by the time I was twenty,' he reflects. For a while, it was, at best, three steps forward, two steps back. But he mentions today that there did come a moment – a moment he can't really explain – when he simply *knew*.

'I remember doing a photo shoot around this time, in a high rise somewhere, and I remember overlooking London, and I had this quiet moment by myself, and I looked over it, and I just thought: "One day, all this is going to be mine." You know, like a film.'

He doesn't say this with excitement. Puzzlement, more like.

'It scared the life out of me,' he says. 'What scared me was the utter belief that that was going to happen. Something about that freaked me out. I thought there was something very weird about it.'

Scary that you felt like you were in the hands of destiny?

'It was kind of like I wasn't alone. It was a rush of euphoria... probably mania, at the time. I can't put my finger on what I was scared of but it did freak me out that that thought was so powerful.'

And in the way that you meant then, it came true, didn't it?

'In the way that I meant then, yeah, it did definitely come true.'

He considers the photos taken for the sleeve of his first album, *Life Thru A Lens*, a portfolio of pictures depicting a day in the life of someone far more famous than he yet was, caught by the camera as every attention was bearing down on them.

'I thought that's where I was headed,' he reflects. 'I thought that was what I wanted.'

And?

'And I was right... and I was right... and I was wrong.'

Glastonbury | 1995

'Just before the end with Take That. That afternoon, we were at the Nordoff Robbins Awards in London, and I'm not sure if they knew I was going to Glastonbury, but I did. I stole all the champagne from the tables – seven bottles – stuck them in the back of this jag, and drove down. I'd been the year before when M People were on, but it didn't cause as much of a stir because most of the time I hid on M People's tour bus. It had felt incredibly naughty – like bobbing off school or sneaking out at dinner time. This time my agenda was to go and hang out with Oasis and get off my head, and fuck the consequences. That was the first time I met Oasis. I was a big fan – they were the biggest thing in the world at the time. I remember being at the side of the stage and just enjoying it, and then Liam beckoning me with his head and me going up on stage with them and doing my best impression of Bez. Twatty dancing. I don't know which song it was. I can't remember much of the whole weekend apart from being paranoid in a catering caravan. I think I was probably at the start of a nervous breakdown. When we all went round to Gary's house for the big talk that they were going to have with me, we went in Gary's back garden and everyone sat round in a sort of powwow. I was resting back on the swing, and all of them individually talked to me – it had gone past a bollocking. I said, "Have you finished?", and they said, "Yeah", and I just lifted my feet up and pushed myself back on the swing and went, "Wheeeeeeeeeee…!" They must have hated me. They were concerned about me being a dysfunctional band member. They weren't really aware of what I was doing to myself. Because I don't think we'd been around people who had lost the plot.'

The Big Breakfast | 1995

'I got paid fifteen grand for the week to present Channel 4's *The Big Breakfast*, which was more than anybody had ever been paid for presenting the programme at the time. I don't think necessarily it was a bad idea – I didn't know what I was going to do, so it was something to fall back on. But that was a bad week. I didn't go to bed. Literally. I can remember thinking I was doing an alright job, but by the end of the week I remember Dani Behr and Keith Chegwin sort of holding me up while I was passing out behind my sunglasses. There was an interview that we had to cancel because I just couldn't speak.'

Barbados | 1996

'Eventually, the record company suggested I record George Michael's "Freedom" as my first single. It was horrific that year. The wasted year. I'm not well in this photo. I'm bloated. I've been eating all the cake. Everything I wasn't allowed to do before, I could now do. There was a time when I went to the fridge at my new flat – 550 quid a week – and I opened the fridge door and there was this Mr Kipling cake. I'd just left Take That and I'd just left my mum's house and there was this cake and I ate the whole of it. It was a massive cake – one of those with currants in that's kind of brown – and I ate it because I now could. And that was the epitome of that year: I did everything because I could, and there was nobody there to tell me no. There was nobody there to guide me. And I wouldn't have taken their guidance if they had been there and tried to intrude on my revelry. It was quite literally my own freedom. Freedom is a bit overrated – I was only free to be my own slave.'

'Freedom' video | 1996

'Miami. A video shoot that nearly didn't happen. I think I'd drunk all of the shorts out of the mini-bar an hour before I was supposed to start the filming. I was in Miami because they'd shipped me out to work with this tunesmith, Desmond Child, to give me some hits. He rubbed me up the wrong way, and the songs he'd play me were these big American-sounding radio tunes. Back then what I wanted on a record was a bit of a brawl. So I left with nothing but "Old Before I Die". On the way over on the plane, I'd seen this advert for Barclaycard or something like that, with Pete Townshend and "*Hope I die before I get old*", and I thought, "Fucking hell, I hope I'm old before I die – I'm going to switch that round."'

London | 1996

'For the cover of *Attitude* magazine. I like that picture. Publicly, I was an angry young man. That was the famous "Gary Barlow's a cunt with a briefcase" interview. I was drinking, and the more provocative and controversial I got, the more it was encouraged and smiled at and laughed at and nodded at, and it went on and it went on and it went on. I got on a roll, and then, as I said, it just became part of my schtick, particularly onstage. But I meant it at the time. From my perspective as a 21-year-old, he was just one notch below Nigel Martin-Smith, and I think people know what I think about him. For me, Gary was like his emotional henchman, and the person I thought Gary was, in my mind, deserved what I was saying. I was incredibly angry with him.'

'Old Before I Die' video | 1997

'I'd grown the beard because I wasn't in Take That, I suppose. I felt overweight then, and I didn't want anyone to see me. I was hungover, because I'd been out the night before. And I'd been out the night before that. And the night before that. And the night before that. I was physically just about young enough to get away with it, but I was killing myself. A new wave of laddish culture had invaded the British shores, the reinvention of what it was meant to be a New Lad, and I was bang up for it. I was reading *Loaded* magazine and wanted to behave as badly and as largely as the people in that magazine were. I'd read their "Rogue's Gallery" every week and was upset if I wasn't in it. It was a year of black cabs, leaving places as the sun was rising, and escalating cocaine prices as the night went on. Cocaine used to be sixty quid, then by five in the morning, it was eighty or ninety. I was kind of happy for the duration that the coke and drink lasted for, and then I was beyond miserable coming down off those substances.'

'Lazy Days' sleeve shoot | 1997

'I'm lying down because I'm hungover. It was a hot day. I went to rehab soon afterwards – I had to be let out of rehab for the day to make the video.'

London | 1997

'I remember the alleyway. It was the East End. There was a train track over the wall. I'm fresh out of rehab, lost a bit of weight. By now, something's happening around me. There's a machine around me. There's something to aim towards. I'm in the comfort of the machine. I have a direction. There's something I care about. And there's a safety in that.'

Life Thru A Lens sleeve shoot | 1997

'It was the condensed a-day-in-the-life-of-a-pop-star. A bizarre day. I was wearing Alexander McQueen. Stylistically, it looked great. I can remember thinking, "Yeah, this is going to be good." But also at the same time feeling uncomfortable that you've got to behave in a manner that's not your normal behaviour. I remember there being a very cool model who was my fake girlfriend for the day, and I didn't have the guts to flirt with her or ask her out, but I really wanted to. She was very pretty. But she showed no interest coming back my way, or at least that's how I read it. She did play backgammon with me, though.'

Paris │ 1997

'The album launch. All I can remember thinking is I was still a big deal. Lots of journalists had turned up to interview me from different countries and I was in Paris! I wasn't in London or Manchester. Back then, I was kind of quick-witted and cocky and svelte, and did an entertaining press conference.'

British tour | 1997

'I performed very often in the early days like my life depended on it. And, very much so, it did. We played Norwich University first. I was nervous before I went on because I'd never done a show by myself before, but then I got wrapped up in the energy of the room. The people in the audience were actually the people that bought the same magazines that I bought, and they weren't bottling or booing me. They were encouraging the way I portrayed myself onstage: high octane, let's-have-it... *bounce!* I just wanted people to be sweaty, and leave with their endorphins kicked in. I wanted to see a room bounce to my music. And it did. And they laughed in the right parts when I did something funny. It was like those sci-fi movies where a computer quickly learns how to be human by watching other humans, and it's that quick on the uptake that it actually becomes human – that was me figuring out how to motivate a crowd, or how to work a room.'

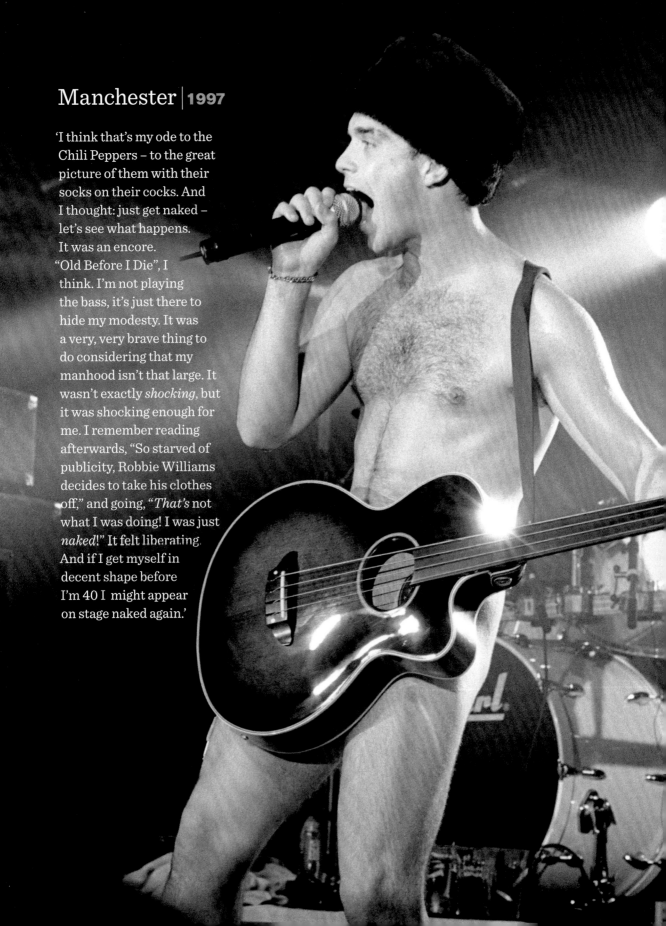

Manchester | 1997

'I think that's my ode to the Chili Peppers – to the great picture of them with their socks on their cocks. And I thought: just get naked – let's see what happens. It was an encore. "Old Before I Die", I think. I'm not playing the bass, it's just there to hide my modesty. It was a very, very brave thing to do considering that my manhood isn't that large. It wasn't exactly *shocking*, but it was shocking enough for me. I remember reading afterwards, "So starved of publicity, Robbie Williams decides to take his clothes off," and going, "*That's* not what I was doing! I was just *naked*!" It felt liberating. And if I get myself in decent shape before I'm 40 I might appear on stage naked again.'

London | 1997

'Me and Guy Chambers, for all intents and purposes, we were a band. He was just about to give everything up and become a music teacher. He was penniless and his band hadn't worked out, his roof was leaking, and all of a sudden we came into each other's lives and things turned around. It was very special coming up with that first album, because I was writing songs – I was *doing* it. And it came quite naturally, and I was very impressed with myself that I'd actually done it, regardless of where it was going to go or what it was going to do. I felt as though I was A Creative. It's a very loving, lovely photo. I love Guy. I still love Guy, and I loved him then. A brilliant, brilliant eccentric. He seemed a lot older than me and he knew all the brushstrokes. He knew the magic chords. And he cared. I was his last line of hope, I suppose. And he was my last line of hope. And we were counting on each other to pull each other through. And we did.'

'Angels' sleeve shoot | 1997

'I felt very nice in that grey suit. I was
probably at my most comfortable with
my physical image at the time. And
I always knew that I had "Angels". I
always knew that in my pocket was
this ballad that was massive. I could
feel it, and I knew it. It took two weeks
to write the whole of *Life Thru A Lens*.
We'd write three songs a day, and one of
them was "Angels", and it made Guy that
ill writing "Angels" that he had to go to
sleep straight afterwards. I remember
walking back from Holloway Road with
a tape in my hand, just staring at it,
walking through the snow. I'd planned
on walking all the way back, but I'd got
a couple of miles and it was cold so I
flagged down a taxi. And I said, "Mate,
just put this on." And he put it on and he
was listening to it and he went, "That's a
fucking number one, that is, son." And I
was, "Yeah, it is, isn't it?" Both wrong.'

'Angels' video | 1997

'Somewhere in Devon – it was beautiful down there. I
remember being in this circle and being confused by
it, thinking: "What does this *mean*? Why *is* this?" And I
remember that Vaughan Arnell, the director, was very,
very encouraging: "You're going to look cool as fuck, you're
going to look like Paul Newman, you're going to look like
Steve McQueen, you're going to look like..." And I was:
"I'm going to look like Steve McQueen!" And that's exactly
what I was thinking when I was walking along the beach:
"Fuck me! I look like Steve McQueen!" And when there's
two helicopters swirling above your head just to take
pictures of you, and you're in a lovely coat, and you're thin
and alone and lithe and young... you think you *are* Steve
McQueen for that moment.'

Top of the Pops | 1998

'*Top of the Pops* was a mainstay of my childhood and everybody's childhood who grew up in Britain during the 60s, 70s, 80s and most of the 90s. Nothing beats the first one you do, when you go in and realise how small the place is. And it was always: "Cliff Richard's next door... Rozalla's over there... that 'Size of a Cow' lead singer's a bit of a grumpy twat... he doesn't like us because we're a boy band..." I'd wander over and talk to Elastica, then you'd have Def Leppard striding down the halls and hear the stories about them paying thirty grand to get this mythical satellite feed for Sheffield United vs. Sheffield Wednesday while on tour in America and think that was amazing. I remember being told off by Take That: "You're making us all look like idiots." There's still leftovers from that: "Don't do that – they'll go off us." It's very sweet now, but at the time it was annoying. I was their little brother, and I didn't like being their little brother. I wanted to be a big boy. But what I didn't like about them first time around, I love about them now. I don't mind being Jay's little brother. He kind of still treats me like a little brother, but whereas before I'd want to punch my own weight and not be talked down to, now I could quite easily nestle into his little shoulder and have him look after me, or even talk down to me. I quite like it. He is my bigger brother.'

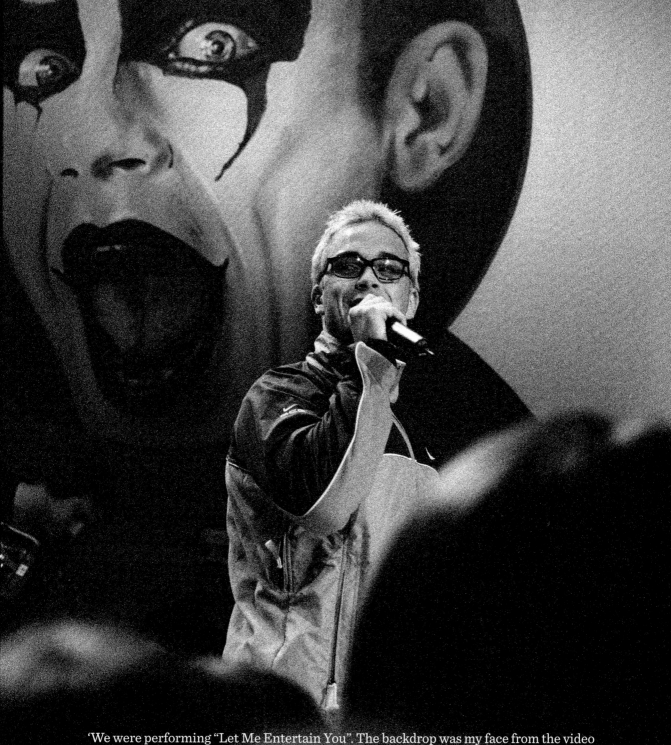

'We were performing "Let Me Entertain You". The backdrop was my face from the video shoot. I was a council estate Mick Jagger. Having the make-up on allowed me to get into character. I was worried about Kiss suing us, because they have sued people for using that make-up before, but fortunately they didn't. The video was shot the day after the Brit Awards, and it was great because I'd just done *Parkinson* and that had gone really well, and then I'd done the Brits, and me and Tom Jones, we'd been the performance of the night and I kind of knew it. So I was kind of at my most confident at the video shoot.'

Glastonbury | 1998

'Glastonbury wasn't something that I was looking forward to. It hadn't been that long ago that I was considered an embarrassment in those circles. Here I was turning up as an act, and I wasn't sure whether they were going to bottle me off stage. It felt like putting your head in the lion's mouth. I remember standing at the side of the stage waiting to go on, with all these thoughts running through my mind about who I was and what I meant to these people, and the anticipation and fear of being accepted or not. I was also in the middle of learning the craft, learning who I am as a performer, and I think after the first or second number I thought: "They're buying this! Great!" It felt very triumphant. And by the time of "Angels" I'm told that it was the biggest ever assembled audience at the main stage: 88,000. It had also been raining, and that was the first time the sun had appeared.'

3

'...life's too short to be afraid...'

He has a better memory for pain than for pleasure, which may be a necessary kind of protection in a world that always assumes fame and success will wipe away all the problems of anyone who comes to possess them. But he realises, too. 'Of course,' he says, 'the upshot of all these pictures is this fantastic house and fantastic lifestyle. It's amazing…' These words are spoken as he floats shoulder-deep in his swimming pool, the location he has chosen today to survey photos and see into the past, a process briefly interrupted when he feels the need to shout indoors and request an adjustment – 'Do you mind turning it up a few notches?' – to the pool temperature.

His house is rarely empty and, as he talks, there are various visitors to the poolside. Ayda wanders by for a while. Kelvin Andrews, who is working on music in one of the bedrooms with his brother Danny, slips into the water behind Rob and starts doing lengths. Several of the dogs running around the garden also scamper or lumber over to investigate. Over recent years, dogs have become an increasingly important part of Rob's everyday life.

Growing up, he only had one dog of his own, and not for too long. 'A poodle, Tammy,' he explains, 'that escaped and got run over, unfortunately.' Instead, his early impression of dogs was largely formed by his sister's Cairn terrier, Trixie. 'And she hated me. She wouldn't let me go upstairs. I actually would have to climb over banisters and up onto landings. There was a circumference around my sister's room that she wouldn't let me step into. Once, she took the end of my finger off – I was trying to get her out from underneath a bed, put my hand out and she just bit it, took the skin clean off.' His sister's next dog, a Jack Russell called Pip, was different. 'She was fucking unbelievable,' he remembers, 'a kind-hearted, very intelligent dog. Me and Pip had an affinity. I would stick her in my rucksack, and she'd stick her little head out, and I'd get on my mountain bike and go round town and she'd come with me, and she'd love it. She was incredibly obedient and just a very, very special dog. And after that I kind of thought all dogs would be like Pip.'

Still, his first attempt at keeping his own dogs as a grown-up was a fiasco. It was when he lived in London. 'In my wisdom,' he says, 'I decided to have two Great Danes in a flat with no garden. And I came down the first night and they'd done twenty human-size shits in the kitchen. Twenty. Ten each. Of course, in my enthusiasm for dog ownership I hadn't played the tape forward.' When Rob took them back to the breeders in Burslem, it was the young daughter who met him at the door: 'You couldn't handle it, could you?'

Now, in Los Angeles, he has eight dogs.

('And yes,' he says, 'I can handle it.')

When he first moved to LA, even though his inspiration for getting a dog was his sister's Jack Russell, he was convinced that the only dogs for him would be big ones. 'I wasn't a small dog person,' he says. 'I thought that all little dogs were Chihuahua-esque. I just saw them as bag companions for women. I didn't think it was a manly dog to have.'

Rob got his first dog from the pound, a German Shepherd called Sammy: 'brilliant, but incredibly jealous'. In the end, Sammy had to go: 'bit the gardener, bit the maid...' Meanwhile, he got Sid the wolf (actually 80 per cent wolf, 20 per cent Malamute Husky) from the local pet store, and he also got Rudy the Alsatian, who was the son of one of Rachel Hunter's dogs, Argos. 'Rudy was the runt of the litter. He was sickly and he's got bad legs, and for a couple of years he couldn't even jump up on the bed,' says Rob. 'But he's a little poet – he's got an amazing soul.' To prove his dominance, Argos had also tried to kill another of Rachel Hunter's dogs, a Bullmastiff called Duke, so Rob took Duke as well: 'That's why he has scars around his legs and chest. But he's the coolest dog ever, Duke. All he does is farts, shits and sleeps.' For a long time, these three big dogs – Sid, Rudy and Duke – were the three Robbie Williams dogs. Until life, and Rob, changed.

'Boy dogs are kind of aloof,' he says. 'They want to be pack leaders, and seldom do they come up for a cuddle or sit with you on the sofa. Especially a wolf that could be pulling a sled up north somewhere. So, because of my sexist thinking, I'd got these three big, aloof male dogs that prefer their company to mine. Then Ayda comes into my life, and she's got little dogs. I'm still a big dog guy, but after we'd been seeing each other for a few months I was, "Yeah, get the little dogs over..." And that was it.'

Her dogs were a Maltipoo called Poupette and a Pekinese called Maggie. 'I'm a small dog guy now. Poupette is heartbreakingly cute and always wants to be with us. When you get your luggage out to travel, she instantly knows that you're going away and tries to get in the luggage with you. Heartbreaking, leaving her. And Maggie doesn't know what time of day it is, where she is, who she is, if she's a dog, if she's not, does she exist. They're a great double act. They're just the cutest, most loving little doggies, and exactly what I was after, which was love bugs, basically. And after a year of me and Aydes seeing each other, we fancied another one. So off we went and got Wall-E.' A Havanese, and dog number six.

Then, in early 2009, Rob and Ayda moved to England. The seed for this abrupt change of plan was planted one day in Los Angeles when Rob gave Ayda a virtual tour of where he comes from on Google Earth. 'I got very nostalgic,' he says. 'I'd show her around the Potteries and she was going, "Oh, it's idyllic," and I thought, "Well, I'll go and take her."'

They flew over for a visit in November 2008. 'A magical trip,' he says. 'I felt like I literally had come home.' While in the Stoke area, they visited his family, and family graves, and even turned up on the doorstep of the house where he lived from the age of three to eighteen: 'An Asian family live there now, and they were really, really lovely. I went in and saw the box room that was my bedroom.' The rest of the trip went well too, and a plan was hatched.

'There's a different soul in England than there is in Los Angeles and I missed that soul,' he explains, 'and we decided that the pair of us would move back to England, have kids, and be amongst that soul.' He bought a large house in Wiltshire, a property once owned by Catherine Parr, and by February they had moved in.

Aside from its other attractions, it was, he says, 'a house with a lot of countryside where we could indulge our dog fetish'. Plans were made to bring the Los Angeles dogs over, but it would be several months before they would be there, and in the meantime there were 70 acres waiting for a dog, and two dog-deprived residents. So they went dog shopping: 'Ayda had always wanted a Chow, and I'd always wanted a Jack Russell, like Pip.' Abba Bear and Baby became dogs seven and eight.

Still, Rob has long known that his ability to make big, life-changing decisions is matched by his ability to un-make, or remake, such decisions. The two of them began to have second thoughts. 'We decided we were in the wrong place,' he says. 'It was lonely there.' (For one thing, Jonathan Wilkes, who lives nearby and who Rob routinely refers to as his best friend, had just left on a nine-month tour in the musical *We Will Rock You*.) Another factor was the weather. 'We decided that it's great to have a little bit of soul,' he says, 'but the shallow's okay too, as long as there's sun with the shallow.' Rob took his Los Angeles home off the market (it had nearly been sold to ex-Guns N' Roses guitarist, Slash), and towards the end of the summer they moved back, their newest companions in tow.

'And that's how we came to have eight dogs.'

Is eight enough?

'Not for us, but for the people that work with me, yeah. Everyone helps out – there's shit everywhere and piss everywhere. But I think if it was down to me, there'd be twenty in this garden.'

What's it like with eight dogs running around?

'You're never alone. They've all got their different personalities, and they all get on really well. We've got beds for them upstairs and now even the big dogs have decided they want to come and stay with us in the evenings, and that's cool because the big dogs used to want to stay downstairs. Now they make their way upstairs into the bedrooms.'

'We have all eight in the room, most nights,' says Ayda.

How many on the bed?

'Five or four, depending on,' says Ayda. 'Abba usually goes on the bed for a little bit.'

'I think she'd stay all night but she gets too hot,' says Rob. 'Even Sid's become a cuddly dog, and he comes into bed with us sometimes, but he's absolutely massive. He gets in the way of the telly.'

* * *

The photos by the poolside today are from the very end of the last millennium, when everything to do with Robbie Williams was getting bigger and bigger, but also weirder and weirder. 'There's a lot of growing pains,' he sighs. 'When the outside world all of a sudden is going mental, and you're in the centre, it does strange things to your mind. And you're trying to make sense of it, because this is exactly what you've been wanting, and exactly what so many people would like. And then you find yourself in a shitstorm, going, "This is totally uncomfortable... this is surreal... but it's real... I can't go to the shops... I can't go out walking... I'm being followed 24/7..." 1999, I suppose, was when I first became a hermit...'

As he rises out of the pool and wraps himself in a dressing gown – it is unusually cold in Los Angeles today – he mentions that Stephen Fry might be coming to quiz night on Sunday. (When he is home, Rob often holds quiz nights. In the end, although around 30 people will show up this Sunday, Fry – who sends his apologies and news of an unavoidable alternative commitment – will not be one of them.) Their paths have crossed in various ways over the years: in Rob's early solo years, Fry would be one of those carousing at The Groucho Club, and in 2006, Fry interviewed Rob for his TV documentary *The Secret Life of the Manic Depressive*. They occasionally correspond. This presents its own challenges.

'He sent me an email once and I spent two hours staring at a blank screen thinking, "What the fuck do I write back?"' says Rob. 'Everything from him is so erudite and witty and concise, and I can't spell and I don't know where the full stops go...'

Unable to overcome his own expectations, he eventually decided it would be easier not to reply at all.

'Elvis'
1998

'Jesus'
1998

Collages | 1998

'When I was sober, I realised there was going to be a lot of time on my hands, so I decided to make some art, and did some collages. I don't know why I was inspired to do them – I just thought it might be therapeutic. They were crap, basically. Anyway, I just did them and gave them to my management and the next minute they were up in the Tate in Liverpool next to Paul McCartney's and John Lennon's, which isn't bad for an afternoon's work, first stab at it.'

(Peter Blake, the artist who curated that Liverpool exhibition, recently shared his own encouraging perspective: 'Robbie's art was good. One of the collages was of Christ, and the other was of Elvis. One had a smashed Take That record in it, so it was about his life at that point. Obviously, there was a lot of interest because it was Robbie, but they still hold up. I don't know if he went on to do more, but he would have done some interesting work if he had.')

'Millennium' video | 1998

'I can't remember whether it was me or Vaughan, the director, who thought of doing James Bond but the sample in the song sort of suggested it. For the final shot, I remember being in that field as all the ground crew scurried off to hide when the helicopter came over. I had to struggle and pretend that the jetpack wasn't working. And I was asking myself: is this silly struggle at the end of a video really how I want to present myself? I just thought it was silly. And I felt terribly self-conscious about my first bit of acting that wasn't sung to camera. Looking back, I think it was the start of things to come. The not-take-yourself-seriously train was leaving the station, and I jumped on it.'

At home | 1998

'This is the chair I bought for my flat opposite Paul Smith's shop in Notting Hill. I liked the retro feel of it. I remember thinking it was *Doctor Who*-y. I also paid way too much for those trainers at a trendy shop in Notting Hill. I think they were £300. I've also got on a pair of Maharishi's, the trousers of the day – that was the fashion influence rubbing off from All Saints there. The top is by a company called Fake. And the look is Blue Steel.

'A few weird things happened in that place. In the flat and in the chair. Upstairs was the playroom. There were decks up there – I decided that I was going to learn how to DJ, and I never did, but there was a great set of decks, loads of vinyl, a nice sound system, a big telly, and a pool table if I remember rightly – proper bachelor stuff. There'd also be lots of paintbrushes and paint, and when the relapse came about six or seven months after, I woke up one morning on the sofa and I looked on the white wooden floor, and I'd painted "0207 312", and underneath "0207 3125", and then "0207 31256". I figured out what I'd done the night before was call Directory Enquiries for Stringfellows, so I could phone the girl I had been talking to there, but I couldn't quite manage to write the number down. Wrote it in paint on the floor. It could have been my greatest work of art. I should have got a chainsaw and seen which gallery I could put it up in.

'The television room was on the bottom floor and you could actually directly look into it from the double-decker bus. It was only about ten foot away from the top floor of the double-decker bus, so I'd be watching television and then I'd turn to the right and there'd be loads of people on the top of the double-decker bus watching Robbie Williams watching the television.'

I've Been Expecting You sleeve shoot | 1998

'You can feel insignificant in a town. I can remember Los Angeles being sparkly and new and much bigger than me. I was dwarfed by the presence of Hollywood and the people who lived here. I thought I wasn't fit to be in their presence at the time. But you stay here a couple of months and that will soon wear off. This shoot carried on the James Bond theme, in a house just above Sunset Strip. It was fun because people were making a fuss of you, and these people who were making a fuss of you had American accents, so it was a novelty. I was being taken seriously and there was once again this machine around me, and inevitably amidst that machine you feel comfortable. It was all about you. Everything is. If you succeed, they succeed.'

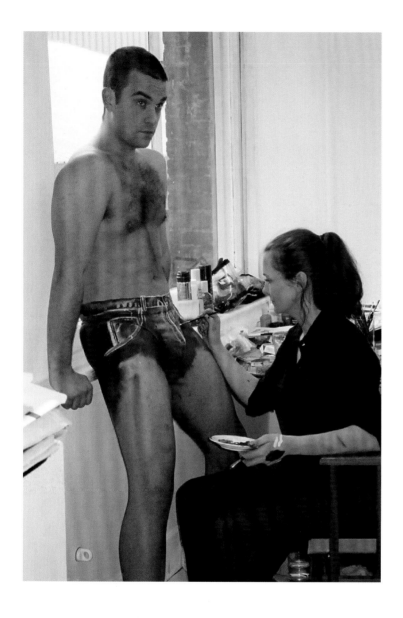

London | 1998

'That's Gina, my long-suffering make-up artist. She got the job because she refused to sleep with me. I didn't ask her, but the management were like, "You can't sleep with him – promise." I've got a canny management who could see a possible pattern emerging. "Yeah, promise." And she's worked with me ever since. There was only one make-up artist before; I hadn't trollopped through loads of them. But he was a lovely lad.'

'Those body painting jobs take hours and hours to do. I literally haven't got the patience, so to sit there for three hours was an accomplishment. But it was for charity, so I managed it. That's me trying my best to concave my stomach and give myself shoulders. I was quite concerned about the size of my legs at the time – I look like I play for Wigan.'

Sri Lanka | 1998

'When I was in Take That I listened to a lot of Ian Dury and the Blockheads. I liked his lyrics and I saw his record "Sex & Drugs & Rock & Roll" as an instruction: "... all my brain and body needs..." I was nineteen, I was: "Yeap. Sex and drugs and rock and roll is *all* my brain and body needs. *Correct*." Gina used to do Ian Dury's make-up, and through Gina he asked me if I wanted to be an ambassador for UNICEF. We went away on a trip together to open polio immunisation centres in Sri Lanka. I was quite scared of him – because of what he meant to me and how great he was, and also because he was a bit drunk and cantankerous. He was a lovely, lovely man but had the ability to lash out. Not at me, but I stayed out of his way.'

'No Regrets' video | 1998

'Every time I get a video of mine and I watch it for the first time, I hate it. It's never until I've seen it ten times that I can separate the fact that it's me and just see it as what it is. It's the same with music. I always pick apart a fraction of it, and that fraction of it I hate, and it makes me hate it all. And unfortunately I said I didn't like this video at the time. It was no reflection on the director's work because Pedro did a really good job – I just didn't like me.'

'No Regrets' video | 1998

'A small crowd gathered to watch us film at a garage we'd rented, and along with that small crowd came some kids with a yo-yo. I wanted to be down with the kids. I wanted the kids to like me: *I can yo-yo!* I think I still thought I was their age, and still wanted to be their age.'

Top of the Pops | 1998

'When I was growing up, I'd see Freddie
Starr on Des O'Connor's show, or Emu on
Parkinson, all of these people who made an
impact with what they did when they went on
stage, or went on television, made a *moment*
in TV. And, rightly or wrongly, I've tried to do
that with every interview I've ever given, or
every performance, up to a point. Up until
recently. To punctuate every performance
with something different, or something that
people would remember. And my idea for this
was wearing a dress. The idea would have
been quite good, but the dress was awful.'

BBC concert | 1998

'This was a gig at the BBC theatre. I'd invited my dad along and we did "That's Life" together, a favourite of my dad's. I think that's probably the first time we'd ever sung together, other than when he did "Little White Bull" when I was eight at Perran Sands. I sat on his knee and he'd sing "Once upon a time there was a little white bull" and I'd do the "... little white bull!"

'The records that caught my fancy when I was a kid, because they were the records that were left behind by my dad, were all swing albums. I used to take myself off into a room of a Sunday or a Saturday afternoon and learn them like books. I'd be swept away into a fantasy world of glamour. All these lush strings, and the magic of those records, kind of pierced my soul when I was a kid. I'd listen to them, and then I'd put on the spoken *Mr. Men*, with Arthur Lowe doing the *Mr. Men* stories. So, in between listening to *Mr. Men*, I'd listen to Nat King Cole or the Nat King Cole Trio, or Tony Bennett, or Jack Jones, or Ella Fitzgerald, and learn the words. I suppose this BBC concert was the first time I performed a swing song. I don't think the thought of recording any of them was there yet, not at that point.'

The Brit Awards | 1999

'I think this was the first time my parents had actually been together at a function in twenty-odd years. And that was weird in itself. It was fine, in a "we don't talk about it" kind of way, but that was another ingredient to the evening. I was drinking again. I had a couple of shots before I went on, and when I came through the centre of the ceiling through this little hole on a harness to make my entrance, I banged my head and nearly knocked myself out, which would have been quite something for a live TV show. But I came down all guns blazing and did "Let Me Entertain You". Muhammad Ali was there. My dad and I are big fans of Muhammad Ali, and my dad looked over at him when I was onstage, and Muhammad Ali looked back at him, looked up at me, and winked. He nodded at my performance, like, "This is good..." That made my dad's life, basically.'

Wembley Arena | 1999

'I love Morecambe and Wise. I always loved the bit at the end with "Bring Me Sunshine" and, if I remember it rightly, Eric Morecambe would be wearing a coat like that, with a cap on and a plastic bag, and he'd be going off home. That's how the show would start on this tour – as an ode to Eric Morecambe. It reminds me of being at my gran's on a Saturday evening. Three television channels. 28 million people watching the show at Christmas. And Morecambe and Wise never failed to deliver a kind of beauty through comedy. Genius daftness. It was a time of: put another ring on the fire and get the broken biscuits out and let's eat them all.

'There would be me in the nearest seat to the television – I could literally change the channels with my fingers, wouldn't have to move. There were no remotes then. My grandad would be sitting in silence on another chair about five feet away from me. He never said a word all his life, really. The only thing he would say when I came in is, "Alright, son, are you well?" He'd sit there, and he'd be taken care of with his food, and he and my nan never talked to each other, never slept in the same room, and stayed together 60 years or something.

'It was a terraced house, you could almost stretch out your arms and touch both walls. The toilet had only just been moved inside. To have a bath, you had to fill up this big iron thing with a bucket because there was no running water for the bath, and wash yourself. I had a few baths in that. And then my nan would put talcum powder on me. My nan was a big exponent of the talcum powder.

'My nan was also a big book reader. That was when I first read about UFOs. And when I was eight, I read David Niven's *The Moon's a Balloon* and Spike Milligan's *Adolf Hitler: My Part in his Downfall*. And every night, when I went to bed, my nan would teach me about history. She knew an awful lot about kings and queens, and I used to love her telling me the stories. She was your archetypal, sun-shines-out-of-your-arse grandmother, and that's how she made me feel.

'On the wall she had Constable's *The Hay Wain*, a print from Woolworths. Next to that was *The Laughing Cavalier*. And I've had those remade in memory of my grandma – I commissioned an artist to do them. *The Laughing Cavalier* now faces you when you walk into my house. *The Hay Wain* hasn't been put up yet because we can't find a wall big enough.

'I did enquire about buying the actual *Hay Wain*. 29 million, apparently. Not this year...'

Use ear protecti

Testicular Cancer Awareness advert | 1999

'This was the trip to Los Angeles when I nearly wasn't allowed to go on the plane because I was that drunk. I remember the BA staff bringing me a phone and it being David Enthoven on the other end: "Listen, old chap, they're not going to let you on the plane unless you sober up a little bit, so I suggest you have a cup of coffee and behave." So I did. For the advert, I had to be naked with a pair of boobs on and I was a bit nervous about showing the top half of my body because I'd been boozing it up. I don't know why I wore a pair of breasts for the advert, but I'm up for that kind of thing. For false boobs. Anyone's. Even my own.'

American tour │ 1999

'I only bought that PC so I could play the Tiger Woods game. I didn't know what an email was at that point, I didn't know what any of that nonsense was. I didn't really know what the internet was – I just wanted to play Tiger Woods. It became the most expensive game of Tiger Woods I'd ever played.'

MTV Movie Awards | 1999

'I think that was just before Kid Rock became major league. He's always been very nice to me and we've always had a chat whenever we've bumped into each other. These awards were kind of mind-blowing, feeling insignificant at this glamorous Hollywood bash where there's no end of stars. When people know who you are, you're allowed to be – or at least act – like a pop star. When people don't know you, you behave in the way that you feel in real life, which is: excuse me, I'll just move out of the way for this famous person to come through. That's how I really feel, but it's just magnified in the States. I also remember meeting Ben Stiller there and telling him I'd just been for a colonic. Wasn't met with enthusiasm at all – he's a pretty serious dude. I'd had a colonic because it was the latest craze sweeping Hollywood, and I'd heard that you feel a million times better, and that it's great for you, it's great for the skin, great for this, that, and the other. I just felt a bit defiled.'

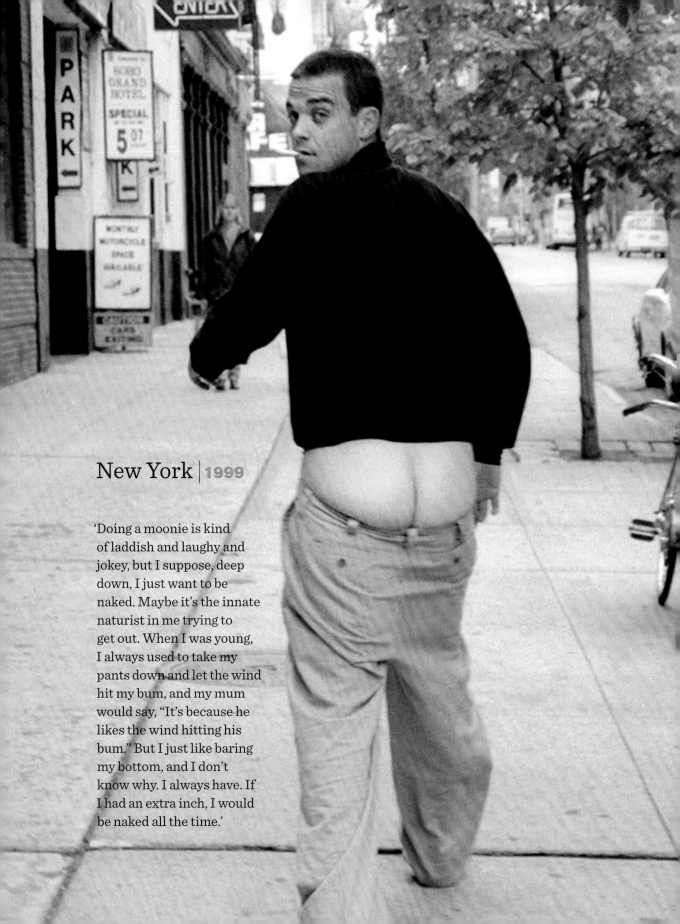

New York | 1999

'Doing a moonie is kind of laddish and laughy and jokey, but I suppose, deep down, I just want to be naked. Maybe it's the innate naturist in me trying to get out. When I was young, I always used to take my pants down and let the wind hit my bum, and my mum would say, "It's because he likes the wind hitting his bum." But I just like baring my bottom, and I don't know why. I always have. If I had an extra inch, I would be naked all the time.'

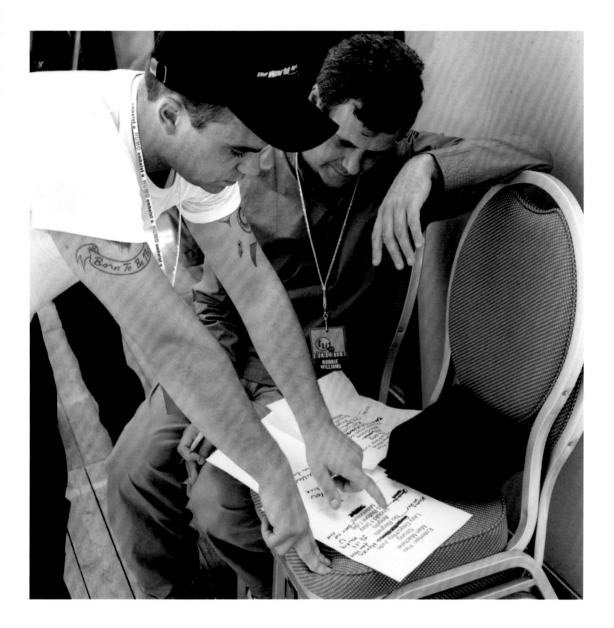

Brussels | 1999

'I'm probably taking songs out of the set list. I always have.
Trying to be on stage as little as I could. But apart from the last
two it's a good set list, that.'

'She's The One' video | 1999

'The nearest ice-skating rink when I was young was
Telford, which is 50 miles away, so we'd go on high
days and holidays, special occasions, maybe once
every two years. But I'd done a ton of rollerblading
and it's pretty similar. It's kind of a weird video
for that kind of song: a comedy video to a serious
ballad. But it worked.'

Slane, Ireland | 1999

'I remember this being a really big deal. I think people had come to have a good time, they wanted me to generate that good time, and they were on my side. And I delivered. Though I remember reading the Irish papers on the day, and one headline was, "Tell This Fat English Waster To Feck Off".'

4

'...every mistake
I've ever made has
been rehashed
and then replayed...'

When he looks back upon his life – and in particular when he is surrounded by the pictures of his life staring back at him – one recurrent theme is the contradiction between the fears he feels and the front he so often and so persuasively presents to the world. If, as he puts it, 'your act is being the most confident person in the world', it is only natural for people to attribute the qualities of the performance to the performer. Natural, but perhaps misleading.

'My confidence has always been a bluff,' he says. 'It's never been real. It's a painted face for entertainment purposes.' It doesn't lessen or disqualify what the most impetuously regal and triumphant version of Robbie Williams has achieved, or meant to people, if it turns out that this Robbie Williams exists, at least in part, only as camouflage for someone very different. 'Ego happens in many different ways to many different people,' he says. 'Mine is an act. There's always a very fragile, unconfident, fat thirteen-year-old beneath the skin.' (Perhaps in any case it is the combination of the two – the strutting, egocentric, overconfident super-performer and his ever-present, semi-visible, fragile twin alter ego – that is so alluring.)

When he first returned last year after his long time away, he discovered that crossing back over to that other Robbie Williams was more awkward and less instinctive than ever. His scheduled comeback performance was to be a live appearance on the TV show *The X Factor*. Singing 'Bodies' onstage in rehearsals, he was slick and persuasive, though his comment immediately afterwards – 'I was just doing an impression of what I used to do' – could be seen in a number of very different ways. His performance on the show itself was less assured, in that it was strangely manic and disjointed. It was as though he, momentarily failing to summon up 'how to charm a TV audience' from his repertoire, had reached into the memory banks and pulled out the wrong file – the one used for encores at the end of stadium shows.

It was only a blip. Within a few days, he was back to performing in ways that convinced everyone that Robbie Williams had truly returned. (Nearly everyone, anyway. There is the one critic he has always struggled, and often failed, to convince – the one who remains when everybody else leaves the room.)

Meanwhile, his comeback interviews were the one area where the whole melange – the doubts, the ego, the performance, the reluctance, the sincerity, the irony, the indifference, the flirtatiousness, the flippancy and the commitment – only served to make a greater whole, a snapshot of all the many Robbie Williams, old, new and future, rolled into one:

British TV interview:

What does it take to make Robbie Williams?

'A little bit of neurosis, a little bit of a music collection, some weird times in your youth, becoming famous really too early, and a big mouth.'

Hong Kong radio interview:

So it sounds like you have a very promising relationship at the moment, right?

'Very promising relationship at the moment. She knows my name. And when I was born. We're getting to grips with each other.'

So how do you know this girlfriend?

'I met her on an online dating agency, match.com. [Ayda silently holds the little finger of his right hand, unseen by the interviewer, who is on the other end of a telephone, as Rob spins these lies.] I signed my profile and ticked all the boxes and she winked me on the site. And you know what? Match.com does get the right people with the right people – it's just amazing.'

Hmmm. Congratulations. You have, like, a very steady relationship?

'Yeah. Yeah.'

Do you ever think about walking down the aisle and getting married?

'Yeah. I mean, she's a Satanist, so we'd have to get married in the church of Satan. Which is alright by me.'

Australian TV interview:

This is your public probe... Here we go! From Ryan in Queensland – what's the weirdest thing a fan has ever said to you?

'"You've given me herpes." Which is weird because I actually hadn't. She sent me a text. She was a mentalist. [Pauses to look round the hotel room he is in, where there has been much half-stifled spluttering.] Shall I not tell this story? Anyway, that's what she said. I hadn't. I was clean as a whistle. Whoo-hoo! So there you go...'

Do you ever have sexy dreams about any celebrities?

'Yeah, quite often. But they've always got to go somewhere, or I just can't get it in... It never gets to the pay-off.'

Argentinian radio interview:

Robbie, why it took you three years to come back?

'This is how the cycle goes with Robbie Williams: release an album, be very excited about it, look healthy, be healthy, promote that album, start eating, tour the album, start going mad, end tour, have a nervous breakdown, end up in rehab... Something had to give.'

International press roundtable interview:

Do you believe in God?

'God? I don't know where I'm at, really, with that sort of stuff... I was raised Catholic... didn't fancy that – it was just boring, damp, and the sex was awful. The minute

I was allowed not to go to church, I was, like, cool, I'll just stay in, thanks – you go to mass. And then I got myself a drink and drug problem, and started to learn about the concept of a higher power that was not religious, that was like an agony aunt in the sky with 55-inch biceps who looks after you, and wants you to do well. And then that drifts away, and then you're kind of part-atheist, part-"the-first-problem-that-comes-up-you-go-straight-to-God" religious. I did pray to archangel Michael the other day – he's a fantastic angel. He is huge. I want him to be my dad. But where I'm at with all that stuff at the minute is: I'm an atheist until the shit hits the fan, and then I'll be on my knees quicker than anyone else.'

Mexican newspaper interview:

Do you think there is any disadvantage in being famous?

'They're only disadvantages if you view them as such. [smiles] And I tend to view them as such.'

Dutch TV interview:

If you had to choose between your career and love, would that be a difficult choice to make?

'Well, yeah. Because I've spent a lot of time working on this album. [Considers it anew.] Career or love? Fortunately, it's not a choice I have to make, but if I had to, yeah, I'd go and be in a tent with Ayda somewhere in the jungle.'

Are you also thinking about family? Children?

'Yup. Talk about it a lot.'

I just had a child. One year.

'Did you think you weren't going to have one?'

Yes.

'Me too. How old are you?'

I'm 32.

'32? It's about time I knocked one out, really, isn't it? I'm 36. [Pauses, momentarily confused] Am I 36?'

[A voice, off camera, correcting him.] '35.'

'I'm 35? Oh. Thank God...'

Swedish newspaper interview:

It's been reported that you have been playing poker in Swindon. I'm a poker player and I'd like to know your style. Are you loose aggressive or sound and tight?

'Robbie "all in" Williams. Does that answer your question? I never fucking win, but I am all in.'

Danish TV interview:

'... I was probably a bit scared to stop, just to go, right, who am I without the Robbie thing? And in the end, I didn't have a choice because I burned myself out.'

So who are you without the Robbie thing?

'A guy who sits on the sofa and watches telly, apparently. That's who I am. That tickles the dogs, strokes the dogs. A guy who finds a girlfriend, settles down. It's been a nice break. I genuinely haven't felt like a pop star for three years, so it's a bit weird doing interviews... It's like riding a very wonky bike at the moment. So who am I without it? I still don't know.'

> *But did you like it, whatever you found?*

'Um. I got really bored. Really, really bored.'

Italian press interview:

> *Do you think Jesus exists?*

'I really don't know. I wouldn't say no. I've got a tattoo of him on my forearm. I'm a big fan of Jesus, whether he existed or not. I'm a big fan of Superman, and he didn't exist.'

Argentinian radio interview:

> *We are now preparing a special show for Christmas, and this year's show title* is For a Better World. *Which thing is your wishes to live in a better world?*

'My wishes to live in a better world? [There are weird codes of interwoven sincerity and insincerity that run through interviews like this. Most interviewees simply go along with them. Some – Rob, for instance – often do not.] My wishes. To live. In a better world. [brightly] They could invent a calorie-free doughnut.'

> *What?* [The interviewer appears astonished, and perhaps also affronted.]

'A calorie-free doughnut. That would make the world a better place. It would for me.'

> *Yeah.* [Looking dumbfounded.]

'Calorie-free cake – that *tastes* like it's full of calories.' [Rob persists as though he has failed to be clear enough about his personal Utopian dream.]

[The interviewer sits there silently, shell-shocked. He obviously believes, quite wrongly, that Rob doesn't realise what was expected of him, and that Rob's failure to deliver is an accidental act of idiocy and self-obsession rather than deliberate. Maybe he's even a little worried, too, about how this answer will make Rob look when stacked up against the other noble soundbites that are probably already being edited together back in Buenos Aires. While he may see a gross insensitivity and triviality in Rob's answer, he is entirely blind to the same qualities in the question that has triggered it. Rob, meanwhile, completes what he has started.]

'I know you probably want "an end to war" and "an end to suffering". "An end to violence." But you can keep that. Just give me cake that doesn't make me fat.'

Mexican press interview:

'I'm all different things every single day. All over the place. Morning amazing, afternoon indifferent, evening miserable. The next day: morning miserable, afternoon indifferent, the evening amazing. Underneath it all, I'm the happiest I've been. Yeah, underneath it all, I'm the happiest I've been. But I'm human, I go up and down, up and down...'

Hook End Studios | 2000

'Recording *Sing When You're Winning*. It was a very exciting time, because I believed I was delivering a great album chock full of hits. The only song that kind of didn't have a lyric was "Rock DJ", and it soon became a bone of contention because I couldn't think of any words for it at all. Here, Guy's probably just told me to do the words again. I've got my hand on my head, and my head's probably hurting from thinking too much, and I'm probably judging myself for it not being natural, and I'm judging myself for it not coming out, and I've probably been thinking for five hours. The brainpower wasn't working. There were about three or four different drafts for what it was going to become, and I wasn't happy with any of them. In fact, I wasn't happy with what we came up with in the end, because I didn't know what I wanted to convey, but as the deadline approached that's what we had so that's what we went with. For somebody that can't concentrate, if a lyric's not coming, it can be very Rubik's Cube-like. I could only ever do two sides of the Rubik's Cube, and that's pretty much what it felt like with "Rock DJ". If you hear where we nicked the tune from, which is "... Ecstasy..." by Barry White, it's like sexy Guinness: thick, very sexual, it's got a lot of earth to it. And I was hoping to create something like that. But I didn't know what to say, so it was: "Me with the floorshow..."'

'Chris Briggs, A & R man. He's been a father figure over the last fifteen years, since I've been solo. He's sober – we probably would have hung out together when we were both using and it would probably have been very messy and one of us would probably have ended up in hospital. I look up to Chris. He's very, very smart, he's been around the block and seen the business inside and out. Good talker, good communicator. I just like him. I still don't know what he does for a living.'

'One of many Silk Cut there. By the looks of it, in my eyes, Guy's annoying me. And I'm probably annoying him too.'

'Rock DJ' video | 2000

'I think this was another tipping point for who I was going to
be as a personality or as an entertainer. To begin with, I kind of
saw myself as the lead singer of a band, and then all of a sudden
I was becoming a pop star. And I didn't notice. I think it was a
natural progression, but looking back now, it's, oh yeah, those
were the videos that did it.'

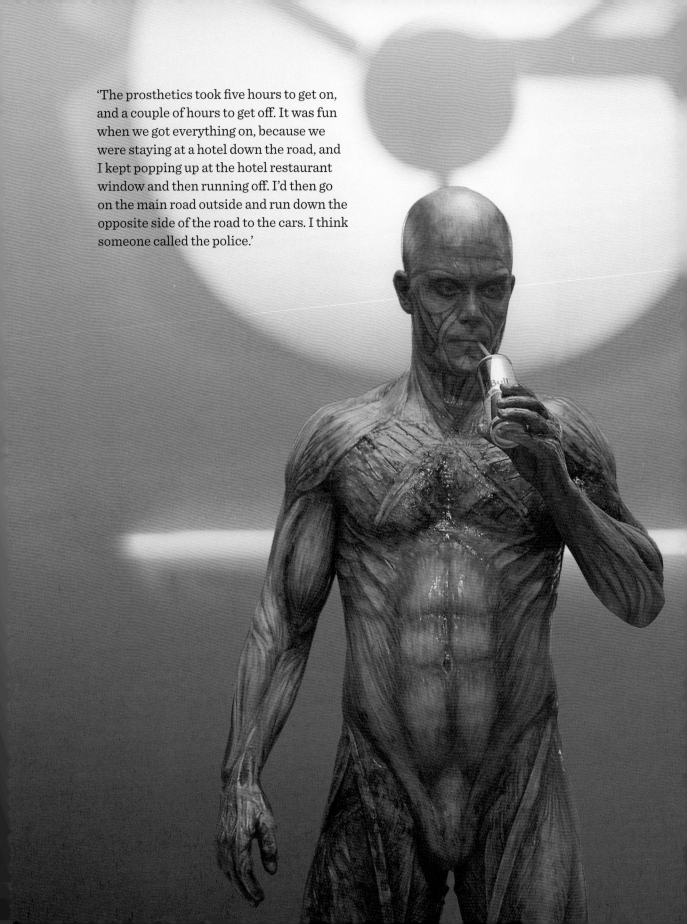

'The prosthetics took five hours to get on, and a couple of hours to get off. It was fun when we got everything on, because we were staying at a hotel down the road, and I kept popping up at the hotel restaurant window and then running off. I'd then go on the main road outside and run down the opposite side of the road to the cars. I think someone called the police.'

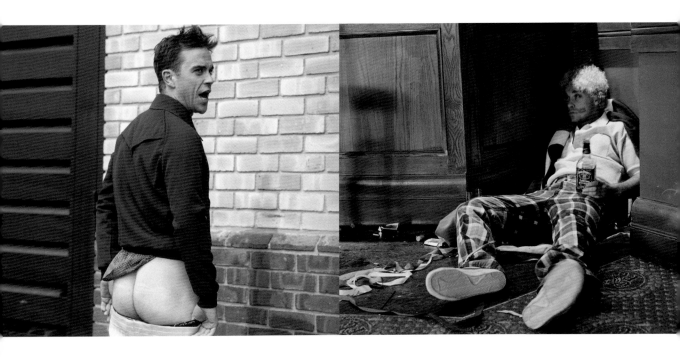

Sing When You're Winning sleeve | 2000

'Definitely my best artwork. Probably one of the best that there's *ever* been. I can remember some guy coming up to me eighteen months after: "I work with the Beastie Boys and they just thought that the artwork on your album was fantastic." Though I just read that as: they didn't like the music, did they? It was a three-day shoot – an awful load of make-up, an awful load of different set ups, a lot of hard work, great end result. I had to play all the characters that were combined on the finished artwork. For instance, I had to be every character in different parts of the wall for the free kick. I'd be one, then I'd move over a person and be the next one. I think I had to be every member of both sides as well. But I enjoyed being on the pitch at Chelsea, and having that to myself. That was fun. There's one of me being a ticket tout outside the game... me playing the foreign manager; I remember the suit was polyester... me as the home manager, a Malcolm Allison kind of character; they made me have ruddy cheeks. I think me pissing up the wall's my favourite. No, actually, the policeman's my favourite. And I liked the 1970s pub scene. It reminds me of my dad, of the pub when I was a kid, the hairstyles and sideburns, the pint pots and the smell of the cigarettes, all the characters. And I was surprised when I played a barmaid how much like my mum I looked.'

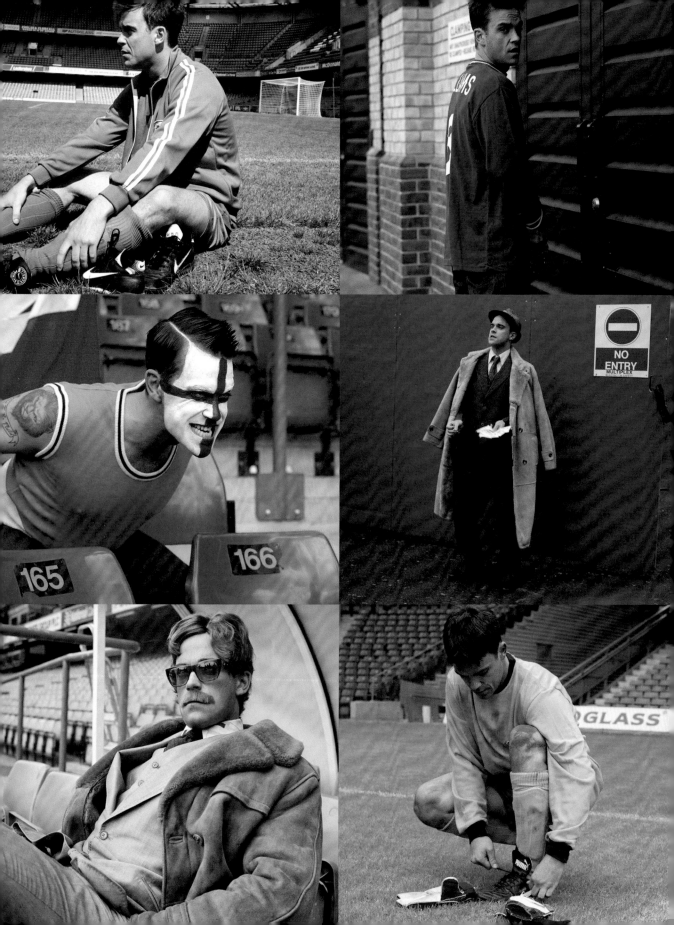

'Kids' video | 2000

'I'd always had a big crush on Kylie, ever since she was a mechanic on *Neighbours*, and here I was doing a video shoot with her. And, as so often happens with the objects of my crushes over the years, you've projected so much onto somebody, about who they could possibly be and what they could possibly mean to you and how they make you feel, that by the time it comes around to meeting them and spending any time with them, you're just a bit of a teenage boy. I just become an inanimate object around them. So I gawped at Kylie, and I couldn't figure out why my banter wouldn't work. Why my natural ability to just be myself went awry.'

'I'd got into the Drambuie by the end of the day. I think I probably started drinking to get some Dutch courage, but it backfired. We were at a health club and I was in this pool, and Kylie was going to come over to me, and that's all I was told. Nobody told me she was going to be naked – top half – as she came over to me. I was drunk, and waiting, and the shot started, and then all of a sudden she disrobed and she's just got a G-string on. And I just burst out laughing. Which I don't think went down well with Kylie. I may have offended her, because she must have felt vulnerable too, being naked on set, and being naked in front of me. But just the thought of Kylie disrobing… and there she was, the naked Kylie, when I was drunk… made me laugh. It was like: "There's Kylie – *naked*! How fucking mental's that?" I think that any chance of anything disappeared when I laughed at her. Perhaps she likes being naked, but she probably doesn't enjoy being laughed at by some Stokie idiot. You know, it's at moments like those that you feel very Stokie. Maybe me saying this here will go some way as an apology – I was too embarrassed to ever bring it up with her. Anyway, the evening ended with Geri Halliwell making a dash through London and out to the countryside to come and whisk me away in her Aston Martin.'

'Supreme' video | 2000

'This was the day that I lost my love for pine nuts. I'd eaten something that had given me food poisoning and I was constantly being sick. Since that day, I haven't been able to eat pine nuts. I think everybody thought I was trying to get off the video shoot early, pretending to be ill. It wasn't until I had to pull up at the side of the motorway to throw up everywhere that everybody was like, "Oh, he really *is* ill."'

'Vaughan had come up with an amazing idea for the video. I think an awful lot of my persona has been driven by Vaughan Arnell. He pushed me towards what he is and what he would like to be, which is like Steve McQueen, and like Paul Newman, but also slapstick, *Carry On* films, and saucy humour, somebody that's from the 1970s, a jack of all trades, a master of many. He came up with great ideas, and it was only in hindsight that I realised that that's shaping who you are and what you come across as. I have no regrets about any of that. I was a willing participant and it was a load of fun. He caught an essence of who I could be. I was now driving the train of pop stardom. I was Being A Pop Star in its many guises, trying to project something that was entertaining, trying to project something that other people weren't doing. It was like *Confessions of a Pop Star*, I suppose. I think that's what Vaughan saw me as, like a Robin Askwith kind of character. And I quite happily played that part. In Vaughan's videos, the character's always bigger than how I really think of me as a person. This guy's a Formula 1 driver, he's got the world on a string, the world's his playground, and so are the women in it. He has a carefree kind of eccentric ego-ness. And the reality is, I'm just in my house having a wank and a cry.'

Tour rehearsals | 2001

'I'm not very good at rehearsing. People want me to show willing, and I kind of want to show willing for them, or I have in the past, and so I've turned up for a day and a half, and then not turned up again. I think: "Well, I've only got to know the words, haven't I?" There isn't an ego ramp in rehearsals, there isn't a hundred-foot-wide stage, there isn't 80,000 people in front ... so what's the point in me being there? My rehearsals really are the first three shows. I also think it's a throwback from being in Take That, because we used to rehearse for two months. Very regimented: we'd get up at 9.00, work till 12.00, eat, work till 5.00, rest, then come in the next day. I used to find it laborious and tiring. I couldn't pick up the steps as quick as the other lads and I'd get confused a lot easier than the other lads, and I'd get annoyed at myself for not picking up the steps. Status Quo came in to rehearse one weekend and they ran through the set twice and went home, and I thought: "One day I'm going to do that."

'But if I toured with Take That again... yeah, I would rehearse for a couple of months again. Just watching their last tour and seeing what they came up with, I'd quite look forward to it, actually. It would be a bit of a relief, having something to do at every moment of the show – a position to be in, a movement to make. I'd look forward to it being structured, instead of the ad libbing that I do. And I'd just have to not find it restrictive, because if I was doing it, I'd want to be part of the band again, doing the thing that they're doing.'

Paris | 2001

'Lovely jacket, great shirt, nice specs, good dye on the hair. It's strange now, because I used to dye my hair all the time – when I was in Take That, I dyed it ten different colours, and at the start of the solo career, I used to dye it dark, because it's mousey. Now, because I've gone grey, or am going grey, I kind of can't dye my hair because people'll go: "He's dyed his hair! Because of the grey! Ah ha ha ha – it's because he's getting older!" And I quite fancy dyeing my hair, not because of the grey, but because of boredom – I like a change.'

Amsterdam | 2001

'It's the no-carb twins.'

Rotterdam | 2001

'In this photo, I'm praying. I don't know if I was praying to Elvis, or praying to God, but I was definitely praying. I had a few pictures up underneath the stage, just for a bit of inspiration. Heroes. And they used to work at the time. There'd be Frank Sinatra, and Muhammad Ali, and maybe Eric Morecambe. I'd look around and see their faces just before I went onstage, and drew on these pictures as inspiration to lift me. And for the majority of that tour, those pictures worked. Muhammad Ali meant an awful lot to me when I was a kid – seeing him on *Parkinson*, watching the Rumble in the Jungle or the Thrilla in Manila, watching him give interviews and knowing what a giant personality he was. There were an awful lot of people waiting for me each night, and in some way they were kind of seeing me as a similar figure. I'm not saying I am or will ever be a Muhammad Ali, or a Frank Sinatra. But just the amount of people that were coming... I would try and get inspiration from my heroes and feel what I thought their confidence must be, or must have been. Try to feel big enough to mean something to the audience.'

Rotterdam | 2001

'This is what we'd do before going back onstage for the encore. We would go: [sings mellifluously] *"Me with the floorshow... kicking with your torso... boys getting hi-igh... girls even more so..."* By then, I was either full of endorphins and pleased to be getting towards the end of the show, or feeling absolutely fucking knackered and drained. I think I'm probably full of endorphins there.'

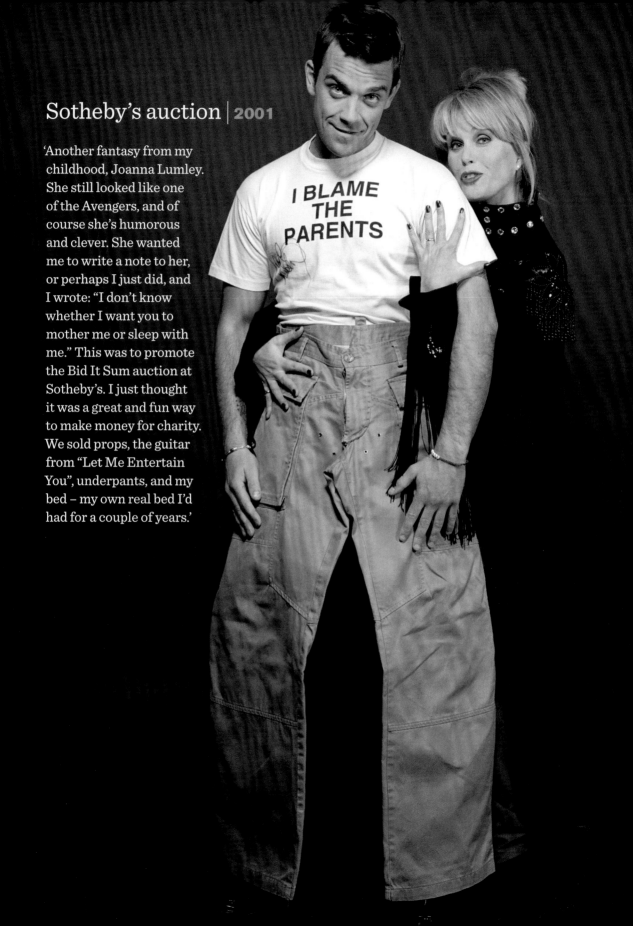

Sotheby's auction | 2001

'Another fantasy from my childhood, Joanna Lumley. She still looked like one of the Avengers, and of course she's humorous and clever. She wanted me to write a note to her, or perhaps I just did, and I wrote: "I don't know whether I want you to mother me or sleep with me." This was to promote the Bid It Sum auction at Sotheby's. I just thought it was a great and fun way to make money for charity. We sold props, the guitar from "Let Me Entertain You", underpants, and my bed – my own real bed I'd had for a couple of years.'

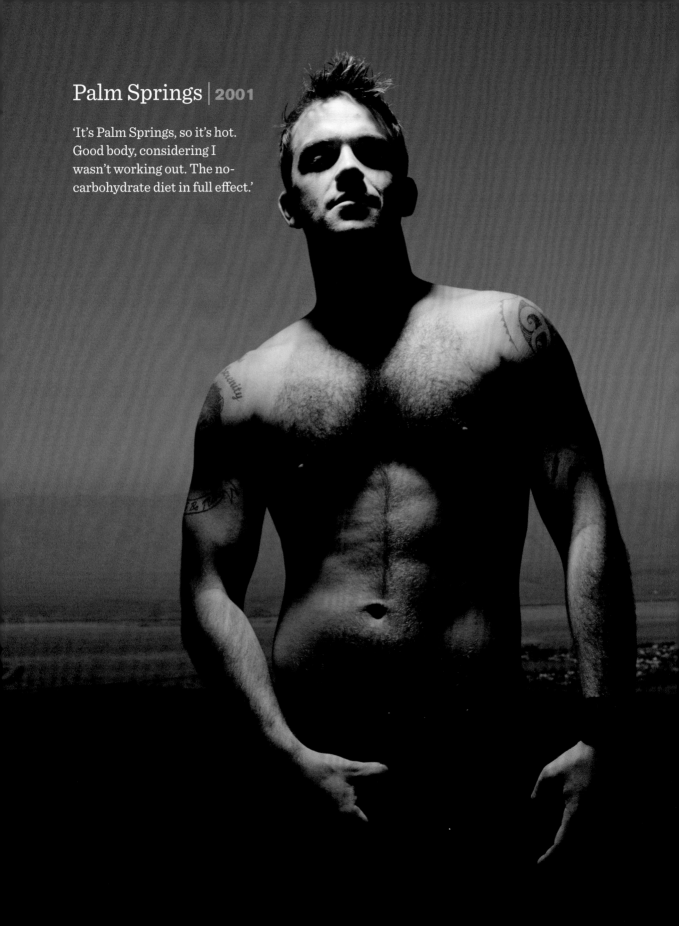

Palm Springs | 2001

'It's Palm Springs, so it's hot. Good body, considering I wasn't working out. The no-carbohydrate diet in full effect.'

'Eternity' sleeve | 2001

'Apparently, this photo was never used
because the coat was real fur. Perhaps
I was really tired and didn't notice.
Fur feels really nice on, I can't deny
that, but I wouldn't want to wear a
fur coat. There's just a part of me that
thinks it's a bit wrong.'

'Eternity'/'The Road To Mandalay' video | 2001

'Oh, *that's* where those are from. I keep finding those pyjama bottoms every now and again and I'm like, these are nice – I can't remember getting these. But they were from that shoot. I enjoyed doing the kissing scenes. They were fun.'

'Here I'm recreating Bros's "Drop The Boy" video. I really am. I always used to do it because it always made people laugh. It made people laugh at school – I used to do it back then by jumping off a wall. And it carried on making people laugh in 2001.'

Dublin | 2001

'I'm so thin there. Gaunt. Underweight. Malnourished. Perfect. I'm walking towards the stage and I can remember a bunch of people being able to see me, and I was in 1-2-3- rock and roll star guise. I can remember phoning my AA sponsor beforehand, because I was absolutely terrified, and he said, "*You're* not there to be entertained." That struck a chord with me. He was absolutely right.'

5

'...trying to understand why he did what he did...'

Sitting in his bedroom one Los Angeles morning, Rob is talking, via Skype on his computer, with Brian Hill, the film director who nearly a decade ago made a documentary about him, *Nobody Someday*. Today, Hill, who is in the early stages of discussing a new and very different kind of documentary, wants to record some of Rob's recollections of performing in front of 375,000 people over three nights at Knebworth in 2003.

Rob's emotions when it comes to that weekend are not simple. Knebworth is a prime example of an event in the Robbie Williams career that might appear from the outside as a straightforward and exhilarating triumph, but which remains a far more complicated experience in his memory. Perhaps because of this, he begins by demurring, and suggesting that he has very little to say.

Hill proposes that they should just talk as they would do when *Nobody Someday* was being made.

'I'm a very different person to how I was in *Nobody Someday* though,' Rob answers.

'I'm sure you are,' says Hill evenly.

'I am,' Rob persists. 'I haven't much to say at all.'

'That's what you said then,' Hill points out. 'That's what you said then.'

'Oh.'

* * *

'... and I got my legs tied to the rope and up I went, and there I was upside down, and the music starts and I haven't got a clue if I'm going to be able to open my mouth, let alone have something come out when I open my mouth...'

If it is Hill's instinct that once Rob has lit a Silk Cut and begun thinking about Knebworth he will find he has far more to tell than he had imagined he might, Hill is right. By the time Rob finally says, 'I think I've told you everything I remember,' he has been talking more or less non-stop for nearly forty minutes, a stream of recollections that takes in Justin from The Darkness's over-persistent child, inter-security-posse death threats, what appears to be a rather manic Eddie Izzard impression, plenty of wryness ('There were 135,000 of them. Having a good time. At my expense.'), the dichotomy between 50 Cent and Norman Wisdom that lies within, tomorrow's therapy session, debating stagecraft with Elton John ('I spoke to Elton John, because sometimes he goes on for three hours. I'm, "Why do you do that?", and he says, "Because I enjoy it." I'm, like, "Oh... that's interesting."'), corresponding with Madonna, dancing in front of the fridge, a new taxonomy of fear, and the demographics of sweat and sex at the very front of an outdoor audience.

He talks of Knebworth as a high point, though also sometimes as the point at which he knew that, in a certain way, it was impossible for things ever to get bigger. There have been other record-breaking achievements since – in 2005, he would enter the *Guinness Book of Records* for selling 1.6 million concert tickets in a single day, for instance, and his unequalled fifteen Brit Awards – but Knebworth still stands as a particular kind of landmark and pinnacle: a weekend of such concentrated immensity and intensity that, even if it were possible to top it or eclipse it, it is quite likely that he would decline to do so. As if it is a magnificent event that still takes his breath away, but in a manner that continues to panic him slightly.

* * *

When asked to celebrate his own career, Rob generally retreats. Sometimes, it can seem as though the only thing he truly likes celebrating is a certain relish in the lengthy elaboration of his own ongoing discomfort. But there are other moments. It is when anybody else is unwise enough to join in with the tirade of disapproval he aims in his own direction that his pride is most likely to fire up; it is when other people echo his lowest opinions of what he has done that he is most likely to rediscover its worth.

On a Tuesday afternoon not too long ago, I find him slightly put off his stride by a column in one of the previous weekend's newspapers in which the writer Miranda Sawyer, musing on some of his myriad contradictions, recounts the following story:

A few years ago, a friend was enjoying a minor film hit. Robbie complimented him on his work, and then said: 'But how good is it really? Is it two nights in Knebworth good?' Oh yes. When Robbie really tried, he could make Jordan look chilled and uncompetitive.

Rob readily acknowledges that he probably did say something of this sort – he believes the conversation in question may have been with Simon Pegg – but that the spirit in which he would have said this has been fundamentally misunderstood. A comment like this is one of his fallback, jokey responses, far more mock-egotistical than the real thing. He tells me he remembers an occasion when a friend's niece was showing off some gymnastic moves in the garden – 'Look at me! I can do this!' – and he similarly responded, deadpan, 'I did Knebworth.'

The question now is: how, if at all, should he deal with the disquiet he feels? This is, of course, a very Robbie Williams predicament – calibrating how over-sensitive and self-obsessed one may permit oneself to be about an article that accuses one of over-sensitivity and self-obsession. And, as is likewise often the case, he settles on a path that is both very and not at all, and is also quite funny.

He sends Sawyer some cakes and, with them, a note that reads: 'Thanks, Miranda. Actually, it's *three* nights at Knebworth...'

Capitol Studios | 2001

'I'd never seen myself as a singer. And here I was in Studio A in the basement of the Capitol Records building in Los Angeles, where Frank Sinatra recorded many of his albums, just about to open my mouth in front of all of these legendary musicians to record *Swing When You're Winning*. That was very, very ballsy. I had a whole orchestra that have played with Tony Bennett, Frank Sinatra and Dean Martin, and there was little old me who used to get up in a pub in Hanley when it was open mike night, and where Bill Pope used to play the organ and I'd sing "Every Time We Say Goodbye". But I managed to lose myself in the performances, and it was kind of like a busman's holiday, really. It felt a bit like *The Generation Game*: "We've seen them do it – now you do it!" It was like I'd won a competition.'

'I made sure that I went round to absolutely everybody in the band and shook their hands and thanked them, and kind of got them on my side. I felt very fortunate, very, very lucky to be in the position that I was, and not completely fouling up.'

Swing When You're Winning
unused sleeve | 2001

'We'd had an idea that Peter Blake would paint the album cover. And it came back, and it's an amazing painting, it was beautiful, but it somehow just wasn't right. I think it hurt his feelings a bit that we didn't use it.'

Swing When You're Winning
sleeve shoot | 2001

'We wanted to capture the environment and the mood of a Frank Sinatra photo shoot. I think we just tried to make it as Frank as possible. I remember my depression was in full swing – excuse the non-pun – at the time. The upside of it is you can fit into any clothes you like. Sample sizes and beyond. The downside is that you want to die.'

Live at the Royal
Albert Hall
rehearsals | 2001

'It's an amazing stage set, that.
Huge. I got that thin with the
worry that the shirt was now
too big for me.'

Live at the Royal Albert Hall rehearsals | 2001

'A friend of mine was good friends with Jon Lovitz.
I never envisioned at the start of the project how
big things were going to be, it was just, "Does Jon
sing? Get Jon to come down..." And he did, and
he did a really, really good job. That's one of my
favourite swing songs: "... have you heard it's in
the stars..." It's Christmas once again, you're off
school, you're watching *High Society* and you're
lost in the glamour of it all. And then there you
are, ten years later, trying to portray the same sort
of glamour that was so infectious when you were
eating clementines and roasting chestnuts.'

Live at the Royal Albert Hall | 2001

'This was beforehand. I had one chance to get it right, nowhere to hide. I performed completely on the tip of my toes on adrenalin. Like my life depended on it. Up onstage you can't read how well it's going, how badly it's going, what you sound like, whether you're in key, whether they're buying it. I didn't actually realise how well I'd done until I saw a version of it back two months later. That night, I got off stage – everybody's going "whhheyyyy!" – went straight back home, had a Chinese and went to bed.'

'Something Stupid' video | 2001

'Another one of those moments where you're lost in little-boy land, sort of very impressed with the glamour of Hollywood that was sat opposite. Moments like that, you very much feel as though you're from Stoke-on-Trent, and what the fuck are you doing here? Nicole Kidman was very kind, she was well up for doing the video, and she did it really well, and sang the song really well. I just felt honoured that somebody with the class and the glamour and the talent and the prestige would do it. I spent the day of the video worrying about not doing anything that she'd disapprove of.'

Stoke | 2002

'Part of my charity work – a day blitzing Stoke, visiting the
places that my money had helped out. This particular place
was an old folks home and they were doing bingo and stuff.
Stoke is, for me, and I would say for the majority of the people
who live there, a very, very special place. You feel proud to be a
Stokie. It's the place where I grew up, and I spent a lot of time in
fantasy there, the way kids can make a dreamland out of places.
Playing army in the fields and in the bushes, or imagining
yourself in Narnia, or as a pop star, or running down the wing at
Port Vale and scoring a goal in the FA Cup to knock Tottenham
out – all of these things I've been in Stoke-on-Trent. So the
place obviously is very important in my heart. I feel like Stoke-
on-Trent's my mum and dad, or my extended family. I decided
that I was going to give a portion of what I'd earned away, and I
wanted to see it in action, so I've given back to Stoke-on-Trent.'

Los Angeles | 2002

'Recording *Escapology*. I don't
know why I bought a Superman
costume. It was just a way to
distract me, I suppose. I like
an all-in-one.'

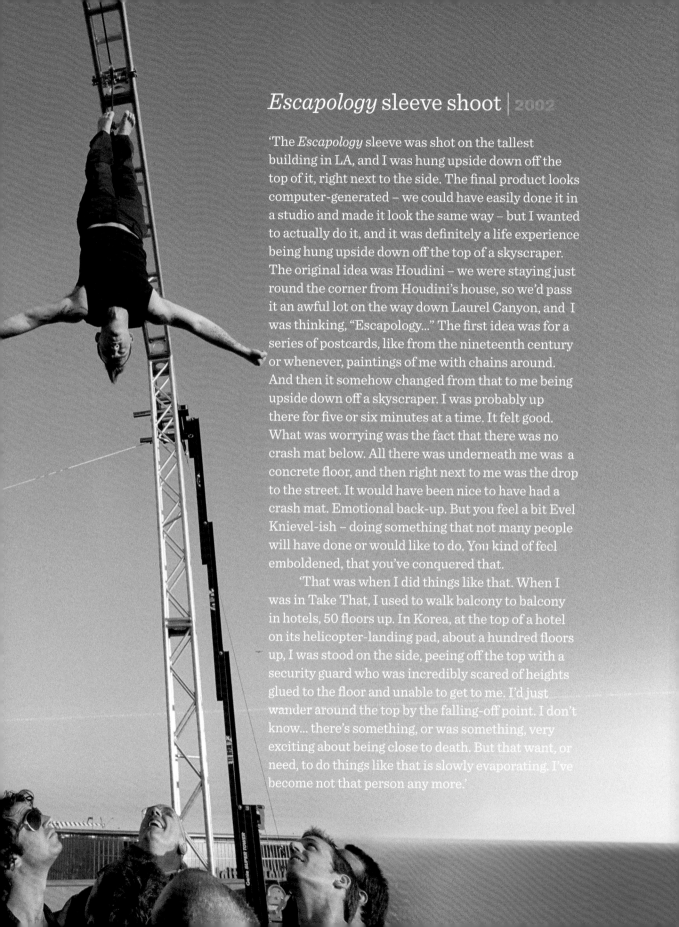

Escapology sleeve shoot |

'The *Escapology* sleeve was shot on the tallest building in LA, and I was hung upside down off the top of it, right next to the side. The final product looks computer-generated – we could have easily done it in a studio and made it look the same way – but I wanted to actually do it, and it was definitely a life experience being hung upside down off the top of a skyscraper. The original idea was Houdini – we were staying just round the corner from Houdini's house, so we'd pass it an awful lot on the way down Laurel Canyon, and I was thinking, "Escapology..." The first idea was for a series of postcards, like from the nineteenth century or whenever, paintings of me with chains around. And then it somehow changed from that to me being upside down off a skyscraper. I was probably up there for five or six minutes at a time. It felt good. What was worrying was the fact that there was no crash mat below. All there was underneath me was a concrete floor, and then right next to me was the drop to the street. It would have been nice to have had a crash mat. Emotional back-up. But you feel a bit Evel Knievel-ish – doing something that not many people will have done or would like to do. You kind of feel emboldened, that you've conquered that.

'That was when I did things like that. When I was in Take That, I used to walk balcony to balcony in hotels, 50 floors up. In Korea, at the top of a hotel on its helicopter-landing pad, about a hundred floors up, I was stood on the side, peeing off the top with a security guard who was incredibly scared of heights glued to the floor and unable to get to me. I'd just wander around the top by the falling-off point. I don't know... there's something, or was something, very exciting about being close to death. But that want, or need, to do things like that is slowly evaporating. I've become not that person any more.'

'I'm having a head massage because there's too much blood in there.'

Los Angeles | 2002

'Another Houdini idea. I'm getting into a cylinder full of water, doing something else that not many people have done.'

'I'd seen a picture of my body, with the optical illusion making it look massive, and so I thought: "I wonder if it'll do that to my cock..."'

Canada | 2002

'The "Feel" video. Miles and miles from anyone and anywhere. Just glorious scenery. And Daryl Hannah, she's lovely. She's a little pixie, a little angelic soul. She was incredibly easy to get along with. Not kind of... a superstar. She was big in my childhood – *Splash* and all the other films that she was in. But there are some people you bump into, particularly in Los Angeles, that are, like, "Fucking hell, you're impressive," and then there's some people out here that are really impressive but are just like, "Fucking hell, you're my mate." She was my mate.'

Canada | **2002**

'I love that picture. It's the only picture I'll have of myself up in the house. I couldn't ride before, but I picked it up very quickly. Me and the horse were one for a bit. It was really cool.'

De-Lovely | 2003

'During those Sunday afternoons listening and learning my dad's records, there were a lot of Cole Porter songs amongst them. I decided to honour what Cole Porter had meant to me when I was a kid when I was asked to be in the film about Cole Porter's life. I was the wedding singer. It was then that I realised that I really, really didn't want to act. You have to get up so early and you go to bed so late, and then there's the amount of time you have to sit around doing nothing. When you do a video shoot, it's based around *you*. I'm so slipshod with an awful lot of things that when I came to lip-sync back to my song in *De-Lovely*, I didn't know the words. I was being shot over the shoulder of Kevin Kline and Ashley Judd, and it was quite obvious that I was getting the words wrong. And to my embarrassment, I got a bit of a bollocking from the director, Irwin Winkler. I got sent home so I would learn the words. I felt like I was at school, as though I'd had a bollocking from a teacher. As though I was in trouble with my mum. It felt horrendous. The *shame*. But I was bang on the next day.'

London | 2003

'Stephen Duffy at Air Studios, Haverstock Hill, the first day we wrote together. It's the boxiest of box rooms, tiny tiny tiny, tucked away at the top of a few staircases – a storage room, really. And that's where we spent a few months knocking together a few songs. The first thing we came up with was "Sin Sin Sin", and I just thought the verse was so brilliant: "*don't let your eyes tell the brain / you should feel ashamed / everyone needs it baby...*" I thought, "Ooh, we're definitely onto something." We're both playing the guitar here – I don't know what we're singing. Stephen hadn't got the memo from Guy that I wasn't supposed to touch the instruments, and I didn't let him know that I couldn't play anything really, and just tried my best to fumble through lots of different instruments. And Stephen had the patience to let me. It was fun. It was my time to come from an art school for a little while .'

Berlin | 2003

'That's how the show started. Most nights, it worked as a shot of adrenalin, the fact that you're upside down and the curtains are going to be drawn back and there's going to be thousands of people staring at you. It certainly is a fantastically weird way to see an audience.'

Europe | 2003

'There are several little bits in a show that keep the momentum going and make it interesting. I'm always glad to do a little bit. The little bit on this tour was getting a fan onstage and kissing them or grinding with them. I thought I'd give it a go, and one particular night it worked and it got a reaction from the crowd, so I thought I'd keep it in. I'd always try to pick one that was attractive but it's difficult to know what's below the barrier. So you never knew what you were going to get. Sometimes it got a bit scary. I'm just *acting*, they're in it for real.'

But you were prepared to take it as far as you could, weren't you?

'Yeah.'

If you fancied kissing them properly and they were into it, you'd do it?

'Yeah. I am a slapper.'

Isn't that weird? Pulling someone out of the crowd and sharing tongues in front of 80,000 people?

'Showmanship. Mixed with a little bit of pleasure. I don't know – you egg yourself on, and it gets more and more provocative each night. And you see how far you can take it. Here I'm doing full-on Mr Casanova.'

How far would be too far?

'I think exposing my genitals in a stadium would be bad.'

Right.

'Maybe in an arena it would be okay.'

Copenhagen | 2003

'That's weird – I just played footie in that top this morning.
Here, I'm probably going through the notes from Lee Lodge
who's behind me – he made notes for me each night: "For
this bit, be here, and for that bit, do this, and for this bit, sing
louder..." By the end of the tour some of it had sunk in. Max
Beesley was on tour with us. It's always good to have a mate
around. Max is a fantastic character and an amazing musician.
The show was a bit long so I cut one of the swing numbers out
and he was devastated – absolutely devastated: "Kid, why don't
you take out 'Rock DJ' or something?"'

Europe | 2003

'At the beginning of the tour, I turned up at the airport – at Luton, I think it was. "We've got a surprise for you..." And I looked on the airfield and there was this massive plane and it had RW on it. Every now and again, I get incredibly embarrassed and shy, and for some reason, it *incredibly* embarrassed me, this big RW sticker. It only took one flight and I was really into it. There's all the dancers at the front there. I didn't sleep with one of them. Big regret.'

Stockholm | 2003

'Me with a sock over my cock.
Nakedness always raises
a laugh. Like farting. And,
once again, if it was a little
bit larger, there would be
no sock, and I would just be
walking around completely
naked an awful lot of the time:
less sock, more cock.'

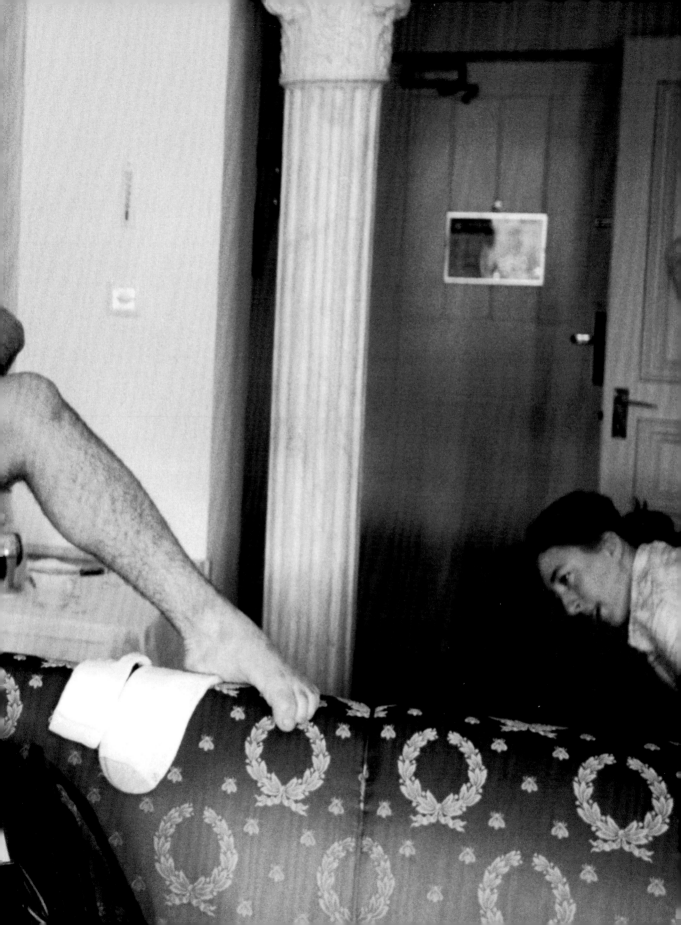

Knebworth | 2003

'Lee Lodge came up with ideas for the graphics for Knebworth; I
think they were very successful, and really good. Kind of pop art,
Andy Warhol-esque, and the early days of Banksy. Lee had given
me a booklet that I think was probably Banksy's first published
whatever. This was way before Blur did *Think Tank*. I realised I'd
seen some of Banksy's art around London – in fact, outside the flat
in Notting Hill he'd sprayed on a big white wall: *Official Graffiti Wall
Sanctioned By The Council*. I didn't realise it wasn't an official graffiti
wall sanctioned by the council, I just thought: "That's cool – it's great
round here." He's my favourite artist. I have about ten of them. Quite
fortunately, I got in before the prices went up. I like the humour, and
the anarchy. I think it appeals to most people's sense of mischief.
They're quite conspiracy-minded as well. And there's one in the
bathroom – a little girl with the balloon – that's just really beautiful.'

Knebworth | 2003

'The fear of what I was about to undertake took hold very quickly that morning. The day before the first show, I'd convinced myself that I wasn't nervous, that it would just be a walk in the park with a few friends and it'd be cool. And then I woke up the next morning and my body ached and my calves were sore and my thighs were like rocks and the base of my spine was sort of welded together in a very uncomfortable way. I got out of the bed and opened the curtains – we were staying at a hotel about fifteen miles away – and it was a beautiful, sunny day in England, the magic kind of sunny day that we get every now and again, and there in front of me was the Harrods helicopter with the two pilots waiting to take me to the gig. Along with the pilots there were a bunch of well-wishers stood next to the helicopter, and of course as soon as I opened the curtains a big cheer went up: "Wheyyyy!" And I really tried my best to convey to them that everything was great, and inside it just wasn't. It felt as though the eyes of the world were just about to set upon me.'

'When the helicopter took off, Jonny turned to me and said, "You know what song's in my head now, youth?" And I said, "What song's in your head?" And he goes, "YMCA! It's fun to stay at the YMCA!", with a big smile on his face. "What song's in your head?" And I went: "Don't give up... you know we'll make it through." Peter Gabriel and Kate Bush.'

Knebworth | 2003

'Jonny saw it before me, and he just went, "Fuck me, youth." I looked over to see what he could see, and there was that sea of people. It looked as though the whole world had come to see me. This awe-inspiring sight. And every part of me wanted to hijack the helicopter and fly somewhere else.'

Knebworth | 2003

'Fortunately, for the longest time in my career, I've been able to count on the fact that, no matter what I'm feeling inside, people can't read it on the outside. Even my best friends and management have never been able to read what's going on on the inside when I'm onstage. Even though the crowd are loving it from the start, it makes no odds. There's still 135,000 of them. I've got to pretend now, as is my act, that I think I'm a hundred men, a caged lion being unleashed on this public that's waiting to be entertained, that I'm so confident that I can hold them all in the palm of my hand, and entertain them each, and make them feel loved, make them feel laughter, make them feel happy, make them cry, make them go home happy. I think it was probably about eight songs into the show until I actually said, "I'm back!"'

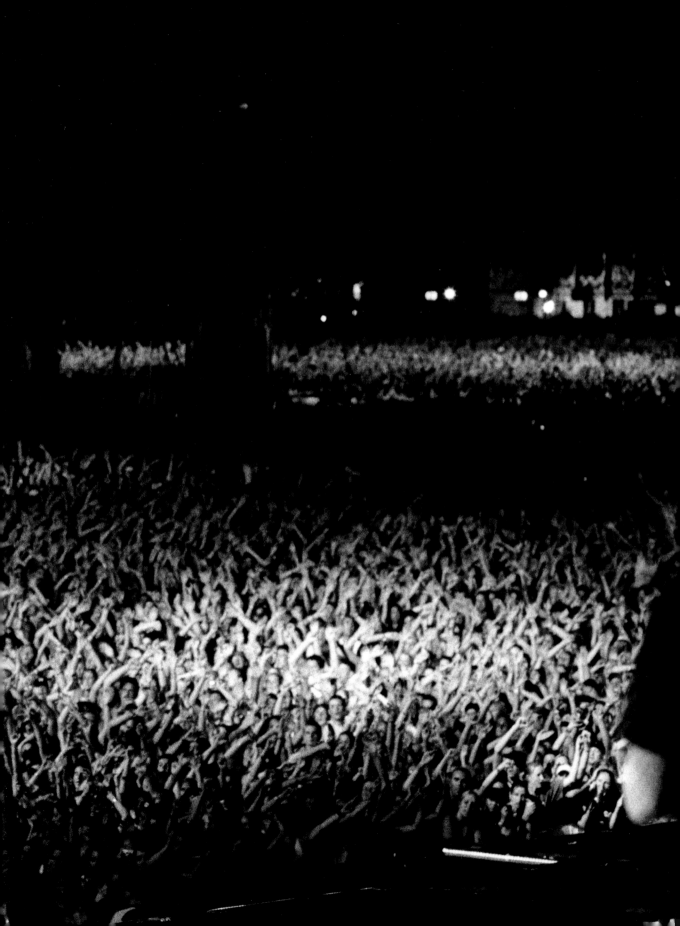

Knebworth | 2003

'Ant and Dec have been a fixture in my life for several years now. They kind of put me to shame, the grounded northern-ness they have and are, and also the perfectionists that they are. It's great having a partner. That was the great bit about being in Take That – that you were bothered because you had to be bothered for the other people. And I think I would work better now if somebody was alongside me that I couldn't let down. Those boys hate letting each other down, so they work really hard and they're incredible at what they do. It looks easy, but it's only easy because of the work they put in.'

'I love Wayne. He's incredibly shy and I am too, but he's more shy than me so I kind of thought I had to take the brunt of both of our shynesses, and at least try and talk.'

'On the last night, Mark Owen came. He was my best mate when I was in Take That but we hadn't seen each other for ages, and I felt kind of embarrassed that I was in such a manic state. I'd bought all his albums and really enjoyed his music, and wished and hoped that more people would appreciate what he was doing.'

Moscow | 2003

'During the tour, I did a UNICEF trip to an orphanage. I sang for them and played the guitar – "Better Man", I think. Played football with them outside. Everybody was lovely but I remember just how harsh it all seemed. Also, it's tradition to have bread and salt, and they gave me some bread and a bowl of salt, and I put too much salt on the bread. It was just horrible. And I remember not being able to spit it out or eat it, because my mouth was too dry, so I was in a bit of a two-and-eight about it. Eventually, I managed to dispose of it without offending anybody.'

6

'...at what point
did you realise...'

One afternoon, Rob and I are sitting in the nook at the far end of his bedroom, talking, when suddenly, unexpectedly:

MR BLUE SKY...

Music blares out from the ceiling at a deafening volume.

... PLEASE TELL US WHY...

We are under attack from ELO.

... YOU HAD TO HIDE AWAY...

It surrounds us, so loud that we can barely hear each other.

... FOR SO LONG...

Even if we shout.

These are the kind of mishaps that can befall you if you live with a sophisticated house-wide entertainment system. Rob gets on the phone. Someone technical, it turns out, is working on the system downstairs and is unaware of the easy-listening havoc he has unleashed in the rooms above.

'Hello? HELLO? "Mr Blue Sky" is on in the bedroom...' Rob pleads. 'Can you turn it off?... Thank you...'

Another unforeseen peril of modern luxury living.

* * *

Rob will often reflect on how lazy he is, and he will also often bemoan the pressure he is under from all he is doing. Strangely, at times these two apparently contradictory impulses make some sort of sense. Right now, for instance, he is supposed to be on a total break, and he is spending a fair amount of time doing little more than playing games, watching reality TV in bed, swimming in the pool, watching football on the TV downstairs, planning more games, watching strange documentaries on the internet, and – in between all of these arduous pursuits, by way of recovering from them – simply lounging around.

And yet, right now, he is also on a manic exercise regime. Most days a trainer comes round and leads him through a long, multi-discipline workout in the basement gym. He also plays football several times a week. (It's when I've passed by those games, and seen him taking quiet enjoyment from slotting into a team, doing his best to fill a useful role with restraint, that I most believe that he would really like to sink into the shared responsibility and teamwork of a band.) And there is also, despite being on a break, a fair amount of what one might call work. Working on this book, for instance. Most days

I arrive with a pile of photographs and ask him to spend a couple of hours remembering, a kind of reflection which can bring out the best of his impishness and playfulness but which also clearly sometimes takes a toll. One more of the many thousands of mixed blessings that comes with celebrity: how little freedom you are allowed to let your past recede. It is always revisiting, disturbing your present, nagging you, reminding you, tugging at your sleeve. Even if one's past was full of nothing but glories – and whose is? – one might well feel harassed by its persistent interruptions.

My visits aside, he is constantly hatching plans: proposals of when to tour, where to tour, how to tour, how not to tour; records to write, records to record, records to release, records not to release; songs to write, songs to rewrite, songs to finish. For every grand scheme that comes to fruition, several others have usually been thought up, plotted out, enthused about, worked through and then, often only at the end of a long process, either set aside, postponed or abandoned. But when inspired by an idea that captivates him, in that particular moment he can be surprisingly hands-on. One day I arrive at the house to find him keenly researching the ticket pricing structures between different tiers at a famous venue in order to work out the feasibility of his most recent masterplan.

Quite often, he is actually working on songs. Sometimes, he is trying to improve lyrics to a near-finished song for his next project, say, but he is just as likely to be writing something new, either with one of the number of more- or less-regular collaborators he now has, or with someone new he has just run into.

More specific one-off commitments come up fairly often, too. (These often have a pattern. He agrees to them. Closer to the time, he'll somewhat regret agreeing to them. He'll wonder if he can get out of them. Usually, if it is important enough and hard to cancel, he nonetheless goes ahead.) Today, he has two such commitments looming. One is a foreign trip of several days. The other is to go round this evening to the studio the producer Trevor Horn has at his Bel Air home (a studio Rob first visited several years back to record his dialogue for *The Magic Roundabout*). Rob is due there to record a vocal for the new version of the England World Cup anthem 'Three Lions'. Russell Brand is also supposed to be recording his contribution today.

As it turns out, their paths don't cross. After Rob returns, he announces, 'I think I may have ballsed it up in a way.' He arrived to discover that the song's chosen key was too low for him to be able to sing the song in the spirit it requires. 'There was nothing to grasp onto,' he explains. So he and Trevor Horn changed the key so he could sing the song as he felt he should. But this may have created its own, new problem. 'Everybody else that's done a vocal on it hasn't sung in that key,' he says. 'So it's either me singing the whole thing, or whoever else was singing on it needs to come and redo the vocals.'

* * *

Trevor Horn, the producer who first became famous for his innovatively lush and vivid widescreen productions for groups such as ABC and Frankie Goes To Hollywood, produced Rob's last album, *Reality Killed The Video Star*. There is a story Rob likes to tell about their first discussion. It is a story that would be easy to misunderstand as simply reflecting not only a certain sloth on Rob's part but a fundamental lack of interest in the record he was making. But bear in mind that before Trevor Horn even got involved, all of the songs on the album had not only been written but also recorded, mostly in Rob's studio bedroom – and not just sketched out, but arranged in some detail. 'That's the part that excites me,' he explains. Hence his initial conversation with his new producer:

'Trevor said to me, "What hours do you like working?" and I said, "Friday." And he sort of laughed, and I went, "No, *Friday*."'

And so in the early stages of recording, the only involvement Rob had was to listen to the progress made at the week's end. 'For the first four weeks in the studio musos are just laying tracks down, of bass, and drums, and whatever, and it's kind of laborious and boring,' he says. 'What am I going to do? I don't know the difference between the hi-hat sound there and the hi-hat sound five minutes later after they've tweaked it. I haven't got a fucking clue. No point in me being there. A waste of time for everyone.'

The process, which eventually ended up involving Rob far more deeply, worked well. For Rob's last birthday, his 36th, he was sent a present by Horn and his manager that sits on a counter next to the table overlooking his back garden at which Rob usually eats his dinner. It is a tank, and in it are two turtles.

'Jonny wanted them to be called Cuff and Link, because of Rocky,' he says. 'Rocky had two turtles that were called Cuff and Link, and Jonny is a ridiculously big Rocky fan. He told Ayda even before I knew that I'd got them that they had to be called Cuff and Link. But I'm not a big Rocky fan. It doesn't mean that much to me. So I called them Giggsy and Rooney. Jonny was quite upset.'

His two new turtles seem to have grown into their assigned roles. 'Rooney's massive, and doesn't want to be fucked with at all – you know, you pick him up and he's so strong, he just wants to get back in the tank. He's not panicking or anything, he's just: "No – fuck off." Giggsy's quite slight and he's more up for being held than Rooney. Rooney's nearly double the size of Giggsy at the minute.'

Rooney and Giggsy remain their names, though during one of my visits Ayda comes up to interrupt Rob as he gazes at another old picture of himself. She has news.

'You know,' she says, 'Giggsy might be a girl.'

Skibo Castle | 2004

'My 30th birthday trip had been a big secret. Skibo was fantastic. It's their M.O. to not say no to anything that you ask. We were, "Can we have some chocolate?", and it came on a silver platter, Dairy Milks built up like Jenga. At one o'clock in the morning we wanted to go and hit some golf balls and they were, "Okay, we can do that," and they were going to get all their Range Rovers and turn all the lights on so we'd have a floodlit driving range. I'd always wanted to be on *Family Fortunes* – I'd got a bit of a *Family Fortunes* fetish. So for my 30th we did a version of it up at Skibo Castle. Ant and Dec came up as a surprise, and hosted the evening, and it was a lot of fun. Jonny still goes on about an answer that I gave in the last round: "Name a way that potatoes are cooked." I said "steamed". And he thinks that's hilarious. I don't think he's ever heard of a steamed potato. And he'll still bring it up, now, six years later.

"*Steamed*... ha ha ha..."

"Well, just because you haven't heard of a steamed potato doesn't mean that they don't exist."

"Course they fucking don't."

"Well, they actually fucking do."

"I can't believe you said 'steamed', you knob."

"Well, 'baked' had been taken."

"*Steamed*...'"

'I had to plant a tree, my very own tree, named after me. There were other trees planted by various celebrities and dignitaries. The last tree had been planted by Madonna – I think she got married there. I didn't see the point of it, to be honest, but I just went along with it.'

'Radio' video | 2004

'I was reading a lot of David Icke stuff at the time, so I think a reptilian kind of motif was running through my head, and that came through in this video. To the uninitiated, David Icke reckons that shape-shifting reptilians run the world. The Queen, Royal Family, MPs, big bankers. Reptilians seem to have gone on the back burner for David over the last few years but at the time they kind of made sense to me – that there's an unfortunate kind of dark imprint on the world running through everything, and the only suitable explanation is that it's unfeeling reptilians. I don't necessarily *believe* it, but I don't necessarily disbelieve it either. I keep an open mind on things... though you do hope your brain doesn't fall out of your very open mind. I think it was also at this point that I wanted actual vampire teeth. I was ahead of the curve by a few years. I was actually going to go to the dentist and have long teeth added. But Josie convinced me not to. At one point I was also going to shave my head and have fire tattooed on it. I was talked out of that too. It was a passing fancy.'

Greatest Hits sleeve shoot | 2004

'In 2004, I was in the midst of my Morrissey phase.
I think a lot of the lyrics on *Intensive Care* were kind
of Morrissey-esque, or me trying to be Morrissey.
And I'd seen a few Morrissey pictures in his younger
days where he was doing kind of homoerotic-by-
a-swimming-pool. It was a good visual, and so
I decided to channel his homoeroticism for the
Greatest Hits cover. You could look at it and think,
that fellow really, really digs himself, but I was just
copying Morrissey. Around this time, there was talk
of us performing together at the Brits. I was told he'd
said, "I'd only do it if Robbie'll kiss me at the end of
it..." There were two stipulations – one, that we'd do
his song "Let Me Kiss You", and the other was that
we kiss each other at the end. I was bang up for that.
Kissing Morrissey. That would have been great.
Because he's just got, like, a fiercely brilliant face.
Watching the idolatry that surrounds him, I think
thousands and thousands of straight men would
sleep with Morrissey. And I might not *sleep* with
Morrissey but I'd have a cuddle and a kiss.'
Would you be doing it for the right reasons?
'What are the wrong reasons?'
So why didn't it happen?
'I don't know. I think he pulled out. I think he was
probably a bit bluffing. Maybe. But I wasn't. I'd have
wrestled him to the floor. And dominated him.'

At home | 2005

'I'm emailing. I email, surf the internet, read about conspiracies, look for interesting documentaries, download music. It would be fair to say that I'm addicted to my computer. But, at the same time, I wasn't allowed my computer in rehab for three weeks and I didn't miss it. Though I did manage to smuggle in an iPod. As I was in the middle of making an album, I was given special dispensation one Sunday to go to a room and listen to music for an hour. Afterwards, I got my wallet, which felt the same weight as the iPod, and I replaced the iPod with my wallet in the box and gave it them back and said "thank you", and kept my iPod and the headphones. Any little bits of naughtiness in rehab just feel tremendous.'

Willow Springs | 2005

'I needed a new hobby. The guy that was working with me at the time, Pomp, had a big love for motorbikes, and it was quite contagious. I'd been watching a lot of hip hop videos and at the time the Ruff Ryders were riding these Suzukis, and I just thought they looked so cool. I thought, "I'll have a bit of that." So I went out to buy myself a big machine, and the first one that I set my eyes on was a Honda, I think it's a CDR 1000, Repsol colours. I just really loved the colours. I got myself leathers and started renting a racetrack out up in Willow Springs, in the nether regions of the Valley here, about 40 minutes away from the house. And it was just a really bad idea, me and anything that goes fast, because I was intent on driving as fast as I could. I'd only been on a motorbike once before, for a couple of days in Bath when I went to pass my motorbike test. And the next time was this: going 174 miles an hour around a racetrack. I went up there a few times, but the whole of my body and the whole of my very being was just going, "Don't do this, Rob, please don't do this, it's not you, you know what's going to happen." I was trying to do things that I wasn't yet capable of doing and shouldn't have even been attempting.'

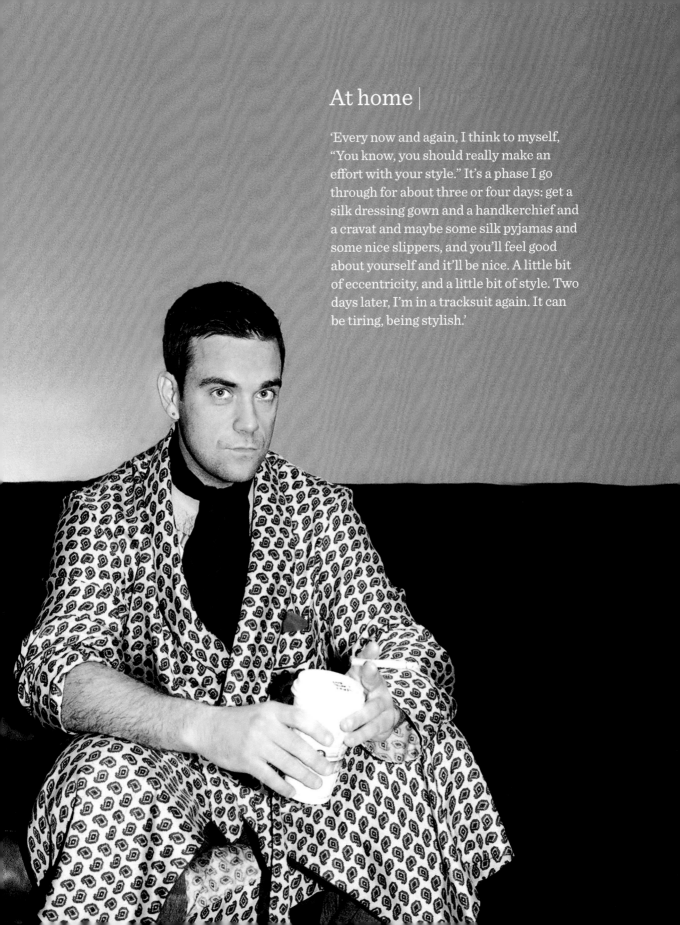

At home |

'Every now and again, I think to myself,
"You know, you should really make an
effort with your style." It's a phase I go
through for about three or four days: get a
silk dressing gown and a handkerchief and
a cravat and maybe some silk pyjamas and
some nice slippers, and you'll feel good
about yourself and it'll be nice. A little bit
of eccentricity, and a little bit of style. Two
days later, I'm in a tracksuit again. It can
be tiring, being stylish.'

Comic Relief | 2005

'Though it's not my bag to be an actor, it's always great to be asked to be in TV sketch shows that you're a big fan of. It's great to do something that you wouldn't normally do, and to be invited into something as brilliant as *Little Britain* is definitely ten Brit Awards. It was also great because I could do it – I could do the character that they do. And the dress was very, very comfortable. I felt at ease all day. There's a lot of room for movement with your legs and stuff. It's just basically a kaftan. With a cinched waist.'

Los Angeles | 2005

'I have a five-a-side field, the field of dreams, up at the top of a
certain mountain in Beverly Hills, and I would say it's definitely
"top five best five-a-side fields in the world". There's a net all over
the top to stop the balls from going out, eight floodlights, eight
speakers for piped music, a club house, and it's exactly what you'd
want if you were a fourteen-year-old boy. I've had a load of pro
players play up there, who have played in the World Cup, won the
World Cup, played for England, played Premier League football,
etc., etc. I'd say I'm average at football. When I'm fit, I'm just a bit
above average, but the times of being fit are few and far between,
and interrupted by injuries, and getting old.'

'Me with a sweat on. It's the best feeling in the world, having a sweat on, only thinking about where your next movement is, where you're going to pick up the ball, where you're going to receive it, where you're going to place it next. The endorphins are going and everything else fades away.'

Los Angeles | 2005

'There's me standing next to a very good-looking man. I remember seeing David Beckham for the first time at *Top of the Pops* with Victoria Beckham. Me and Jonny are such big fans, and Jonny famously said he didn't know whether to shake his hand or lick his face. I kind of felt the same way, and still did when he was in the room with me and I was sharing space with him here, just talking to him, the unbelievable fan boy that I am as regards to footballers or anything to do with football. I just wanted Dave to like me and to do my best for Dave. These photos were for UNICEF. We went out on the pitch and LA Galaxy's third string-goalie was in goals and we took shots at him, and David Beckham showed me how to take a free kick. It was incredible watching him, because the only thing I can do with a free kick is try to bend it slowly, but it more *floats*. He hits it as hard as he can, and it goes up and down. It's quite amazing. He has practised and practised and practised and practised. It was quite funny because Dean, a mate of mine at the time, had been teaching me football, how to take free kicks, and he was, "You know, with Dave, if you look, he does the same thing every time – he puts the ball down, he looks at the goalkeeper, he takes a sidestep, he takes three paces back, he deh deh deh deh…' So now I'm with David Beckham and I'm like, "Yeah, so you go…" and tell him. And he says, "No, I don't do any of that. I just hit it."'

'I was supposed to interview Dave walking onto the pitch. I was, "I don't know what the fuck I'm going to say." So I asked him if he liked butter. He said, "Yeah, I like butter."'

Intensive Care sleeve shoot | 2005

'I got a DVD from The Disinformation Society and on the bonus disc there was a guy called Grant Morrison who gave this amazing, inspiring speech about the wonders of Sigil Magic and magic in general. So I got in touch with him, met up with him, and did a bit of magic myself. And he worked on the sleeve of *Intensive Care*, which is a kind of graphic novel. I also bought Aleister Crowley's books. I remember seeing and hearing about Aleister Crowley when I was a kid and being absolutely terrified of him, so I found myself visiting occult bookshops and wanting to learn about why I was scared. And wanting to overcome it, and maybe use it for my own purposes.'

What purposes did you have in mind?

'I think I just wanted to create a girlfriend, to be honest with you, at the time.'

What magic did you actually do?

'I did some Sigil Magic.'

What does that involve?

'People would have to find out for themselves – google "Sigil Magic" and have a go.'

Did it involve rituals and substances?

'It involved a ritual, yes. Not substances, no. It involves an intention, and an invocation invoking that intention, and you can invoke that intention by many means. It's always extremes.'

Why did you stop doing it?

'Because you don't really know what you're dealing with, to be honest. I mean, you could invoke magic to sell five or six million albums but you might be doing it at the expense of your own life. But there's a little symbol on the finger on the *Intensive Care* sleeve and it's Sigil Magic. And it worked.'

What did it mean?

'I'm not saying.'

Berlin | 2005

'A one-off, big, gig-sized venue for a TV special, in my pink *Hi-de-Hi!* suit. I broke my arm playing football a couple of nights before, so I had to have one of those injections footballers have because I was in pain. Fracturing your arm, you feel nauseous all the time. And I did this gig with a fractured arm.'

'Advertising Space' video |2005

'This was David LaChapelle's idea, who directed it. I'm an Elvis impersonator. Elvis is so beautiful that, although bits and bobs of it were fun, you feel yourself at all times paling in comparison to anything that the King can do, or radiate. A radio station in Blackpool quite kindly announced exactly where I was, so I'd be walking down one side of the road by myself in my leathers with my guitar pretending that I was lost and lonely but there were two thousand people on the other side of the road. I was, "I should do something for them," so I sang "Angels" over the megaphone. They didn't join in. I was like, "Okay, I tried." The weirdest thing was that on Blackpool Pier there was this massive advert for a show with lookalikes, and it was Michael Jackson, Tina Turner, Freddie Mercury... and me. That was a wobbly moment of: "That's too much to take in."'

Los Angeles | 2005

'The tour programme photo shoot. I think it was supposed to be a mixture of *Signs* and *Close Encounters of the Third Kind*. People think I grew a beard and started my interest in aliens a couple of years back, but my interest in extraterrestrials has been ever since I can remember. I think there's lots of contributing factors, like when I first watched *The Hitchhiker's Guide to the Galaxy*, the TV series, and that spaceship came over to blow up the planet. That kind of blew my mind as a ten-year-old. It opened up a whole range of possibilities. This tour was called Close Encounters because of my interest in extraterrestrials and also because of me having close encounters with the public. Or the public having close encounters with me.'

Cape Town | 2006

'That's cool – I look a bit like Johnny Cash. We rehearsed in a winery. I must have been some kind of worried because I turned up a lot of the days to rehearse. What goes along with the factoid that three million tickets had been sold for this tour was that three million people were on the way to see me. And it's very difficult to articulate how small one feels up against that fact, walking into it. And I find it very difficult to separate each day as it comes and whatnot, so I felt the weight of three million people... and it's just *me*. It's just me by myself. If I don't turn up and do it, it all falls to shit. I was scared.'

Cape Town | 2006

'While we were rehearsing, I discovered
Photo Booth on my computer, which kept me
entertained for at least a week. It's the equivalent
of the green laserlight pens when they came out.
Just some stupid way to pass the time. In some
of them, I actually look like the people I think
live in the sky.'

'Sin Sin Sin' video | 2006

'Meanwhile videos
have just descended
into excuses for me to
kiss a lot of girls, really.
It wasn't a very tough
assignment. I loved
being a guru. It makes
me laugh.'

'Sin Sin Sin' video | 2006

'There's the guru meditating, standing on his head. It's something I've always been able to do. I used to be incredible at walking on my hands. Me and Jason Orange would have competitions to see who could stay up the longest. We'd stay up there for ages, but he'd always win. I don't stand on my head enough nowadays. You know, there's a time in your young life – and I don't know when it ends and I didn't notice it go – where you just jump over shit to see if you can jump over it. And then all of a sudden it stops and you don't see it leave.'

Durban | 2006

'The Zondi family and their friends. This was a UNICEF
visit. We all loved football, so we had something in common.
These lads just spent all day, every day, in a very confined
space, kicking the ball to each other in a small circle, while
both parents are dead in the front garden, buried in makeshift
graves. On visits like this, at some point you just feel like a silly
white man. I know that inevitably the visit draws attention to
what's going on, and that that's how charities work... but even I
sometimes feel like, "Who's this white dude coming into town?"
And I'm the white dude.'

Soccer Aid | 2006

'An amazing week, Soccer Aid. Just a week from heaven, really. It just
started with me and Jonny by the pool one day – we literally went,
"Let's get a game together, England versus The Rest Of The World,
have it for UNICEF, do it at Old Trafford, and put it on the telly, raise
some money...' And we did. This is from training. What can you say
about it, really? You've got the England training kit on, you're playing
with England players. Gazza! Terry Venables as your manager... It's
like some weird parallel universe you're stepping into. It's the lifelong
ambition of pretending to be a professional footballer for a week.
There's nothing better than that.'

Soccer Aid | 2006

'Gordon Ramsay was the opposing captain. Big boy. He's good to be around. He's inspirational. A huge character, and a really good footballer. I remember about two weeks before Soccer Aid, I was lying in bed on a Sunday, eleven o'clock in the morning, and I think I'd just tucked into my third Easter egg, and I'd got a can of Coke and a Silk Cut on, and I was feeling lethargic... and I turned the television on and Gordon Ramsay was just finishing the marathon. Yeah. That was a bit of a reality check.'

'Against The Rest Of The World, we won 2-1 and Bobby Charlton gave me the cup. This is the practice game, England versus The Legends, at Fulham. There's a shirt with "Williams" on, and I'm in it, and there's a shirt with "Beardsley" on, and he's in it. Just amazing. When we were waiting to go on the pitch, I had gone into this kind of comatose staring, and I just looked to my left and there was Peter Beardsley, and I went, "Hiya, Peter Beardsley." And I realised what I'd done, and I looked round to Dave Seaman who was behind me, and he just looked at me and shook his head, really disappointed.'

Dublin | 2006

'I'd felt nerves before but something about these nerves was different on this tour. Beforehand I was feeling absolutely horrendous.'

Dublin | 2006

'For the encore on that tour, a little lift took me to the top of the scaffolding where I'd start "Let Me Entertain You" before coming down on a gondola. This was the first night, I'm 120 foot up in the air in a gondola, the audience below... and the gondola doesn't move. I'm in front of 80,000 people. There was nothing to do but go back down the lift, still singing the song. It just capped off a very, very nervous night. I thought I wasn't at my best, and after coming down in the lift, I said, "I haven't been very good tonight – I'll come back and do you a free show." I think they're still holding me to that. And so they should – I promised them. But I didn't realise what was to come on the tour. I didn't realise that that evening wasn't a one-off – that was pretty much how my nerves wouldn't be holding up for the rest of the tour.'

Rudebox sleeve | 2006

'It was funny the first time I performed the song "Rudebox" live, at Hampden Park. In my mind, it was: "It's going to be another glorious victory for the boy Williams who reinvents himself so majestically again and again and again." But when it started, the whole of the stadium kind of collectively took one step back and just looked at me with bewilderment, just a lot of Scots with puzzlement on their faces. As much as frighten me, it actually made me giggle, the response that it got. You have to understand that we'd been having a very magical time in the studio in my bedroom in Los Angeles, just having a laugh, and the process had been easier than for any of the other albums. I just thought that, because of the enjoyment that we got out of it, that would be translated to my audience. I thought I'd made a brilliant album and I still do. I think it is my favourite me album.'

Vienna | 2006

'I've always loved playing Vienna. It's one that I always look forward to. The first time we went there, we were told that the crowds were notoriously quiet, and I was quite overwhelmed by how boisterous the crowd was, and how willing they were to have a good time. And then every time I go back, the Viennese go mental. It's a special gig.'

Vienna | **2006**

'Did she have that prepared? Because how could
she possibly *know*? Perhaps she had two signs
ready: YOU'RE SHIT TONIGHT or YOU WERE
FUCKIN' GREAT! THANKS BABY. I'm glad to see
that she used the YOU WERE FUCKIN' GREAT!
THANKS BABY one.'

Leeds | **2006** 'Because Knebworth had been so big, when I got to the UK on this tour I kind of undermined myself, thinking that I had to be as good as that again. I was overwhelmed.'

'She's Madonna' video | 2006

'It can be a bit too easy doing generic aftershave commercials for your song, and there was an eclectic weirdness for this video that I liked. It was different and pierced the screen in a different kind of way. It was also weird and wonderful being around a load of trannies, and it was nice to be a tranny for a little bit, even though I don't make the best woman. I'd like to be more beautiful as a woman.'

Mexico | 2006

'Fannying about on a moped. There's Manny – he's passed away, bless him. Member of a notorious biker gang, German security, a great bloke, the coolest German I knew. He had become a kind of mainstay in my life over the last fifteen years. Sad that he won't be there the next time we go out on tour.'

Buenos Aires | 2006

'Buenos Aires is completely fucking mental and wonderful. Just to think that I was doing stadiums in South America… that's incredible. I'm very proud of that – very proud of how it all went over and of how it was received. I think for that year I was the biggest-selling Anglo-Saxon solo artist in South America. And they used to say, "Of course Robbie Williams the phenomena won't travel…"'

Sydney | 2006

'Australia's always great to visit – it's a place where I could see myself living. I love the people down there. It's a bit like England in the 70s.'

Sydney | 2006

'When I was in Australia on tour, it was just after Take That's comeback album had come out. I remember being in the same hotel as Elton John and he sent a note down to my room and it said: "Take That, number one album, number one single – funny how things work out. Elton." And I read that and I thought, "What a bizarre way to think about things." When the boys had a number one album and a number one single, I was stood in front of 60,000, 70,000 people a night myself. I'm trying to think if there was even a part of me that wasn't pleased for them, and I can't recognise me having that. So when I read that note, I just thought, "Well, you live in a world that I don't live in..."'

Melbourne | 2006

'I recognise how I felt there. Last show of the tour. I hadn't slept the night before. And it wasn't for partying or being nefarious, it was just because I couldn't. Proper insomnia. It was crazy-making how fucking knackered I was on that tour. Even once the tour was finished, I didn't feel relieved because I knew I'd been spending energy that I didn't have, and I knew there was going to be some sort of payment – spiritually, physically and mentally – for what I'd just been through. If you go on tour and come off tour and you're sober, it's a horrendous comedown anyway. At eight o'clock your body switches on and goes, "Hey! Hey, *everybody*! LET ME ENTERTAIN *YOUUUUUU!!!!!*" You don't know *what* to do. You're bouncing off walls for at least a month. This time, I was that, but with the added, "Oh, I've got a dependency as well." It was really bad. I was pretty broken. I suppose there was a breakdown. I stayed in a lot. Watched TV. Did drugs. The week before rehab, I just lived on chocolate éclairs. For eight days, the only thing I ate was chocolate éclairs. For *eight days*. And I'm serious – nothing other than éclairs. By the beginning of 2007, I didn't care if I was dead or not. There's no photos from then. At least I had the sense to not do it in public.'

7

'...in my own way
I haven't changed...'

As he is well aware, there is a popular notion that one day a few years ago Robbie Williams went mad, grew a beard, became obsessed by UFOs, and remained lost to sanity and pop music until, thankfully, he somehow snapped to his senses, shaved, and put such lunacy behind him, once more becoming the beloved Robbie Williams of old.

It's a potent storyline, and a reasonably entertaining one, too (especially if it's not about you), but it's one that misunderstands almost everything that actually happened. It just wasn't like that. To begin with, as he has pointed out, Rob's curiosity about such things didn't suddenly emerge. 'I've always had an interest in the paranormal, ever since I was a kid,' he says. 'It wasn't like it sprang up as soon as I grew a beard.' (And so, if his interest in this stuff made him a nutter, it was a nutter he had always been.) It was this very same world-view, these very same interests, that many years ago inspired his most famous and most universal song. 'I believed that stuff when I wrote "Angels" – that's why I wrote it,' he points out. '"Angels" isn't *about* anybody, it's about the thoughts that loved ones who have passed on come back and take care of you.'

Nor has this kind of curiosity since abated. Asked to explain some of what currently fascinates him, the reasonably clean-shaven 2010 pop star version of Robbie Williams reels off a comprehensive list including conspiracies, UFOs, religions, weather manipulation and 2012 phrophecy. 'I'm open to a lot of possibilities that are unseen. I'm sure a lot of people would find that bonkers. I personally don't.'

What was distinct about the time between the end of his 2006 world tour and the release of *Reality Killed The Video Star* in the autumn of 2009 was that, having decided to stay away from the pop music merry-go-round for a while, he had the opportunity and time to indulge his fascination in such things. He also had a girlfriend who was happy to explore them with him. For most of one summer, they slept in a tent in the back garden. 'We'd listen to radio shows and scour the internet. Mainly for stuff to do with the paranormal. We'd have books on tape, watch DVDs and then pop out the tent and jump in the pool and then come back and cuddle and do all those things that people do when they're new and in love.' They also went on trips – 'Myself and Ayda and a few friends went to Morocco, Holland, Egypt, Arizona, Mexico, the Caribbean, and out into the desert a lot in California' – and some of these further fed or satisfied his curiosities.

He had a practical agenda, too, although it wasn't one that was fully formed. He sometimes imagined that instead of being a pop star he might do something else, and one notion was that he might host a TV documentary series about UFOs and the paranormal. 'I used to love Arthur C. Clarke's *Mysterious World* when I was a kid. And I thought: "I could do that." I was finding a ton of really incredible and interesting theories and stories on the internet and I thought they deserved a bigger audience.' To test the water, he made a BBC Radio 4 documentary with the journalist Jon Ronson about their visit to a UFO conference in Laughlin, Nevada. 'I wanted to see which avenues would open,' he says. 'There was something in me that wanted to go "I'm into this – I'll put it out into the universe and see what it attracts." It attracted very little, really.' Not in the way he had hoped, anyway. Anyone who listened to the documentary would have heard a man who seemed empathetic and non-judgmental without offering a naive, foolhardy blanket endorsement of those believers he spoke with, but I think for many people it was enough simply to know that the documentary existed. For the most part, it was greeted as one of those foolish, feckless moments when a celebrity goes public with a kind of private madness.

Although he has had several experiences over the years that he cannot explain but loves to describe, his journeys into the world of those who believe has left him somewhat less of a believer. 'I wanted to go and be with the people who have experienced amazing things, and research these amazing things, and be presented with the proof. But then every avenue that you turn down, unfortunately you invariably come across a charlatan selling snake oil. A lot of them don't even know that they're selling snake oil. I went into it with an open mind, erring on the side of the believer. The more I looked into it, the more sceptical I became about the stuff that's provided as evidence.' Though that's no reason to stop looking. 'I'd be sad if there wasn't anything out there that was a bit tinfoil hat and woo-ey and weird-y, but I actually don't *believe* in any of that. That's why I put myself out there – to see if I could find some truth, either way. When you've had a taste of weird things happening, you want weird things to happen again. You want to experience the things that you can't explain.'

And he would still *like* to believe.

'Am I eight years old?' he says. 'Of course. I think everybody loves a bit of magic, and sometimes I hope for that magic to be real.' One does not need to be recklessly credulous to entertain hope. 'If anything did come to pass and they did exist and there was disclosure,' he says, breaking into a smile, 'I'll be dancing a merry dance.'

A merry dance of simply being thrilled or a merry dance of 'I told you so'?

He grins. 'Both.'

* * *

Here's another way of putting it: although his scepticism endures, so does his faith that the world remains a place stranger and more shadowy than allowed by inflexible, rational modes of thought. For he knows that he himself, in his own lifetime, has seen clear evidence that such faith is not always unrewarded.

'Other unnatural things have happened,' he says. 'Me selling 60 million records is one of them.'

He giggles.

'If I can do *that*, then the possibility of life on other planets...'

Los Angeles | 2007

'In February, Tim and David, my managers, came: "There's a plane waiting. You need to pack your bags, you're going to Arizona." And it was *infuriating,* because I'd got in that place again. I'd got to where I'd been so many times before. And it's embarrassing to have to go to rehab again, knowing that you've already been, and knowing what's to come, and knowing the *boredom* that you're going to have while you're there, and being scared about the people who are going to be in there. Are you going to get on with anybody? Is anybody going to be *your* kind of nutter? Because they're all nutters, including myself. Are you going to meet a nutter who you like? And it's really fucking scary. I think everybody thinks that rehab's this place that's a bit like a health farm where you go and get pampered. I was in a hospital in a ward with four other people who were also in hospital, in single beds, being treated for an illness. It's absolutely horrendous in there. And there I was on this aeroplane being flown to Arizona, kicking the fucking seat in front of me so many times because I couldn't believe I'd allowed myself to get in that position again. I fucking hated it. Absolutely hated it.

'But I sorted it out to the best of my abilities at the time, and then couldn't wait to get back to Los Angeles. I wanted to drop out completely and not be seen and go under the radar. I wasn't thinking about coming back to my career. In July, I had a Christmas party at my house for about 70 people with snow and Father Christmas and presents. There was a snow machine and an ice bar and lots of girls dressed up in short skirts, faux Santas. Snow was over the garden. There was Father Christmas's sleigh outside, and Father Christmas, and a Christmas tree. That's me greeting people at the door – nice silk pyjamas. It was great. I don't know why I wanted Christmas in summer. There doesn't always have to be a reason. And a lot of the time, with me, there just isn't one.'

Los Angeles | 2007

'A lot of football this year. I had my own team, LA Vale. I'd set about not being a pop star, and I had no plans to do it again at this point, so I think this was my pre-UFOs UFOs. Filling the "gnawing at your own elbow with boredom" void. Because you've got to do something – entertain yourself somehow, do a little bit of work, fill in the cracks somewhere. You can't be retired at 32. It all started when a group of lads who used to come up and play at my pitch, one of them used to play for Des Moines Menace in Iowa, and he got invited to bring a team to play the Des Moines Menace pre-season. So we became LA Vale. We got a private jet and Adidas did our kits and we went to Des Moines, and had the best time. It was just brilliant – boys' own stuff. We got smashed 6–1, but the comradeship was brilliant, and it was great just to pretend to be a professional outfit for a little bit. We'd had that much fun that when we came back I thought: "I'm going to build my own team." It started out really well. But then it went west so quickly. There were factions, and a whole bunch of egos turned up. The more competitive and the more professional it got, the less of a laugh it was, so that was it.'

Story starts: *

A MAN REALLY, REALLY <u>FARAWAY</u>

Yesterday i had a profound
Observation on life
i was so proud i wrote IT
DOWN.
but i think my accountant's got
it cos i wrote it down on a
recipt.. And they all got handed
in..
shit!

he'll read it and pretend
its his.

TWO MEN HOLDING A MASSIVE
TIT.....

A: is It him?
B: cant tell.

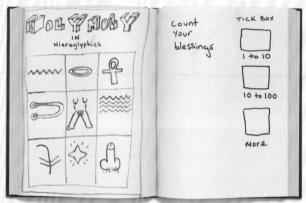

Notebook | 2007

'There's this artist I like called David Shrigley and some of these are a bit like that.'

Egypt | 2007

'I decided to grow a beard when I split up Robbie Williams. When the Beatles split up, Paul McCartney went off and grew a little beard, and I just got it in my mind that I'd grow a little beard since I was splitting me up. It was kind of like the giving up of peacocking. I suppose subconsciously I'd found the mate that I'd been trying to look good for. And I'd never been a holiday person – I always thought that living in Los Angeles was an extended vacation. It was only after I started going out with Ayda, who's from Los Angeles, and she talked about "going on holiday". So this year I really got into holidaying. I was catching up on all the holidays that I hadn't had. Before, my perfect holiday was skiing, because there was an *activity*. If you're skiing it takes your mind off feeling lonely, I suppose. If you're on a beach and you're bored, you get a bit lonely. I wasn't very good at just sitting down and doing nothing. But since the arrival of Ayda I've become quite good at it. I'm not lonely any more.'

'I've always had a big connection with Egypt because I had quite a few freaky things happen to me there the first time I went. Just after Take That, I think. And of course with me being into UFOs and weirdness, the pyramids really interest me and excite me. The plan at the time was to travel round the world – we went to Amsterdam and then to Egypt. It was majestic and other-worldly being at the pyramids but there were just way too many people there that day, and the only space you could get was by actually going into the pyramid itself. It was great just being inside the middle of a pyramid. And it did make you wonder how the fuck they built it. I would hope that there was alien handiwork. There's a possibility that none of it is alien handiwork – I do understand that. But I think there's still a lot about me that's seven, that's just come out of *Flash Gordon* at the cinema and just seen him go into space and fight some baddies, and I think there's still an awful lot of me that wants those films to be real. I understand that about myself too.'

Egypt | 2008

'We rented a boat and went down the Nile.
Danny, out of Kelv and Danny, would say,
"I just woke up in the Bible – it's fucking
amazing." It's very Miss Marple, too, isn't it?
It was absolutely wonderful. That was Ackee,
our guide for the trip. I kept beating him at
backgammon and he accused me of cheating.'

'This was the year of the kaftan. We'd been in Morocco and just saw everybody wearing these kaftans, and I thought, "Wicked! Obi-Wan Kenobi! Great! I'm going to get loads!" So I got four or five cashmere kaftans. And then in Egypt I bought myself some low-quality kaftans, linen that ripped easily. But even a low-quality kaftan's fun when you can breathe out. You kind of don't have to worry that the T-shirt's getting a bit smaller. Around this time a friend came up to the house in LA for some food one night and he was staying at a hotel down in town so I dropped him off, and as I dropped him off Ant and Dec were getting out of a car. And I'm thinking, "I'm in a kaftan... oh, fuck it, I'll go and have a drink with them in the bar." I think they definitely thought I'd gone mad. They are the most normal blokes in the world, and then their crazy pop star friend turns up with 45 extra pounds and a big beard and a kaftan. Somebody from Newcastle's not going to have that, really, are they?'

Mexico | 2008

'We rented a ruddy big yacht and we were supposed to do some music writing – never got round to it. We went fishing, scuba-diving, jet skiing, and then when it'd get dark we'd just take a little skiff and go out to sea for a little bit in the dark. It was just really magical, one of those "how small are we?" moments when all you've got is the moonlight and a little skiff and the coastline's in the distance. Scary and beautiful all at the same time. I'm like the Wild Man of Borneo or something. You see some pictures of my dad at the same age – he kind of calls it his wilderness years – where he wasn't with my mum and wasn't with us, and he was still reeling from that, and he was living in a pub, and he was a big lad. I never want to be that big again, but I think if it was the Med and I'd got a real healthy tan I think I'd be a very interesting sexy man, the big charismatic 70s guy. I caught a load of puffer fish. You can't eat them so I put them back.'

Mexico | 2008

'A 47 foot jump. I used to have no problems with that kind of stuff. I used to throw myself in off everything at any available moment. This is the moment where I think I went from "young and daft" to "old and unsteady". Because I jumped 47 foot and I thought, "I didn't like that." I only did it once. I hit the sea, went in, didn't hurt anything, but I just didn't enjoy the process any more. And I've been a bit more cautious since. I do think twice or three times these days. I've got the fear, which I never had when I was growing up. But I love looking at this photo. It's an impressive jump. If and when we do have kids, that's a picture they'd love to see: "Look! Daddy's *flying...*!"'

Mexico | 2008

'*Great* picture. Very Oliver Reed.'

Indigo Island | 2008

'I shaved off the beard on Indigo Island. I was talking to Max Beesley, and he was, "It's weird, kid...*weird.*" He kind of thinks anything weird is weird. Also, we had to stay at a hotel the night before being transported to Indigo Island, and it was the first time that I'd been out in public like that for a long time, and there was one of those classic examples of a British couple having a conversation about me even though I was there. "Oh God, he's let himself go so badly..." They didn't know I could hear, but I could hear. "He looks like a tramp..." I think that got into my head, along with Max saying, "It's weird, kid..." That's why the beard went. The year after this Lee Lodge was telling me about Stephen Duffy's new beard. I said, "Oh, does it look good?" He said, "Yes, it looks like Paul McCartney's beard just after he left the Beatles." I said, "Oh, a bit like mine last year?" And Lee replied, "No, yours made you look like you eat people."'

Trout Lake, Washington | 2008

'I quite regularly visit a site called Above Top Secret: abovetopsecret.com for all your conspiracy needs. It's my favourite website, and there's tons of information and great documentaries and talk about things that interest and excite me. I went with the Above Top Secret website owners and some friends to Gilliland ranch, the owner of which claims it's been visited by interplanetary craft. The vibe that surrounded the place was ethereal, let's say, magical, and I kind of thought there was all kind of possibilities for anything there. You look up in the sky and see the weirdest-shaped clouds that you've ever seen, and have never seen again. The weirdest grey hues, mixed with purples, mixed with bubbles and globulations and weird patterns. At 8 o'clock each evening, the sun would go down, night would start and we'd see lights in the sky moving in patterns that we'd find unfamiliar: zigzagging, moving in opposite directions. One night, I saw something just appear from out the back of two stars. It was just a fantastic trip – really, really special.'

Trout Lake, Washington | 2008

'I'm being Alan Partridge here, because I was up a ruddy big tree. It was just off the ranch at a coffee shop just down the road. It's like an amateur operatic society photo.'

Mustique | 2008

'Another holiday. Mustique is an island where no paparazzi are allowed. Mick Jagger's got a place there. Princess Margaret used to own a place out there and I think used to take her men there. It's quite a place to visit. Great picture. It was the rainy season, and we were swimming in the rain: Jamo, Danny, Kelv, Ayda and me.'

Los Angeles | 2009

'This is when Wall-E had just arrived on the scene. We used to have Krispy Kreme Doughnut Friday, which was our regular and only weekly sugary indulgence. My favourites: anything with custard in, really, and icing. I think we'd ordered that many doughnuts that they gave us the hat for free. Krispy Kreme Doughnut Friday lasted for five weeks, and then we kind of overdosed on Krispy Kremes and we've never had one since. I find them quite sickly now, I'm pleased to say.'

Comic Relief | 2009

'Once again, just to be associated with a programme like *Little Britain*, holding your own with these titans of comedy, it's fun. I had to be a little girl that very innocently said some very, very rude things. I think I said, "I suck Satan's cock in hell." It's nice to play dress up and see people's reaction to it, raising a laugh just because of what you're wearing. I actually didn't see myself as a little girl, I just saw myself as a woman with kid's clothes on.'

Wiltshire | 2009

'I had three or four close friends all do some weird stuff, and LA cracked for me. It just completely shrivelled up. And I'm like, "Babe, come home with me." So off we went, saw Compton Bassett, house of our dreams, and close to where Jonny lives, bought it, and that was where we were going to raise kids and be happy ever after. This is on a walk there with Baby. Baby's one of those dogs that runs off, and she was brand new to the world so she was struggling with the concept of leads. She didn't understand that what was choking her was herself trying to get away. We sometimes had to walk past some quail, and she used to go for them. So I just stuck her in my body warmer. Or... that was the day I grew a Jack Russell out of my breasts. Again.'

Wiltshire | 2009

'Kelv, my mate from Stoke, had come down for Ayda's birthday, with Danny. They're just the nicest people I've ever met – such good souls and good hearts. I knew of Danny first because he was kind of like a teenage legend, the best break-dancer I'd ever seen live. Not long after, he was on *Top of the Pops* with his brother as Candy Flip. He was from a mile away from where I lived and it was incredible that these guys were on the television. And I met Kelv, who was Danny's big brother, probably just after I'd left school. I used to go drinking up Hanley and he was DJing and he always looked really cool: leather pants, pair of boots and a boa.'

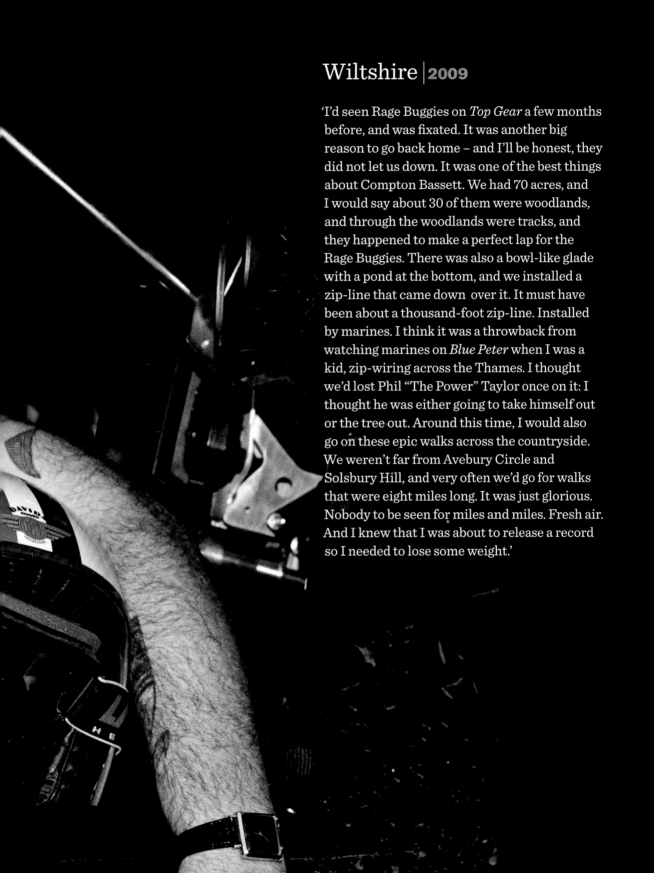

Wiltshire | 2009

'I'd seen Rage Buggies on *Top Gear* a few months before, and was fixated. It was another big reason to go back home – and I'll be honest, they did not let us down. It was one of the best things about Compton Bassett. We had 70 acres, and I would say about 30 of them were woodlands, and through the woodlands were tracks, and they happened to make a perfect lap for the Rage Buggies. There was also a bowl-like glade with a pond at the bottom, and we installed a zip-line that came down over it. It must have been about a thousand-foot zip-line. Installed by marines. I think it was a throwback from watching marines on *Blue Peter* when I was a kid, zip-wiring across the Thames. I thought we'd lost Phil "The Power" Taylor once on it: I thought he was either going to take himself out or the tree out. Around this time, I would also go on these epic walks across the countryside. We weren't far from Avebury Circle and Solsbury Hill, and very often we'd go for walks that were eight miles long. It was just glorious. Nobody to be seen for miles and miles. Fresh air. And I knew that I was about to release a record so I needed to lose some weight.'

8

'...there is no finish line...'

There is usually some kind of semi-competitive obsession – backgammon, Scrabble, Uno, table tennis, golf, underwater swimming – going on in Rob's life. Partly these pursuits offer a context in which someone like Rob, who considers himself far shyer and more socially awkward than people usually assume him to be, can easily enjoy socialising. 'I think I'm best with people when there's something between me and them,' he considers. 'A competition, a quiz, a "folf".'

The last of these – folf – is the current craze: a revitalised version of a golf-football hybrid he and Jonny invented as a distraction on tour in 2006, and which has been recently reimagined as a convoluted eighteen-hole game which utilises the full topography of his Los Angeles back garden. Right now, he's not too keen on going out, but frequently in the afternoon the house fills with arriving folf players.

'That's why I like so many people being in the house – nice people,' he rationalises. 'Because I'm not going to hang out with them out there. But I love games and people being happy and relaxed, and I love relaxing with people. I love the house full. Gary Barlow said to me the other day when everybody was round the house: "I bet you'll be glad when everybody's cleared off." I was like, "No. I'll be sad when everybody's cleared off."'

Today's visitors include some real footballers: the ex-England player Barry Venison, and Chris Birchall, now with LA Galaxy but at one time a player for Rob's team, Port Vale (although real football skills offer only a modest advantage in the surreal folf world). As Rob folfs alongside Chris Birchall, they talk about a place they've both known in Stoke.

'I went in there once, drunk, coming back from the pub,' says Rob, 'and bought a car. It was yellow.'

* * *

In the middle of April, his routine – most often looking through old photographs before the late-afternoon folf kick-off – has to be suspended for a short while. Rob has somewhere he has to go: one more aspect of the life fame brings you, another responsibility you realise you couldn't possibly refuse. This week he must visit Haiti on a UNICEF trip to see the recent earthquake's devastating impact and to be filmed for this summer's Soccer Aid.

'We live in such a fucked up world that if you allow your ears to fall on negative words you can really judge yourself for going and doing charity work,' he reflects. '"Look at me! Who the fuck do I think I am out here, helping these kids?" Also, people go: "Pop star guilt", "celeb guilt"... and, yeah, that's *exactly* what I've got. I feel shit if I don't do it. Because I'm in a position where I can, and I'd judge myself even more harshly if I didn't.'

In the days before his trip, one of his friends asks Rob exactly what he will be doing over there.

'Getting in the way of people working,' he replies.

* * *

He flies into Haiti's capital, Port-au-Prince, feeling ill all the way. 'Totally psychological,' he concludes. Originally, the plan was to stay in Port-au-Prince, but it has been decided that the area isn't safe enough. Instead, there is a drive three hours south to the coastal town of Jacmel. The whole way there, he says, he saw the same damage: 'one house safe, two houses knocked down...' Around Jacmel, he visits tent cities of displaced Haitians set out on football pitches, and listens to horrendous tales of hardship and heart-warming tales of hope. He skips with some kids until his Achilles tendons begin to give out and he has to stop. 'I nearly ended up face down,' he says. The days go smoothly and successfully, the UNICEF filming is completed as planned, and soon he is home.

Ayda accompanied him to Haiti. 'We were the naïve Westerners who straightaway wanted to bring back a grandmother and some kids with us,' he says, 'though of course we didn't say it. Ayda's got no filter for harrowing scenes. She's just porous when it comes to grief. She was constantly in tears. But all the kids loved Ayda. She's great with everybody.'

Before he met Ayda in early 2007, Rob had pretty much come around to thinking that he neither wanted nor expected to have a long-term relationship. 'I spent a lot of my twenties wanting a maid, really,' he reflects. 'I thought I wanted a relationship but I just wanted somebody to fix and nurse me, and I'd take her hostage for six months. When you're 23, 24, you want to be in a relationship because they look brilliant – you've heard all the songs about it and seen all the movies and it looks great. Little did I know that I was nowhere near being in a relationship with anyone. I only had a couple, and after that realised that, until I was really ready, it was going to be a pain in the ass for the other person.'

He says that in his late twenties he became further disillusioned with the whole idea of relationships because he saw so little he envied in those around him, in his friends', and those he'd see on TV: 'Things like *Loose Women* – everybody's always falling out or at each other, and that's not what I wanted for myself. I didn't want to be in an argumentative relationship or a stressful relationship, and I actually started to think: "Yeah, I'm better off out..." There was a period in my life which seemed to go on forever where I'd write songs called "If She Exists" and literally be pining for a relationship, but then it was: "I've got none of these burdens everyone seems to be having."' He had an exemplar close to hand of someone who had long embraced this way of thinking: 'My dad's a big believer in being single and not having commitments and being free to go here and there, and it's sort of been indoctrinated in me.'

Nonetheless, for a role he didn't want filled, he assiduously undertook many years of vigorous auditioning: 'For a lot of reasons. Company. Instant gratification. With a view to long-term gratification.' He recognises that for a long time he rarely gave anyone he was with much of a chance for things to develop. Nor himself. 'I was always expecting to be completely and utterly bowled over, like the movies, and because I didn't think that I was getting that feeling, I'd move on very quickly.'

The way he describes it, it almost seems a miracle that this relationship didn't founder in similar waters. Even though he and Ayda got on from the moment they met – 'I made her laugh and she made me laugh' – they were on-and-off for several months. It was as though he couldn't shake his expectation that if he liked someone he was with this much then it was only a matter of time until she revealed herself as someone completely different. The more wonderful she seemed, the more he was convinced that it must be some kind of trick. Eventually, he says, 'I got rid of all the excuses not to stay.' They've been together ever since. 'For me, she's incredible. For anybody, she'd be incredible, really. We don't fall out – never have done. If there's ever a grumpy situation, I'm the grumpy one – which I apologise for as soon as anything comes out of my mouth. Or at least five hours later.'

Even his father gave his own roundabout blessing. 'He was like, "You're in trouble there, son,"' says Rob. 'He means it as a nice thing: "She's amazing. So that's a problem for you."'

This change in circumstance is another reason he is so rarely seen in the kind of places in Los Angeles that he would once frequent. As he often remarks: 'I only used to go out to find somebody to stay in with.'

* * *

A few days after returning from Haiti, his back garden is home to the inaugural folf tournament. A small plaque has been bought from a trophy shop in the Valley for the occasion. (It's quite clearly a golf plaque that has been hastily customised.). The first hole begins from his bedroom balcony and requires a controlled kick over the railing towards an open patch of lawn, between the swimming pool and some plant beds, towards the 'hole', a large, shiny-metal garbage can, now dented. The ball is a slightly-deflated football. Before kick-off he announces, 'There are no friends in folf,' but the over-competitiveness is mostly theatre and bluff. When it comes to competition, he has very precisely calibrated feelings. He clearly relishes the pointless, melodramatic, childish over-caring about something essentially meaningless that is at the heart of the typically male competitive instinct, but he has equally great distaste for any behaviour that takes that too far, or carries it on with too much edge or pride once any kind of game has been

concluded. It can be great fun to take something silly much too seriously, but in the end it is just fun.

He far from always wins the games in which he takes part, but today – despite fierce competition from Barry Venison and, before she fades, Ayda – he does. He makes a brief, mock-earnest speech – 'Folf was the winner today' – expressing preposterous magnanimity at the end of an enjoyably absurd afternoon.

Earlier, as he lines up for one hole, where the ball is kicked from the rock feature above the jacuzzi at the back of the pool, I hear him reminisce with Barry Venison's son, Max, about how he had wanted to be a footballer.

'But I was in Take That by the time I was sixteen,' he says, ruefully.

'So you didn't have a chance?' says Max.

Rob nods. But he's too honest to allow this implication – of a destiny thwarted – to stand.

'I wasn't good enough, either,' he adds.

So, he explains, drawing back his foot to punt a football across his garden, he took a different road.

He acts out how it started:

'Naked with jelly and a mop...?'

'... okay!'

'Bondage gear...?'

'... okay!'

Wiltshire | 2009

'All of a sudden it was time to be a pop star again, and it was terrifying, three years down the line. This was the first proper photo session I'd done for years. It was shot in the Compton Bassett grounds. The hammock was put up for the photos but we did have a yurt in the garden with a bed in it. When the press discovered where I was, their version was that I'd moved to Wiltshire to be amongst the crop circles. It was more of a story than "Bloke buys house closer to friend to enjoy friendship between them more frequently than when bloke lived in LA." To be honest I have very little interest in crop circles. There were loads laid nearby while we were there, and we didn't go to see any of them.'

Wiltshire | 2009

'The inspiration for the shoot was a Steve McQueen photo book. Because he looks cool and effortless and timeless in everything he wore and everything he created.'

'Bodies' video | 2009

'It felt really strange dancing on the wing of the plane at the end of the video. I didn't realise it was going to feel so weird. It felt like I'd just had the training wheels taken off my tricycle. I was trying to remember what I used to do.'

Electric Proms rehearsals | 2009

'I'd just done *The X-Factor*. To this day I haven't even seen the performance back, but afterwards I had emails from a whole lot of people going, "You were great tonight, well done," and I didn't read the press. And then the album's coming out, and it does pique your interest what people are saying about it, because you've spent three years with it, so I went to look. I know it's not the greatest idea because people who write and talk about my music in England quite often are very disparaging and kind of relentlessly ruthless in fine detail about why I'm wank. And when I went to look, every single review started with: "After the disastrous performance on *The X Factor*..." And I was, "Wow – I didn't even know that it was bad." By then, the Electric Proms gig was coming up, with a massive orchestra and a big band. If I could have pulled out without pissing off a huge load of people, I would have done. So the pressure was on.'

Electric Proms | 2009

'Gandalf was there in the audience. Playing the role of some actor. A load of celebrities came to see me, which was a blessing and a curse. The blessing was that they were interested enough to come and see what I was doing, and hear the new stuff, and I was thrilled about that, but the curse was that I could potentially fall on my face in front of them. Anyway, I sort of worried myself into oblivion so much that by the time it came to walking down the stairs to go and sing, I was kind of numb to anything. I just thought: "Alright, well, if this is my last performance ever, all I've got to do is stand there and sing the songs." And it went really well. "He's back!" – it was all of that afterwards.'

Reality Killed The Video Star sleeve | 2009

'This was carrying on the Steve McQueen idea, even more so. It was in the middle of the Californian desert somewhere, 100-degree heat, like being in a sauna. But it was a fun day – I got to fanny about on motorbikes, even if I was ill-equipped to ride them the way I was riding them. Give me a toy to play with and I'll be happy.'

'You Know Me' video | 2009

'Me and Ayda had watched *Big Brother* that summer – I hadn't watched it since the first season but we really enjoyed it, got engrossed and got taken on the ride. One of the tasks was *Alice in Wonderland* and Siavash was the white rabbit and he had a nice tweed suit on with plus fours, and he looked really cool. I just thought: "I want to be a rabbit in my next video."'

London | 2010

'This was a very quick photo shoot when I was rehearsing for the Brits, for the *Radio Times*, tied in with Sport Relief. The interview caused a bit of fuss – I was in a conversation with the interviewer about smoking weed on a human level before the interview started and I kind of thought we were just chatting. But I'm not bothered. I said what I said. All I said was that marijuana was a lovely drug, but it was a shame because it gave me psychosis and it made me fat. I mean, it goes without saying – nobody starts taking drugs because they're shit. But it does give you psychosis and make you fat. That's the truth – what's wrong with that? And I don't take it, and I haven't for a long time, because I can't. Because it doesn't suit me. No drugs do.'

The Brit Awards | 2010

'It's a good and great thing to do, and it's an honour to be given the Outstanding Contribution Award, but it's a terrifying place to be in. It was important that I did a good job. Trevor Horn did all the thinking, and God bless him for it – he came up with the medley, and arranged it. It went down really well. I'd have been mortified if it hadn't. Backstage, I saw Nicole Appleton. It'd been maybe ten years. It was really nice, actually, and really sweet. Because I think when you've finished with somebody, you look at every opportunity to think of the negative about them, to make it okay in your mind about how much you've hurt them, or how much it's hurt you. I think that's naturally what I've done over the years, and I think that's human but I think it's unfair. I haven't said or been unkind really about Nic, but it was nice to grow up a little bit and go: "You were really great – thank you." Afterwards, Ayda and I went home and I ate cake – some leftover birthday cake. I allowed myself a massive slice that evening. I knew that I was on my way to LA and that I was going to start training again, so those last few days were kind of like when you know you're going to rehab: you drink an awful lot and do a load of drugs because it's going to be your last time. So that night was cake night.'

Over the Atlantic, 2010

'India, a friend of ours, had an all-in-one pink Primark costume, a onesie. And I used to have a yellow all-in-one with a budgerigar on when I was a kid, and loved it – I suppose wearing an all-in-one's very soothing – so I asked India the next time she was in Primark to get me one. This is a big girl's one, and it's very, very comfortable. Ayda's got one, too. My feet get a bit too hot, so I'm going to cut holes in the feet. I just wore it for a little bit on the flight back to LA... I've got a big camel toe here.'

'Morning Sun' video | 2010

'This was a costume fitting for the video – I'm holding Poupette. That suit was worn in the film *Space Cowboys* where all the old guys go up as astronauts. It felt great in there. There's something about being cocooned in one of those helmets that feels very safe.'

London | 2010

'The press continually do the same story, the headline that should be, "Guy That Used To Be Young Gets Progressively Older...", "Hair Turns A Different Colour", etc., etc. So I was just trying out different colours to see what would suit me if I dyed my hair. Using the dogs as colour pods. I think there could be a new website in there somewhere where people send pictures of themselves with their dogs as wigs. (1) This is Poupette. Very Louis XIVth. And this is... (2) ...Wall-E. It's Andy Warhol-esque and New Romantic 80s movement. Put a bit of a wedge in it and I'm in Visage... and this is... (3) ... Maggie. I think that one makes me look demure. Or like Davy Crockett... and this is... (4) ... Abba. This one's just afro-tastic. That's amazing, that. I want to be that guy. It'd be ace. You'd be the only guy in the world like that. I'm sure that when you were a kid you'd think you were a freak, but then you'd really grow into it and really love your individuality.'

In and Out of Consciousness sleeve shoot | 2010

'We did this in Malibu, California with Julian Broad. It is said that a man's face is his autobiography and a woman's face is a work of fiction. I am fast becoming part of the latter.'

EPILOGUE

This is who Robbie Williams has been, or, at the very least, what he has looked like while he was being it. This has been the view looking in on him as he has been looking out at us – or, perhaps more often, looking out past us to somewhere beyond the horizon. It has been twenty years since he joined Take That, an eager teenager innocently clamouring for the world's attention. What he received was more scrutiny than he could ever have possibly anticipated. These images sit as evidence of that scrutiny, and of its consequences – but also of the enduring and often glorious reasons why anyone ever chose to cast their eye his way.

It is in his nature to sidestep moments of reflection and celebration. He finds it hard to appreciate what he has done, and what he has accomplished. One more layer of self-protection, no doubt. 'I get more of a sense in Take That of what we achieved,' he demurs, 'than by myself...'

That may come in time. For now, it is as though he instinctively feels that just living this kind of remarkable, outsized, see-saw life messes with your head quite enough; why risk discovering what might happen to you if you started to celebrate it as well?

Still, don't misread him. Don't confuse his complicated thoughts about the voyage he has been on, and about the voyage that continues, with the worth of the voyage itself.

'If I had to do it all again,' he says, 'I'd do it all again.'

Picture credits: Photographs were supplied by and reproduced by kind permission of the following: **Chapman Bahler** 98, 100, 140, 141; **Frank Bauer** 162, 163, 167; **The Big Breakfast, Planet 24 Productions for Channel 4** 53; **Peter Blake** 142; **Julian Broad** 9, 11, 13, 18, 258, 259, 260, 266, 267, 270, 271, 272, 273, 274, 275, 278, 279, 284, 285 and 286; **Hamish Brown** 62, 63, 64, 65, 68, 70, 71, 72, 73, 85, 90, 91, 92, 93, 94, 96, 99, 120, 121, 122, 123, 129, 130, 136, 143, 148, 149, 150, 152, 153, 154, 156, 158, 159, 172, 173, 174, 175, 176, 177, 178, 179, 182, 189, 190, 191, 200, 202, 203, 237, 268, 269, 276, commissioned from Hamish Brown by Radio Times to mark Comic Relief 277; **Johnny Buzzerio** 224, 225; **Lee Carter** 76, 99, 101, 102; **Gabby Chelmicka** 74, 75, 83, 88, 95; **Josie Cliff** 160, 281; **Chris Clunn** 106, 112, 113, 114, 115, 116, 117, 118, 119; **David Constantine** 90; **Elaine Constantine** 86; **Victoria Dawe** 255; **Suki Dhanda** 82; **Do What U Like Video Stills** 30, 31; **Andy Earl** 60; **Fred&Nick** 16, 17; **Sean Gleason** 165, 166, 167, 168, 169, 181, 196, 197, 198, 199; **Rick Guest** 204; **Hammer & Tongs** 55; **Austin Hargrave** 6; **Dave Hogan** 32, 33, 54; **Joey Kelly** 20, 34, 35, 36, 37, 38, 39, 40, 41; **Phil Knott** 57, 59; **Lisa Marie Kurbikoff** 132, 133; **Graham Kuhn** 201; **Charlie Lightening** 218, 219; **Lee Lodge** & **Hamish Brown** 170, 171; **Hamilton Lund** 227; **Tiziano Magni** 42, 43, 44, 45; **Tony McGee** 89; **Simon Niblett** 205, 208, 209, 210, 214, 215, 216, 217, 220, 221, 222, 226, 228, 230, 231; **Phil Ollerenshaw** 47; **Scarlett Page** 126, 127, 128, 134, 135, 144, 145, 146, 147, 151; **RETNA UK** 29, 52; **RW Personal** 12, 26, 28, 161, 187, 206, 207, 232, 236, 238, 239, 240, 241, 242, 243, 244, 245, 246, 247, 248, 249, 251, 252, 253, 254, 256, 257, 280, 282; **Luis Sanchis** 131, 155; **Roger Sargent** 103; **Mary Scanlon** 58; **Diana Scrimgeour** 104, 105, 124, 125; **David Sitwell** 164, 188, 223; **Socceraid/ITV** 211, 212, 213; **Lee Strickland** 56; **Chris Taylor** 61; **Mark W. Allin** 250; **Norman Watson** 48, 66; **Des Willie** 195; **Retts Wood** 192, 193, 194.

Music credits: 'Being Boring' Words and Music Neil by Tennant/Chris Lowe © Cage Music Ltd and Sony/ATV Music Publishing (UK) Ltd. Used by permission. • 'Mr Blue Sky' Words and Music by Jeff Lynne © EMI April Music Inc and EMI Music Publishing. Used by permission. • 'Well Did You Evah' Words and Music by Cole Porter © Chappell Co Inc and Warner Chappell North America Ltd. Used by permission. • 'My Generation' Words and Music by Peter Townshend © Fabulous Music Ltd. Used by permission. Every effort has been made to clear relevant copyright permissions. Please contact the publishers with any queries or corrections.

Acknowledgements: Editors for IE Music: Josie Cliff, Tim Clark and David Enthoven • Picture research: Sarah Carmody and Vince Sievers.

I have written many novel _____ st ten years and am probably best known _____ omedies under the name Sophie Kinsella. Howe _____, long before I dreamed up the *Shopaholic* series I wrote seven books under the name Madeleine Wickham (my real name).

I'm often asked why I write under two names and the reason is that these books are in a different style from my Sophie Kinsella books.

Although I have not written as Madeleine Wickham for several years, I am immensely fond of these novels and hope you enjoy this one!

Madeleine Wickham

aka Sophie Kinsella

Madeleine Wickham was born in London and published her first novel, *The Tennis Party*, while working as a financial journalist. Under the name of Sophie Kinsella she is the author of many number one bestselling novels including the *Shopaholic* series, now filmed as *Confessions of a Shopaholic*. She lives in London with her husband and children.

Her **Madeleine Wickham** novels:
THE TENNIS PARTY

A DESIRABLE RESIDENCE

SWIMMING POOL SUNDAY

THE GATECRASHER

THE WEDDING GIRL

COCKTAILS FOR THREE

SLEEPING ARRANGEMENTS

Her **Sophie Kinsella** novels:
THE SECRET DREAMWORLD OF A SHOPAHOLIC
(also published as CONFESSIONS OF A SHOPAHOLIC)

SHOPAHOLIC ABROAD

SHOPAHOLIC TIES THE KNOT

SHOPAHOLIC & SISTER

SHOPAHOLIC & BABY

MINI SHOPAHOLIC

CAN YOU KEEP A SECRET?

THE UNDOMESTIC GODDESS

REMEMBER ME?

TWENTIES GIRL

For more information on Sophie Kinsella and her books,
see her website at **www.sophiekinsella.co.uk**

THE WEDDING GIRL

Madeleine Wickham

BLACK SWAN

TRANSWORLD PUBLISHERS
61–63 Uxbridge Road, London W5 5SA
A Random House Group Company
www.rbooks.co.uk

THE WEDDING GIRL
A BLACK SWAN BOOK: 9780552776738

First publication in Great Britain
Black Swan edition published 1999
Black Swan edition reissued 2010

Addresses for Random House Group Ltd companies outside the UK
can be found at: www.randomhouse.co.uk
The Random House Group Ltd Reg. No. 954009

The Random House Group Limited supports The Forest Stewardship
Council (FSC), the leading international forest certification organisation.
All our titles that are printed on Greenpeace approved FSC certified paper
carry the FSC logo. Our paper procurement policy can be found at
www.rbooks.co.uk/environment

Typeset in 11/14.5pt Giovanni Book by
Falcon Oast Graphic Art Ltd.
Printed in the UK by CPI Cox & Wyman, Reading, RG1 8EX.

2 4 6 8 10 9 7 5 3

For Hugo, who arrived in the middle

PROLOGUE

A group of tourists had stopped to gawp at Milly as she stood in her wedding dress on the registry office steps. They clogged up the pavement opposite while Oxford shoppers, accustomed to the yearly influx, stepped round them into the road, not even bothering to complain. A few glanced up towards the steps of the registry office to see what all the fuss was about, and tacitly acknowledged that the young couple on the steps did make a very striking pair.

One or two of the tourists had even brought out cameras, and Milly beamed joyously at them, revelling in their attention; trying to imagine the picture she and Allan made together. Her spiky, white-blond hair was growing hot in the afternoon sun; the hired veil was scratchy against her neck, the nylon lace on her dress felt uncomfortably damp wherever it touched her body. But still she felt light-hearted and full of a euphoric energy. And whenever she glanced up at Allan – at her husband – a new, hot thrill of excitement coursed through her body, obliterating all other sensation.

She had only arrived in Oxford three weeks ago. School had finished in July – and while all her friends had planned trips to Ibiza and Spain and Amsterdam, Milly had been packed off to a secretarial college in Oxford. 'Much more useful than some silly holiday,' her mother had announced firmly. 'And just think what an advantage you'll have over the others when it comes to job-hunting.' But Milly didn't want an advantage over the others. She wanted a suntan and a boyfriend, and beyond that, she didn't really care.

So on the second day of the typing course, she'd slipped off after lunch. She'd found a cheap hairdresser and, with a surge of exhilaration, told him to chop her hair short and bleach it. Then, feeling light and happy, she'd wandered around the dry, sun-drenched streets of Oxford, dipping into cool cloisters and chapels, peering behind stone arches, wondering where she might sunbathe. It was pure coincidence that she'd eventually chosen a patch of lawn in Corpus Christi College; that Rupert's rooms should have been directly opposite; that he and Allan should have decided to spend that afternoon doing nothing but lying on the grass, drinking Pimm's.

She'd watched, surreptitiously, as they sauntered onto the lawn, clinked glasses and lit up cigarettes; gazed harder as one of them took off his shirt to reveal a tanned torso. She'd listened to the snatches of their conversation which wafted through the air towards her and found herself longing to know these debonair, good-looking men. When, suddenly, the older one addressed her, she felt her heart leap with excitement.

'Have you got a light?' His voice was dry, American, amused.

'Yes,' she stuttered, feeling in her pocket. 'Yes, I have.'

'We're terribly lazy, I'm afraid.' The younger man's eyes met hers: shyer; more diffident. 'I've got a lighter; just inside that window.' He pointed to a stone mullioned arch. 'But it's too hot to move.'

'We'll repay you with a glass of Pimm's,' said the American. He'd held out his hand. 'Allan.'

'Rupert.'

She'd lolled on the grass with them for the rest of the afternoon, soaking up the sun and alcohol; flirting and giggling; making them both laugh with her descriptions of her fellow secretaries. At the pit of her stomach was a feeling of anticipation which increased as the afternoon wore on: a sexual frisson heightened by the fact that there were two of them and they were both beautiful. Rupert was lithe and golden like a young lion; his hair a shining blond halo; his teeth gleaming white against his smooth brown face. Allan's face was crinkled and his hair was greying at the temples, but his grey-green eyes made her heart jump when they met hers, and his voice caressed her ears like silk.

When Rupert rolled over onto his back and said to the sky, 'Shall we go for something to eat tonight?' she'd thought he must be asking her out. An immediate, unbelieving joy had coursed through her; simultaneously she'd recognized that she would have preferred it if it had been Allan.

But then Allan rolled over too, and said 'Sure thing.' And then he leaned over and casually kissed Rupert on the mouth.

The strange thing was, after the initial, heart-stopping shock, Milly hadn't really minded. In fact, this way was almost better: this way, she had the pair of them to herself. She'd gone to San Antonio's with them that night and basked in the jealous glances of two fellow secretaries at another table. The next night they'd played jazz on an old wind-up gramophone and drunk mint juleps and taught her how to roll joints. Within a week, they'd become a regular threesome.

And then Allan had asked her to marry him.

Immediately, without thinking, she'd said yes. He'd laughed, assuming she was joking, and started on a lengthy explanation of his plight. He'd spoken of visas, of Home Office officials, of outdated systems and discrimination against gays. All the while, he'd gazed at her entreatingly, as though she still needed to be won over. But Milly was already won over, was already pulsing with the excitement at the thought of dressing up in a wedding dress, holding a bouquet; doing something more exciting than she'd ever done in her life. It was only when Allan said, half frowning, 'I can't believe I'm actually asking someone to break the law for me!' that she realized quite what was going on. But the tiny qualms which began to prick her mind were no match for the exhilaration pounding through her as Allan put his arm around her and said quietly into her ear, 'You're an angel.' Milly had smiled breathlessly back, and said, 'It's nothing,' and truly meant it.

And now they were married. They'd hurtled through the vows: Allan in a dry, surprisingly serious voice; Milly quavering on the brink of giggles. Then they'd signed the register. Allan first, his hand quick and deft, then Milly, attempting to produce a grown-up signature for the occasion. And then, almost to Milly's surprise, it was done, and they were husband and wife. Allan had given Milly a tiny grin and kissed her again. Her mouth still tingled slightly from the touch of him; her wedding finger still felt self-conscious in its gold-plated ring.

'That's enough pictures,' said Allan suddenly. 'We don't want to be too conspicuous.'

'Just a couple more,' said Milly quickly. It had been almost impossible to persuade Allan and Rupert that she should hire a wedding dress for the occasion: now she was wearing it, she wanted to prolong the moment for ever. She moved slightly closer to Allan, clinging to his elbow, feeling the roughness of his suit against her bare arm. A sharp summer breeze had begun to ripple through her hair, tugging at her veil and cooling the back of her neck. An old theatre programme was being blown along the dry empty gutter; on the other side of the street the tourists were starting to melt away.

'Rupert!' called Allan. 'That's enough snapping!'

'Wait!' said Milly desperately. 'What about the confetti!'

'Well, OK,' said Allan indulgently. 'I guess we can't forget Milly's confetti.'

He reached into his pocket and tossed a multi-coloured handful into the air. At the same time, a gust of wind caught Milly's veil again, this time ripping it away from the tiny plastic tiara in her hair and sending it spectacularly up into the air like a gauzy plume of smoke. It landed on the pavement, at the feet of a dark-haired boy of about sixteen, who bent and picked it up. He began to look at it carefully, as though examining some strange artefact.

'Hi' called Milly at once. 'That's mine!' And she began running down the steps towards him, leaving a trail of confetti as she went. 'That's mine,' she repeated clearly as she neared the boy, thinking he might be a foreign student; that he might not understand English.

'Yes,' said the boy, in a dry, well-bred voice. 'I gathered that.'

He held out the veil to her and Milly smiled self-consciously at him, prepared to flirt a little. But the boy's expression didn't change; behind the glint of his round spectacles, she detected a slight teenage scorn. She felt suddenly aggrieved a little foolish, standing bare-headed, in her ill-fitting nylon wedding dress.

'Thanks,' she said, taking the veil from him. The boy shrugged.

'Any time.'

He watched as she fixed the layers of netting back in

place, her hands self-conscious under his gaze. 'Congratulations,' he added.

'What for?' said Milly, without thinking. Then she looked up and blushed. 'Oh yes, of course. Thank you very much.'

'Have a happy marriage,' said the boy in deadpan tones. He nodded at her and before Milly could say anything else, walked off.

'Who was that?' said Allan, appearing suddenly at her side.

'I don't know,' said Milly. 'He wished us a happy marriage.'

'A happy divorce, more like,' said Rupert, who was clutching Allan's hand. Milly looked at him. His face was glowing; he seemed more beautiful than ever before.

'Milly, I'm very grateful to you,' said Allan. 'We both are.'

'There's no need to be,' said Milly. 'Honestly, it was fun!'

'Well, even so. We've bought you a little something.' Allan glanced at Rupert, then reached in his pocket and gave Milly a little box. 'Freshwater pearls,' he explained as she opened it. 'We hope you like them.'

'I love them!' Milly looked from one to the other, eyes shining. 'You shouldn't have!'

'We wanted to,' said Allan seriously. 'To say thank you for being a great friend – and a perfect bride.' He fastened the necklace around Milly's neck, and she flushed with pleasure. 'You look beautiful,' he said softly. 'The most beautiful wife a man could hope for.'

'And now,' said Rupert, 'how about some champagne?'

They spent the rest of that day punting down the Cherwell, drinking vintage champagne and making extravagant toasts to each other. In the following days, Milly spent every spare moment with Rupert and Allan. At the weekends they drove out into the countryside, laying sumptuous picnics out on checked rugs. They visited Blenheim, and Milly insisted on signing the visitors' book, Mr and Mrs Allan Kepinski. When, three weeks later, her time at secretarial college was up, Allan and Rupert reserved a farewell table at the Randolph, made her order three courses and wouldn't let her see the prices.

The next day, Allan took her to the station, helped her stash her luggage on a rack, and dried her tears with a silk handkerchief. He kissed her goodbye, and promised to write and said they would meet in London soon.

Milly never saw him again.

ONE

Ten Years Later

The room was large and airy and overlooked the biscuity streets of Bath, coated in a January icing of snow. It had been refurbished some years back in a traditional manner, with striped wallpaper and a few good Georgian pieces. These, however, were currently lost under the welter of bright clothes, CDs, magazines and make-up piled high on every available surface. In the corner a handsome mahogany wardrobe was almost entirely masked by a huge white cotton dress carrier; on the bureau was a hat box; on the floor by the bed was a suitcase half full of clothes for a warm-weather honeymoon.

Milly, who had come up some time earlier to finish packing, leaned back comfortably in her bedroom chair, glanced at the clock, and took a bite of toffee apple. In her lap was a glossy magazine, open at the problem pages. 'Dear Anne,' the first began. 'I have been keeping a secret from my husband.' Milly rolled her eyes. She didn't even have to look at the advice. It was always the same. Tell the truth. Be honest. Like some sort of secular catechism, to be learned by rote and repeated without thought.

Her eyes flicked to the second problem. 'Dear Anne. I earn much more money than my boyfriend.' Milly crunched disparagingly on her toffee apple. Some problem. She turned over the page to the homestyle section, and peered at an array of expensive waste-paper baskets. She hadn't put a waste-paper basket on her wedding list. Maybe it wasn't too late.

Downstairs, there was a ring at the doorbell, but she didn't move. It couldn't be Simon, not yet; it would be one of the bed and breakfast guests. Idly, Milly raised her eyes from her magazine and looked around her bedroom. It had been hers for twenty-two years, ever since the Havill family had first moved into 1 Bertram Street and she had unsuccessfully petitioned, with a six-year-old's desperation, for it to be painted Barbie pink. Since then, she'd gone away to school, gone away to college, even moved briefly to London – and each time she'd come back again; back to this room. But on Saturday she would be leaving and never coming back. She would be setting up her own home. Starting afresh. As a grown-up, bona fide, married woman.

'Milly?' Her mother's voice interrupted her thoughts, and Milly's head jerked up. 'Simon's here!'

'What?' Milly glanced in the mirror and winced at her dishevelled appearance. 'He can't be.'

'Shall I send him up?' Her mother's head appeared round the door and surveyed the room. 'Milly! You were supposed to be clearing this lot up!'

'Don't let him come up,' said Milly, looking at the toffee apple in her hand. 'Tell him I'm trying my dress on. Say I'll be down in a minute.'

Her mother disappeared, and Milly quickly threw her toffee apple into the bin. She closed her magazine and put it on the floor, then, on second thoughts, kicked it under the bed. Hurriedly she peeled off the denim-blue leggings she'd been wearing and opened her wardrobe. A pair of well-cut black trousers hung to one side, along with a charcoal grey tailored skirt, a chocolate trouser suit and an array of crisp white shirts. On the other side of the wardrobe were all the clothes she wore when she wasn't going to be seeing Simon: tattered jeans, ancient jerseys, tight bright miniskirts. All the clothes she would have to throw out before Saturday.

She put on the black trousers and one of the white shirts, and reached for the cashmere sweater Simon had given her as a Christmas present. She looked at herself severely in the mirror, brushed her hair – now buttery blond and shoulder-length – till it shone, and stepped into a pair of expensive black loafers. She and Simon had often agreed that buying cheap shoes was a false economy; as far as Simon was aware, her entire collection of shoes consisted of the black loafers, a pair of brown boots, and a pair of navy Gucci snaffles which he'd bought for her himself.

Sighing, Milly closed her wardrobe door, stepped

over a pile of underwear on the floor, and picked up her bag. She sprayed herself with scent, closed the bedroom door firmly behind her and began to walk down the stairs.

'Milly!' As she passed her mother's bedroom door, a hissed voice drew her attention. 'Come in here!'

Obediently, Milly went into her mother's room. Olivia Havill was standing by the chest of drawers, her jewellery box open.

'Darling,' she said brightly, 'why don't you borrow my pearls for this afternoon?' She held up a double pearl choker with a diamond clasp. 'They'd look lovely against that jumper!'

'Mummy, we're only meeting the vicar,' said Milly. 'It's not that important. I don't need to wear pearls.'

'Of course it's important!' retorted Olivia. 'You must take this seriously, Milly. You only make your marriage vows once!' She paused. 'And besides, all upper-class brides wear pearls.' She held the necklace up to Milly's throat. 'Proper pearls. Not those silly little things.'

'I like my freshwater pearls,' said Milly defensively. 'And I'm not upper class.'

'Darling, you're about to become Mrs Simon Pinnacle.'

'Simon isn't upper class!'

'Don't be silly,' said Olivia crisply. 'Of course he is. His father's a multimillionaire.' Milly rolled her eyes.

'I've got to go,' she said.

'All right.' Olivia put the pearls regretfully back into her jewellery box. 'Have it your own way. And, darling, do remember to ask Canon Lytton about the rose petals.'

'I will,' said Milly. 'See you later.'

She hurried down the stairs and into the hall, grabbing her coat from the hall stand by the door.

'Hi!' she called into the drawing room, and as Simon came out into the hall, glanced hastily at the front page of that day's *Daily Telegraph*, trying to commit as many headlines as possible to memory.

'Milly,' said Simon, grinning at her. 'You look gorgeous.' Milly looked up and smiled.

'So do you.' Simon was dressed for the office, in a dark suit which sat impeccably on his firm, stocky frame, a blue shirt and a purple silk tie. His dark hair sprang up energetically from his wide forehead and he smelt discreetly of aftershave.

'So,' he said, opening the front door and ushering her out into the crisp afternoon air. 'Off we go to learn how to be married.'

'I know,' said Milly. 'Isn't it weird?'

'Complete waste of time,' said Simon. 'What can a crumbling old vicar tell us about being married? He isn't even married himself.'

'Oh well,' said Milly vaguely. 'I suppose it's the rules.'

'He'd better not start patronizing us. That *will* piss me off.'

Milly glanced at Simon. His neck was tense and his eyes fixed determinedly ahead. He reminded her of a young bulldog ready for a scrap.

'I know what I want from marriage,' he said,

frowning. 'We both do. We don't need interference from some stranger.'

'We'll just listen and nod,' said Milly. 'And then we'll go.' She felt in her pocket for her gloves. 'Anyway, I already know what he's going to say.'

'What?'

'Be kind to one another and don't sleep around.' Simon thought for a moment.

'I expect I could manage the first part.'

Milly gave him a thump and he laughed, drawing her near and planting a kiss on her shiny hair. As they neared the corner he reached in his pocket and bleeped his car open.

'I could hardly find a parking space,' he said, as he started the engine. 'The streets are so bloody congested.' He frowned. 'Whether this new bill will really achieve anything . . .'

'The environment bill,' said Milly at once.

'That's right,' said Simon. 'Did you read about it today?'

'Oh yes,' said Milly. She cast her mind quickly back to the *Daily Telegraph*. 'Do you think they've got the emphasis quite right?'

And as Simon began to talk, she looked out of the window and nodded occasionally, and wondered idly whether she should buy a third bikini for her honeymoon.

Canon Lytton's drawing room was large, draughty and full of books. Books lined the walls, books covered every surface, and teetered in dusty piles on the floor. In addition, nearly everything in the room that wasn't a book, looked like a book. The teapot was shaped like a book, the firescreen was decorated with books; even the slabs of gingerbread sitting on the tea-tray resembled a set of encyclopaedia volumes.

Canon Lytton himself resembled a sheet of old paper. His thin, powdery skin seemed in danger of tearing at any moment; whenever he laughed or frowned his face creased into a thousand lines. At the moment – as he had been during most of the session – he was frowning. His bushy white eyebrows were knitted together, his eyes narrowed in concentration and his bony hand, clutched around an undrunk cup of tea, was waving dangerously about in the air.

'The secret of a successful marriage,' he was declaiming, 'is trust. Trust is the key. Trust is the rock.'

'Absolutely,' said Milly, as she had at intervals of three minutes for the past hour. She glanced at Simon. He was leaning forward, as though ready to interrupt. But Canon Lytton was not the sort of speaker to brook interruptions. Each time Simon had taken a breath to say something, the clergyman had raised the volume of his voice and turned away, leaving Simon stranded in frustrated but deferential silence. He would have liked to take issue with much of what Canon Lytton was saying, she could tell. As for herself, she hadn't listened to a word.

Her gaze slid idly over to the glass-fronted bookcase to her left. There she was, reflected in the glass. Smart and shiny; grown-up and groomed. She felt pleased with her appearance. Not that Canon Lytton appreciated it. He probably thought it was sinful to spend money on clothes. He would tell her she should have given it to the poor instead.

She shifted her position slightly on the sofa, stifled a yawn, and looked up. To her horror, Canon Lytton was watching her. His eyes narrowed, and he broke off mid-sentence.

'I'm sorry if I'm boring you, my dear,' he said sarcastically. 'Perhaps you are familiar with this quotation already.'

Milly felt her cheeks turn pink.

'No,' she said, 'I'm not. I was just . . . um . . .' She glanced quickly at Simon, who grinned back and gave her a tiny wink. 'I'm just a little tired,' she ended feebly.

'Poorly Milly's been frantic over the wedding arrangements,' put in Simon. 'There's a lot to organize. The champagne, the cake . . .'

'Indeed,' said Canon Lytton severely. 'But might I remind you that the point of a wedding is not the champagne, nor the cake; nor is it the presents you will no doubt receive.' His eyes flicked around the room, as though comparing his own dingy things with the shiny, sumptuous gifts piled high for Milly and Simon, and his frown deepened. 'I am grieved,' he continued, stalking over to the window, 'at the casual approach taken by many young couples to the wedding ceremony. The sacrament of marriage should not be viewed as a formality.'

'Of course not,' said Milly.

'It is not simply the preamble to a good party.'

'No,' said Milly.

'As the very words of the service remind us, marriage must not be undertaken carelessly, lightly, or selfishly, but—'

'And it won't be!' Simon's voice broke in impatiently; he leaned forward in his seat. 'Canon Lytton, I know you probably come across people every day who are getting married for the wrong reasons. But that's not us, OK? We love each other and we want to spend the rest of our lives together. And for us, that's a serious matter. The cake and the champagne have got nothing to do with it.'

He broke off and for a moment there was silence. Milly took Simon's hand and squeezed it.

'I see,' said Canon Lytton eventually. 'Well, I'm glad to hear it.' He sat down, took a sip of cold tea and winced. 'I don't mean to lecture you unduly,' he said, putting down his cup. 'But you've no idea how many unsuitable couples I see coming before me to get married. Thoughtless young people who've barely known each other five minutes; silly girls who want an excuse to buy a nice dress . . .'

'I'm sure you do,' said Simon. 'But Milly and I are the real thing. We're going to take it seriously. We're going to get it right. We know each other and we love each other and we're going to be very happy.' He leaned over and kissed Milly gently, then looked up at Canon Lytton, as though daring him to reply.

'Yes,' said Canon Lytton. 'Well. Perhaps I've said enough. You do seem to be on the right track.' He picked up his folder and began to rifle through it. 'There are just a couple of other matters . . .'

'That was beautiful,' whispered Milly to Simon.

'It was true,' he whispered back, and gently touched the corner of her mouth.

'Ah yes,' said Canon Lytton, looking up. 'I should have mentioned this before. As you will be aware. Reverend Harries neglected to read your banns last Sunday.'

'Did he?' said Simon.

'Surely you noticed?' said Canon Lytton looking beadily at Simon. 'I take it you were at morning service?'

'Oh yes,' said Simon after a pause. 'Of course. Now you mention it, I thought something was wrong.'

'He was most apologetic – they always are.' Canon Lytton gave a tetchy sigh. 'But the damage has been done. So you will have to be married by special licence.'

'Oh,' said Milly. 'What does that mean?'

'It means, among other things,' said Canon Lytton, 'that I must ask you to swear an oath.'

'Zounds damnation,' said Milly.

'I'm sorry?' He looked at her in puzzlement.

'Nothing,' she said. 'Carry on.'

'You must swear a solemn oath that all the information you've given me is true,' said Canon Lytton. He held out a bible to Milly, then passed her a piece of paper. 'Just run your eyes down it, check that it's all correct, then read the oath aloud.'

Milly stared down at the paper for a few seconds, then looked up with a bright smile.

'Absolutely fine,' she said.

'Melissa Grace Havill,' said Simon, reading over her shoulder. 'Spinster.' He pulled a face. 'Spinster!'

'OK!' said Milly sharply. 'Just let me read the oath.'

'That's right,' said Canon Lytton. He beamed at her. 'And then everything will be, as they say, above board.'

By the time they emerged from the vicarage, the air was cold and dusky. Snowflakes were falling again; the street lamps were already on; a row of fairy lights from Christmas twinkled in a window opposite. Milly took a deep breath, shook out her legs, stiff from sitting still for so long, and looked at Simon. But before she could speak, a triumphant voice came ringing from the other side of the street.

'Aha! I just caught you!'

'Mummy!' exclaimed Milly.

'Olivia,' said Simon. 'What a lovely surprise.'

Olivia crossed the street and beamed at them both. Snowflakes were resting lightly on her smartly cut blond hair and on the shoulders of her green cashmere coat. Nearly all of Olivia's clothes were in jewel colours – sapphire blue, ruby red, amethyst purple – accented by shiny gold buckles, gleaming buttons and gilt-trimmed shoes. She had once secretly toyed with the idea of turquoise-tinted contact lenses but had been unable to reassure herself that she wouldn't become the subject of smirks behind her back. And so instead she made the most of her natural blue by pasting a bright gold on her eyelids and visiting a beautician once a month to have her lashes dyed black.

Now her eyes were fixed affectionately on Milly.

'I don't suppose you asked Canon Lytton about the rose petals, did you?' she said.

'Oh!' said Milly. 'No, I forgot.'

'I knew you would!' exclaimed Olivia. 'So I thought I'd better pop round myself.' She smiled at Simon. 'Isn't my little girl a scatterhead?'

'I wouldn't say so,' said Simon in a tight voice.

'Of course you wouldn't! You're in love with her!' Olivia smiled gaily at him and ruffled his hair. In high heels she was very slightly taller than Simon, and he'd noticed – though nobody else had – that since he and Milly had become engaged, Olivia wore high heels more and more frequently.

'I'd better be going,' he said. 'I've got to get back to the office. We're frantic at the moment.'

'Aren't we all!' exclaimed Olivia. 'There are only four days to go, you know! Four days until you walk down that aisle! And I've a thousand things to do!' She looked at Milly. 'What about you, darling? Are you rushing off?'

'Not me,' said Milly. 'I took the afternoon off.'

'Well then, how about walking back into town with me? Perhaps we could have . . .'

'Hot chocolate at Mario's,' finished Milly.

'Exactly.' Olivia smiled almost triumphantly at Simon. 'I can read Milly's mind like an open book!'

'Or an open letter,' said Simon. There was a short, tense pause.

'Right, well,' said Olivia eventually, in clipped tones. 'I won't be long. See you this evening, Simon.' She opened Canon Lytton's gate and began to walk quickly up the path, skidding slightly on the snow.

'You shouldn't have said that,' said Milly to Simon, as soon as she was out of earshot. 'About the letter. She made me promise not to tell you.'

'Well, I'm sorry,' said Simon. 'Milly, you must be joking. It was addressed to you and it was in your bedroom!'

'Oh well,' said Milly good-naturedly. 'It doesn't really matter.' She gave a sudden giggle. 'It's a good thing you didn't write anything rude about her.'

'Next time I will,' said Simon. He glanced at his watch. 'Look, I've really got to go.'

He took hold of her chilly fingers, kissed them gently one by one, then pulled her towards him. His mouth was soft and warm on hers; as he drew her gradually closer to him, Milly closed her eyes. Then, suddenly he let go of her, and a blast of cold snowy air hit her in the face.

'I must run. See you later.'

'Yes,' said Milly. 'See you then.'

She watched, smiling to herself, as he bleeped open the door of his car, got in and, without pausing, zoomed off down the street. Simon was always in a hurry. Always rushing off to do; to achieve. Like a puppy, he had to be out every day, either doing something constructive or determinedly enjoying himself. He couldn't bear wasting time; didn't understand how Milly could spend a day happily doing nothing, or approach a weekend with no plans made. Sometimes he would join her in a day of drifting indolence, repeating several times that it was nice to have a chance to relax. Then, after a few hours, he would leap up and announce he was going for a run.

The first time she'd ever seen him, in someone else's kitchen, he'd been simultaneously conducting a conversation on his mobile phone, shovelling crisps into his mouth, and bleeping through the news headlines on Teletext. As Milly had poured herself a glass of wine, he'd held his glass out too and, in a gap in his conversation, had grinned at her and said, 'Thanks.'

'The party's happening in the other room,' Milly had pointed out.

'I know,' Simon had said, his eyes back on the Teletext. 'I'll be along in a minute.' And Milly had rolled her eyes and left him to it, not even bothering to ask his name. But later on that evening, when he'd rejoined the party, he'd come up to her, introduced himself charmingly, and apologized for having been so distracted.

'It was just a bit of business news I was particularly interested in,' he'd said.

'Good news or bad news?' Milly had enquired, taking a gulp of wine and realizing that she was rather drunk.

'That depends,' said Simon, 'on who you are.'

'But doesn't everything? Every piece of good news is

someone else's bad news. Even . . . ' She'd waved her glass vaguely in the air. 'Even world peace. Bad news for arms manufacturers.'

'Yes,' Simon had said slowly. 'I suppose so. I'd never thought of it like that.'

'Well, we can't all be great thinkers,' Milly had said, and had suppressed a desire to giggle.

'Can I get you a drink?' he'd asked.

'Not a drink,' she'd replied. 'But you can light me a cigarette if you like.'

He'd leaned towards her, cradling the flame carefully, and she'd registered that his skin was smooth and tanned, and his fingers strong, and he was wearing an aftershave she liked. Then, as she'd inhaled on the cigarette, his dark brown eyes had locked into hers, and to her surprise a tingle had run down her back, and she'd slowly smiled back at him.

Later on, when the party had turned from bright, stand-up chatter into groups of people sitting on the floor and smoking joints, the discussion had turned to vivisection. Milly, who had happened to see a *Blue Peter* special on vivisection the week before while at home with a cold, had produced more hard facts and informed reasoning than anyone else, and Simon had gazed at her in admiration.

He'd asked her out to dinner a few days later and talked a lot about business and politics. Milly, who knew nothing about either subject, had smiled and nodded and agreed with him; at the end of the evening, just before he kissed her for the first time, Simon had told her she was extraordinarily perceptive and understanding. When, a bit later on, she'd tried to tell him that she was woefully ignorant on the subject of politics – indeed, on most subjects – he'd chided her for being modest. 'I saw you at that party,' he'd said, 'destroying that guy's puerile arguments. You knew exactly what you were talking about. In fact,' he'd added, with darkening eyes, 'it was quite a turn-on.' And Milly, who'd been about to admit to her source of information, had instead moved closer so that he could kiss her again.

Simon's initial impression of her had never been corrected. He still told her she was too modest; he still thought she liked the same highbrow art exhibitions he did; he still asked her opinion on topics such as the American presidency campaign and listened carefully to her answers. He thought she liked sushi; he thought she had read Sartre. Without wanting to mislead him, but without wanting to disappoint him either, she'd allowed him to build up a picture of her which – if she were honest with herself – wasn't quite true.

Quite what was going to happen when they started living together, she didn't know. Sometimes she felt alarmed at the degree to which she was being misrepresented; felt sure she would be exposed as a fraud the first time he caught her crying over a trashy novel. At other times, she told herself that his picture of her wasn't so inaccurate. Perhaps she wasn't quite the sophisticated woman he thought she was – but she could be. She would be. It was simply a matter of discarding all her old clothes and wearing only the new ones. Making the odd intelligent comment – and staying discreetly quiet the rest of the time.

Once, in the early days of their relationship, as they lay together in Simon's huge double bed at Pinnacle Hall, Simon had told her that he'd known she was someone special when she didn't start asking him questions about his father. 'Most girls' he'd said bitterly, 'just want to know what it's like, being the son of Harry Pinnacle. Or they want me to get them a job interview or something. But you . . . you've never even mentioned him.'

He'd gazed at her with incredulous eyes, and Milly had smiled sweetly and murmured an indistinct, sleepy response. She could hardly admit that the reason she'd never mentioned Harry Pinnacle was that she'd never heard of him.

'So – dinner with Harry Pinnacle tonight! That should be fun.' Her mother's voice interrupted Milly's thoughts, and she looked up.

'Yes,' she said. 'I suppose so.'

'Has he still got that wonderful Austrian chef?'

'I don't know,' said Milly. She had, she realized, begun to imitate Simon's discouraging tone when talking about Harry Pinnacle. Simon never prolonged a conversation about his father if he could help it; if people were too persistent he would change the subject abruptly, or even walk away. He had walked away from his future mother-in-law plenty of times as she pressed him for details and anecdotes about the great man. So far she had never seemed to notice.

'The really lovely thing about Harry,' mused Olivia, 'is that he's so normal.' She tucked Milly's arm cosily under her own and they began to walk down the snowy street together. 'That's what I say to everybody. If you met him, you wouldn't think, here's a multimillionaire tycoon. You wouldn't think, here's a founder of a huge national chain. You'd think, what a charming man. And Simon's just the same.'

'Simon isn't a multimillionaire tycoon,' said Milly. 'He's an ordinary advertising salesman.'

'Hardly ordinary, darling!'

'Mummy . . .'

'I know you don't like me saying it. But the fact is that Simon's going to be very wealthy one day.' Olivia's arm tightened slightly around Milly's. 'And so are you.' Milly shrugged.

'Maybe.'

'There's no point pretending it's not going to happen. And when it does, your life will change.'

'No it won't.'

'The rich live differently, you know.'

'A minute ago,' pointed out Milly, 'you were saying how normal Harry is. He doesn't live differently, does he?'

'It's all relative, darling.'

They were nearing a little parade of expensive boutiques; as they approached the first softly lit window, they both stopped. Inside the window was a single mannequin, exquisite in heavy white velvet.

'That's nice,' murmured Milly.

'Not as nice as yours,' said Olivia at once. 'I haven't seen a single wedding dress as nice as yours.'

'No,' said Milly slowly. 'Mine is nice, isn't it?'

'It's perfect, darling.'

They lingered a little at the window, sucked in by the rosy glow of the shop; the clouds of silk, satin and netting lining each wall; the dried bouquets and tiny embroidered bridesmaids' shoes. At last Olivia sighed.

'All this wedding preparation has been fun, hasn't it? I'll be sorry when it's all over.'

'Mmm,' said Milly. There was a little pause, then Olivia said, as though changing the subject, 'Has Isobel got a boyfriend at the moment?'

Milly's head jerked up.

'Mummy! You're not trying to marry Isobel off, too.'

'Of course not! I'm just curious. She never tells me anything. I asked if she wanted to bring somebody to the reception . . .'

'And what did she say?'

'She said no,' said Olivia regretfully.

'Well then.'

'But that doesn't prove anything.'

'Mummy,' said Milly. 'If you want to know if Isobel's got a boyfriend, why don't you ask her?'

'Maybe,' said Olivia in a distant voice, as though she wasn't really interested any more. 'Yes, maybe I will.'

An hour later they emerged from Mario's Coffee House, and headed for home. By the time they got back, the kitchen would be filling up with bed and breakfast guests, footsore from sightseeing. The Havills' house in Bertram Street was one of the most popular bed and breakfast houses in Bath: tourists loved the beautifully furnished Georgian townhouse; its proximity to the city centre; Olivia's charming, gossipy manner and ability to turn every gathering into a party.

Tea was always the busiest meal in the house; Olivia adored assembling her guests round the table for Earl Grey and Bath buns. She would introduce them to one another, hear about their day, recommend diversions for the evening and tell them the latest gossip about people they had never met. If any guest expressed a desire to retreat to his own room and his mini-kettle, he was given a look of disapproval and cold toast in the morning. Olivia Havill despised mini-kettles and tea-bags on trays; she only provided them in order to qualify for four rosettes in the *Heritage City Bed and Breakfast Guide*. Similarly she despised, but provided, cable television, vegetarian sausages and a rack of leaflets about local theme parks and family attractions – which, she was glad to note, rarely needed replenishing.

'I forgot to say,' said Olivia, as they turned into Bertram Street. 'The photographer arrived while you were out. Quite a young chap.' She began to root around in her handbag for the doorkey.

'I thought he was coming tomorrow.'

'So did I!' said Olivia. 'Luckily those nice Australians have had a death in the family, otherwise we wouldn't have had room. And speaking of Australians . . . look at this!' She put her key in the front door and swung it open.

'Flowers!' exclaimed Milly. On the hall stand was a huge bouquet of creamy white flowers, tied with a dark green silk ribbon bow. 'For me? Who are they from?'

'Read the card,' said Olivia. Milly picked up the bouquet and reached inside the cracking plastic.

' "To dear little Milly," ' she read slowly. ' "We're so proud of you and only wish we could be there at your wedding. We'll certainly be thinking of you. With all our love from Beth, Scott and Adrian." ' Milly looked at Olivia in amazement.

'Isn't that sweet of them! All the way from Sydney. People are so kind.'

'They're excited for you, darling,' said Olivia. 'Everyone's excited. It's going to be such a wonderful wedding!'

'Why, aren't those pretty,' came a pleasant voice from above. One of the bed and breakfast guests, a middle-aged woman in blue slacks and sneakers, was coming down the stairs. 'Flowers for the bride?'

'Just the first,' said Olivia, with a little laugh.

'You're a lucky girl,' said the middle-aged woman to Milly.

'I know I am,' said Milly and a pleased grin spread over her face. 'I'll just put them in some water.'

Still holding her flowers, Milly pushed open the door to the kitchen, then stopped in surprise. Sitting at the table was a young man wearing a shabby denim jacket.

He had dark brown hair and round metal spectacles and was reading the *Guardian*.

'Hello,' she said politely. 'You must be the photographer.'

'Hi there,' said the young man, closing his paper. 'Are you Milly?'

He looked up, and as she saw his face, Milly felt a jolt of recognition. Surely she'd met this guy before somewhere?

'I'm Alexander Gilbert,' he said in a dry voice, and held out his hand. Milly advanced politely and shook it.

'Nice flowers,' he said, nodding to her bouquet.

'Yes,' replied Milly, staring curiously at him. Where on earth had she seen him before? Why did his face feel etched in her memory?

'That's not your wedding bouquet, though.'

'No, it's not,' said Milly. She bent her head slightly and inhaled the sweet scent of the flowers. 'These were sent by some friends in Australia. It's really thoughtful of them, considering—'

Suddenly she broke off, and her heart began to beat faster.

'Considering what?' said Alexander.

'Nothing,' said Milly, backing away. 'I mean – I'll just go and put them away.'

She moved towards the door, her palms sweaty against the crackling plastic. She knew where she'd seen him before. She knew exactly where she'd seen him before. At the thought of it, her heart gave a terrified lurch and she gritted her teeth, forcing herself to stay calm. Everything's OK, she told herself as she reached for the door handle. Everything's OK. As long as he doesn't recognize me . . .

'Wait.' His voice cut across her thoughts as though he could read her mind. Feeling suddenly sick, she turned round, to see him staring at her with a slight frown. 'Wait a minute,' he said. 'Don't I know you?'

TWO

Sitting in a traffic jam on his way home that night, watching the endlessly falling snow and rhythmic sweeping of his windscreen wipers, Simon reached for his phone to dial Milly's number. He pressed the first two digits, then changed his mind and switched the phone off. He had only wanted to hear her voice; make her laugh; picture her face as she spoke. But she might be busy, or she might think him ridiculous, phoning on a whim with nothing to say. And if she was still out, he might find himself talking to Mrs Havill, instead.

Her mother was the only thing about Milly that Simon would have changed if he could. Olivia was a pleasant enough woman, still attractive, charming and amusing; he could see why she was a popular figure at social events. But the way she treated Milly irritated him intensely. She seemed to think Milly was still a six-year-old – helping her choose her clothes, telling her to wear a scarf, wanting to know exactly what she was doing, every minute of every day. And the worst thing was, Simon thought, that Milly didn't seem to mind. She allowed her mother to smooth her hair and say, 'Good little girl'; she telephoned dutifully when she thought she might be late home. Unlike her older sister Isobel, who had long ago bought her own flat and moved out, Milly seemed to have no natural desire for independence.

The result was that her mother continued to treat her like a child, instead of the mature adult she really was. And Milly's father and sister Isobel were nearly as bad. They laughed when Milly expressed views on current issues, they joked about her career, they discussed important matters without consulting her. They refused to see the intelligent, passionate woman he saw; refused to take her seriously; refused to elevate her to grown-up status.

Simon had tried to talk to Milly about her family; tried to make her see how they patronized and limited her. But she had simply shrugged and said they weren't so bad, and when he'd strengthened his attack on them, had got upset. She was too good-natured and affectionate a creature to see any faults in them, thought Simon, turning off the main road out of Bath, towards Pinnacle Hall. And he loved her for it. But things would have to alter when they were married, when they set up their own home together. Milly's focus would have to change, and her family would have to respect that. She would be a wife; maybe some day a mother. And the Havills would just have to realize that she was no longer their little girl.

As he approached Pinnacle Hall he pressed the security code on his bleeper, then sat, waiting impatiently for the gates to swing open – heavy, iron gates, with the word 'Pinnacle' wrought into the design. Lights were blazing from every window of the house; cars were parked in the allocated spaces and the office wing was still buzzing. His father's red Mercedes was parked bang in front of the house; a big shiny, arrogant car. Simon loathed it.

He parked his own Golf in an unobstructive spot and crunched over the snow-covered gravel towards Pinnacle Hall. It was a large, eighteenth-century house which had been a luxury hotel during the eighties, complete with a leisure complex and a tastefully added wing of extra bedrooms. Harry Pinnacle had bought it when the owners had gone bust and turned it back into a private home, with his company headquarters housed in the extra wing. It suited him, he would tell visiting reporters, to be out of London. He was, after all, getting old and past it. There would be a beat of silence – then everyone would laugh, and Harry would grin, and press the bell for more coffee.

The panelled hall was empty and smelt of beeswax. From his father's study came a light; Simon could hear his voice, muffled behind the door, then a burst of low laughter. Resentment, never far from the surface, began to crackle at Simon's skin, and his hands clenched tightly inside his pockets.

For as long as he could remember, Simon had hated his father. Harry Pinnacle had disappeared from the family home when Simon was three, leaving his mother to bring up Simon alone. His mother had never elaborated on exactly why the marriage had broken down, but Simon knew it had to be the fault of his father. His overbearing, arrogant, obnoxious father. His driven, creative, incredibly successful father. It was the success that Simon hated the most.

The story was well known by all. In the year that Simon had turned seven, Harry Pinnacle had opened a small juice bar called Fruit 'n Smooth. It served healthy drinks at chrome counters and was an instant hit. The next year, he opened another, and the year after that, another. The year after that, he began selling franchises. By the mid-eighties, there was a Fruit 'n Smooth in every town and Harry Pinnacle was a multimillionaire.

As his father had grown in wealth and stature, as he'd leapt from the inside business pages to the front-page headlines, the young Simon had watched his progress with fury. Cheques arrived every month, and his mother always exclaimed over Harry's generosity. But Harry never appeared in person, and Simon hated him for it. And then, when Simon was nineteen, his mother had died and Harry Pinnacle had come back into his life.

Simon frowned, and felt his nails digging into the flesh of his hands as he remembered the moment, ten years ago, when he'd seen his father for the first time. He'd been pacing the corridor outside his mother's hospital room, desperate with grief, with anger, with tiredness. Suddenly he'd heard a voice calling his name, and he'd looked up to see a face which was familiar from a thousand newspaper photographs. Familiar – and yet strange to him. as he'd stared at his father in silent shock, he'd realized for the first time that he could see his own features in the older man's face. And in spite of himself he'd felt emotional tentacles reaching out; instinctive feelers like a baby's. It would have been so easy to fall on his father's neck, to allow the burden to be shared, to accept his overtures and make him a friend. But even as he'd felt himself beginning to soften, Simon had stamped on his feelings and ground them back into himself. Harry Pinnacle didn't deserve his love, and he would never have it.

After the funeral, Harry had welcomed Simon into his house. He'd given him his own room, his own car; taken him on expensive holidays. Simon had accepted everything politely. But if Harry had thought that by showering him with expensive gifts he would buy his son's affection, he had thought wrong. Although Simon's adolescent fury had soon simmered down, there had arisen in its place a determination to outdo his father on every front. He would run a successful business and make money – but, unlike his father, he would also marry happily; bring up his children to love him; become the figurehead of a contented, stable family. He would have the life that his father had never had – and his father would envy and hate him for it.

And so he'd begun, by launching his own little

publishing company. He'd started with three specialist newsletters, a reasonable profit and high expectations. Those expectations had never been realized. After three years of struggle his profits were down to nothing; at the end of the fourth year he went into liquidation.

Humiliation still burned through Simon as he remembered the day he'd had to admit to his father that his business had gone bust; the day he'd had to accept his father's offer, sell his flat and move back into Pinnacle Hall. His father had poured him a deep glass of whisky, had uttered clichés about the rough and the smooth, had offered him a job with Pinnacle Enterprises. Simon had immediately turned it down with a few muttered words of thanks. He could barely look his father in the eye; could barely look anyone in the eye. At that low point he'd despised himself almost as much as he despised his father. His whole being was wrought with embarrassed disappointment.

At last he'd found himself a job selling advertising on a small, low-profile business magazine. He'd winced as Harry congratulated him; winced as he watched his father leafing through the drab little publication and trying to find some words of praise. 'It's not much of a job,' he'd said defensively. 'But at least I'm in work.' At least he was in work, at least the days were filled, at least he could begin to pay off his debts.

Three months after starting on the magazine, he'd met Milly. A year later he'd asked her to marry him. His father had again congratulated him; had offered to help out with the engagement ring. But Simon had refused his offer. 'I'll do this my way,' he'd said, and looked his father straight in the eye with a new confidence, almost a challenge. If he couldn't beat his father in business, then he would beat him at family life. He and Milly would have a perfect marriage. They would love each other, help each other, understand each other. Worries would be discussed; decisions would be made jointly; affection would be expressed freely. Children would enhance the bliss. Nothing was allowed to go wrong. Simon had experienced failure once; he never wanted to experience it again.

Suddenly his thoughts were interrupted by another burst of laughter from inside his father's room, a mumble of conversation, and then the sharp ping which meant his father had replaced the old-fashioned receiver of his private-line telephone. Simon waited a minute or two, then took a deep breath, approached his father's door and knocked.

As Harry Pinnacle heard the knock at his door he gave an uncharacteristic start. Quickly he put the tiny photograph he was holding into the desk drawer in front of him and closed it. Then, for good measure, he locked the drawer. For a few moments he sat, staring at the drawer key, lost in thoughts.

There was another knock, and he looked up. He swivelled his chair away from the desk and ran his hands through his silvering hair.

'Yes?' he said and watched the door open.

Simon came in, took a few paces forward and looked

angrily at his father. It was always the same. He would knock on his father's door and would be kept waiting outside, like a servant. Never once had Harry exhorted him not to knock; never once had he even looked pleased to see Simon. He always looked impatient, as though Simon were interrupting crucial business. But that's bullshit, thought Simon. You're not in the middle of crucial business. You're just an arrogant bastard.

His heart was beating quickly; he was in the mood for a confrontation. But he couldn't bring himself to say any of the words of attack circling his mind.

'Hi,' he said in a tense voice. He gripped the back of a leather chair and glared at his father, somehow hoping to provoke a reaction. But his father simply stared back at him. After a few moments he sighed, and put down his pen.

'Hello,' he said. 'Good day?' Simon shrugged and looked away. 'Feel like a whisky?'

'No. Thanks.'

'Well, I do.'

As he got up to pour himself a drink, Harry caught a glimpse of his son's unguarded face: tense, miserable, angry. The boy was full of anger; he'd been carrying the same anger around ever since Harry had first seen him, standing outside his mother's hospital room. That day he'd spat at his father's feet and stalked away before Harry could say anything. And a wretched guilt had begun to grow inside Harry, a guilt which stabbed him every time the boy looked at him with his mother's blasted eyes.

'Good day?' he said, lifting the whisky glass to his lips.

'You already asked that.'

'Right. So I did.' Harry took a slug of the fiery liquid and immediately felt a little better. He took another.

'I came,' said Simon, 'to remind you about dinner tonight. The Havills are coming.'

'I remember,' said Harry. He put down his glass and looked up. 'Not long now till the big day. Are you nervous?'

'No, not at all,' said Simon at once. Harry shrugged.

'It's a big commitment.'

Simon stared at his father. He could feel a string of words forming at his lips; pent-up words which he'd carried around for years like a constant weight.

'Well,' he found himself saying, 'you wouldn't know much about commitment, would you?'

A flash of anger passed across his father's face, and Simon felt a sudden fearful thrill. He waited for his father to shout at him, winding himself up to an even angrier response. But as suddenly as it had appeared, the animation vanished from his father's face and he walked away, towards the huge sash windows. Simon felt himself tense up with frustration.

'What's wrong with commitment?' he shouted. 'What's wrong with loving one person all your life?'

'Nothing,' said Harry, without turning.

'Then why . . .' began Simon, and stopped. There was a long silence, punctuated only by the crackles of the fire. Simon gazed at his father's back. Say something, he thought desperately. Say something, you fucker.

'I'll see you at eight,' said Harry at last.

'Fine,' said Simon, in a voice scored with hurt. 'See you then.' And without pausing, he left the room.

Harry gazed at the glass in his hand and cursed himself. He hadn't meant to upset the boy. Or maybe he had. He couldn't trust his own motives any more, couldn't keep tabs on his feelings. Sympathy so quickly turned into irritation; guilt so quickly transformed into anger. Good intentions towards his son disappeared the minute the boy opened his mouth. Part of him couldn't wait for the moment when Simon married; left his house; became swallowed up by another family; finally gave him some peace. And part of him dreaded it; didn't even want to think about it.

Frowning, Harry poured himself another whisky and went back to his desk. He reached for the phone, dialled a number and listened impatiently to the ringing tone. Then, with a scowl, crashed the received down again.

Milly sat at the kitchen table with a thumping heart, wishing she could run away and escape. It was him. It was the boy from Oxford. The boy who had seen her marrying Allan; who had picked up her wedding veil and handed it back to her. He was older now. His face was harder and there was stubble over his chin. But his round metal spectacles were just the same, and so was his arrogant, almost scornful expression. Now he was leaning back in his chair, staring at her curiously.

Just don't remember, thought Milly, not daring to meet his gaze. For God's sake don't remember who I am.

'Here we are,' said Olivia, coming over to the table. 'I've arranged your flowers for you, darling. You can't just dump them and forget about them!'

'I know,' muttered Milly. 'Thanks.'

'Now, would you like some more tea, Alexander?'

'Yup,' said the boy, holding out his cup. 'Thanks very much.' Olivia poured the tea, then sat down and smiled around the table.

'Isn't this nice,' she said. 'I'm starting to feel as though this wedding is really happening!' She took a sip of tea, then looked up. 'Milly, have you shown Alexander your engagement ring?'

Slowly, feeling her insides clenching, Milly held out her left hand to Alexander. His gaze passed inscrutably over the antique diamond cluster, then he raised his eyes to hers.

'Very nice,' he said and took a sip of tea. 'You're engaged to Harry Pinnacle's son. The heir to Fruit 'n Smooth. Is that right?'

'Yes,' said Milly reluctantly.

'Quite a catch,' said Alexander.

'He's a sweet boy,' said Olivia at once, as she always did when anyone referred to Simon's money or family background. 'Quite one of us, now.'

'And what does he do?' Alexander's voice was faintly mocking. 'Work for his father?'

'No,' said Milly. Her voice felt awkward and unfamiliar. 'He sells advertising.'

'I see,' said Alexander. There was a pause. He took another sip of tea and frowned at Milly. 'I'm still sure I recognize you from somewhere.'

'Do you really?' said Olivia. 'How funny!'

'Well, I'm afraid I don't recognize you,' said Milly, trying to sound light-hearted.

'Yes, darling,' said Olivia, 'but you're not very good with faces, are you?' She turned to Alexander. 'Now, I'm just the same as you, Alexander. I never forget a face.'

'Faces are my business,' said Alexander. 'I spend my life looking at them.' His eyes ran over Milly's face and she felt herself flinching. 'Have you always had your hair like that?' he suddenly asked. Milly's heart lurched in fright.

'Not always,' she said, and gripped her cup tightly. 'I . . . I once dyed it red.'

'Not a success,' said Olivia emphatically. 'I told her to go to my salon, but she wouldn't listen. And then of course—'

'That's not it,' said Alexander, cutting Olivia off. He frowned again at Milly. 'You weren't at Cambridge, were you?'

'No,' said Milly.

'But Isobel was,' said Olivia triumphantly. 'Perhaps you're thinking of her!'

'Who's Isobel?' said Alexander.

'My sister,' said Milly, gripped by sudden hope. 'She . . . she looks just like me.'

'She read modern languages,' said Olivia. 'And now she's doing *terribly* well. Flies all over the world, interpreting at conferences. You know, she's met all the world leaders. Or at least . . .'

'What does she look like?' said Alexander.

'That's a picture of her there,' said Olivia, pointing to a photograph on the mantelpiece. 'You and she should really meet before the wedding,' she added lightly, watching Alexander scan the picture. 'I'm sure you've got lots in common!'

'It wasn't her,' said Alexander, turning back to Milly. 'She looks nothing like you.'

'She's taller than Milly,' said Olivia, then added thoughtfully, 'You're quite tall, aren't you, Alexander?' He shrugged, and stood up.

'I've got to go. I'm meeting a friend in town.'

'A friend,' said Olivia. 'How nice. Someone special?'

'An old mate from school,' said Alexander, looking at Olivia as though she were mad.

'Well, have fun!' said Olivia.

'Thanks,' said Alexander. He paused by the door. 'I'll see you tomorrow, Milly. I'll take a few informal shots and we can have a little chat about what you want.' He nodded at her, then disappeared.

'Well!' exclaimed Olivia, as soon as he had gone. 'What an interesting young man.'

Milly didn't move. She stared straight at the table, hands still clenched round her cup, her heart beating furiously.

'Are you all right, darling?' said Olivia, peering at her.

'Fine,' said Milly. 'I'm fine.' She forced herself to smile at her mother and take a sip of tea. It was OK, she told herself firmly. Nothing had happened. Nothing was going to happen.

'I was looking at his portfolio earlier on,' said Olivia. 'He's really very talented. He's won awards, and everything!'

'Really,' said Milly in a dry voice. She picked up a biscuit, looked at it and put it down again, feeling a sudden swoop of fear. But what if it came back to him? What if he remembered – and told someone exactly what he'd seen her doing ten years ago? What if it all came out? Her stomach curdled at the thought; she felt suddenly ill with panic.

'He and Isobel really should meet each other,' Olivia was saying. 'As soon as she gets back from Paris.'

'What?' Milly's attention was momentarily drawn. 'Why?' She stared at Olivia, who gave a tiny shrug. 'Mummy, no! You don't mean it!'

'It's just a thought,' said Olivia defensively. 'What chance has poor Isobel got to meet men, stuck in dreary conference rooms all day?'

'She doesn't want to meet men. Not your men! Milly gave a tiny shudder. 'And especially not him!'

'What's wrong with him?' said Olivia.

'Nothing,' said Milly quickly. 'He's just . . . not Isobel.'

An image of her sister came into Milly's mind – clever, sensible Isobel. Suddenly she felt a surge of relief. She would talk to Isobel. Isobel always knew what to do. Milly looked at her watch.

'What time is it in Paris?'

'Why? Are you going to make a call?'

'Yes,' said Milly. 'I want to speak to Isobel.' Suddenly she felt desperate. 'I need to speak to Isobel.'

Isobel Havill arrived back at her hotel room at eight o'clock to find the message light on her telephone furiously blinking. She frowned, rubbed a weary hand over her brow, and opened the minibar. The day had been even more draining than usual. Her skin felt parched from the dry atmosphere of the conference room; her mouth tasted of coffee and cigarette smoke. She had spent all day listening, translating and speaking into her microphone in the low, measured tones that made her so highly sought after. Now her throat felt sore and her mouth incapable of further speech; her head was still a maelstrom of furious, multilingual discussion.

Holding a glass of vodka, she went slowly into the white marble bathroom, switched on the light and looked for a few silent seconds at her red-rimmed eyes. She opened her mouth to say something, then feebly closed it again. She felt unable to think; unable to initiate a single idea of her own. For too many hours, her brain had been acting as nothing but a high-powered conduit of information. She was still geared up only to channel words back and forth; not to interrupt the flow with her own thoughts; not to sully the translation with her own opinions. She had operated immaculately all day, never flagging, never losing her cool. And now she felt like a dried-out, empty shell.

She drained her glass of vodka and put it down on the glass bathroom shelf. The clinking sound made her wince. In the mirror, her reflection stared back at her with an apprehensive expression. All day, she'd managed to put this moment from her mind. But now she was alone and her work was finished, and there was no longer any excuse. With a trembling hand she reached into her bag and pulled out a crackly pharmacist's bag; took out a little oblong box. Inside was a leaflet bearing instructions printed in French, German, Spanish and English. Her eyes flicked impatiently over each of them, noticing that the Spanish paragraph was poorly constructed and there was a discrepancy in the German version. But all seemed agreed on the short time span of the test. Only one minute. *Une minute. Un minuto.*

She carried out the test, scarcely able to believe what she was doing, then left the little phial on the edge of the bath and went back into the bedroom. Her jacket was still lying on the huge hotel bed; the telephone was still furiously bleeping. She pressed the button for messages, went to the minibar and poured herself another vodka. Thirty seconds to go.

'Hi, Isobel. It's me.' A man's low voice filled the room, and Isobel flinched. 'Call me if you have time. Bye.'

Isobel looked at her watch. Fifteen seconds to go.

'Isobel, it's Milly. Listen, I really need to speak to you. Please, please can you call me back as soon as you get this? It's really really urgent.'

'Isn't it always urgent?' said Isobel aloud.

She looked at her watch, took a deep breath and strode towards the bathroom. The little blue stripe was visible before she even reached the door. Suddenly she felt sick.

'No,' she whispered. 'I can't be.' She backed away from the pregnancy test, as though from something contaminated, and shut the bathroom door. She took a deep, shuddering breath, and reached automatically for her glass of vodka. Then, in sudden realization, her hand stopped. A lonely dismay crept over her.

'Isobel?' the machine was saying brightly. 'It's Milly again. I'll be at Simon's tonight, so maybe you could call me there?'

'No,' shouted Isobel, and she felt a sudden pricking of tears. 'I couldn't, all right?' She picked up the vodka, drained it in one, and crashed the glass defiantly down on the bedside table. But suddenly more tears were filling her eyes, suddenly she was unable to control her breath. Like a wounded animal, she crawled into bed, buried her head in her hotel pillow. And as the telephone rang again, she silently began to cry.

THREE

At eight-thirty, Olivia and Milly arrived at Pinnacle Hall. They were met at the door by Simon and shown into the large baronial drawing room.

'Well,' said Olivia, wandering over to the crackling fire. 'Isn't this nice!'

'I'll get some champagne,' said Simon. 'Dad's still on the phone.'

'Actually,' said Milly faintly, 'I think I'll try Isobel again. I'll use the phone in the games room.'

'Can't it wait?' said Olivia. 'What do you to speak to her about?'

'Nothing,' said Milly at once. 'Nothing, I just . . . need to talk to her.' She swallowed. 'I won't be long.'

When they'd gone, Olivia settled herself into a chair, admiring the portrait above the fireplace. It was a grandly framed oil painting which looked as though it could have been bought along with the house; in fact it was a picture of Harry's grandmother as a girl. Harry Pinnacle was so famous as a self-made man that it was widely assumed he'd started from nothing. The fact that he'd attended an expensive public school only spoiled the story, as did the hefty parental loans which had got him started – so these were generally brushed over by everyone, including Harry himself.

The door opened, and a pretty blond girl in a smart trouser suit entered, holding a tray of champagne glasses.

'Simon's just coming,' she said. 'He just remembered a fax he had to send.'

'Thank you,' said Olivia, taking a glass and giving a small, regal smile.

The girl left the room, and Olivia took a sip of champagne. The fire was warm on her face; her chair was comfortable; classical music was playing pleasantly through concealed speakers. This, she thought, was the life. A pang went through her – part delight, part envy – at the knowledge that soon her daughter would be entering this kind of existence. Milly was already as much at home at Pinnacle Hall as she was at 1 Bertram Street. She was used to dealing easily with Harry's staff; was used to sitting alongside Simon at grand dinner parties. Of course she and Simon could maintain that they were just like any other young couple, that the money wasn't theirs – but who were they kidding? They would be rich one day. Fabulously rich. Milly would be able to have anything she wanted.

Olivia clenched her hand more tightly around her

glass. When the engagement had first been announced, she'd been overcome by an astonished, almost giddy delight. For Milly to have any kind of connection with the son of Harry Pinnacle was good enough. But for them to be marrying – and so quickly – was unasked-for bliss. As the wedding plans had progressed and become more concrete, she'd prided herself on keeping her triumph concealed; on treating Simon as casually as any other young beau; on playing down – to herself as much as anyone else – the significance of the match.

But now, with only a few days to go, her heart was beginning to beat quickly again with jubilation. In only a few days the whole world would see her daughter marrying one of the most eligible bachelors in the country. All her friends – indeed, everyone she had ever known – would be forced to admire as she presided over the biggest, glitziest, most romantic wedding any of them had ever seen. This was an event which Olivia felt as though she had been building up to all her life; an event surpassing even her own wedding. That had been a modest, anonymous little affair. Whereas this occasion would be crammed with important, in-fluential, wealthy people, all forced to take a back seat as she – and of course Milly – strolled prominently, centre stage.

In just a few days' time she would be donning her designer outfit and smiling at massed rows of cameras and watching as all her friends and acquaintances and jealous relatives goggled at the lavishness of Milly's reception. It would be a beautiful day, a day they would all carry in their thoughts for ever. Like some wonderful movie, thought Olivia happily. Some wonderful, romantic Hollywood movie.

James Havill arrived at the front door of Pinnacle Hall and tugged at the heavy wrought-iron bell-pull. As he waited for an answer he looked around and frowned. The place was too beautiful, too perfect. It was a cliché of opulence, more like some ghastly Hollywood movie than a real place. If this is what money can buy, he thought dishonestly, then you can keep it. I'd rather have real life.

The front door was, he realized, slightly ajar, and he pushed it open. A fire was blazing cheerily in a huge fireplace and the chandeliers were all lit up, but no-one was about. He gazed cautiously around, trying to distinguish the panelled doors from each other. One of these doors was the huge drawing room with the deers' heads. He remembered it from previous visits. But which was it? For a few seconds he dithered, then, suddenly irritated with himself, he stepped towards the nearest door and pushed it open.

But he'd got it wrong. The first thing he saw was Harry. He was sitting at an enormous oak desk, listening intently to a phone conversation. He raised his silvery head at the sound of the door opening, narrowed his eyes, then waved James away in irritation.

'Sorry,' said James quietly, backing out.

'Mr Havill?' came a low voice behind him. 'I'm sorry I didn't answer the door more quickly.' James turned to see a blond girl he recognized as one of Harry's assistants behind him. 'If you'd like to come with me . . .' she said, tactfully guiding him out of the room and closing the study door.

'Thank you,' said James, feeling patronized.

'The others are in the drawing room. Let me take your coat.'

'Thank you,' said James again.

'And if you need anything else,' said the girl pleasantly, 'just ask me. All right?' In to her words – thought James resentfully – don't go wandering about. The girl gave him a smooth smile, opened the door of the drawing room and ushered him in.

Olivia's pleasant dreamworld was interrupted as the door suddenly opened. She quickly smoothed down her skirt and looked up with a smile, expecting to see Harry. But it was the pretty blond girl again.

'Your husband's here, Mrs Havill,' she said, and stepped aside.

Into the room walked James. He'd come straight from the office; his dark grey suit was crumpled and he looked tired.

'Been here long?' he said.

'No,' said Olivia with a forced cheerfulness. 'Not very.'

She rose from her seat and walked towards James, intending to greet him with a kiss. Just before she reached him, the girl tactfully withdrew, and closed the door.

Olivia stopped in her tracks, suddenly feeling

self-conscious. Physical contact between herself and James had, over the last few years, become something which only happened in front of other people. Now she felt awkward, standing this close to him without an audience; without a reason. She looked at him, hoping he would help her out, but his face was blank; she couldn't read it. Eventually she leaned forward, flushing slightly, and gave him a peck on the cheek – then immediately stepped backwards and took a gulp of champagne.

'Where's Milly?' said James in an expressionless voice.

'She's popped off to make a telephone call.'

Olivia watched as James helped himself to a glass of champagne and took a deep swig. He walked over to the sofa and sat down, stretching his legs out comfortably in front of him. Olivia gazed down at his head. His dark hair was damp from the snow but neatly combed, and she found herself running her eyes idly along his side parting. Then, as he turned his head, she quickly looked away.

'So,' she began – then stopped and took a sip of champagne. She wandered over to the window, pulled open the heavy brocade curtain and looked out into the snowy night. She could barely remember the last time she'd been alone in a room with James; certainly couldn't recall the last time they'd talked together naturally. Topics of conversation passed through her mind like shrink-wrapped food on a conveyor belt, each as unappealing and difficult to get into as the next. If she told James the latest piece of Bath gossip, she would have to begin by reminding him who all the main characters were. If she told him about the wedding shoe fiasco, she would first have to explain the difference between duchesse satin and slub silk. Nothing she could think of to say seemed quite worth the effort of starting.

Once, long ago, their conversation had flowed like a seamless length of ribbon. James had listened to her stories in genuine amusement; she'd laughed at his dry wit. They'd entertained each other, had fun together. But these days all his jokes seemed tinged with a bitterness she didn't understand, and a tense boredom crept over his face as soon as she began to speak.

So they remained in silence, until finally the door opened and Milly came in. She gave James a brief, strained smile.

'Hello, Daddy,' she said. 'You made it.'

'Did you get through to Isobel?' said Olivia.

'No,' said Milly shortly. 'I don't know what she can be doing. I had to leave another message.' Her eye fell on the tray. 'Oh good. I could do with a drink.'

She took a glass of champagne and raised it. 'Cheers.'

'Cheers!' echoed Olivia.

'Your good health, my darling,' said James. All three drank; there was a little silence.

'Did I interrupt something?' said Milly.

'No,' said Olivia. 'You didn't interrupt anything.'

'Good,' said Milly without really listening, and walked over to the fire, hoping no-one would talk to her.

*　*　*

For the third time, she'd got through to Isobel's message machine. As she'd heard the tinny tones she'd felt a spurt of anger, an irrational conviction that Isobel was there and just wasn't answering. She'd left a brief message, then remained staring at the phone for a few minutes, biting her lip, hoping desperately that Isobel would call back. Isobel was the only one she could talk to – the only one who would listen calmly; who would think of a solution rather than lecturing.

But the phone had remained silent. Isobel hadn't called back. No Milly's hand tightened around her champagne glass. She couldn't stand this niggling, secret panic. On the way over to Pinnacle Hall she'd sat silently in the car, gathering reassuring thoughts around herself like sandbags. Alexander would never remember, she'd told herself again and again. It had been a two-minute encounter, ten years ago. He couldn't possibly remember that. And even if he did, he wouldn't say anything about it. He would just keep quiet and get on with his job. Civilized people didn't deliberately cause trouble.

'Milly?' Simon's voice interrupted her thoughts and she jumped guiltily.

'Hi,' she said. 'Did you send your fax all right?'

'Yes.' He took a sip of champagne and looked more closely at her. 'Are you OK? You're looking tense.'

'Am I?' She smiled at him. 'I don't feel it.'

'You're tense,' persisted Simon, and he began to

massage her shoulders gently. 'Worrying about the wedding. Am I right?'

'Yes,' said Milly.

'I knew it.'

Simon sounded satisfied and Milly said nothing. Simon liked to think that he was in tune with her emotions; that he knew her likes and dislikes; that he could predict her moods. And she'd got into the habit of agreeing with him, even when his assertions were wildly inaccurate. After all, it was sweet of him to have a go. Most men wouldn't have bothered.

And to have expected him to get it right all the time would have been unreasonable. Most of the time she herself was unsure exactly how she was feeling. Emotions shaded her mind like colours on a palette – some lingering, some momentary, but all blended together in an inseparable wash. Whereas Simon's moods seemed to march through him, distinct and uniform, like a row of children's building blocks. When he was happy, he smiled. When he was angry, he frowned.

'Let me guess what you're thinking,' murmured Simon against her hair. 'You're wishing it was just the two of us tonight.'

'No,' said Milly honestly. She turned round and looked straight up at him, breathing in his musky, familiar scent. 'I was thinking how much I love you.'

It was nine-thirty before Harry Pinnacle strode into the room. 'My apologies,' he said. 'This is unforgivable of me.'

'Harry, it's utterly forgivable!' exclaimed Olivia, who was by now on her fifth glass of champagne. 'We know what it's like!'

'I don't,' muttered Simon.

'And I'm sorry about earlier,' said Harry to James. 'It was an important call.'

'That's quite all right,' said James stiffly. There was a slight pause.

'Well, let's not hang about,' said Harry. He turned politely to Olivia. 'After you.'

They slowly made their way across the hall, into the dining room.

'All right, sweetheart?' said James to Milly as they sat down round the magnificent mahogany dining table.

'Fine,' she said, and gave him a taut smile.

But she wasn't, thought James. He'd watched her knocking back glasses of champagne as though she were desperate; watched her jump every time the phone rang. Was she having second thoughts? He leaned towards her.

'Just remember, darling,' he said in an undertone. 'You don't have to go through with it if you don't want to.'

'What?' Milly's head jerked up as though she'd been stung, and James nodded reassuringly.

'If you change your mind about Simon – now, or even on the day itself – don't worry. We can call the whole thing off. No-one will mind.'

'I don't want to call the whole thing off!' hissed Milly. Suddenly she looked close to tears. 'I want to get married! I love Simon.'

'Good,' said James. 'Well, that's fine then.'

He sat back in his chair, glanced across the table at Simon and felt unreasonably irritated. The boy had everything. Good looks, a wealthy background, an annoyingly calm and balanced personality. He quite obviously adored Milly; he was polite to Olivia; he was thoughtful towards the rest of the family. There was nothing to complain about. And tonight, James admitted to himself, he was in a mood for complaint.

He'd had a grisly day at work. The engineering firm in whose finance department he worked had undergone restructuring in recent months. Endless rumours had that day culminated in the announcement that there would have to be four junior redundancies in his department. The news was supposed to be confidential but it had obviously spread: as he'd left the office, all the younger members of the team had still been hunched dutifully over their desks. Some had kept their heads down; others had looked up with scared eyes as he passed. Every single one of them had a family and a mortgage. None of them could afford to lose their job. None of them deserved to.

By the time he'd arrived at Pinnacle Hall he'd felt unspeakably depressed by the whole thing. As he had parked his car he had made up his mind that when Olivia asked how his day had been, he would, for once, tell her the truth. Perhaps not everything straight away, but enough to make her concerned; enough to make her realize what a burden he was struggling with. But she had not asked – and a certain pride had stopped him from volunteering his story; from admitting to her his vulnerability. He didn't want his wife turning her mind to him as if he were just another one of her charity projects. Abandoned ponies, handicapped children, a miserable husband.

He should, thought James, be used to Olivia by now. He should be used to the fact that she was not very interested in him; that her life was full enough of other concerns; that she paid more attention to the problems of her chattering girlfriends than she ever did to him. after all, they had managed to carve out a stable, workable life together. If they weren't soulmates there was at least some sort of symbiosis between them. She had her life and he had his – and where they overlapped they were always perfectly amicable. James had resigned himself to this arrangement long ago, had thought it would be all that he ever needed. But it wasn't. He needed more; he wanted more. He wanted a different life, before it was too late.

'I'd like to propose a toast.'

Harry's voice interrupted James's thoughts and he looked up, frowning slightly. There he was. Harry Pinnacle, one of the most successful men in the country, and his own daughter's prospective father-in-law. James was aware that this alliance made him the envy of his peers and knew that he should be pleased at Milly's future financial security. But he refused to rejoice in the fact of his daughter becoming a Pinnacle; refused to bask, as his wife did, in the fascinated

66

curiosity of their friends. He'd heard Olivia on the phone, dropping Harry's name into the conversation, assuming an intimacy with the great man that he knew she did not have. She was milking the situation for all it was worth – and her behaviour made him curl up with shame. There were days when he wished Milly had never met the son of Harry Pinnacle.

'To Milly and Simon,' declaimed Harry, in the gravelly voice which made all his utterances sound more significant than everyone else's.

'To Milly and Simon,' echoed James, and picked up the heavy Venetian glass in front of him.

'Simply delicious wine,' said Olivia. 'Are you a wine expert as well as everything else, Harry?'

'Christ, no,' replied Harry. 'I rely on people with taste to tell me what to buy. It's all the same to me.'

'Now, I don't believe that! You're too modest,' exclaimed Olivia. James watched in disbelief as she reached over and patted Harry intimately on the hand. Just who did she think she was? He turned away, slightly sickened, and caught Simon's eye.

'Cheers, James,' he said, and raised his glass. 'Here's to the wedding.'

'Yes,' said James, and took a huge gulp of wine. 'To the wedding.'

As he watched everyone drinking his father's wine, Simon felt a sudden tightening in his throat. He coughed and looked up.

'There's someone missing here tonight,' he said. 'And

I'd like to propose a toast to her.' He raised his glass. 'To my mother.'

There was a slight pause and he was aware of eyes darting towards the head of the table. Then Harry raised his glass.

'To Anne,' he said gravely.

'To Anne,' echoed James and Milly.

'Was that her name?' said Olivia, looking up with flushed cheeks. 'I always thought it was Louise.'

'No,' said Simon. 'Anne.'

'Oh well,' said Olivia, 'if you say so.' She raised her glass. 'To Anne. Anne Pinnacle.' She drank from her glass, then looked at Milly, as though struck by a sudden thought. 'You're not planning to keep your own name, are you, darling?'

'I don't think so,' said Milly. 'Although I might stay as Havill for work.'

'Oh no!' exclaimed Olivia. 'Too confusing. Just be Pinnacle through and through!'

'I think it's a good idea,' said James. 'Keep your independence. What do you think, Simon? Would you mind if Milly stayed Havill?'

'To be honest,' said Simon, 'I'd prefer it if we shared a name. We'll be sharing everything else.' He turned towards Milly and smiled. 'But I'll be sad to lose Milly Havill, too. After all, it was Milly Havill I fell in love with.'

'Very touching,' said James.

'Would you consider changing your name to Havill?' said Harry, from the end of the table. Simon looked at him steadily.

'Yes, I would,' he said. 'If Milly really wanted it.'

'No!' exclaimed Olivia. 'You don't, do you, darling?'

'I don't suppose you would have changed your name for Mum, would you, Dad?' said Simon.

'No,' said Harry. 'I wouldn't.'

'Yes well,' said Simon tautly, 'the difference is that I'm prepared to put my marriage before everything else.'

'The difference is,' Harry said, 'that your mother's maiden name was Parry.' Olivia laughed and Simon shot her a furious look.

'The point is,' he said loudly, 'names are irrelevant. It's people that make a marriage work. Not names.'

'And you, of course, are an expert on marriage,' said Harry.

'I'm more of an expert than you! At least I haven't screwed mine up yet!' There was a short silence. The Havills, all looked at their plates. Simon gazed at his father, breathing hard. Then Harry shrugged.

'I'm sure you and Milly will be very happy,' he said. 'We can't all be so lucky.'

'It's not a matter of luck,' retorted Simon angrily. 'Luck doesn't come into it!' He looked at James and Olivia. 'What would you say makes a successful marriage?'

'Money,' said Olivia, then laughed brightly. 'Only joking!'

'It's communication, isn't it?' said Simon. He leaned forward earnestly. 'Sharing, talking, knowing each other inside out. Wouldn't you agree, James?'

'I'll take your word for it,' said James, and took a swig of wine.

'You're absolutely right, Simon,' said Olivia. 'I was actually going to say communication.

'I'd put sex above communication,' said Harry. 'Good sex, and plenty of it.'

'Well, I wouldn't know much about that, either,' said James drily.

'James!' exclaimed Olivia, and gave a tinkling laugh. Simon gave James a curious look, then glanced at Milly. But she didn't seem to be listening to the conversation at all.

'What about you, Harry?' Olivia was saying, gazing up at him through her lashes.

'What about me?'

'Aren't you ever tempted to marry again?'

'I'm too old to marry,' said Harry shortly.

'Nonsense!' exclaimed Olivia gaily. 'You could easily find yourself a lovely wife.'

'If you say so.'

'Of course you could.' Olivia took another sip of wine. 'I'd marry you myself!' She gave a little laugh.

'Very kind of you,' said Harry.

'Oh no,' said Olivia, waving her glass in the air. 'It would be a pleasure. Really.'

There was a choice of puddings.

'Oh!' said Olivia, looking from lemon mousse to chocolate torte and back again. 'Oh dear, I can't decide.'

'Then have both,' said Harry.

'Really? Would that be all right? Is anyone else going to have both?' Olivia looked around the table.

'I'm not going to have any,' said Milly, pleating her napkin nervously between her fingers.

'You're not slimming, are you?' said Harry.

'No,' said Milly. 'I'm just not very hungry.' She managed a smile at Harry and he nodded pleasantly back. He was basically a kind man, thought Milly. She could see it, even if Simon couldn't.

'You're as bad as Isobel!' said Olivia. 'Isobel eats like a little bird.'

'She's too busy to eat,' said James.

'How is she?' asked Harry politely.

'She's great!' said James with sudden animation. 'Forging ahead with her career, travelling the world . . .'

'Does she have a boyfriend?'

'Oh no,' James laughed. 'She's too busy doing her own thing. Isobel's always been an independent spirit. She's not going to get tied down in a hurry.'

'She's might,' objected Olivia. 'She might meet someone tomorrow! Some nice businessman.'

'God help us,' said James. 'Can you really see Isobel settling down with some dreary businessman? Anyway, she's far too young still.'

'She's older than me,' said Milly.

'Yes,' said James, 'but the two of you are very different.'

'How?' said Milly. She looked at her father. The tensions of the day were throbbing unbearably inside her head; she felt suddenly on edge. 'How are we different? Are you saying I'm too stupid to do anything but get married?'

'No!' said James. He looked shocked. 'Of course not! All I mean is that Isobel's a bit more adventurous than you. She likes taking risks.'

'I've taken risks in my time!' cried Milly. 'I've taken risks you know nothing about!' She broke off, and stared at her father, breathing hard.

'Milly, don't get upset,' said James. 'All I'm saying is that you and Isobel are different.'

'And I prefer you,' whispered Simon to Milly. She gave him a grateful smile.

'Anyway, James, what's wrong with businessmen?' said Olivia. 'You're a businessman, aren't you, and I married you.'

'I know, my love,' said James tonelessly. 'But I'm hoping Isobel might do a little better than someone like me.'

Later on, as the pudding plates were being removed, Harry cleared his throat for attention.

'I don't want to make a big thing of this,' he said. 'But I've got a bit of a present for the happy couple.'

Simon looked up defensively. He'd bought a present of his own to give Milly this evening and had planned to spring it on her while they were all drinking coffee. But whatever Harry had bought, it would undoubtedly be more expensive than the ear-rings he'd chosen. Surreptitiously he felt for the small leather box, safely in his pocket, and wondered whether to leave it for another day – a day without competition from his father. But then a small wave of indignation rose through him. Why should he be ashamed? Perhaps his father could afford to spend a bit more than him – but then, what did everyone expect?

'I've got a present too,' he said, trying to sound casual. 'For Milly.'

'For me?' said Milly confusedly. 'But I haven't got anything for you. At least, not anything to give you tonight.'

'This is something extra,' said Simon.

He leaned over and gently pushed Milly's blond hair back behind her shoulders, exposing her little pink ears. As he did so, the gesture seemed suddenly erotic; and as he stared at her flawless skin, breathing in her sweet, musky scent, a proud desire surged through him. sod the rest of them, he thought – Olivia with her unbearable smugness, Harry with all his cash. He had Milly's divine body all to himself, and that was all that counted.

'What is it?' said Milly.

'Dad first,' said Simon, feeling magnanimous. 'What have you got us, Dad?'

Harry felt in his pocket, and for a mad moment, Simon thought he was going to produce an identical pair of ear-rings. But instead, Harry dropped a key on the table.

'A key?' said Milly. 'What's it for?'

'A car?' said Olivia in incredulous tones.

'Not a car,' said Harry. 'A flat.'

There was a unanimous gasp. Olivia opened her mouth to speak, then closed it again.

'You're joking,' said Simon. 'You've bought us a flat?'

Harry pushed the key across the table.

'All yours.'

Simon stared at his father, feeling all the wrong emotions rise to the surface. He tried to locate a feeling of gratitude, but all he could feel was shock – and the beginnings of a defensive, smarting anger. He glanced at Milly. She was gazing at Harry with shining eyes. Simon felt a sudden despair.

'How . . .' he began, trying to summon the correct, grateful tones, but only managing to sound peevish. 'How do you know we'll like it?'

'It's the one you wanted to rent.'

'The one in Marlborough Mansions?'

Harry shook his head.

'The one you *wanted* to rent. The one you couldn't afford.'

'The flat in Parham Place?' whispered Milly. 'You *bought* it for us?'

Simon stared at his father, and felt like punching him. Fuck him for being so thoughtful.

'This is very good of you, Harry,' said James. 'Incredibly generous.' Harry shrugged.

'One less thing for them to worry about.'

'Oh darling!' said Olivia, clasping Milly's hand. 'Won't it be lovely? And you'll be so near us.'

'Well now, there's a plus,' said Simon, before he could stop himself. James glanced at him, and cleared his throat tactfully.

'And now,' he said, 'what about Simon's present?'

'Yes,' said Milly. She turned to Simon and touched his hand gently. 'What is it?'

Simon reached into his pocket and silently presented her with the little box. Everyone watched as she opened it to reveal two tiny, twinkling diamond studs.

'Oh Simon,' said Milly. She looked at him, her eyes suddenly glittering with unshed tears. 'They're beautiful.'

'Pretty,' said Olivia dismissively. 'Oh Milly! Parham Place!'

'I'll put them on,' said Milly.

'You don't have to,' said Simon, trying to control himself. His heart pounded with a raw, hurt anger; it seemed to him that everyone was laughing at him. Even Milly. 'They're nothing very special.'

'Of course they are,' said Harry gravely.

'No they're not!' Simon found himself shouting. 'Not compared with a piece of fucking real estate!'

'Simon,' said Harry calmly, 'no-one is making that comparison.'

'Simon, they're lovely!' said Milly. 'Look.' She smoothed her hair back and the little diamonds sparkled in the candlelight.

'Great,' said Simon without looking up. He was making things worse, he knew, but he could not help himself. He felt like a small, humiliated schoolboy.

Harry caught James's eye, then rose to his feet.

'Let's have coffee,' he said. 'Nicki will have put it in the drawing room.'

'Absolutely,' said James, taking his cue. 'Come on, Olivia.'

The three parents moved out of the dining room, leaving Milly and Simon together in silence. After a few moments Simon looked up, to see Milly gazing at him. She wasn't laughing, she wasn't pitying. Suddenly he felt ashamed.

'I'm sorry,' he muttered. 'I'm being a complete prick.'

'I haven't said thank you for my present yet,' said Milly.

She leaned forward and kissed him with warm, soft lips, Simon closed his eyes and cupped her face, feeling nothing but sweet sensation. Gradually, his father receded from his thoughts; his soreness began to lessen. Milly was all his – and nothing else really mattered.

'Let's elope,' he said suddenly. 'Sod the wedding. Let's just go and do it on our own in a registry office.' Milly pulled away.

'Do you really want to?' she said. Simon stared back at her. He had been only half-serious, but she was staring at him intently. 'Shall we, Simon?' she said, and there was a slight edge to her voice. 'Tomorrow?'

'Well,' he said, feeling a little taken aback. 'We could do. But wouldn't everyone get a bit pissed off? Your mother would never forgive me.' Milly stared at him for a moment, then bit her lip.

'You're right,' she said. 'It's a stupid idea.' She pushed her chair back and stood up. 'Come on. Are you ready to be grateful to your father yet? He's very kind, you know.'

'Wait,' said Simon. He reached out and grasped her hand tightly. 'Would you really elope with me?'

'Yes,' said Milly simply. 'I would.'

'I thought you were looking forward to the wedding. The dress, and the reception, and all your friends . . .'

'I was,' said Milly. 'But . . .' She looked away and shrugged slightly.

'But you'd give it all up and elope,' said Simon in a shaking voice. 'You'd give it all up.' He gazed at Milly and thought he'd never known such love, such generosity of spirit. 'No other girl would do that,' he said, his voice thick with emotion. 'God, I love you. I don't know what I've done to deserve you. Come here.'

He pulled her down onto his knee and began kissing her neck; feeling for her bra strap; tugging urgently at the zip of her skirt.

'Simon . . .' began Milly.

'We'll close the door,' he whispered. 'Put a chair under the door handle.'

'But your father . . .'

'He made us wait for him,' said Simon, against Milly's warm, scented skin. 'And how he's going to wait for us.'

FOUR

The next morning, Milly woke feeling refreshed. The rich food, wine and conversation from the night before seemed to have disappeared from her system; she felt light and energetic.

As she went into the kitchen for breakfast, a couple of guests from Yorkshire, Mr and Mrs Able, looked up from their coffee and nodded pleasantly.

'Morning, Milly!' said her mother, looking up from the phone. 'There's another special delivery for you.' She pointed to a large cardboard box on the floor. 'And someone's sent you a bottle of champagne. I've put it in the fridge.'

'Champagne!' said Milly in delight. 'And what's this?' She poured herself a cup of coffee, sat down on the floor and began to rip open the cardboard.

'It looks exciting,' said Mrs Able encouragingly.

'And Alexander says he'll meet you at ten-thirty,'

said Olivia. 'To take some shots and have a little chat.'

'Oh,' said Milly, suddenly feeling sick. 'Good.'

'You'd better put on some make-up first,' said Olivia. She looked critically at Milly. 'Darling, is something wrong?'

'No,' said Milly. 'Of course not.'

'Ah, Andrea,' said Olivia, turning to the phone. 'Yes, I got your message. And, frankly, it perturbed me.'

Milly began to tug at the plastic wrapping with shaky hands, feeling bubbles of panic rise inside her. She didn't want to see him. She wanted to run away like a child and block him out of her mind.

'Well then, perhaps Derek will have to *buy* a morning suit,' Olivia was saying sharply. 'Andrea, this is a society wedding. Not some dismal affair in a church hall. No, a good lounge suit certainly would not do.' She rolled her eyes at Milly. 'What is it?' she mouthed, gesturing to the present.

Silently, Milly pulled out a pair of Louis Vuitton travel bags and stared at them. Another sumptuous gift. She tried to smile, tried to look pleased. But all she could think of was the thudding fear growing inside her. She didn't want to feel his scrutinizing eyes on her face again. She wanted to hide herself until she was safely married to Simon.

'Well!' said Olivia.

'I've never seen anything like it,' said Mrs Able. 'Geoffrey! Just look at that for a wedding gift. Who are they from, dear?'

Milly looked at the card. 'Someone I've never even heard of.'

'One of Harry's friends, I expect,' said Olivia, putting down the phone.

'I've never known a wedding like this,' said Mrs Able, shaking her head. 'The stories I'm going to tell when I get back home!'

'I told you about the procession, didn't I?' said Olivia complacently going over to the Aga. 'We're having an organist specially flown in from Geneva. He's the best, apparently. And three trumpeters are going to play a fanfare as Milly arrives at the Church.'

'A fanfare!' said Mrs Able to Milly. 'You'll feel like a princess.'

'Darling, have an egg,' said Olivia.

'No thanks,' said Milly. 'I'll just have coffee.'

'Still a little fragile after last night,' said Olivia airily, cracking eggs into a pan. 'It was a wonderful dinner, wasn't it, Milly?' She smiled at Mrs Able. 'I have to say, Harry's a wonderful host.'

'I've heard his business dinners are quite something,' said Mrs Able.

'I'm sure they are,' said Olivia. 'But of course, it's different when it's just us.' She gave a reminiscent little smile. 'We never have any of that formality – we just all enjoy ourselves. We eat, we drink, we talk . . .' She glanced over at Mr and Mrs Able to make sure they were listening. 'After all, Harry is one of our closest friends. And soon he'll be family.'

'Think of that,' said Mr Able. 'Harry Pinnacle, part of

your family. And you just running a bed and breakfast house.'

'An *upmarket* bed and breakfast,' snapped Olivia. 'There's a difference!'

'Geoff!' whispered Mrs Able crossly. 'You must dine with him often,' she said quickly to Olivia. 'Being such close friends.'

'Oh well . . .' said Olivia in mollified tones. She waved her egg-slice vaguely in the air.

Twice, thought Milly. You've been twice.

'It really depends,' said Olivia, smiling kindly at Mrs Able. 'We don't have any hard and fast arrangements. Sometimes he'll be out of the country for weeks – then he'll come back and just want to spend a quiet few days with friends.'

'Have you visited his London home?' asked Mrs Able.

'No, I haven't,' said Olivia regretfully. 'Milly has, though. And his villa in France. Haven't you, darling?'

'Yes,' said Milly tightly.

'Quite a jump for you, love,' said Mr Able. 'Joining the jet set overnight.' Olivia bridled.

'It's hardly as though Milly comes from a deprived family,' she exclaimed. 'You're used to mingling with all sorts of people, aren't you, darling? At Milly's school,' she added, giving Mr Able a satisfied glance, 'there was an Arab princess. What was her name, now?'

'I've got to go,' said Milly, unable to bear any more. She stood up, leaving her coffee undrunk.

'That's right,' said Olivia. 'Go and put some make-up on. You want to look your best for Alexander.'

'Yes,' said Milly faintly. She paused by the kitchen door. 'Isobel hasn't called for me this morning, has she?' she asked casually.

'No,' said Olivia. 'I expect she'll ring you later.'

At ten-forty, Alexander appeared at the door of the drawing room.

'Hi, Milly,' he said. 'Sorry I'm a bit late.'

Milly felt a sickening thud of nerves, as though she were being called for an exam or the dentist.

'It doesn't matter,' she said, putting down the copy of *Country Life* she had been pretending to read.

'That's right,' said Olivia, following in behind Alexander. 'By the window, do you think, Alexander, or by the piano?'

'Just where you are, I think,' said Alexander, looking critically at Milly's position on the sofa. 'I'll need to put up a couple of lights . . .'

'Would anyone like a cup of coffee?' said Olivia.

'I'll make it,' said Milly quickly and, without looking back, scuttled out of the room. On the way into the kitchen she glanced at herself in the mirror. Her skin was dry, her eyes had a frightened look in them; she looked nothing like a happy bride. Digging her nails into her palms, she forced herself to smile brightly at her reflection. Everything would be fine. If she could just force herself to act confidently, everything would be fine.

By the time she got back, the room had been transformed into a photographer's studio. A white cloth was draped on the floor and white umbrellas and light stands surrounded the sofa on which Olivia sat, smiling self-consciously at Alexander's camera.

'I'm being your stand-in, darling!' she said brightly.

'Nervous?' said Alexander to Milly.

'Not at all,' she said coolly.

'Let me see your nails, darling,' said Olivia, standing up. 'If we're going to see your engagement ring . . .'

'They're fine,' snapped Milly, whipping her hands away from her mother's grasp. She picked her way over the white cloth, sat down on the sofa and looked up at Alexander with all the calmness she could muster.

'That's right,' said Alexander. 'Now just relax. Sit back a bit. Loosen your hands.' He stared critically at her for a while. 'Could you sweep your hair back, off your face?'

'That reminds me!' exclaimed Olivia. 'Those photographs I was telling you about. I'll fetch them.'

'OK,' said Alexander absently. 'Now, Milly, I want you to lean back a little and smile.'

Without intending to, Milly found herself obeying his commands. As she smiled, she felt her body relax; felt herself sink into the cushions of the sofa. Alexander seemed utterly preoccupied with his camera. Any suggestion that they'd met before seemed to have been forgotten. She'd been worrying over nothing, she told herself comfortably. Everything was going to be all right. She glanced at her ring, sparkling prettily on her hand, and shifted her legs slightly, to a more flattering position.

'Here we are!' said Olivia, bustling up beside Alexander with a photograph album. 'These are of Isobel, just before she graduated, now we thought they were marvellous shots – but then, we don't have the expert's eye. What do you think?'

'Nice,' said Alexander, glancing briefly down.

'Do you really think so?' said Olivia, pleased. She flipped the page backwards. 'Here she is again. And again.' She flipped the pages back further. 'And this is one of Milly at around the same time. It must be ten years ago, now. Just look at her hair!'

'Nice,' said Alexander automatically. He turned his head to look, then, as his eyes fell on the picture of Milly, stopped still. 'Wait,' he said. 'Let me see that.' He took the album from Olivia, stared for a few seconds at the photograph, then looked incredulously at Milly.

'She cut all her hair off and bleached it without telling us!' Olivia was saying brightly. 'She was quite a wild little thing back then! You'd never believe it, looking at her now, would you?'

'No,' said Alexander. 'You'd never believe it.' He gazed down, mesmerized, at the album. 'The wedding girl,' he said softly, as though to himself.

Milly felt her insides turn to ice. She stared at him helplessly, feeling sick with fright, not daring to move a muscle. He remembered. He remember who she was. But if he would just keep his mouth shut, everything could still be all right. If he would just keep his mouth shut.

'Well,' said Alexander, finally looking up. 'What a

difference.' He looked at Milly with a small, amused smile and she stared back, her stomach churning.

'It's the hair,' said Olivia eagerly. 'That's all it is. If you change your hairstyle, everything else seems to change too. You should have seen me with a beehive!'

'I don't think it's just the hair,' said Alexander. 'What do you think, Milly? Is it just the hair? Or is it something else completely?'

He met her eyes and she gazed at him in terror.

'I don't know,' she managed eventually.

'It's a mystery, isn't it?' said Alexander. He gestured to the album. 'There you are, ten years ago . . . and here you are, now, a different woman completely.' He paused, loading film into his camera. 'And here I am.'

'Here's a super picture of Isobel in her school play,' said Olivia, holding the album out to Alexander. He ignored her.

'By the way, Milly,' he said conversationally. 'I never asked you. Is this your first marriage?'

'Of course it's her first marriage!' exclaimed Olivia, laughing slightly. 'Does Milly look old enough to be on her second marriage?'

'You'd be surprised,' said Alexander, adjusting something on the camera. 'These days.' A sudden white flash went off, and Milly flinched as though she were being attacked. Alexander looked up at her.

'Relax,' he said, and the flicker of a smile passed across his face. 'If you can.'

'You look lovely, darling,' said Olivia, clasping her hands together.

'I only asked,' continued Alexander, 'because I seem to do a lot of second marriages these days.' He paused, and surveyed Milly over his camera. 'But that's not you.'

'No,' said Milly in a strangled voice. 'That's not me.'

'Interesting,' said Alexander.

Milly glanced at her mother apprehensively. But Olivia had on her face the same look of polite incomprehension which appeared when business guests started discussing computer software or the yen. As she caught Milly's eye she nodded and started backing deferentially away.

'I'll see you later, shall I?' she whispered.

'That's good,' said Alexander. 'Now turn your head to the left. Lovely.' The room flashed again. In the corner the door closed softly behind Olivia.

'So, Milly,' said Alexander. 'What have you done with your first husband?'

The room swam around Milly's head; every muscle in her body tightened. She stared fixedly at the camera lens without speaking.

'Loosen your hands,' instructed Alexander. 'They're gripping too tightly. Try to relax.' He took another couple of shots. 'Come on, Milly. What's the story?'

'I don't know what you're talking about,' said Milly in a dry voice. Alexander laughed.

'You're going to have to do better than that.' He reached across and adjusted one of the white umbrellas. 'You know exactly what I'm talking about. And it's obvious no-one knows about it except me. I'm intrigued. Try crossing your legs,' he added, looking at

86

her through the lens. 'Left hand on your knee so we can see the ring. And the other under your chin.'

The white flash went off again. Milly stared desperately ahead, trying to frame in her mind a reply, a put-down, a witty riposte. But her thoughts were inarticulate and feeble, as though her brain-power had been sapped by panic. She felt pinned to the sofa by fear, unable to do anything but follow his commands.

'A first marriage isn't against the law, you know,' observed Alexander. 'So what's the problem? Would your bridegroom disapprove? Or his father?' He took another few shots, then loaded a new reel of film. 'Is that why you're keeping it secret?' He eyed her thoughtfully. 'Or maybe there's a bit more to the story.' He lowered his eye to the lens. 'Can you come slightly forward?'

Milly edged forward. Her stomach was tense, her skin felt prickly.

'I've still got an old photograph of you, by the way,' said Alexander. 'In your wedding dress, on the steps. It made a good shot. I almost framed it.'

The room flashed again. Milly felt giddy with fright. Her mind scurried back to that day in Oxford; to the crowd of tourists who had taken photographs of her and Allan on the steps, as she prinked and smiled and encouraged them. How could she have been so stupid? How could she have . . .

'Of course, you look very different now,' said Alexander. 'I nearly didn't recognize you.'

Milly forced herself to look up and meet his eye.

'You didn't recognize me,' she said. A tiny note of pleading entered her voice. 'You didn't recognize me.'

'Well, I don't know about that,' said Alexander, shaking his head. 'Keeping secrets from your future husband, Milly. Not a good sign.' He peeled off his jersey and threw it into a corner. 'Doesn't the poor guy deserve to know? Shouldn't someone tell him?'

Milly moved her lips to speak but no sound came out. She had never felt so scared in all her life.

'That's great,' said Alexander, looking into the camera again. 'But try not to frown.' He looked up at her and grinned. 'Think happy thoughts.'

After what seemed like hours, he came to an end.

'OK,' he said. 'You can go now.' Milly got up from the sofa and stared at him speechlessly. If she appealed to him – told him everything – he might relent. Or he might not. A tremor ran through her. She couldn't risk it.

'Did you want something?' said Alexander, looking up from his camera case.

'No,' said Milly. For an instant her eyes met his and a bolt of fear went through her. 'Thank you,' she added.

She walked to the door as quickly as she could without looking rushed, forced herself to turn the door knob calmly, and slipped out into the hall. As the door closed behind her, she felt almost tearful with relief. But what should she do now? She closed her eyes for a second, then opened them and reached for the phone. By now she knew the number off by heart.

'Hello,' came a voice. 'If you would like to leave a message for Isobel Havill, please speak after the tone.'

Milly crashed the receiver back down in frustration and stared at it. She had to talk to someone. She couldn't stand this any more. Then a sudden note of inspiration hit her, and she picked up the phone again.

'Hello?' she said, as it was answered. 'Esme? It's Milly. Can I come and see you?'

Milly's godmother lived in a large, elegant house to the north of the city, set back from the road and enclosed in a walled garden. As Milly walked up the path to her house, Esme opened the door and her two lean, pale whippets bounded out into the snow, jumping up at Milly and placing their paws lightly on her chest.

'Get down, you brutes,' exclaimed Esme, from the doorway. 'Leave poor Milly alone. She's feeling sensitive.' Milly looked up.

'Is it that obvious?'

'Of course it isn't,' said Esme. She inhaled on her cigarette and leaned against the door frame. Her dark eyes met Milly's appraisingly. 'But you don't normally ring me in the middle of the day with requests for immediate meetings. I imagine something must be wrong.'

Milly looked into Esme's scrutinizing eyes and suddenly felt shy.

'Not exactly,' she said. She rubbed the dogs' heads absently. 'I just felt like talking to someone, and Isobel's away . . .'

'Talking about what?'

'I don't know really,' said Milly. She swallowed. 'All sorts of things.' Esme puffed again at her cigarette.

'All sorts of things. I'm intrigued. You'd better come in.'

A fire was crackling in the drawing room and a jug of mulled wine was sending fragrant steam into the air. As Milly gave Esme her coat and sank down gratefully into the sofa, she found herself marvelling again that such an urbane, sophisticated woman could be related to her own dull father.

Esme Ormerod was the second half-cousin of James Havill. She had been brought up in London by a different, wealthier side of the family, and James had never known her well. But then, at around the time Milly was born, she had moved to Bath, and had made courteous contact with James. Olivia, impressed by this new, rather exotic relation of James's, had immediately asked her to be Milly's godmother, thinking that this might promote some intimacy between the two women. It had not done so. Esme had never become intimate with Olivia; she was not, as far as Milly knew, intimate with anyone particularly. Everyone in Bath knew of the beautiful Esme Ormerod. Many had attended parties in her house, admired her unusual clothes and the constantly changing collection of *objets* strewn around her rooms, but few could boast that they knew Esme well. Even Milly, who was closest to her of all the Havills, was often at a loss to know what she was thinking or what she might say next.

Neither did she know quite how Esme made her money. Although Esme's branch of the family was wealthy, it was generally agreed that it couldn't be wealthy enough to have funded Esme's easy existence for all these years. The few paintings which Esme occasionally sold were, as Milly's father put it, not even enough to keep her in velvet scarfs; apart from that she had no obvious income. The subject of Esme's money was the source of much speculation. One of the latest rumours circulating Bath was that she travelled to London once a month to perform unspeakable sexual acts with an ageing millionaire, who paid her a handsome allowance in return. 'Honestly, what rubbish,' Olivia had said when she'd heard the rumour – then, in the next breath, 'But I suppose it's possible . . .'

'Have one of these.' Esme passed Milly a plate of biscuits, each a beautifully made, individual creation.

'Gorgeous,' said Milly, hovering between one dusted with swirls of cocoa powder and another strewn with almond flakes. 'Where did you get these from?'

'A little shop I know,' said Esme. Milly nodded, and bit into the cocoa swirls; a heavenly, chocolatey taste immediately filled her mouth. Esme seemed to buy everything from tiny, unnamed shops – the opposite of her mother, who preferred large establishments with names that everyone recognized. Fortnum and Mason. Harrods. John Lewis.

'So, how are the wedding preparations going?' said Esme, sitting on the floor in front of the fire and pushing back the sleeves of her grey cashmere sweater. The opal pendant which she always wore glowed in the firelight.

'Fine,' said Milly. 'You know what it's like.' Esme shrugged noncommitally, and it occurred to Milly that she hadn't seen or talked to her godmother for weeks. If not months. But that was not unusual. Their relationship had always gone in phases, ever since Milly was a teenager. Whenever things had gone badly at home, Milly would head straight for Esme's house. Esme always understood her; Esme always treated her like an adult. Milly would spend days in her god-mother's company, soaking up her thoughts, adopting her vocabulary, helping her prepare interesting meals filled with ingredients of which Olivia had never heard. They would sit in Esme's drawing room drinking pale, chilled wine, listening to chamber music. Milly would feel grown-up and civilized, and vow to live more like Esme in future. Then, after a day or two, she would return home and pick up her old life exactly where she had left off – and Esme's influence would amount to little more than the odd new word or bottle of cold-pressed olive oil.

'So, darling,' Esme was saying. 'If it's not the wedding, then what is it?'

'It is the wedding,' said Milly. 'But it's a bit compli-cated.'

'Simon? Have you argued?'

'No,' said Milly at once. 'No. I just . . .' She exhaled sharply and put her biscuit down. 'I just need some advice. Some . . . hypothetical advice.'

'Hypothetical advice?'

'Yes,' said Milly desperately. She met Esme's eyes. 'Hypothetical.'

There was a little pause, then Esme said, 'I understand.' She gave Milly a cat-like smile. 'Continue.'

At one o'clock a call came through to Simon's desk from Paris.

'Simon? It's Isobel.'

'Isobel! How are you?'

'Do you know where Milly is? I've been trying to ring her.' Isobel's voice sounded ridiculously distant and tinny, thought Simon. She was only in Paris, for God's sake.

'Isn't she at work?' said Simon.

'Apparently not. Listen, have you two had a row? She's been trying to call me.'

'No,' said Simon, taken aback. 'Not that I know of.'

'Must be something else then,' said Isobel. 'I'll try at home. OK, well, I'll see you when I get back.'

'Wait!' said Simon suddenly. 'Isobel – I want to ask you something.'

'Yes?' She sounded suspicious. Or maybe that was just his paranoia. Simon always found Isobel a little tricky to deal with. For a start, she always said so little. Whenever he spoke to her he ended up feeling self-conscious under her intelligent scrutiny, and wondering what on earth she thought of him. of course he was fond of her – but he also found her very slightly scary.

'It was a favour, actually,' he said. 'I wondered if you would pick me up a present for Milly.'

'What sort of present?' said Isobel.

If it had been Milly, thought Simon, she would have cried 'Of course I will!' straight away – and then asked for details.

'I want to get her a Chanel bag.' He swallowed. 'So maybe you could choose her one.'

'A Chanel bag?' said Isobel incredulously. 'Do you know how much they cost?'

'Yes,' said Simon.

'Hundreds.'

'Yes.'

'Simon, you're mad. Milly doesn't want a Chanel bag.'

'Yes she does!'

'It's not her style.'

'Of course it is,' retorted Simon. 'Milly likes elegant, classic pieces.'

'If you say so,' replied Isobel drily. Then she sighed. 'Simon, is this about your father buying you a flat?'

'No!' said Simon. 'Of course not.' He hesitated. 'How did you know about that?'

'Mummy told me. And she told me about the earrings.' Isobel's voice softened. 'Look, I can guess it wasn't an easy moment for you. But that's no reason to go and spend all your money on an expensive bag.'

'Milly deserves the best.'

'She's got the best. She's got you!'

'But—'

'Look, Simon. If you really want to buy Milly something, buy something for the flat. A sofa. Or a rug. She'd love that.'

There was silence.

'You're right,' said Simon eventually.

'Of course I'm right.'

'It's just . . .' Simon exhaled. 'My fucking father!'

'I know,' said Isobel. 'But what can you do? He's a generous millionaire. It's a bummer.' Simon winced.

'God, you're harsh, aren't you? I think I prefer your sister.'

'Fine by me. Look, I've got to go. I've got a plane to catch.'

'OK. Listen, thanks, Isobel. I'm really grateful.'

'Yeah, yeah. I know. Bye.' And she was gone before Simon could say anything more.

'All right,' said Milly. She hunched her shoulders up, staring away from Esme, into the flickering fire. 'Suppose there was a person. And suppose that person had a secret.'

'A person,' said Esme, looking at her quizzically. 'And a secret.'

'Yes,' said Milly, still staring at the fire. 'And suppose she'd never told anyone about it. Not even the man she loved.'

'Why not?'

'Because he didn't need to know,' said Milly defensively. 'Because it was just some stupid, irrelevant thing which happened ten years ago. And if it came out, it would ruin everything. Not just for her. For everybody.'

'Ah,' said Esme. 'That kind of secret.'

'Yes,' said Milly. 'That kind of secret.' She took a deep breath. 'And suppose . . .' She bit her lip. 'Suppose someone came along who knew about the secret. And he started threatening to say something.'

Esme exhaled softly.

'I see.'

'But she didn't know if he was serious or not. She thought he might just be joking.'

Esme nodded.

'The thing is,' said Milly, 'what should she do?' She looked up. 'Should she tell the . . . the partner? Or should she just keep quiet and hope that she'd get away with it?'

Esme reached for her cigarette case.

'Is it really a secret worth keeping?' she said. 'Or is it just some silly little indiscretion that no-one would mind about? Might this person be overreacting?'

'No,' said Milly, 'she's not overreacting. It's a very bit secret. Like a . . .' She paused. 'Like a previous marriage. Or something.'

Esme raised her eyebrows.

'That *is* a big secret.'

'Or something,' repeated Milly. 'It doesn't matter what it is.' She met Esme's eyes steadily. 'The point is, she's kept it secret for ten years. No-one's ever known about it. No-one needs to know.'

'Yes,' said Esme. 'I see.' She lit a fresh cigarette and inhaled deeply.

'So what would you do, if you were that person?' said Milly. Esme blew out a cloud of smoke thoughtfully.

'What is the risk of this other character giving her away?'

'I don't know,' said Milly. 'Quite small at the moment, I think.'

'Then I would say nothing,' said Esme. 'For the moment. And I would try to think of a way of keeping the other one quiet.' She shrugged. 'Perhaps the whole thing will quietly fade away.'

'Do you think so?' Milly looked up. 'Do you really think so?'

Esme smiled.

'Darling, how many times have you tossed and turned at night, worried about something, only to find in the morning that there was nothing to fear? How many times have you rushed in with an excuse for some misdemeanour, only to find no-one realized you'd done anything wrong?' She took a deep drag on her cigarette. 'Nine times out of ten, it's better to say nothing and keep your head down and hope that every-thing will proceed smoothly. And no-one need ever know.' She paused. 'Hypothetically speaking, of course.'

'Yes, of course.'

There was silence, broken only by the crackle and spitting of the fire. Outside, it had begun to snow again, in thick, blurry flakes.

'Have some more mulled wine,' suggested Esme. 'Before it gets cold. And another biscuit.'

'Thanks,' murmured Milly. She picked up a disk of smooth clementine fondant and gazed at it. 'You don't think I . . . the person should be honest with her partner.'

'Why should she?'

'Because . . . because she's going to marry him!' Esme smiled. 'Darling, it's a nice idea. But a woman should never try to be honest with a man. It's quite impossible.'

Milly looked up. 'What do you mean, impossible?'

'Of course, one can try,' said Esme. 'But essentially, women and men speak different languages. They have . . . different senses. Put a man and a woman in exactly the same situation and they'll perceive it entirely differently.'

'So?'

'So, they're foreign to each other,' said Esme. 'And the truth is, you can't be completely honest with someone you don't properly understand.'

Milly thought for a few moments.

'People who've been happily married for years understand each other,' she said at last.

'They muddle through,' said Esme, 'with a mixture of sign language and goodwill and the odd phrase picked up over the years. But they don't understand each other. They don't have access to the rich depths of each other's spirits. The common language simply isn't there.' She inhaled on her cigarette again. 'And there aren't any interpreters. Or at least, very few.'

Milly stared at her. 'So you're saying there's no such thing as a happy marriage.'

'I'm saying there's no such thing as an honest marriage,' said Esme. 'Happiness is something else.' She blew out a cloud of smoke.

'I suppose you're right,' said Milly doubtfully, and glanced at her watch. 'Esme, I've got to go.'

'So soon?'

'We're having a wedding present given to us at Simon's work.'

'I see.' Esme tapped her cigarette ash into a mother of pearl dish. 'Well, I hope I've been some help with your little problem.'

'Not really,' said Milly bluntly. 'If anything, I'm more confused than before.' Esme smiled amusedly.

'Oh dear. I'm sorry.' She surveyed Milly' face. 'So – what do you think your . . . hypothetical person will do?'

There was silence.

'I don't know,' said Milly eventually. 'I really don't know.'

James Havill had left the office at lunchtime that day and headed for home. As he let himself in, the house was steeped in a midday quiet, silent apart from the odd creak. He stood for a few moments in the hall, listening for voices. But the house seemed as empty as he had hoped it would be. At this time of day, the guests would be out, sightseeing. Milly would still be at work; the daily woman would have finished. The only person in the house now would be Olivia.

He climbed the stairs as soundlessly as possible. As he rounded the corner to the second floor his heart began to beat in anticipation. He had planned this encounter all morning; had sat in meetings thinking of nothing except what he would say to his wife that afternoon. What he would say – and how he would say it.

The door to her room was closed. James stared for a moment at the little porcelain plaque bearing the word PRIVATE, before knocking.

'Yes?' Her voice sounded startled.

'It's only me,' he said and pushed the door open. The room was warm from an electric fire; too warm, he thought. Olivia was sitting in her faded chintz armchair in front of the television. Her feet were resting on the tapestry footstool she had upholstered herself. A cup of tea was at her elbow, and her hands were full of pale pink silk.

'Hello,' said James. He glanced at the screen where a black and white Bette Davis was talking frostily to a man with a square jaw. 'I didn't mean to disturb you.'

'Don't worry,' said Olivia. She picked up the remote control and reduced Bette Davis's voice to an almost inaudible murmur. 'What do you think?'

'What do you mean?' said James, taken aback.

'Isobel's dress!' said Olivia, holding up the pink silk. 'I thought it looked a little plain, so I'm just trimming it with some roses.'

'Lovely,' said James, still gazing at the screen. He couldn't quite make out what Bette Davis was saying. She had unbuttoned her gloves; was she about to challenge the square-jawed man to a fight? He looked up. 'I wanted to talk to you.'

'And I wanted to talk to you,' said Olivia. She picked up a red exercise book lying near her chair and consulted it. 'First, have you checked the route to the church with the council?'

'I know the route,' said James. Olivia sighed exasperatedly.

'Of course you do. But do you know if any roadworks or demonstrations are going to spring up on Saturday? No! That's why we have to ring the council. Don't you remember?' She began to write in the exercise book. 'Don't worry. I'll do it myself.'

James said nothing. He looked around for somewhere to sit, but there were no other chairs. After a pause he sat down on the edge of the bed. Olivia's duvet was soft and smelt faintly of her perfume. It was spread evenly over her bed and anchored down with lacy cushions, neat and sexless as though she never slept in it. For all she knew, she didn't. James had not seen the underside of Olivia's duvet for six years.

'The other thing,' said Olivia, 'is about presents for the guests.'

'Presents *for* the guests?'

'Yes, James,' said Olivia impatiently. 'Presents for the guests. Everyone gives their guests a present these days.'

'I thought it was the other way around.'

'It's both. The guests give presents to Milly and Simon, and we give presents to the guests.'

'And who gives presents to us?' asked James. Olivia rolled her eyes.

'You're not helping, James. Milly and I have already organized for each guest to receive a champagne flute.'

'Well then, that's fine.' James took a deep breath. 'Olivia—'

'But I was wondering, wouldn't a flowering rose bush

be more original? Look.' She gestured to an open magazine on the floor. 'Isn't that pretty?'

'A flowering rose bush for each guest? The place will be a bloody forest.'

'A *mini* rose bush,' said Olivia impatient. 'Purse-sized, they call it.'

'Olivia, haven't you got enough to do without organizing last-minute purse-sized rose bushes?'

'Maybe you're right,' said Olivia regretfully. She reached for her pen and scored out an entry in her exercise book. 'Now, what else was there?'

'Olivia, listen for a moment,' said James. He cleared his throat. 'I wanted to talk about—' He broke off. 'About what's going to happen. After the wedding.'

'For goodness' sake, James! Let's just get the wedding safely over before we start talking about what happens next. As if I haven't got enough to think about!'

'Just hear me out.' James closed his eyes and took a deep breath. 'I think we both realize that things will be different when Milly's gone, don't we? When it's just the two of us in this house.'

'Fees for the choir . . .' murmured Olivia, ticking off on her fingers. 'Buttonholes . . .'

'There's no pretending things are the same as they were.'

'Cake stand . . .'

'We've been drifting apart for years now. You've got your life, I've got mine . . .'

'Speech!' said Olivia, looking up triumphantly. 'Have you composed your speech?'

'Yes,' said James, staring at her. 'But no-one seems to be listening.'

'Because what I suggest is that you write *two* sets of notes. Then I can keep one, just in case.' She smiled brightly at him.

'Olivia . . .'

'And I'm going to suggest the same to Simon. Let me just write that down.'

She began to scribble and James's eyes drifted towards the television screen. Bette Davis was falling into the arms of the square-jawed man; tears glistened on her lashes.

'Right,' said Olivia. 'Well, that's it.' She looked at her watch and stood up. 'And now I must pop along to see the choirmaster. Was there anything else?'

'Well—'

'Because I am running a little late. Excuse me.' She gestured to James to stand up, and laid the pink silk carefully on the bed. 'See you later!'

'Yes,' said James. 'See you later.'

The door closed behind him and he found himself staring again at Olivia's little plaque.

'So what I'm saying,' he said to the door, 'is that after the wedding, I want to move out. I want a new life. Do you understand?'

There was silence. James shrugged, turned on his heel and walked away.

FIVE

As Milly arrived at the offices where Simon worked, there was a small shriek from the reception desk.

'She's here!' cried Pearl, one of the middle-aged receptionists. 'Milly's here!' She beamed as Milly approached the desk. 'How are you, dear? Not too nervous about Saturday?'

'There's nothing to be nervous about,' exclaimed another of the receptionists, a woman in a pale blue cardigan and matching eye shadow. 'Just make sure you enjoy the day, darling. It'll go by so fast!'

'It'll be a blur,' said Pearl, nodding seriously. 'What you need to do is, every so often, stop still and look around, and say to yourself: this is my wedding day. Just say it. This is my wedding day. And then you'll enjoy yourself!' She smiled at Milly. 'I'll buzz Simon for you, then I'll take you up.'

'It's all right,' said Milly. 'I know the way.'

'No trouble!' exclaimed Pearl. She tapped at her keyboard. 'Margaret, keep trying Simon, will you? And tell him I'm on my way up with Milly.'

To a chorus of good lucks, the two of them walked across the reception area to the lifts.

'We're coming to watch you on Saturday,' said Pearl, as the lift doors closed behind them. 'Outside the church. You don't mind, do you, dear?'

'Of course not,' said Milly confusedly. 'You mean you're just going to stand there and watch?'

'Beryl's bringing camp-chairs!' said Pearl triumphantly. 'And we'll have a thermos of coffee. We want to see everyone arrive. All the VIPs. It'll be just like a royal wedding!'

'Well,' said Milly, embarrassed. 'I don't know about—'

'Or that lovely wedding on the television,' said Pearl. 'On *EastEnders* the other day. Did you see it?'

'Oh, yes!' said Milly enthusiastically. 'Wasn't it romantic?'

'Those two little bridesmaids,' Pearl sighed fondly. 'Weren't they a picture?'

'Gorgeous,' agreed Milly. 'Not,' she added quickly, as the lift approached Simon's floor, 'that I really knew who any of the characters were. I don't normally watch *EastEnders*. I prefer . . . documentaries.'

'Do you, dear? I couldn't live without my soaps,' said Pearl comfortably. 'Your Simon teases me about them. Quizzes me on all the plots.' She smiled at Milly. 'He's a lovely boy really. So down-to-earth. You wouldn't think he was who he is. If you know what I mean.' The lift pinged. 'Here we are.' She peered down the carpeted corridor. 'Now, where's he got to?'

'Here I am,' said Simon, suddenly appearing round the corner. He held out a bottle of wine and some plastic cups to Pearl. 'Take these down for everyone on reception.'

'That's very kind!' said Pearl. 'And make sure you come down and show us your present.' She took one of Milly's hands and pressed it hard. 'Good luck, my dear,' she said. 'You deserve nothing but happiness.'

'Thank you,' said Milly, feeling tears prick the backs of her eyes. 'You're very kind.'

The lift doors closed, and Simon grinned at Milly. 'Come on,' he said. 'They're all waiting for you.'

'Don't say that!' said Milly. 'You're making me nervous.'

'Nervous?' Simon laughed. 'There's nothing to be nervous about!'

'I know,' said Milly. 'I'm just . . . a bit on edge at the moment.'

'Wedding jitters,' said Simon.

'Yes,' said Milly. She smiled at him. 'That must be it.'

Simon's department had clustered self-consciously in the office he shared with four other advertising sales-people. As they arrived, bottles of fizzy wine were being passed around in plastic cups, and a woman in a red jacket was hastily collecting some last-minute signatures on an outsize card.

'What shall I put?' a girl was wailing as Milly passed. 'Everyone else has been really witty.'

'Just put your name!' snapped the woman in the red jacket. 'And hurry up.'

Milly clutched her plastic cup and fixed a smile to her face. She felt vulnerable under the gaze of so many people, so many strangers. She sipped at the fizzy wine and took a crisp from the plate offered to her by one of Simon's cheery colleagues.

'Aha!' A deep voice interrupted the general chatter, and she looked up. A man in a brown suit with receding hair and a moustache was bearing down on her. 'You must be Simon's fiancée.' He grasped her hand. 'Mark Taylor. Head of publications. Very pleased to meet you.'

'Hello,' said Milly politely.

'Now, where's he got to? We've got to get this presentation done. Simon! Over here!'

'Have you two met?' said Simon, coming up. 'Sorry, I should have introduced you properly.'

Mark Taylor was clapping his hands.

'All right, everyone. Hush up, hush up. On behalf of us all here at Pendulum, I'd like to wish Simon and Mandy all the very best for their future together.' He raised his glass.

'Milly!' shouted someone.

'What?' said Mark Taylor, screwing up his face puzzledly.

'It's Milly, not Mandy!'

'It doesn't matter,' said Milly, going red.

'What are they saying?' said Mark Taylor.

'Nothing,' said Milly. 'Carry on.'

'To Mandy and Simon! May they have a long, happy and prosperous life together.' A telephone began to ring in the corner of the room. 'Get that, somebody, would you?'

'Where's the present?' shouted someone.

'Yes,' said Mark Taylor. 'Where is the present?'

'It's being delivered,' said a woman to Milly's left. 'It's off the list. A covered vegetable dish. I've got a picture of it.'

'Very nice,' said Mark Taylor. He raised his voice. 'The present is a covered vegetable dish off the list! Sally's got a picture, if anyone's interested.'

'But there should be a card,' said Sally. 'Where's the card?'

'Here it is!' said the woman in the red jacket.

There was a small silence as Simon ripped open the huge envelope and opened a large card with two teddy bears on the front. He scanned the signatures, laughing every so often; looking up and nodding to people as he read their messages. Milly looked over his shoulder. Most of the jokes were about targets and quarter-pages and, bewilderingly, something called Powerlink.

'Great,' said Simon eventually. 'I'm really touched.'

'Speech!' yelled someone.

'I'm not going to make a speech,' said Simon.

'Thank the Lord!' interjected someone else.

Simon took a sip of fizzy wine.

'But I just wanted to say,' he said, 'for those of you

who thought the most important thing in my life was beating Eric's insane monthly targets' – there was a small laugh – 'or demolishing Andy at darts . . .'

There was a bigger laugh, and Simon smiled.

'For all of you,' he said, 'I've got some news. 'You're wrong.' He paused. 'The most important thing in my life is standing next to me.' He took Milly's hand, and there was a small sigh from some of the girls. 'This woman,' he said, 'for those of you who don't know her, is the most beautiful, sweet-natured, open and giving woman in the world – and I'm truly honoured that, on Saturday, she will become my wife. I feel very lucky.'

There was a short silence, then in muted tones someone said, 'To Milly and Simon.'

'To Milly and Simon,' chorused the others obediently. Milly looked up at Simon's happy, unaware face and felt a sudden misery come over her.

'I'll see you all in the pub!' added Simon. The crowd began to disperse and he smiled down at Milly.

'Did I embarrass you?'

'Just a bit,' said Milly, trying to smile back. Her skin was prickling with guilt and her insides felt clenched by a strong, bony hand.

'I just had to tell everyone how I feel,' said Simon. He stroked her hair tenderly. 'Sometimes I can't believe how much I love you.' A sudden rush of tears came to Milly's eyes.

'Don't,' she said. 'Don't.'

'Look at you!' said Simon, tracing her tears with his thumb. 'Oh, sweetheart. Do you want a hanky?'

'Thanks,' gulped Milly. She mopped at her face and took a couple of deep breaths.

'Simon!' A cheerful voice interrupted them. 'Your round, I believe!'

'OK!' said Simon, grinning. 'Give me a minute.'

'Simon,' said Milly quickly. 'Would you mind if I didn't come to the pub?'

'Oh,' said Simon. His face fell.

'I'm just feeling a bit tired,' said Milly. 'I don't really feel up to' – she gestured – 'all of this.'

'Simon!' yelled someone. 'You coming or what?'

'Hang on!' called Simon. He touched Milly's face gently. 'Would you rather we went off somewhere, just the two of us?'

Milly looked at him and had a sudden vision of the two of them in a secluded restaurant. They would sit tucked away at a corner table. They would eat risotto and drink mellow red wine. And slowly, quietly, she would tell him the truth.

'No,' she said. 'You go and have fun. I'll have an early night.'

'You're sure?'

'Yes.' She pulled his face down and kissed it. 'Go on. I'll talk to you tomorrow.'

She arrived home wanting to go straight to bed. As she took off her coat she heard voices in the kitchen, and winced as it occurred to her that Aunt Jean might have arrived early. But when she pushed open the door, it was Isobel she saw, standing on a kitchen chair, wearing a pink bridesmaid's dress and with a garland of dried flowers in her hair.

'Isobel!' she exclaimed, feeling sudden, almost tearful relief. 'When did you get back?' Isobel looked up and grinned.

'This afternoon. I got back home, and what do I find? My bloody pipes have gone.'

'Pipes?'

'Water pipes,' said Isobel. 'What did you think I meant? Bagpipes?'

'Isobel's going to stay here until the wedding,' said Olivia, with a mouthful of kirby grips. 'Although of course we'll be a bit squashed when Aunt Jean and the cousins arrive . . .'

'Get rid of Alexander,' said Milly. She sat down at the table and began to fiddle with a stray rosebud. 'Then there'll be room.'

'Don't be silly, darling,' said Olivia. 'He's got to stay here.' She shoved another kirby grip into Isobel's hair and poked at the garland. 'There. That's better.'

'If you say so,' said Isobel. She grinned at Milly. 'What do you think?'

Milly looked up and for the first time registered what Isobel was wearing.

'What happened to your dress?' she asked, trying not to sound appalled.

'I added some silk roses,' said Olivia. 'Aren't they pretty?' Milly met Isobel's eye.

'Beautiful,' she said. Isobel grinned.

'Be honest. Do I look like an idiot?'

'No,' said Milly. She looked at Isobel and frowned. 'You look . . . tired.'

'That's what I said!' exclaimed Olivia triumphantly. 'She looks washed-out and peaky.'

'I don't look washed-out and peaky,' said Isobel impatiently. Milly gazed at her sister. Isobel's skin was almost grey; her fair, straight hair was lank. The flowers in her hair only emphasized the lack of bloom in her cheeks.

'You'll look fine on the day,' she said uncertainly. 'Once you're wearing some make-up.'

'She's lost weight, too,' said Olivia disapprovingly. 'We could almost do with taking this dress in.'

'I haven't lost that much,' said Isobel. 'Anyway, it doesn't matter what I look like. It's Milly's day, not mine.' She looked at Milly. 'How are you doing?'

'I'm OK,' said Milly. She met her sister's eyes. 'You know.'

'Yup,' said Isobel. She began to slip the pink dress off. 'Well, I might go upstairs and get sorted out.'

'I'll come and help you,' said Milly at once.

'That's right,' said Olivia. 'Good little girl.'

Isobel's room was next door to Milly's, at the top of the house. Now that she had left home it was occasionally used by bed and breakfast guests, but more often than not remained empty, clean and neat, waiting for her return.

'Jesus!' said Isobel, as she opened the door. 'What's all this?'

'Wedding presents,' said Milly. 'And this is just a few of them.'

They both looked silently around the room. Every spare piece of floor was piled high with boxes. A few had been opened: they spilled shredded paper and bubble wrap; glimpses of glass and china.

'What's this?' said Isobel, prodding one of them.

'I don't know,' said Milly. 'I think it's a soup tureen.'

'A soup tureen,' echoed Isobel disbelievingly. 'Are you planning to cook soup when you're married?'

'I suppose so,' said Milly.

'You'll have to, now you've got a special soup tureen to put it in.' Isobel caught Milly's eye and she began to giggle, in spite of herself. 'You'll have to sit in every night, and ladle soup out of your soup tureen.'

'Shut up!' said Milly.

'And drink sherry out of your eight sherry glasses,' said Isobel, reading the label on another parcel. 'Married life is going to be a riot.'

'Don't!' said Milly. She was shaking with giggles; her eyes were bright.

'Electric breadmaker. Now, I wouldn't mind one of those.' Isobel looked up. 'Milly, are you OK?'

'I'm fine,' said Milly. 'I'm fine.' But her giggles were turning into sobs; suddenly a pair of tears landed on her cheeks.

'Milly! I knew there was something.' Isobel came over and put her hands on Milly's shoulders. 'What's wrong? What did you want to talk to me about in Paris?'

'Oh God, Isobel!' More tears landed on Milly's face. 'It's all gone wrong!'

'What?'

'I'm in real trouble!'

'What do you mean?' Isobel's voice rose in alarm. 'Milly, tell me! What's happened?'

Milly looked at her for a long time.

'Come here,' she said at last. She went back into her own room, waited until Isobel had followed her inside, and closed the door. Then, as Isobel watched silently, she reached up inside the chimney, scrabbled for a bit, and pulled down an old school shoe-bag, drawn tightly at the neck.

'What—'

'Wait,' said Milly, groping inside. She pulled out a smaller bag – then, from that, produced a box tied tightly with string. She tugged at the string and wrenched it off, taking the lid off with it. For a few moments she stared at the open box. Then she held it out to Isobel.

'OK,' she said. 'This is what's happened.'

'Blimey,' said Isobel. Staring up at them from inside the box was a photograph of Milly in a wedding dress, beaming through a cloud of confetti. Isobel picked it up and stared at it more closely. Glancing at Milly, she put it down, and picked up the photograph underneath. It was a picture of two men standing side by side, one dark-haired, the other fair. Beneath that was a shot of the dark-haired man kissing Milly's hand. Milly was simpering at the camera. Her veil was tossed over her shoulder; she looked wildly happy.

Without speaking, Isobel leafed through to the end of the pile of pictures. Underneath the photographs were some old faded confetti and a little flowered card.

'Can I?' said Isobel, touching the card.

'Go ahead.'

Silently, Isobel opened the card and read the inscription: 'To the best bride in the world. Yours ever, Allan.' She looked up.

'Who the hell is Allan?'

'Who do you think he is, Isobel?' said Milly in a ragged voice. 'He's my husband.'

As Milly came to the end of her faltering story, Isobel exhaled sharply. She got up, strode to the fireplace and stood for a moment, saying nothing. Milly, who was sitting in an armchair, hugging a cushion to her chest, watched her apprehensively.

'I can't quite get my head round this,' said Isobel eventually.

'I know,' said Milly.

'You really married a guy to keep him in the country?'

'Yes,' said Milly. She glanced at the wedding pictures, still spread over the floor; at herself, young and vibrant and happy. As she had told the story, all the romance and adventure of what she'd done had flooded back into her, and for the first time in years she'd felt a nostalgia for those heady, magical Oxford days.

'Those bastards!' Isobel was shaking her head. 'They must have seen you coming!' Milly stared at her sister.

'It wasn't like that,' she said. Isobel looked up.

'What do you mean, it wasn't like that? Milly, they used you!'

'They didn't!' said Milly defensively. 'I helped them because I wanted to. They were my friends.'

'Friends,' echoed Isobel scathingly. 'Is that what you think? Well, if they were such great friends, how come I never met them? Or even heard about them?'

'We lost touch.'

'When did you lose touch? As soon as you'd signed on the dotted line?'

Milly was silent.

'Oh, Milly,' said Isobel. She sighed. 'Did they pay you?'

'No,' said Milly. 'They gave me a necklace.' Her hands reached for the little pearls.'

'Well, that's a lot of compensation,' said Isobel sarcastically. 'Bearing in mind you broke the law for them. Bearing in mind you could have been prosecuted. The Home Office investigates phoney marriages, you know! Or didn't you know?'

'Don't go on about it, Isobel,' said Milly in a trembling voice. 'It's done, OK? And there's nothing I can do about it.'

'OK,' said Isobel. 'Look. I'm sorry. This must be awful for you.' She picked up one of the pictures and stared at it for a few moments. 'I have to say, I'm surprised you risked keeping these.'

'I know,' said Milly. 'It was stupid. But I couldn't bear to throw them out. They're all I've got left of the whole thing.' Isobel sighed, and put the photographs down.

'And you've never told Simon about it.'

Milly shook her head, lips clamped together tightly.

'Well, you've got to,' said Isobel. 'You do know that?'

'I can't,' said Milly, closing her eyes. 'I can't tell him. I just can't.'

'You're going to have to!' said Isobel. 'Before this Alexander character decides to say something to him.'

'He might not say anything,' said Milly in a small voice.

'But he might!' retorted Isobel. 'And it's not worth the risk.' She sighed. 'Look, just tell him. he won't mind! Plenty of people are divorced these days.'

'I know they are,' said Milly.

'There's no shame in it! So you're divorced.' She shrugged. 'It could be worse.'

'But I'm not,' said Milly tightly.

'What?' Isobel stared at her.

'I'm not divorced,' said Milly. 'I'm still married.'

There was a still silence.

'You're still married?' said Isobel in a whisper. 'You're still *married*? But Milly, your wedding's on Saturday!'

'I know!' cried Milly. 'Don't you think I know that?' And as Isobel gazed at her in horror, she buried her head in the cushion and sank into blinding tears.

The brandy was in the kitchen. As Isobel opened the door, hoping no-one was about, Olivia raised her head from the phone.

'Isobel!' she said in a stage whisper. 'The most ghastly thing's happened!'

'What?' said Isobel, feeling a beat of fear.

'There aren't enough orders of service. People are going to have to share!'

'Oh,' said Isobel. She felt a sudden, terrible desire to cackle. 'Well, never mind.'

'Never mind?' hissed Olivia. 'The whole event will look shoddy!' Her eyes narrowed as she watched Isobel pour out a glass of brandy. 'Why are you drinking brandy?'

'It's for Milly,' said Isobel. 'She's a bit tense.'

'Is everything all right?'

'Yes,' said Isobel, backing away. 'Everything's just fine.'

She went back up to the bedroom, closed the door and tapped Milly on the shoulder.

'Drink this,' she said. 'And calm down. It'll be OK.'

'How can it be OK?' sobbed Milly. 'It's all going to come out! Everything's going to be ruined.'

'Come on,' said Isobel. She put an arm round Milly's shoulders. 'Come on. We'll sort it out. Don't worry.'

'I don't see how we can,' said Milly, looking up with a tear-stained face. She took a sip of brandy. 'I've completely messed things up, haven't I?'

'No,' said Isobel. 'Of course you haven't.' Milly gave a shaky laugh.

'Nice try, Isobel.' She took another sip of brandy. 'God, I need a cigarette. Do you want one?'

'No thanks,' said Isobel.

'Come on,' said Milly, pushing open the sash window with shaking hands. 'One cigarette won't give you bloody lung cancer.'

'No,' said Isobel after a pause. 'No, I suppose one cigarette can't hurt.' She sat down on the windowsill. Milly passed her a cigarette and they both inhaled deeply. As the smoke hit her lungs, Milly felt her whole body expand and relax.

'I needed that,' she said with a sigh. She blew out a cloud of smoke and wafted it with her hand out of the window. 'Oh God. What a mess.'

'What I don't understand,' said Isobel carefully, 'is why you didn't get a divorce.'

'We were always going to,' said Milly, biting her lip. 'Allan was going to sort it out. I even got some papers from his lawyers. But then it all fizzled out and I didn't hear any more. I never went to court, nothing.'

'And you never chased it up?'

Milly was silent.

'Not even when Simon asked you to marry him?' Isobel's voice sharpened. 'Not even when you started planning the wedding?'

'I didn't know how to! Allan left Oxford, I didn't know where he was, I lost all the papers . . .'

'You could have gone to a lawyer, couldn't you? Or the Citizens' Advice Bureau?'

'I know.'

'So why—'

'Because I didn't dare, OK? I didn't dare rock the boat.' Milly puffed quickly on her cigarette. 'I know what I'd done was dodgy. People might have started poking around and asking questions. I couldn't risk it!'

'But Milly . . .'

'I just didn't want anyone else to know. Not a single person. While no-one else knew, I felt . . . safe.'

'Safe!'

'Yes, safe!' said Milly defensively. 'No-one in the world knew about it. No-one asked any questions; no-one suspected anything!' She raised her eyes to Isobel's. 'I mean, did *you* suspect anything?'

'I suppose not,' said Isobel reluctantly.

'Of course you didn't. No-one did.' Milly took another shaky drag. 'And the more time went on, the more it was as though the whole thing had never happened. A few years went by, and still nobody knew about it, and gradually it just . . . stopped existing.'

'What do you mean, it stopped existing?' said Isobel impatiently. 'Milly, you married the man! You can't change that.'

'It was three minutes in a registry office,' said Milly. 'One tiny signature, ten years ago. Buried on some legal document which no-one's ever going to see again. That's not a marriage, Isobel. It's a piece of dust. A nothing!'

'And what about when Simon asked you to marry him?'

There was a sharp silence.

'I thought about telling him,' said Milly at last. 'I really did. But in the end, I just couldn't see the point. It's got nothing to do with us. It would just have complicated things. He didn't need to know.'

'So what were you going to do?' said Isobel incredulously. 'Commit *bigamy*?'

'The first one wasn't a proper marriage,' said Milly, looking away. 'It wouldn't have counted.'

'What do you mean?' exclaimed Isobel. 'Of course it would have counted! Jesus, Milly, how can you be such a moron? I don't believe you sometimes!'

'Oh shut up, Isobel!' cried Milly furiously.

'Fine. I'll shut up.'

'Fine.'

There was silence for a while. Milly finished her cigarette, then stubbed it out on the windowsill.

'Aren't you going to smoke yours?' she said, not looking at Isobel.

'I don't think I want the rest of it. You can have it.'

'OK.' Milly took the half-burned cigarette, then glanced at her sister, momentarily distracted. 'Are you OK?' she said. 'Mummy's right, you look awful.'

'I'm fine,' said Isobel shortly.

'You're not anorexic, are you?'

'No!' Isobel laughed. 'Of course I'm not.'

'Well, you've been losing weight . . .'

'So have you.'

'Have I?' said Milly, plucking at her clothes. 'It's probably all this stress.'

'Well, don't stress,' said Isobel firmly. 'OK? Stressing is useless.' She pulled her knees up and hugged them. 'If only we knew how far your divorce had actually got.'

'It didn't get anywhere,' said Milly hopelessly. 'I told you, I never went to court.'

'So what? You don't have to go to court to get a divorce.'

'Yes you do.'

'No you don't.'

'Yes you do!' said Milly. 'They did in *Kramer versus Kramer*.'

'For God's sake, Milly!' exclaimed Isobel. 'Don't you know anything? That was for a custody battle.'

There was a little pause, then Milly said, 'Oh.'

'If it's just a divorce, your lawyer goes for you.'

'What lawyer? I didn't have a lawyer.'

Milly took a final drag on Isobel's cigarette, then stubbed it out. Isobel was silent, her brow wrinkled perplexedly. Then suddenly she looked up.

'Well, maybe you didn't need one. Maybe Allan did all the divorcing for you.'

Milly stared at her.

'Are you serious?'

'I don't know. It's possible.' Milly swallowed.

'So I might be divorced after all?'

'I don't see why not. In theory.'

'Well, how can I find out?' said Milly agitatedly. 'Why didn't I hear? Is there some official list of divorces somewhere? My God, if I found out I was actually divorced . . .'

'I'm sure there is,' said Isobel. 'But there's a quicker way.'

'What?'

'Do what you should have done bloody ten years ago. Phone your husband.'

'I can't,' said Milly at once. 'I don't know where he is.'

'Well then, find him!'

'I can't.'

'Of course you can!'

'I don't even know where to start! And anyway—' Milly broke off and looked away.

'What?' There was silence as Milly lit another cigarette with trembling hands. 'What?' repeated Isobel impatiently.

'I don't want to speak to him, OK?'

'Why not?' Isobel peered at Milly's downcast face. 'Why not, Milly?'

'Because you're right,' said Milly suddenly, tears springing to her eyes. 'You're right, Isobel! Those two were never my friends, were they? They just used me. They just took what they could get. All these years, I've thought of them as my friends. They loved each other so much, and I wanted to help them . . .'

'Milly . . .'

'You know, I wrote to them when I got back,' said Milly, staring into the darkness. 'Allan used to write back. I always planned to go back one day and surprise them. Then gradually we lost touch. But I still thought of them as friends.' She looked up at Isobel. 'You don't know what it was like in Oxford. It was like a whirlwind romance between the three of us. We went punting, and we had picnics, and we talked into the night . . .' She broke off. 'And they were probably just laughing at me the whole time, weren't they?'

'No,' said Isobel. 'I'm sure they weren't.'

'They saw me coming,' said Milly bitterly. 'A naive, gullible little fool who would do anything they asked.'

'Look, don't think about it,' said Isobel, putting her arm around Milly's shoulders. 'That was ten years ago.

It's over. Finished with. You have to look ahead. You have to find out about your divorce.'

'I can't,' said Milly, shaking her head. 'I can't talk to him. He'll just be . . . laughing at me.' Isobel sighed.

'You're going to have to.'

'But he could be anywhere,' said Milly helplessly. 'He just vanished into thin air!'

'Milly, this is the age of information,' said Isobel. 'Thin air doesn't exist any more.' She took out a pen from her pocket and tore a piece of card off one of the wedding present boxes. 'Now come on,' she said briskly. 'Tell me where he used to live. And his parents. And Rupert, and Rupert's parents. And anyone else they used to know.'

An hour later, Milly looked up from the phone with triumph on her face.

'This could be it!' she exclaimed. 'They're giving me a number!'

'Hallelujah!' said Isobel. 'Let's hope this is him.' She gazed down at the road map in her lap, open at the index. It had taken Milly a while to remember that Rupert's father had been a headmaster in Cornwall, and another while to narrow the village name down to something beginning with T. Since then they had been working down the index, asking Directory Enquiries each time for a Dr Carr.

'Well, here it is,' said Milly, putting down the receiver and staring at the row of digits.

'Great,' said Isobel. 'Well, get dialling!'

'OK,' said Milly, taking a deep breath. 'Let's see if we've got the right number.'

I should have done this before, she thought guiltily, as she picked up the phone. I could have done this any time. But even as she dialled, she felt a painful dismay at what she was being forced to do. She didn't want to speak to Rupert. She didn't want to speak to Allan. She wanted to forget the bastards had ever existed; wipe them out of her memory.

'Hello?' Suddenly a man's voice was speaking in her ear and Milly gave a jump of fright.

'Hello?' repeated the man. Milly dug her nails into the palm of her hand.

'Hello,' she said cautiously. 'Is that Dr Carr?'

'Yes, speaking.' He sounded agreeably surprised that she should know his name.

'Oh good,' said Milly, and cleared her throat. 'May I . . . may I talk to Rupert, please?'

'He's not here, I'm afraid,' said the man. 'Have you tried his London number?'

'No, I haven't got it,' said Milly, amazed at how natural her voice sounded. She glanced over at Isobel, who nodded approvingly. 'I'm an old friend from Oxford. Just catching up.'

'Ah, well he's in London now. Working as a barrister, you know, in Lincoln's Inn. But let me give you his home number.'

As Milly wrote down the number, she felt a bubble of astonishment expanding inside her. It was that simple. For years she'd thought of Rupert and Allan as people

125

out of her life for ever; misty figures who might be any-where in the world by now, whom she would never see again. And yet here she was, talking to Rupert's father, a phone call away from talking to Rupert himself. In a few minutes she would hear his voice. Oh God.

'Have I met you?' Rupert's father was saying. 'Were you at Corpus?'

'No, I wasn't,' said Milly hurriedly. 'Sorry, I must go. Thank you so much.'

She put the receiver down and stared at it for a few seconds. Then she took a deep breath, lifted it again and, before she could change her mind, tapped in Rupert's telephone number.

'Hello?' A girl's voice answered pleasantly.

'Hello,' said Milly, before she could chicken out. 'May I talk to Rupert, please? It's quite important.'

'Of course. Can I say who's calling?'

'It's Milly. Milly from Oxford.'

While the girl was gone, Milly twirled the telephone cord round her fingers and tried to keep her breathing steady. She didn't dare meet Isobel's eye in case she collapsed with nerves. Ten years was a long time. What was Rupert like now? What would he say to her? She could hear faint music in the background, and pictured him lying on the floor, smoking a joint, listening to jazz. Or perhaps he was sitting on an old velvet chair, playing cards, drinking whisky. Perhaps he was playing cards with Allan. A dart of nerves went through Milly. Maybe, any moment, Allan would be on the line.

Suddenly the girl was speaking again.

'I'm sorry,' she said, 'but Rupert's a bit tied up at the moment. Can I take a message?'

'Not really,' said Milly. 'But maybe he could call me back?'

'Of course,' said the girl.

'The number's Bath 89406.'

'Got it.'

'Great,' said Milly. She looked down at the doodles on her notepad, feeling a sudden relief. She should have done all this years ago; it was easier than she'd thought. 'Are you Rupert's flat-mate?' she added, conversationally. 'Or just a friend?'

'No, I'm neither,' said the girl. She sounded surprised. 'I'm Rupert's wife.'

SIX

Rupert Carr sat by the fire of his Fulham house, shaking with fear. As Francesca put down the phone she gave him a curious look, and Rupert felt his insides turn to liquid. What had Milly said to his wife? What exactly had she said?

'Who's Milly?' said Francesca, picking up her glass of wine and taking a sip. 'Why don't you want to talk to her?'

'Just a weird g-girl I once knew,' said Rupert, cursing himself for stammering. He tried to shrug casually, but his lips were shaking and his face was hot with panic. 'I've no idea what she wants. I'll call her tomorrow at the office.' He forced himself to look up ant meet his wife's eyes steadily. 'But now I want to go over my reading.'

'OK,' she said, and smiled. She came over and sat down beside him on the sofa – a smart Colefax and Fowler sofa that had been a wedding present from one of her rich uncles. Opposite was a matching sofa which they'd bought themselves; on it sat Charlie and Sue Smith-Halliwell, their closest friends. The four of them were enjoying a quick glass of wine before leaving for the evening service at St Catherine's, at which Rupert would be reading. Now he avoided their eyes and stared down at his bible. But the words swam before his eyes; his fingers sweated on the page.

'Sorry, Charlie,' said Francesca. She reached behind her and turned Kiri te Kanawa fractionally down. 'What were you saying?'

'Nothing very profound,' said Charlie, and laughed. 'I simply feel that it's up to people like us' – he gestured to the four of them – 'to encourage young families into the church.'

'Instead of spending their Sunday mornings at Homestore,' said Francesca, then frowned. 'Do I mean Homestore?'

'After all,' said Charlie, 'families are the core structure of society.'

'Yes, but Charlie, the whole point is, they're not!' exclaimed Sue at once, in a way which suggested the argument was not new. 'Families are old news! It's all single parents and lesbians these days . . .'

'Did you read,' put in Francesca, 'about that new gay version of the New Testament? I have to say, I was quite shocked.'

'The whole thing makes me feel physically sick,' said Charlie, and gripped his wine glass tightly. 'These people are monsters.'

'Yes but you can't ignore them,' said Sue. 'Can you? You can't just discount a whole section of society. However misguided they are. What do you think, Rupert?'

Rupert looked up. His throat felt tight.

'Sorry,' he managed. 'I wasn't really listening.'

'Oh sorry,' said Sue. 'You want to concentrate, don't you?' She grinned at him. 'You'll be fine. You always are. And isn't it funny, you never stutter when you're reading!'

'I'd say you're one of the best readers in the church, Rupe,' said Charlie cheerfully. 'Must be that university education. We didn't get taught much elocution at Sandhurst.'

'That's no excuse!' said Sue. 'God gave us all mouths and brains, didn't he? What's the reading?'

'Matthew 26,' said Rupert. 'Peter's denial.' There was a short silence.

'Peter,' echoed Charlie soberly. 'What can it have been like, to be Peter?'

'Don't,' said Francesca, and shuddered. 'When I think how close I came to losing my faith altogether . . .'

'Yes, but you never denied Jesus, did you?' said Sue. She reached over and took Francesca's hand. 'Even the day after it happened, when I visited you in hospital.'

'I was so angry,' said Francesca. 'And ashamed. I felt as though I somehow didn't deserve a child.' She bit her lip.

'Yes but you do,' said Charlie. 'You both do. And you'll have one. Remember, God's on your side.'

'I know,' said Francesca. She looked at Rupert. 'He's on our side, isn't he, darling?'

'Yes,' said Rupert. He felt as though the word had been forced off his tongue with a razor. 'God's on our side.'

But God wasn't on his side. He knew God wasn't on his side. As they left the house and headed towards St Catherine's Church – ten minutes away in a little Chelsea square – Rupert found himself lagging behind the others. He felt like lagging so slowly that he would be left behind altogether. He wanted to be overlooked; to be forgotten about. But that was impossible. No-one at St Catherine's was ever forgotten. Anyone who ventured through its portals immediately became part of the family. The most casual visitors were welcomed in with smiling enthusiasm, were made to feel important and loved, were exhorted to come again. Most did. those who didn't reappear were cheerfully telephoned – 'Just checking you're OK. You know, we care about you. We really care.' Sceptics were welcomed almost more keenly than believers. They were encouraged to stand up and express their reservations; the more convincing their arguments, the broader the smiles all around. The members of St Catherine's smiled a lot. They wore their happiness visibly; they walked around in a shiny halo of certainty.

It had been that certainty which had attracted Rupert to St Catherine's. during his first year in chambers, miserably riddled with self-doubt, he had met Tom

Innes, another barrister. Tom was friendly and out-going. He had a secure social life built around St Catherine's. He knew all the answers – and when he didn't know the answer, he knew where to look. He was the happiest man Rupert had ever met. And Rupert, who at that time had thought he would never be happy again, had fallen with an almost desperate eagerness into Tom's life; into Christianity; into marriage. Now his life had a regular pattern, a meaning to it which he relished. He'd been married to Francesca for three contented years, his house was comfortable, his career was going well.

No-one knew about his past life. No-one knew about Allan. He had told nobody. Not Francesca, not Tom, not the vicar. He hadn't even told God.

Tom was waiting for them at the door as they arrived. He was dressed, like Rupert and Charlie, in work clothes – well-cut suit, Thomas Pink shirt, silk tie. All the men at St Catherine's had the same clothes, the same haircuts, the same heavy gold signet rings. At the weekends they all wore chinos and casual Ralph Lauren shirts, or else tweeds for shooting.

'Rupert! Good to see you. All set to read?'

'Absolutely!' said Rupert.

'Good man.' Tom smiled at Rupert and Rupert felt a tingle go up his spine. The same tingle he'd experienced when he met Tom for the first time. 'I'm hoping you'll read at the next chambers bible study group, if that's OK?'

'Of course,' said Rupert. 'What do you want me to do?'

'We'll talk about it later,' said Tom. He smiled again and moved away – and ridiculously, Rupert felt a small dart of disappointment.

In front of him, Francesca and Sue were greeting friends with warm hugs; Charlie was vigorously shaking the hand of an old schoolfriend. Everywhere he looked, well-dressed professionals were thronging.

'I just asked Jesus,' a voice behind him said. 'I asked Jesus, and the next day I woke up with the answer fully formed in my head. So I went back to the client, and I said . . .'

'Why these people can't control themselves, I just don't know!' Francesca was exclaiming. Her voice was sharp and her eyes were shining slightly. 'All these single mothers, with no means to provide for themselves . . .'

'But then, think of the backgrounds they come from,' replied a blond woman in an Armani jacket. She smiled blandly at Francesca. 'They need our support and guidance. Not our condemnation.'

'I know,' muttered Francesca. 'But it's very difficult.' Unconsciously her hand stroked her flat stomach and Rupert felt a wave of compassion for her. He hurried forward and kissed the back of her neck.

'Don't worry,' he whispered in her ear. 'We'll have a baby. You just wait.'

'But what if God doesn't want me to have a baby?' said Francesca, turning round and meeting his eyes. 'What then?'

'He does,' said Rupert, trying to sound sure of himself. 'I'm sure he does.'

Francesca sighed and turned away again, and Rupert felt a stab of panic. He didn't know the answers. How could he? He'd been a born-again Christian for less time than Francesca, was less familiar with the bible than she was, had achieved an inferior degree to hers, even earned less money than she did. And yet she deferred to him constantly. She had insisted on promising to obey him; she looked to him for guidance in everything.

Gradually the crowd dispersed, filing into pews. Some knelt, some sat looking expectantly ahead, some were still chatting. Many were holding crisp notes, ready for collection. The amount of money generated by St Catherine's at each service was approximately the same as that gathered in a whole year at the small Cornish church Rupert had attended as a boy. The congregation here could afford to give extravagantly without their lifestyles being affected; they still drove expensive cars, ate good food, travelled abroad. They were a ready-made advertisters' dream audience, thought Rupert; if the church would only sell space on its walls, it would make a fortune. An unwilling grin passed over his face. That was the sort of remark Allan would have made.

'Rupert!' Tom's voice interrupted his thoughts. 'Come and sit at the front.'

'Right you are,' said Rupert. He sat down on his allotted chair and looked at the congregation facing him. Familiar faces looked back at him; there were a few friendly smiles. Rupert tried to smile back. But suddenly he felt conspicuous under the scrutiny of five hundred Christian eyes. What did they see? What did they think he was? A childish panic went through him. They all think I'm like them, he suddenly found himself thinking. But I'm not. I'm different.

Music struck up, and everybody got to their feet. Rupert stood up too, and looked obediently at his yellow sheet of paper. The tune of the hymn was jaunty; the words were happy and uplifting. But he didn't feel uplifted, he felt poisoned. He couldn't sing, couldn't free his thoughts from the same circular path. They all think I'm the same as them, he kept thinking. But I'm not. I'm different.

He had always been different. As a child in Cornwall he'd been the headmaster's son; he had been set apart before he even had a chance. While other boys' fathers drove tractors and drank beer, his father read Greek poetry and gave Rupert's friends detention. Mr Carr had been a popular headmaster – the most popular the school had ever had – but that hadn't helped Rupert, who was by nature academic, poor at games and shy. The boys had scoffed at him, the girls had ignored him. Gradually Rupert had developed a defensive stutter and a taste for being on his own.

Then, at around the age of thirteen, his childish features had matured into golden good looks, and things had become even worse. Suddenly the girls were following him around, giggling and propositioning him; suddenly the other boys were gazing at him in envy. It was assumed, because he was so good-looking, that he could sleep with any girl he wanted to; that indeed he had already done so. Nearly every Saturday night Rupert would take some girl or other to the cinema, sit with her at the back and put his arm around her for all to see. The next Monday she would giggle hysterically with her friends, flutter her eyelashes and drop hints. His reputation grew and grew. To Rupert's astonishment, not one of the girls ever gave away the fact that his sexual prowess stopped at a goodnight kiss. By the time he was eighteen he had taken out all the girls in the school and was still a virgin.

He'd thought that at Oxford it would be different. That he would fit in. That he would meet another kind of girl; that everything would fall into place. He'd arrived tanned and fit after a summer on the beach, and immediately attracted attention. Girls had flocked round him; intelligent, charming girls. The sort of girls he'd always longed for.

Except that now he'd got them, he didn't want them. He couldn't desire the girls he met, with their high foreheads and flicking hair and intellectual gravitas. It was the men in Oxford who has fascinated him. The men. He'd stared at them surreptitiously in lectures, watched them in the street, edged closer to them in pubs. Foppish law students in waistcoats; crop-haired French students in Doc Martens. Members of the dramatic society piling into the pub after a show, wearing make-up and kissing each other playfully on the lips.

Occasionally one of these men would look up, notice Rupert staring, and invite him to join the group. A few times he'd been openly propositioned. But each time he'd backed away, full of terror. He couldn't be attracted to these men. He couldn't be gay. He simply couldn't.

By the end of the first year at Oxford he was still a virgin and lonelier than ever before. He belonged to no particular set; he didn't have a girlfriend; he didn't have a boyfriend. Because he was so good-looking, others in his college read his shyness as aloofness. They imbued him with a self-confidence and arrogance he didn't have, assumed his social life was catered for out of college; left him alone. By the end of Trinity term, he was spending most nights drinking whisky alone in his rooms.

And then he'd been sent for an extra tutorial to Allan Kepinski, an American junior research fellow at Keble. They'd discussed *Paradise Lost*; had grown more and more intense as the afternoon wore on. By the end of the tutorial Rupert was flushed in the face, utterly caught up in the debate and the charged atmosphere between them. Allan was leaning forward in his chair, close to Rupert; their faces were almost touching.

Then, silently, Allan had leaned a little further and brushed his lips against Rupert's. Excitement had seared Rupert's body. He'd closed his eyes and willed Allan to kiss him again, to come even closer. And slowly, gently, Allan had put his arms around Rupert and pulled him down, off his armchair, onto the rug, into a new life.

Afterwards, Allan had explained to Rupert exactly

how much of a risk he'd been taking by making the first move.

'You could have had me slung in jail,' he'd said in his dry voice, caressing Rupert's rumpled hair. 'Or at least sent home on the first plane. Coming on to undergraduates isn't exactly ethical.'

'Fuck ethical,' Rupert had said, and flopped backwards. He felt shaky with relief; with liberation. 'Christ, I feel incredible. I never knew—' He broke off.

'No,' Allan had said amusedly. 'I didn't think you did.'

That summer remained etched in Rupert's memory as a perfect bubble of intoxication. He'd subsumed himself entirely to Allan, had spent the entire summer vacation with him. He'd eaten with him, slept with him, respected and loved him. No-one else had seemed to matter, or even exist.

The girl Milly had not interested him in the slightest. Allan had been quite taken with her – he'd thought her naively charming; had been amused by her innocent babble. But to Rupert, she had been just another shallow, silly girl. A waste of time, a waste of space, a rival for Allan's attention.

'Rupert?' The woman next to him nudged him and Rupert realized that the hymn was over. Quickly he sat down, and tried to compose his thoughts.

But the thought of Milly had unsettled him; now he couldn't think of anything else. 'Milly from Oxford', she'd called herself tonight. A spasm of angry fear went through Rupert as he thought of her name on his wife's lips. What was she doing, ringing him after ten years?

How had she got his number? Didn't she realize that everything had changed? That he wasn't gay? That it had all been a terrible mistake?

'Rupert! You're reading!' The woman was hissing at him, and abruptly Rupert came to. He carefully put down his yellow sheet of paper, picked up his bible and stood up. He walked slowly to the lectern, placed his bible on it and faced his audience.

'I am going to read from St Matthew's Gospel,' he said. 'The theme is denial. How can we live with ourselves if we deny the one we truly love?'

He opened the Bible with trembling hands, and took a deep breath. I'm reading this for God, he told himself – as all the readers at St Catherine's did. I'm reading this for Jesus. The picture of a grave, betrayed face filled his mind, and he felt a familiar stab of guilt. But it wasn't the face of Jesus he saw. It was the face of Allan.

SEVEN

The next morning, Milly and Isobel waited until a four-some of guests descended on the kitchen, then slipped out of the house before Olivia could ask them where they were going.

'OK,' said Isobel, as they reached the car. 'I think there's an eight-thirty fast to London. You should catch that.'

'What if he says something?' said Milly, looking up at Alexander's curtained window. Her lips began to shiver in the icy morning air. 'What if he says something to Simon while I'm away?'

'He won't,' said Isobel firmly. 'Simon will be at work all morning, won't he? Alexander won't even be able to get to him. and by that time, at least you'll know.' She opened the car door. 'Come on, get in.'

'I didn't sleep all night,' said Milly, as Isobel began to drive off. 'I was so tense.' She wound a strand of hair tightly round her finger, then released it. 'For ten years I've thought I was married. And now . . . maybe I'm not!'

'Milly, you don't know for sure,' said Isobel.

'I know,' said Milly. 'But it makes sense, doesn't it? Why would Allan begin divorce proceedings and not see them through? Of *course* he would have seen it all through.'

'Maybe.'

'Don't be so pessimistic, Isobel! You were the one who said—'

'I know I was. And I really hope you are divorced.' She glanced at Milly. 'But I wouldn't celebrate until you actually find out.'

'I'm not celebrating,' said Milly. 'Not yet. I'm just . . . hopeful.'

They paused at a traffic light and watched a crocodile of children in matching red duffel coats cross the road.

'Of course,' said Isobel, 'if your charming friend Rupert had bothered to call back, you might be in contact with Allan by now. You might know, one way or the other.'

'I know,' said Milly. 'Bastard. *Ignoring* me like that. He must know I'm in some kind of trouble. Why else would I ring him?' Her voice rose incredulously. 'How can someone be so selfish?'

'Most of the world is selfish,' said Isobel. 'Take it from me.'

'And how come he's suddenly got a wife?'

Isobel shrugged.

'There's your answer. That's why he didn't call back.'

Milly drew a circle on the fogged-up passenger window and looked out of it at the passing streets. Commuters were hurrying along the pavements, scuffing the new morning snow into slush; glancing at garish Sale signs in closed shop windows as they passed.

'So, what are you going to do?' said Isobel suddenly. 'If you find out you are divorced?'

'What do you mean?'

'Will you tell Simon?'

There was silence.

'I don't know,' said Milly slowly. 'Maybe it won't be necessary.'

'But Milly—'

'I know I should have told him in the first place,' interrupted Milly. 'I should have told him months ago, and sorted it all out.' She paused. 'But I didn't. And I can't change that. It's too late.'

'So? You could tell him now.'

'But everything's different now! Our wedding is in three days' time. Everything's perfect. Why ruin it all with . . . this?'

Isobel was silent and Milly looked round defensively. 'I suppose you think I should tell him anyway. I suppose you think you can't have secrets from someone you love.'

'No,' said Isobel. 'Actually, I don't think that.' Milly looked at her in surprise. Isobel's gaze was averted; her hands gripped the steering wheel tightly. 'You can easily love someone and still keep a secret from them,' she said.

'But—'

'If it's something that would trouble them needlessly. If it's something they don't need to know.' Isobel's voice grew slightly harsher. 'Some secrets are best left unsaid.'

'Like what?' Milly gazed at Isobel. 'What are you talking about?'

'Nothing.'

'Have you got a secret?'

Isobel was silent. For a few minutes Milly stared at her sister, scanning her face, trying to read her expression. Then suddenly it came to her. A thunderbolt of horrific realization.

'You're ill, aren't you?' she said shakily. 'God, it all makes sense. That's why you're so pale. You've got something terrible wrong with you – and you're not telling us!' Milly's voice rose. 'You think it's best left unsaid! What, until you *die*?'

'Milly!' Isobel's voice snapped curtly across the car. 'I'm not going to die. I'm not ill.'

'Well, what's your secret, then?'

'I never said I had one. I was talking theoretically.' Isobel pulled into the station car park. 'Here we are.' She opened the car door and, without looking at Milly, got out.

Reluctantly, Milly followed. As she reached the station concourse, a train pulled out from one of the platforms, and a trail of arriving passengers began to appear. Unconcerned, happy people, holding bags

143

and waving to friends. People to whom the word 'wedding' meant happiness and celebration.

'Oh God,' she said, catching up with Isobel. 'I don't want to go. I don't want to find out. I want to forget about it.'

'You've got to go. You haven't got any choice.' Suddenly Isobel's face changed colour. 'Get your ticket,' she said in a gasp. 'I'll be back in a moment.' And to Milly's astonishment, she began running towards the Ladies. Milly gazed after her for a moment, then turned round.

'A day return to London, please,' she said to the girl behind the glass. What on earth was wrong with Isobel? She wasn't ill, but she wasn't normal, either. She couldn't be pregnant – she didn't have a boyfriend.

'Right,' said Isobel, reappearing by her side. 'Got everything?'

'You're pregnant!' hissed Milly. 'Aren't you?' Isobel took a step back. She looked as though she'd been slapped in the face.

'No,' she said.

'Yes you are. It's obvious!'

'The train goes in a minute,' said Isobel, looking at her watch. 'You'll miss it.'

'You're pregnant, and you didn't even tell me! Bloody hell, Isobel, you should have told me. I'm going to be an aunt!'

'No,' said Isobel tightly. 'You're not.'

Milly stared at her uncomprehendingly. Then, with a sudden shock, she realized what Isobel was saying.

'No! You can't do that! You can't Isobel, you're not serious?'

'I don't know. I don't know, OK?' Isobel's voice rose savagely. She took a couple of paces towards Milly, clenched her hands, then took a couple of paces back, like a caged animal.

'Isobel—'

'You've got a train to catch,' said Isobel. 'Go on.' She looked up at Milly with glittering eyes. 'Go on!'

'I'll catch a later train,' said Milly.

'No! You haven't got time for that. Go on!'

Milly stared at her sister for a few silent seconds. She had never seen Isobel looking vulnerable before; it made her feel uneasy.

'OK,' she said. 'I'll go.'

'Good luck,' said Isobel.

'And we'll talk about . . . about it – when I get back.'

'Maybe,' said Isobel. When Milly looked back from the ticket barrier to wave goodbye, she had already gone.

Isobel arrived back home to find Olivia waiting for her in the kitchen.

'Where's Milly?' she demanded.

'She's gone to London for the day,' said Isobel.

'To London? What on earth for?'

'To get a present for Simon,' said Isobel, reaching for the biscuit tin. Olivia stared at her.

'Are you serious? All the way to London? She can get a perfectly good present for him in Bath!'

145

'She just felt like going to London,' said Isobel, ripping open a packet of digestives. 'Does it matter?'

'Yes,' said Olivia crossly. 'Of course it matters! Do you know what day it is today?'

'Yes, I do,' said Isobel, biting into a biscuit with relish. 'It's Thursday.'

'Exactly! Only two days to go! I've a thousand things to do, and Milly was supposed to be helping me. She's such a thoughtless girl.'

'Give her a break,' said Isobel. 'She's got a lot on her mind.'

'So have I, darling! I've got to organize extra orders of service, and check all the place settings – and to top it all, the marquee's just arrived. Who's going to come with me to see it?'

There was silence.

'Oh God,' said Isobel, stuffing another biscuit into her mouth. 'All right.'

Simon and Harry were walking along Parham Place. It was a wide road, civilized and expensive and, at this time in the morning, busy – as its residents left for their jobs in the professions and the law and the higher echelons of industry. A pretty brunette getting into her car smiled at Simon as they walked by; three doors down a group of builders sat on the doorstep and drunk steaming cups of tea.

'Here we are,' said Harry as he stopped by a flight of stone steps leading to a glossy blue door. 'Have you got the keys?'

Silently, Simon walked up the steps and put the key in the lock. He stepped into a spacious hall and opened another door, to the left.

'Go on then,' said Harry. 'In you go.'

As he stepped inside, Simon immediately remembered why he and Milly had fallen in love with the flat. He was surrounded by space; by white walls and high, distant ceilings and acres of wooden floor. Nothing else they'd looked at had come close to this; nothing else had been so prohibitively expensive.

'Like it?' said Harry.

'It's great,' Simon said, wandering over to a mantelpiece and running his hand along it. 'It's great,' he repeated. He didn't trust himself to say any more. The flat was more than great. It was beautiful, perfect. Milly would adore it. But as he stood, looking around, all he could feel was resentful misery.

'Nice high ceilings,' said Harry. He opened an empty, panelled cupboard, looked inside, and closed it again. As he wandered over to a window, his steps echoed on the bare floor. 'Nice wooden shutters,' he said, tapping one appraisingly.

'The shutters are great,' said Simon. Everything was great. He couldn't locate a single fault.

'You'll have to get some decent furniture,' said Harry. He looked at Simon. 'Need any help with that?'

'No,' said Simon, 'thank you.'

'Well anyway, I hope you like it.' Harry gave a little shrug.

'It's a beautiful flat,' said Simon stiffly. 'Milly will love it.'

'Good,' said Harry. 'Where is she today?'

'In London. Some mysterious mission. I think she's buying me a present.'

'All these presents,' said Harry lightly. 'You'll be getting quite spoilt.'

'I'll bring her round this evening to see it,' said Simon, 'if that's OK?'

'Your flat. Do what you like.'

They wandered out of the main room into a light, wide corridor. The biggest bedroom overlooked the garden: long windows opened onto a tiny wrought-iron balcony.

'You don't need more than two bedrooms,' said Harry. There was a slight question mark in his voice. 'Not thinking of having children straight away.'

'Oh no,' said Simon. 'Plenty of time for that. Milly's only twenty-eight.'

'Still . . .' Harry turned a switch by the door and the bare bulb swinging from the ceiling suddenly came alive with light. 'You'll need lampshades. Or whatever.'

'Yes,' said Simon. He looked at his father. 'Why?' he said. 'Do you think we should have children straight away?'

'No,' said Harry emphatically. 'Definitely not.'

'Really? But you did.'

'I know. That was our mistake.'

Simon stiffened.

'I was a mistake, was I?' he said. 'A product of human error?'

'You know that's not what I meant,' said Harry irritably. 'Stop being so bloody touchy.'

'What do you expect? You're telling me I wasn't wanted.'

'Of course you were wanted!' Harry paused. 'You just weren't wanted right then.'

'Well, I'm sorry for gatecrashing the party,' said Simon furiously. 'But I didn't exactly have a choice abut when I arrived, did I? It wasn't exactly up to me, was it?' Harry winced.

'Listen, Simon. All I meant was—'

'I know what you meant!' said Simon, striding to the window. He stared out at the snowy garden, trying to keep his voice under control. 'I was an inconvenience, wasn't I? I still am.'

'Simon—'

'Well, look, Dad. I won't inconvenience you any more, OK?' Simon wheeled round, his face trembling. 'Thanks very much, but you can keep your flat. Milly and I will make our own arrangements.' He tossed the keys onto the polished floor and walked quickly to the door.

'Simon!' said Harry angrily. 'Don't be so fucking stupid!'

'I'm sorry I've been in your way all these years,' said Simon at the door. 'But after Saturday, I'll be gone. You'll never have to see me again. Maybe that'll be a relief for both of us.'

And he slammed the door, leaving Harry alone, staring at the keys winking in the winter sunlight.

*　*　*

The Family Registry was large and light and softly carpeted in green. Rows and rows of indexes were stored on modern beechwood shelves, divided into births, marriages and deaths. The marriage section was by far the busiest. As Milly self-consciously edged her way towards the shelves, people milled around her, clanking indexes of paper, and talking to each other in low voices. On the wall was a notice headlined WE WILL HELP YOU TRACE YOUR FAMILY TREE. Two middle-aged ladies were poring over an index from the 1800s. 'Charles Forsyth!' one was exclaiming. 'But is that *our* Charles Forsyth?' Not one person looked anxious or guilty. For everybody else, thought Milly, this was a pleasurable morning's occupation.

Without daring to look anyone in the eye, she headed towards the more recent indexes, and pulled one down, scarcely daring to look inside. For a moment, she couldn't see it, and she was filled with ridiculous hope. But then, suddenly, it jumped up at her. HAVILL, MELISSA G – KEPINSKI. OXFORD.

Milly's heart sank. In spite of herself she'd harboured a secret, tiny belief that her marriage to Allan might have slipped through the legal net. But there it was, typed in black and white, for anyone to look up. A few thoughtless minutes in a registry office in Oxford had led to this lasting piece of evidence: an indelible record which would never, ever disappear. She stared down the page, unable to tear herself away, until the words began to dance in front of her eyes.

150

'You can get a certificate, you know.' A cheery voice startled her and she jumped up in fright, covering her name with her hand. A friendly young man wearing a name badge was standing opposite her. 'We provide copies of marriage certificates. You can also have them framed. They make a very nice gift.'

'No thank you,' said Milly. The idea made her want to laugh hysterically. 'No thanks.' She looked at her name one last time, then slammed the book shut, as though trying to quash the entry and kill it. 'I was actually looking for the list of divorces.'

'Then you've come to the wrong place!' The young man grinned at her, triumphant at her ignorance. 'You want Somerset House.'

It was the biggest marquee Isobel had ever seen. It billowed magnificently in the wind, a huge white mushroom, dwarfing the cars and vans parked next to it.

'Bloody hell!' she said. 'How much is this costing?' Olivia winced.

'Quiet, darling!' she said. 'Someone might hear.'

'I'm sure they all know how much it costs,' said Isobel, staring at the stream of young men and women coming in and out of the marquee. They looked busy and purposeful; many were carrying crates or lengths of flex or pieces of wooden boarding.

'Over there we'll have a tube linking the marquee to the back of Pinnacle Hall,' said Olivia, gesturing. 'And cloakrooms.'

'Bloody hell,' said Isobel again. 'It looks like a circus.'

'Well, you know, we did think of having an elephant,' said Olivia. Isobel goggled at her.

'An elephant?'

'To take the happy couple away.'

'They wouldn't get very far on an elephant,' said Isobel, beginning to laugh.

'But they're having a helicopter instead,' said Olivia. 'Don't tell Milly. It's a surprise.'

'Wow,' said Isobel. 'A helicopter.'

'Have you ever been in a helicopter?' asked Olivia.

'Yes,' said Isobel. 'A few times. It's quite nerve-racking, actually.'

'I haven't,' said Olivia. 'Not once.' She gave a small sigh, and Isobel giggled.

'Do you want to take Milly's place? I'm sure Simon wouldn't mind.'

'Don't be silly,' snapped Olivia. 'Come on, let's look inside.'

The two of them picked their way over the snowy ground towards the marquee and lifted a flap.

'Blimey,' said Isobel slowly. 'It looks even more enormous on the inside.' They both gazed around the massive space. People were everywhere, carrying chairs, setting up heaters, fixing lights.

'It's not so big,' said Olivia uncertainly. 'Once the chairs and tables are all in, it'll be quite cosy.' She paused. 'Perhaps not cosy, exactly . . .'

'Well, I take my hat off to Harry!' said Isobel. 'This is something else.'

'We've contributed too!' exclaimed Olivia crossly. 'More than you might realize. And anyway, Harry can afford it.'

'I don't doubt that.'

'He's very fond of Milly, you know.'

'I know,' said Isobel. 'Gosh . . .' She looked around the marquee and bit her lip.

'What?' said Olivia suspiciously.

'Oh, I don't know,' said Isobel. 'All this preparation, all this money. All for one day.'

'What's wrong with that?'

'Nothing. I'm sure it'll all go swimmingly.'

Olivia stared at her.

'Isobel, what's wrong with you? You're not jealous of Milly, are you?'

'Probably,' said Isobel lightly.

'You could get married, you know! But you've chosen not to.'

'I've never been asked,' said Isobel.

'That's not the point!'

'I think it is,' said Isobel, 'very much the point.' And to her horror she suddenly felt tears pricking her eyes. What the hell was she crying for? She turned away before her mother could say anything else, and stalked off, towards the far end of the marquee. Olivia hurried obliviously after her.

'This is where the food will be,' she called excitedly. 'And that's where the swans will be.'

'The swans?' said Isobel, turning round.

'We're going to have swans made out of ice,'

said Olivia. 'And each one will be filled with oysters.'

'No!' Isobel's laugh pealed around the marquee. 'Whose idea was that?'

'Harry's,' said Olivia defensively. 'What's wrong with it?'

'Nothing. It's just the tackiest thing I've ever heard of.'

'That's what I said,' said Olivia eagerly. 'But Harry said he thought weddings were such tacky affairs anyway, there was no point trying to be tasteful. So we decided to go for broke!'

'He will be broke,' said Isobel, 'by the time he's finished feeding all his guests oysters.'

'No he won't!' snapped Olivia. 'Stop saying things like that, Isobel.'

'All right,' said Isobel in mollifying tones. 'Truthfully, I think it's going to be a lovely wedding.' She looked around the vast tent and, for the hundredth time that day, wondered how Milly was getting on. 'Milly will have the time of her life.'

'She doesn't deserve the time of her life,' said Olivia crossly. 'Rushing off to London like this. There are only two days to go, you know! Two days!'

'I know,' said Isobel. She bit her lip. 'I know. And believe me, so does Milly.'

By the time Milly reached the Strand, a winter sun had begun to shine and she could feel an optimistic excitement rising through her. Within minutes she would know, one way or the other. And suddenly she felt sure she knew which way the answer would be. The burden which had been pressing down on her for the last ten years would be lifted. At last she would be free.

She sauntered along, feeling her hair lifted slightly by the breeze, enjoying the sun on her face.

'Excuse me,' said a girl suddenly, tapping her shoulder. Milly looked round. 'We're looking for hair models. I work for a salon in Covent Garden.' She smiled at Milly. 'Would you be interested?'

A sparkle of delight ran through Milly.

'I'm sorry,' she said regretfully, 'but I'm a bit busy.' She paused, and a faint smile came to her lips. 'I'm getting married on Saturday.'

'Are you?' exclaimed the girl. 'Are you really? Congratulations! You'll make a lovely bride.'

'Thanks,' said Milly, blushing. 'Sorry I can't stop. But I've just got some things to tidy up.'

'No, no,' said the girl, rolling her eyes sympathetically. 'I know what it's like! All those tiny things that you always leave till last!'

'Exactly,' said Milly, walking away. 'Just a few last-minute details.'

As she entered Somerset House and found the department she needed, her spirits were lifted further. The man in charge of divorce decrees was round and cheerful, with twinkling eyes and a quick computer.

'You're in luck,' he said, as he tapped in her details. 'All records since 1981 are on computer file. Before that, and we have to search by hand.' He winked at her. 'But you would have been just a baby then! Now, just bear with me, my dear . . .'

Milly beamed back at him. already she was planning what she would do when she'd received confirmation of her divorce. She would take a taxi to Harvey Nichols and go straight up to the fifth floor, and buy herself a buck's fizz. And then she would call Isobel. And then she would—

Her thoughts were interrupted as the computer pinged. The man peered at the screen, then looked up.

'No,' he said in surprise. 'Not found.'

A stone dropped through Milly's stomach.

'What?' she said. Her lips felt suddenly dry. 'What do you mean?'

'There's no decree absolute listed,' said the man, tapping again. The computer pinged again and he frowned. 'Not in that period, for those names.'

'But there has to be,' said Milly. 'There *has* to be.'

'I've tried twice,' said the man. He looked up. 'Are you sure the spellings are correct?'

Milly swallowed.

'Quite sure.'

'And you're sure the petitioner applied for a decree absolute?' Milly looked at him numbly. She didn't know what he was talking about.

'No,' she said. 'I'm not sure.' The man nodded back at her, cheerful as a puppet.

'Six weeks after the decree nisi is issued, the petitioner has to apply for a decree absolute.'

'Yes,' said Milly. 'I see.'

'You were issued with a decree nisi, weren't you, dear?'

Milly looked up blankly and met the man's eyes, regarding her with a sudden curiosity. A quick stab of fear hit her in the chest.

'Yes,' she said quickly, before he could ask anything else. 'Of course I was. It was all in order. I'll . . . I'll go back and check up on what happened.'

'If you require any legal advice—'

'No thank you,' said Milly, backing away. 'You've been very kind. Thank you so much.'

As she turned to grasp the door handle, a voice hit the back of her head.

'Mrs Kepinski?'

She wheeled round with a white face.

'Or is it Ms Havill now?' said the man, smiling. He came round the counter. 'Here's a leaflet explaining the whole procedure.'

'Thank you,' said Milly desperately. 'That's lovely.'

She shot him an over-bright smile as she pocketed the leaflet and walked out of the room, feeling sick and panicky. She'd been right all along. Allan was a selfish unscrupulous bastard. And he'd left her well and truly in the lurch.

She reached the street and began to walk blindly, aware of nothing but the seeds of panic already sprouting rapaciously inside her mind. She was only back where she'd been before – but somehow her position now seemed infinitely worse; infinitely more precarious. An image came to her of Alexander's malicious, gleaming smile, like the grin of a vulture. And Simon, waiting unsuspectingly in Bath. The very thought of the two of them in the same city made her feel sick. What was she to do? What *could* she do?

A pub sign caught her eye and without considering further, she slipped inside. She headed straight for the bar and ordered a gin and tonic. When that was gone, she ordered another, and then another. Gradually, as the alcohol dulled her nerves, the adrenalin pounding round her body began to slow, and her legs stopped shaking. Standing in this warm, beery atmosphere, downing gin, she was anonymous; the real world was far away. She could put everything from her mind except the sharp taste of the gin and the feeling of the alcohol as it hit her stomach, and the saltiness of the nuts which were provided on the bar in little metal bowls.

For half an hour she stood mindlessly, allowing the crush of people to ebb and flow around her. Girls gave her curious looks; men tried to catch her eye: she ignored them all. Then after a while, as she began to feel both hungry and slightly sick, she found herself putting down her glass, picking up her bag and walking out of the pub, onto the street. She stood, swaying slightly, and wondered where to go next. It was lunchtime, and the pavement was crammed with people hurrying briskly along, hailing taxis, crowding into shops and pubs and sandwich bars. Church bells began to peal in the distance, and as she heard the sound, she felt tears starting to her eyes. What was she going to do? She could barely bring herself to think about it.

She gazed at the blurry crowd of people, wishing with all her heart to be one of them, and not herself. She would have liked to be that cheerful-looking girl eating a croissant, or that calm-looking lady getting onto a bus, or . . .

Suddenly Milly froze. She blinked a few times, wiped the tears from her eyes, and looked again. But the face she'd glimpsed was already gone, swallowed up by the surging crowds. Filled with panic, she hurried forward, peering all around her. For a few moments she could see nothing but strangers: girls in brightly coloured coats, men in dark suits, lawyers still in their courtroom wigs. They thronged past her, and she thrust her way impatiently through them, telling herself feverishly she must have been mistaken; she must have seen someone else. But then her heart stopped. There he was again, walking along the other side of the street, talking to another man. He looked older than she remembered, and fatter. But it was definitely him. It was Rupert.

A surge of white-hot hatred rose through Milly as she stared at him. how dared he sauntered along the streets of London, so happy and at ease with himself? How dared he be so oblivious of all that she was going through? Her life was in disarray because of him. Because of him and Allan. And he wasn't even aware of it.

With a pounding heart, she began to run towards him, ignoring the beeps of angry taxis as she crossed the road; ignoring the curious looks of passers-by. Within a couple of minutes she'd caught up with the two men.

She strode along behind him, gazed for a moment of loathing at Rupert's golden head, then poked his back hard.

'Rupert,' she said. 'Rupert!' He turned round and looked at her with friendly eyes devoid of recognition.

'I'm sorry,' he said. 'Do I . . .'

'It's me,' said Milly, summoning up the coldest, bitterest voice she possessed. 'It's Milly. From Oxford.'

'What?' Rupert's face drained of colour. He took a step back.

'Yes, that's right,' said Milly. 'It's me. I don't suppose you thought you'd ever see me again, did you, Rupert? You thought I'd vanished out of your life for good.'

'Don't be silly!' said Rupert in jocular tones. He glanced uneasily at his friend. 'How are things going, anyway?'

'Things,' said Milly, 'could not be going more badly, thanks for asking. Oh, and thanks for calling back last night. I really appreciated it.'

'I didn't have time,' said Rupert. His blue eyes flashed a quick look of hatred at her and Milly glared back. 'And now, I'm afraid I'm a bit busy.' He looked at his friend. 'Shall we go, Tom?'

'Don't you dare!' exclaimed Milly furiously. 'You're not going anywhere! You're going to listen to me!'

'I haven't got time—'

'Well then, make time!' shouted Milly. 'My life is in ruins, and it's all your fault. You and bloody Allan Kepinski. Jesus! Do you realize what the pair of you did to me? Do you realize the trouble I'm in, because of you?'

'Rupert,' said Tom. 'Maybe you and Milly should have a little talk?'

'I don't know what she's going on about,' said Rupert angrily. 'She's mad.'

'Even more reason,' said Tom quietly to Rupert. 'Here is a truly distressed soul. And perhaps you can help.' He smiled at Milly. 'Are you an old friend of Rupert's?'

'Yes,' said Milly curtly. 'We knew each other at Oxford. Didn't we, Rupert?'

'Well, look,' said Tom. 'Why don't I do your reading, Rupert? And you can catch up with Milly.' He smiled at her. 'Maybe next time, you could come along, too.'

'Yes,' said Milly, not having a clue what he was talking about. 'Why not.'

'Good to meet you, Milly,' said Tom, grasping Milly's hand. 'Perhaps we'll see you at St Catherine's.'

'Yes,' said Milly. 'I expect so.'

'Excellent! I'll give you a call, Rupert,' said Tom, and he was off, across the road.

Milly and Rupert looked at each other.

'You bitch,' hissed Rupert. 'Are you trying to ruin my life?'

'Ruin your life?' exclaimed Milly in disbelief. 'Ruin *your* life? Do you realize what you did to me? You used me!'

'It was your choice,' said Rupert brusquely, starting to walk away. 'If you didn't want to do it, you should have said no.'

'I was eighteen years old!' shrieked Milly. 'I didn't know anything about anything! I didn't know that one day I'd want to marry someone else, someone I really loved . . .'

'So what?' said Rupert tersely, turning back. 'You got a divorce, didn't you?'

'No!' sobbed Milly, 'I didn't! and I don't know where Allan is! And my wedding's on Saturday?'

'Well, what am I supposed to do about it?'

'I need to find Allan! Where is he?'

'I don't know,' said Rupert, beginning to walk off again. 'I can't help you. Now, leave me alone.' Milly gazed at him, anger rising through her like hot lava.

'You can't just walk away!' she shrieked. 'You've got to help me!' She began to run after him; he quickened his pace. 'You've got to help me, Rupert!' With a huge effort, she grabbed his jacket and managed to force him to a standstill.

'Get off me!' hissed Rupert.

'Listen,' said Milly fiercely, gazing up into his blue eyes. 'I did you and Allan a favour. I did you a huge, huge, enormous favour. And now it's time for you to do me a tiny little one. You owe it to me.'

She stared hard at him, watching as thoughts ran through his head; watching as his expression gradually changed. Eventually he sighed, and rubbed his forehead.

'OK,' he said. 'Come with me. We'd better talk.'

EIGHT

They went to an old pub on Fleet Street, full of winding stairs and dark wood and little, hidden nooks. Rupert bought a bottle of wine and two plates of bread and cheese and set them down on a tiny table in an alcove. He sat down heavily, took a deep slug of wine and leaned back. Milly looked at him calmly. And something, she thought, was wrong. He was still handsome, still striking – but his face was pinker and more fleshy than it had been at Oxford, and his hand shook when he put down his glass. Ten years ago, she thought, he had been a golden, glowing youth. Now he looked like a middle-aged man. And when his eyes met hers they held a residual, permanent unhappiness.

'I can't be long,' he said. 'I'm very busy. So – what exactly do you want me to do?'

'You look terrible, Rupert,' said Milly frankly. 'Are you happy?'

'I'm very happy. Thank you.' He took another deep slug of wine, practically draining the glass, and Milly raised her eyebrows.

'Are you sure?'

'Milly, we're here to talk about you,' said Rupert impatiently. 'Not me. What precisely is your problem?'

Milly looked at him for a silent moment, then sat back.

'My problem,' she said lightly, as though carefully considering the matter. 'What's my problem? My problem is that on Saturday I'm getting married to a man I love very much. My mother has organized the hugest wedding in the world. It's going to be beautiful and romantic and perfect in every single detail.' She looked up with bright eyes like daggers. 'Oh, except one. I'm still married to your friend Allan Kepinski.'

Rupert winced.

'I don't understand,' he said. 'Why aren't you divorced?'

'Ask Allan! He was supposed to be organizing it.'

'And he didn't?'

'He started to,' said Milly. 'I got some papers through the post. And I signed the slip and sent them back. But I never heard anything more'

'And you never looked into it?'

'No-one knew,' said Milly. 'No-one ever asked any questions. It didn't seem to matter.'

'The fact that you were married didn't seem to matter?' said Rupert incredulously. Milly looked up and caught his expression.

'Don't start blaming *me* for this!' she said. 'This isn't my fault!'

'You leave it until a couple of days before your wedding to chase up your divorce and you say it's not your fault?'

'I didn't think I needed to chase it up,' said Milly furiously. 'I was fine. No-one knew! No-one suspected anything!'

'So what happened?' said Rupert. Milly picked up her wine glass and cradled it in both hands.

'Now someone knows,' she said. 'Someone saw us in Oxford. And he's threatening to say something.'

'I see.'

'Don't you dare look at me like that,' said Milly sharply. 'OK, I know I should have done something about it. But so should Allan. He said he would sort it all out and I trusted him! I trusted you both. I thought you were my friends.'

'We were,' said Rupert after a pause.

'Bullshit!' cried Milly. Her cheeks began to pinken. 'You were just a couple of users. You just used me for what you wanted – and then as soon as I was gone, you forgot about me. You never wrote, you never called . . .' She crashed her glass down on the table. 'Did you get all those letters I wrote to you?'

'Yes,' said Rupert, running a hand through his hair. 'I'm sorry. I should have replied. But . . . it was a difficult time.'

'At least Allan wrote. But you couldn't even be bothered to do that. And I still believed in you.' She shook her head. 'God, I was a little fool.'

'We were all fools,' said Rupert. 'Look, Milly, for what it's worth, I'm sorry. I honestly wish none of it had ever happened. None of it!'

Milly stared at him. His eyes were darting miserably about; fronds of golden hair were quivering above his brow.

'Rupert, what's going on?' she demanded. 'How come you're married?'

'I'm married,' said Rupert, giving a stiff little shrug. 'That's all there is to it.'

'But you were gay. You were in love with Allan.'

'No I wasn't. I was misguided. I was . . . it was a mistake.'

'But you two were perfect for one another!'

'We weren't!' snapped Rupert. 'It was all wrong. Can't you accept my word on it?'

'Well, of course I can,' said Milly. 'But you just seemed so right together.' She hesitated. 'When did you realize?'

'Realize what?'

'That you were straight?'

'Milly, I don't want to talk about it,' said Rupert. 'All right?' He reached for his glass with a trembling hand and took a gulp of wine.

Milly gave a little shrug and leaned back in her chair. Idly she allowed her eyes to roam around the alcove. To her left, on the rough plaster wall, was a game of noughts and crosses which someone had begun in pencil and then abandoned. A game already destined, she could see, to end in stalemate.

'You've changed a lot since Oxford, you know,' said

Rupert abruptly. 'You've grown up. I wouldn't have recognized you.'

'I'm ten years older,' said Milly.

'It's not just that. It's . . . I don't know.' He gestured vaguely. 'Your hair. Your clothes. I wouldn't have expected you to turn out like this.'

'Like what?' said Milly defensively. 'What's wrong with me?'

'Nothing!' said Rupert. 'You just look more . . . groomed than I would have thought you'd be. More polished.'

'Well, this is what I am now, all right?' said Milly. She gave him a hard look. 'We're all allowed to change, Rupert.'

'I know,' said Rupert, flushing. 'And you look . . . great.' He leaned forward. 'Tell me about the guy you're marrying.'

'He's called Simon Pinnacle,' said Milly, and watched as Rupert's expression changed.

'No relation to—'

'His son,' said Milly. Rupert stared at her.

'Seriously? Harry Pinnacle's son?'

'Seriously.' She gave a half-smile. 'I told you. This is the wedding of the century.'

'And nobody has any idea.'

'Nobody.'

Rupert stared at Milly for a moment, then sighed. He pulled out a little leather-bound notebook and a pen.

'OK. Tell me exactly how far your divorce got.'

'I don't know,' said Milly. 'I told you. I got some

papers through the post and I signed something and sent it back.'

'And what precisely were these papers?'

'How should I know?' said Milly exasperatedly. 'Would you be able to tell one legal document from another?'

'I'm a lawyer,' said Rupert. 'But I get your point.' He put away his notebook and looked up. 'You need to speak to Allan.'

'I know that!' said Milly. 'But I don't know where he is. Do you?'

A look of pain flashed briefly across Rupert's face.

'No,' he said shortly. 'I don't.'

'But you can find out?'

Rupert was silent. Milly stared at him in disbelief.

'Rupert, you have to help me! You're my only link with him. Where did he go after Oxford?'

'Manchester,' said Rupert.

'Why did he leave Oxford? Didn't they want him any more?'

'Of course they wanted him,' said Rupert. He took a gulp of wine. 'Of course they *wanted* him.'

'Then why—'

'Because we split up,' said Rupert, his voice suddenly ragged. 'He left because we split up.'

'Oh,' said Milly, taken aback. 'I'm sorry.' She ran a finger lightly around the rim of her glass. 'Was that when you realized that you didn't . . . that you were . . .' She halted.

'Yes,' said Rupert, staring into his glass.

'And when was that?'

'At the end of that summer,' said Rupert, in a low voice. 'September.' Milly stared at him in disbelief. Her heart began to thump.

'The summer I met you?' she said. 'The summer we got married?'

'Yes.'

'Two months after I married Allan, you split up?'

'Yes.' Rupert looked up. 'But I'd rather not—'

'You're telling me you were only together for two months?' cried Milly in anguish. 'I wrecked my life to keep you together for two months?' Her voice rose to a screech. 'Two *months*?'

'Yes!'

'Then fuck you!' With a sudden surge of fury, Milly threw her wine at Rupert. It hit him straight in the face, staining his skin like blood. 'Fuck you,' she said again, trembling, watching the dark red liquid drip down his gasping face onto his smart lawyer's shirt. 'I broke the law for you! Now I'm stuck with a first husband I don't want! And all so you could change your mind after two months.'

For a long while, neither of them spoke. Rupert sat motionless, staring at Milly through a wet mask of red.

'You're right,' he said finally. He sounded broken. 'I've fucked it all up. I've fucked up your life, I've fucked up my life. And Allan . . .'

Milly cleared her throat uncomfortably.

'Did he . . .'

'He loved me,' said Rupert, as though to himself. 'That's what I didn't get. He loved me.'

'Look, Rupert, I'm sorry,' said Milly awkwardly. 'About the wine. And – everything.'

'Don't apologize,' said Rupert fiercely. 'Don't apologize.' He looked up. 'Milly, I'll find Allan for you. And I'll clear up your divorce. But I can't do it in time for Saturday. It isn't physically possible.'

'I know.'

'What will you do?'

There was a long silence.

'I don't know,' said Milly eventually. She closed her eyes and massaged her brow. 'I can't cancel the wedding now,' she said slowly. 'I just can't do that to my mother. To everyone.'

'So you'll just go ahead?' said Rupert incredulously. Milly gave a tiny shrug. 'But what about whoever it is who's threatening to say something?'

'I'll . . . I'll keep him quiet,' said Milly. 'Somehow.'

'You do realize,' said Rupert, lowering his voice, 'that what you're proposing is bigamy. You would be breaking the law.'

'Thanks for the warning,' said Milly sarcastically. 'But I've been there before, remember?' She looked at him silently for a moment. 'What do you think? Would I get away with it?'

'I expect so,' said Rupert. 'Are you serious?'

'I don't know,' said Milly. 'I really don't know.'

A while later, when the wine was finished, Rupert went and collected two cups of noxious black coffee from the bar. As he returned, Milly looked up at him. His face was clean but his shirt and jacket were still spattered with red wine.

'You won't be able to go back to work this afternoon,' she said.

'I know,' said Rupert. 'It doesn't matter. Nothing's happening.' He handed Milly a cup of coffee and sat down. There was silence for a while.

'Rupert?' said Milly.

'Yes?'

'Does your wife know? About you and Allan?'

Rupert looked at her with bloodshot eyes. 'What do you think?'

'But why?' said Milly. 'Are you afraid she wouldn't understand?' Rupert gave a short little laugh.

'That's underestimating it.'

'But why not? If she loves you . . .'

'Would you understand?' Rupert glared at her. 'If your Simon turned round and told you he'd once had an affair with another man?'

'Yes,' said Milly uncertainly. 'I think I would. As long as we talked about it properly . . .'

'You wouldn't,' said Rupert scathingly. 'I can tell you that now. You wouldn't even begin to understand. And neither would Francesca.'

'You're not giving her a chance! Come on, Rupert, she's your wife! Be honest with her.'

'Be honest? You're telling me to be honest?'

'That's my whole point!' said Milly, leaning forward earnestly. 'I should have been honest with Simon from the start. I should have told him everything. We could have cleared up the divorce together; everything would be fine. But as it is . . .' She spread her hands helplessly on the table. 'As it is, I'm in a mess.' She paused and took a sip of coffee. 'What I'm saying is, if I had the chance to go back and tell Simon the truth, I would grab it. And you've got that chance, Rupert! You've got the chance to be honest with Francesca before . . . before it all starts going wrong.'

'It's different,' said Rupert stiffly.

'No is isn't. It's just another secret. All secrets come out in the end. If you don't tell her, she'll find out some other way.'

'She won't.'

'She might!' Milly's voice rose in conviction. 'She might easily! And do you want to risk that? Just tell her, Rupert! Tell her.'

'Tell me what?'

A girl's voice hit Milly's ears like a whiplash, and her head jerked round in shock. Standing at the entrance to the alcove was a pretty girl, with pale red hair and conventionally smart clothes. Next to her was Rupert's friend Tom.

'Tell me what?' the girl repeated in high, sharp tones, glancing from Rupert to Milly and back again. 'Rupert what's happened to you?'

'Francesca,' said Rupert shakily. 'Don't worry, it's just wine.'

'Hi, Rupe!' said Tom easily. 'We thought we'd find you here.'

'So this is Milly,' said the girl. She looked at Rupert

with gimlet eyes. 'Tom told me you'd met up with your old friend. Milly from Oxford.' She gave a strange little laugh. 'The funny thing is, Rupert, you told me you didn't want to talk to Milly from Oxford. You told me to ignore all her messages. You told me she was a nut.'

'A nut?' cried Milly indignantly.

'I didn't want to talk to her!' said Rupert. 'I don't.' He looked at Milly, blue eyes full of dismay.

'Look,' she said hurriedly. 'Maybe I'd better go.' She stood up and picked up her bag. 'Nice to meet you,' she said to Francesca. 'Honestly, I am just an old friend.'

'Is that right?' said Francesca. Her pale eyes bored into Rupert's. 'So what is it that you've got to tell me?'

'Bye, Rupert,' said Milly hastily. 'Bye, Francesca.'

'What have you got to tell me, Rupert? What is it? And you –' She turned to Milly. 'You stay here!'

'I've got a train to catch,' said Milly. 'Honestly, I've got to go. So sorry!'

Avoiding Rupert's eyes, she quickly made her way across the bar and bounded up the wooden steps to the street. As she stepped into the fresh air she realized that she'd left her cigarette lighter on the table. It seemed a small price to pay for her escape.

Isobel was sitting in the kitchen at 1 Bertram Street, stitching blue ribbon onto a lace garter. Olivia sat opposite her, folding bright pink silk into a elaborate bow. Every so often she looked up at Isobel with a dissatisfied expression, then looked down again. Eventually she put down the bow and stood up to fill the kettle.

'How's Paul?' she said brightly.

'Who?' said Isobel.

'Paul! Paul the doctor. Do you still see much of him?'

'Oh, him,' said Isobel. She screwed up her face. 'No, I haven't seen him for months. I only went out with him a few times.'

'What a shame,' said Olivia. 'He was so charming. And very good-looking, I thought.'

'He was OK,' said Isobel. 'It just didn't work out.'

'Oh, darling. I'm so sorry.'

'I'm not,' said Isobel. 'It was me who finished it.'

'But why?' Olivia's voice rose in irritation. 'What was wrong with him?'

'If you must know,' said Isobel, 'he turned out to be a bit weird.'

'Weird?' said Olivia suspiciously. 'What kind of weird?'

'Just weird,' said Isobel.

'Wacky?'

'No!' said Isobel. 'Not wacky. Weird! Honestly, Mummy, you don't want to know.'

'Well, I thought he was very nice,' said Olivia, pouring boiling water into the teapot. 'A very nice young man.'

Isobel said nothing, but her needle jerked savagely in and out of the fabric.

'I saw Brenda White the other day,' said Olivia, as though changing the subject. 'Her daughter's getting married in June.'

'Really?' Isobel looked up. 'Is she still working for Shell?'

174

'I've no idea,' said Olivia testily. Then she smiled at Isobel. 'What I was going to say was, she met her husband at an evening function organized for young professionals. In some smart London restaurant. They're very popular these days. Apparently the place was *packed* full of interesting men.'

'I'm sure.'

'Brenda said she could get the number if you're interested.'

'No thanks.'

'Darling, you're not giving yourself a chance!'

'No!' snapped Isobel. She put down her needle and looked up. '*You're* not giving me a chance! You're treating me as though I don't have any function in life except to find a husband. What about my work? What about my friends?'

'What about babies?' said Olivia sharply.

Colour flooded Isobel's face.

'Maybe I'll just have a baby without a husband,' she said after a pause. 'People do, you know.'

'Oh, now you're just being silly,' said Olivia crossly. 'A child needs a proper family.' She brought the teapot over to the table, sat down, and opened her red book. 'Right. What else needs doing?'

Isobel stared at the teapot without moving. It was large and decorated with painted ducks; they'd used it at family teas ever since she could remember ever since she and Milly had sat side by side in matching smocks, eating Marmite sandwiches. A child needs a proper family. What the hell was a proper family?

'Do you know?' said Olivia, looking up in surprise. 'I think I've done everything for today. I've ticked everything off my list.'

'Good,' said Isobel. 'You can have an evening off.'

'Maybe I should check with Harry's assistant . . .'

'Don't check anything,' said Isobel firmly. 'You've checked everything a million times. Just have a nice cup of tea and relax.'

Olivia poured out the tea, took a sip and sighed.

'My goodness!' she said, leaning back in her chair. 'I have to say, there have been times when I thought we would never get this wedding organized in time.'

'Well, now it is organized,' said Isobel. 'So you should spend the evening doing something fun. Not hymn sheets. Not shoe trimmings. Fun!' She met Olivia's eyes sternly and, as the phone rang, they both began to giggle.

'I'll get that,' said Olivia.

'If it's Milly,' said Isobel quickly, 'I'll speak to her.'

'Hello, 1 Bertram Street,' said Olivia. She pulled a face at Isobel. 'Hello, Canon Lytton! How are you? Yes . . . Yes . . . No!'

Her voice suddenly changed, and Isobel looked up.

'No, I don't. I've no idea what you're talking about. Yes, perhaps you'd better. We'll see you then.'

Olivia put the phone down and looked perplexedly at Isobel.

'That was Canon Lytton,' she said.

'What did he want?'

'He's coming to see us.' Olivia sat down. 'I don't understand it.'

'Why?' said Isobel. 'Is something wrong?'

'Well, I don't know! He said he'd received some information, and he'd like to discuss it with us.'

'Information,' said Isobel. Her heart started to thump. 'What information?'

'I don't know,' said Olivia. She raised puzzled blue eyes to meet Isobel's. 'Something to do with Milly. He wouldn't say what.'

NINE

Rupert and Francesca sat silently in their drawing room, looking at each other. On Tom's suggestion, they had both phoned their offices to take the rest of the afternoon off. Neither had spoken in the taxi back to Fulham. Francesca had shot Rupert the occasional hurt, bewildered glance; he had sat, staring at his hands, wondering what he was going to say. Wondering whether to concoct a story or to tell her the truth about himself.

How would she react if he did? Would she be angry? Distraught? Revolted? Perhaps she would say she'd always known there was something different about him. Perhaps she would try to understand. But how could she understand what he didn't understand himself?

'Right,' said Francesca. 'Well, here we are.' She gazed at him expectantly and Rupert looked away. From outside he could hear birds singing, cars starting, the wailing of a toddler as it was thrust into its pushchair by its nanny. Mid-afternoon sounds that he wasn't used to hearing. He felt self-conscious, sitting at home in the winter daylight; self-conscious, facing his wife's taut, anxious gaze.

'I think,' said Francesca suddenly, 'we should pray.'

'What?' Rupert looked up, astounded.

'Before we talk.' Francesca gazed earnestly at him. 'If we said a prayer together it might help us.'

'I don't think it would help me,' said Rupert. He looked at the drinks cabinet, then looked away again.

'Rupert, what's wrong?' cried Francesca. 'Why are you so strange? Are you in love with Milly?'

'No!' exclaimed Rupert.

'But you had an affair with her when you were at Oxford.'

'No,' said Rupert.

'No?' Francesca stared at him. 'You never went out with her?'

'No.' He would have laughed if he hadn't felt so nervous. 'I never went out with Milly. Not in that sense.'

'Not in that sense,' she repeated. 'What does that mean?'

'Francesca, you're on the wrong track completely.' He tried to smile. 'Look, can't we just forget all this? Milly is an old friend. Full stop.'

'I wish I could believe you,' said Francesca. 'But it's obvious that something's going on.'

'Nothing's going on.'

'Then what was she talking about?' Francesca's voice rose in sudden passion. 'Rupert, I'm your wife! Your loyalty is to me. If you have a secret, then I deserve to know it.'

Rupert stared at his wife. Her pale eyes were shining slightly; her hands were clasped tightly in her lap. Round her wrist was the expensive watch he'd bought her for her birthday. They'd chosen it together at Selfridges, then gone to see *An Inspector Calls*. It had been a happy day of safe, unambitious treats.

'I don't want to lose you,' he found himself saying. 'I love you. I love our marriage. I'll love our children, when we have them.' Francesca stared at him with anxious eyes.

'But?' she said. 'What's the but?'

Rupert gazed back at her silently. He didn't know how to reply, where to start.

'Are you in trouble?' said Francesca suddenly. 'Are you hiding something from me?' Her voice rose in alarm. 'Rupert?'

'No!' said Rupert. 'I'm not in trouble. I'm just . . .'

'What?' said Francesca impatiently. 'What are you?'

'Good question,' said Rupert. Tension was building up inside him like a coiled spring; he could feel a frown furrowing his forehead.

'What?' said Francesca. 'What do you mean?'

Rupert dug his nails into his palms and took a deep breath. There seemed no way but forward.

'When I was at Oxford,' he said, and stopped. 'There was a man.'

'A man?'

Rupert looked up and met Francesca's eyes. They were blank, unsuspecting, waiting for him to go on. She had no idea what he was leading up to.

'I had a relationship with him,' he said, still gazing at her. 'A close relationship.'

He paused, and waited, willing her brain to process what he had said and make a deduction. For what seemed like hours, her eyes remained empty.

And then suddenly it happened. Her eyes snapped open and shut like a cat's. She had understood. She had understood what he was saying. Rupert gazed at her fearfully, trying to gauge her reaction.

'I don't understand,' she said at last, her voice suddenly truculent with alarm. 'Rupert, you're not making any sense! This is just a waste of time!'

She got up from the sofa and began to brush imaginary crumbs off her lap, avoiding his eye.

'Darling, I was wrong to doubt you,' she said. 'I'm sorry. I shouldn't mistrust you. Of course you have the right to see anybody you like. Shall we just forget this ever happened?'

Rupert stared at her in disbelief. Was she serious? Was she really willing to carry on as before? To pretend he'd said nothing; to ignore the huge questions that must already be gnawing at her brain? Was she really so afraid of the answers she might hear?

'I'll make some tea, shall I?' continued Francesca with a bright tautness. 'And get some scones out of the freezer. 'It'll be quite a treat!'

'Francesca,' said Rupert, 'stop it. You heard what I said. Don't you want to know any more?' He stood up and took her wrist. 'You heard what I said.'

'Rupert!' said Francesca, giving a little laugh. 'Let go! I – I don't know what you're talking about. I've already apologized for mistrusting you. What else do you want?'

'I want . . .' began Rupert. His grip tightened on her wrist; he felt a sudden certainty anchoring him. 'I want to tell you everything.'

'You've told me everything,' said Francesca quickly. 'I understand completely. It was a silly mix-up.'

'I've told you nothing.' He gazed at her, suddenly desperate to talk; desperate for relief. 'Francesca—'

'Why can't we just forget it?' said Francesca. Her voice held an edge of panic.

'Because it wouldn't be honest!'

'Well, maybe I don't want to be honest!' Her face was flushed; her eyes darted about. She looked like a trapped rabbit.

Leave her alone, Rupert told himself. Don't say any more; just leave her alone. But the urge to talk was unbearable; having begun, he could no longer contain himself.

'You don't want to be honest?' he said, despising himself. 'You want me to bear false witness? Is that what you want, Francesca?'

He watched as her face changed expression, as she struggled to reconcile her private fears with the law of God.

'You're right,' she said at last. 'I'm sorry.' She looked at him apprehensively, then bowed her head in submission. 'What do you want to tell me?'

Stop now, Rupert told himself. Stop now before you make her life utterly miserable.

'I had an affair with a man,' he said.

He paused, and waited for a reaction. A scream; a gasp. But Francesca's head remained bowed. She did not move.

'His name was Allan.' He swallowed. 'I loved him.'

He gazed at Francesca, hardly daring to breathe. Suddenly she looked up. 'You're making it up,' she said.

'What?'

'I can tell,' said Francesca quickly. 'You're feeling guilty about this girl Milly, so you've made up this silly story to distract me.'

'I haven't,' said Rupert. 'It's not a story. It's the truth.'

'No,' said Francesca, shaking her head. 'No.'

'Yes.'

'No!'

'Yes, Francesca!' shouted Rupert. 'Yes! It's true! I had an affair with a man. His name was Allan. Allan Kepinski.'

There was a long silence, then Francesca met his eyes. She looked ill.

'You really . . .'

'Yes.'

'Did you actually . . .'

'Yes,' said Rupert. 'Yes.' As he spoke he felt a mixture of pain and relief – as though heavy boulders were being ripped from his back, lightening his burden but leaving his skin sore and bleeding. 'I had sex with him.' he closed his eyes. 'We made love.' Suddenly memories flooded his mind. He was with Allan again in the darkness, feeling his skin, his hair, his tongue. Shivering with delight.

'I don't want to hear any more,' Francesca whispered. 'I don't feel very well.' Rupert opened his eyes to see her standing up; making uncertainly for the door. Her face was pale and her hands shook as they grasped the door handle. Guilt poured over him like hot water.

'I'm sorry,' he said. 'Francesca, I'm sorry.'

'Don't say sorry to me,' said Francesca in a jerky, scratchy voice. 'Don't say sorry to me. Say sorry to our Lord.'

'Francesca . . .'

'You must pray for forgiveness. 'I'm going—' She broke off and took a deep breath. 'I'm going to pray too.'

'Can't we talk?' said Rupert desperately. 'Can't we at least talk about it?' He got up and came towards her. 'Francesca?'

'Don't!' she shrieked as his hand neared her sleeve. 'Don't touch me!' She looked at him with glittering eyes in a sheet-white face.

'I wasn't—'

'Don't come near me!'

'But—'

'You made love to me!' she whispered. 'You touched me! You—' She broke off and retched.

'Francesca—'

'I'm going to be sick,' she said shakily, and ran out of the room.

Rupert remained by the door, listening as she ran up the stairs and locked the bathroom door. He was trembling all over; his legs felt weak. The revulsion he'd seen in Francesca's face made him want to crawl away and hide. She'd backed away from him as though he were contaminated; as though his evilness might seep out from his pores and infect her, too. As though he were an untouchable.

Suddenly he felt that he might break down and weep. But instead he made his way unsteadily to the drinks cabinet and took out a bottle of whisky. As he unscrewed the cap he caught sight of himself in the mirror. His eyes were veined with red, his cheeks were flushed, his face was full of miserable fear. He looked unhealthy inside and out.

Pray, Francesca had said. Pray for forgiveness. Rupert clutched the bottle tighter. Lord, he tried. Lord God, forgive me. But the words weren't there; the will wasn't there. He didn't want to repent. He didn't want to be redeemed. He was a miserable sinner and he didn't care.

God hates me, thought Rupert, staring at his own reflection. God doesn't exist. Both seemed equally likely.

A bit later on Francesca came downstairs again. She had brushed her hair and washed her face and changed into jeans and a jersey. Rupert looked up from the sofa, where he was still sitting with his bottle of whisky. It was half empty, and his head was spinning but he didn't feel any happier.

'I've spoken to Tom,' said Francesca. 'He's coming round later.' Rupert's head jerked up.

'Tom?'

'I've told him everything,' said Francesca, her voice trembling. 'He says not to worry. He's known other cases like yours.' Rupert's head began to thump hard.

'I don't want to see Tom,' he said.

'He wants to help!'

'I don't want him to know! This is private!' Rupert felt a note of panic edging into his voice. He could just imagine Tom's face, looking at him with a mixture of pity and disgust. Tom would be revolted by him. They would all be revolted by him.

'He wants to help,' repeated Francesca. 'And darling . . .' Her tone changed and Rupert looked up in surprise. 'I just want to apologize. I was wrong to react so badly. I just panicked. Tom said that's perfectly normal. He said—' Francesca broke off and bit her lip. 'Anyway. We can get through this. With a lot of support and prayer . . .'

'Francesca—' began Rupert. She raised her hand.

'No, wait.' She came slowly forward, towards him. Rupert stared at her. 'Tom said I must try not to allow my own feelings to get in the way of our . . .' she paused '. . . of our physical love. I shouldn't have rejected you. I put my own selfish emotions first, and that was wrong

186

of me.' She swallowed. 'I'm sorry. Please forgive me.'

She edged even closer until she was standing inches from him.

'It's not up to me to hold back from you,' she whispered. 'You have every right to touch me. You're my husband. I promised before God to love you and obey you and give myself to you.'

Rupert gazed at her. He felt too shocked to speak. Slowly he reached out a hand and put it gently on her sleeve. A look of repulsion passed over her face, but she continued staring at him steadily, as though she was determined to see this through; as though she had no other choice.

'No!' said Rupert suddenly and pulled his hand away. 'I won't do this. This is wrong! Francesca, you're not a sacrificial lamb! You're a human!'

'I want to heal our marriage,' said Francesca in a shaking voice. 'Tom said—'

'Tom said if we went to bed then everything would be sorted, did he?' Rupert's voice was harsh with sarcasm. 'Tom told you to lie back and think of Jesus.'

'Rupert!'

'I won't allow you to subjugate yourself like that. Francesca, I love you! I respect you!'

'Well, if you love me and respect me,' said Francesca in suddenly savage tones, 'then why did you lie to me!' Her voice cracked. 'Why did you marry me, knowing what you were?'

'Francesca, I'm still me! I'm still Rupert!'

'You're not! Not to me!' Her eyes filled with tears. 'I

can't see you any more. All I can see is . . .' She gave a little shudder of disgust. 'It makes me sick to think about it.'

Rupert stared at her miserably.

'Tell me what you want me to do,' he said eventually. 'Do you want me to move out?'

'No,' said Francesca at once. 'No.' She hesitated. 'Tom suggested—'

'What?'

'He suggested,' she said, gulping slightly, 'a public confession. At the evening service. If you confess your sins aloud to the congregation and to God, then perhaps you'll be able to start afresh. With no more lies. No more sin.'

Rupert stared at her. Everything in his body resisted what she was proposing.

'Tom said you might not yet fully realize the wrong you'd done,' continued Francesca. 'But once you do, and once you've properly repented, then we'll be able to start again. It'll be a rebirth. For both of us.' She looked up and wiped the wetness from her eyes. 'What do you think? What do you think, Rupert?'

'I'm not going to repent,' Rupert found himself saying.

'What?' A look of shock came over Francesca's face.

'I'm not going to repent,' repeated Rupert shakily. He dug his nails into the palms of his hands. 'I'm not going to stand up in public and say that what I did was wicked.'

'But . . .'

188

'I loved Allan. And he loved me. And what we did wasn't evil or wicked. It was . . .' Tears suddenly smarted at Rupert's eyes. 'It was a beautiful, loving relationship. Whatever the Bible says.'

'Are you serious?'

'Yes,' said Rupert. He exhaled with a shudder. 'I wish, for both our sakes, that I wasn't. But I am.' He looked her straight in the eye. 'I don't regret what I did.'

'Well then, you're sick!' cried Francesca. A note of panic entered her voice. 'You're sick! You went with a man! How can that be beautiful? It's disgusting!'

'Francesca—'

'And what about me?' Her voice rose higher. 'What about when we were in bed together? All this time, have you been wishing you were with him?'

'No!' cried Rupert. 'Of course not.'

'But you said you loved him!'

'I did. But I didn't realize it at the time.' He stopped. 'Francesca, I'm sorry.'

She stared at him for a silent, aching moment, then backed away, reaching blindly for a chair.

'I don't understand,' she said in a subdued voice. 'Are you really homosexual? Tom said you weren't. He said lots of young men went the wrong way at first.'

'What would Tom know about it?' snapped Rupert. He felt trapped; as though he were being pinned into a corner.

'Well – are you?' persisted Francesca. 'Are you homosexual?'

There was a long pause.

'I don't know,' said Rupert at last. He sank down heavily onto a sofa and buried his head in his hands. 'I don't know what I am.'

When, after a few minutes, he looked up again, Francesca had disappeared. The birds were still twittering outside the window; cars were still roaring in the distance. Everything was the same. Nothing was the same.

Rupert stared down at his trembling hands. At the signet ring Francesca had given him for the wedding. With a sudden flash, he recalled the happiness he'd felt that day; the relief he'd experienced as, with a few simple words, he'd become part of the legitimate married masses. When he'd led Francesca out of the church, he'd felt as though he finally belonged; as though at last he was normal. Which was exactly what he wanted to be. He didn't want to be gay. He didn't want to be a minority. He just wanted to be like everybody else.

It had all happened just as Allan had predicted. Allan had understood; Allan had known exactly how Rupert felt. He'd watched as, over those late summer weeks, Rupert's feeling had gradually turned from ardour to embarrassment. He'd waited patiently as Rupert tried to abandon his company, ignoring him for days on end, only to succumb with more passion than ever before. He'd been sympathetic and supportive and understanding. And in return, Rupert had fled from him.

The seeds of his defection had been sown at the beginning of September. Rupert and Allan had been walking down Broad Street together, not quite holding hands, but brushing arms; talking closely, smiling the smiles of lovers. And then someone had called Rupert's name.

'Rupert! Hi!'

His head had jerked up. Standing on the other side of the road, grinning at him, was Ben Fisher, a boy from the year below at school. Suddenly Rupert had remembered his father's letter of a few weeks before. The wistful hope that Rupert might come home for some of the vacation; the triumphant news that another boy from the little Cornish school would soon be joining him at Oxford.

'Ben!' Rupert had exclaimed, hurrying across the street. 'Welcome! I heard you were coming.'

'I'm hoping you'll show me around the place,' Ben had replied, his dark eyes twinkling. 'And introduce me to some girls. You must have the whole place after you. Stud!' Then his eyes had swivelled curiously towards Allan, still standing on the other side of the road. 'Who's that?' he'd asked. 'A friend?'

Rupert's heart had given a little jump. Suddenly, with a flurry of panic, he saw himself in the eyes of his friends at home. His teachers. His father.

'Oh him?' he'd said after a pause. 'That's no-one. Just one of the tutors.'

The next night he'd gone to a bar with Ben, drunk Tequila slammers and flirted furiously with a couple of

191

pretty Italian girls. On his return, Allan had been waiting for him in his room.

'Good evening?' he'd said pleasantly.

'Yes,' Rupert had replied, unable to meet his gaze. 'Yes. I was with – with friends.' He'd stripped quickly, got into bed and closed his eyes as Allan came towards him; had emptied his mind of all thought or guilt as their physical delight had begun.

But the next night he'd gone out again with Ben, and this time had forced himself to kiss one of the pretty young girls who hung around him like kids round a sweet counter. She'd responded eagerly, encouraging his hands to roam over her soft, unfamiliar body. At the end of the evening she'd invited him back to the house she shared on the Cowley Road.

He'd undressed her slowly and clumsily, taking his cue from scenes in films, hoping her obvious experience would see him through. Somehow he'd managed to acquit himself successfully; whether her cries were real or false he didn't know and didn't care. The next morning he'd woken up in her bed, curled up against her smooth female skin, breathing in her feminine smell. He'd kissed her shoulder as he always kissed Allan's shoulder, reached out experimentally to touch her breast – and then realized with a sudden jolt of surprise that he felt aroused. He wanted to touch this girl's body. He wanted to kiss her. The thought of making love to her again excited him. He was normal. He could be normal.

'Are you running away from me?' Allan had said a

few days later, as they ate pasta together. 'Do you need some space?'

'No!' Rupert had replied, too heartily. 'Everything's fine.' Allan had looked silently at him for a moment, then put down his fork.

'Don't panic,' he said, reaching for Rupert's hand, then flinching as Rupert moved it away. 'Don't give up something that could be wonderful, just because you're scared.'

'I'm not scared!'

'Of course you're scared. Everyone's scared. *I'm* scared.'

'You?' Rupert had said, trying not to sound truculent. 'Why on earth are you scared?'

'I'm scared,' Allan had said slowly, 'because I understand what you're doing, and I know what it means for me. You're trying to escape. You're trying to discard me. In a few weeks you'll walk past me in the street and look away. Am I right?'

He'd gazed at Rupert with dark eyes asking for an answer, a rebuttal. But Rupert had said nothing. He hadn't had to.

After that, things had deteriorated swiftly. They'd had one final conversation in a deserted Keble College bar, the week before the new term began.

'I just can't . . .' Rupert had muttered, stiff with self-consciousness, one eye on the incurious gaze of the barman. 'I'm not—' He'd broken off and taken a deep gulp of whisky. 'You do understand.' He'd looked up pleadingly at Allan, then looked quickly away again.

'No,' Allan had said quietly, I don't understand. We were happy together.'

'It was a mistake. I'm not gay.'

'You're not attracted to me?' Allan had said, and his eyes had fixed on Rupert's. 'Is that what you're saying? You're not attracted to me?'

Rupert had gazed back at him, feeling as though something inside him were being wrenched in two. Waiting in a pub were Ben and a pair of girls. Tonight he would almost certainly have sex with one of them. But he wanted Allan more than he wanted any girl.

'No,' he said at last. 'I'm not.'

'Fine,' Allan had said, his dry voice cracking with anger. 'Lie to me. Lie to yourself. Get married. Have a kid. Play at being straight. But you'll know you're not, and I'll know you're not.'

'I am,' Rupert had retorted feebly, then wished he hadn't as Allan's eyes flashed with contempt.

'Whatever.' He'd drained his glass and got to his feet.

'Will you be all right?' Rupert had said, watching him.

'Don't patronize me,' Allan had snapped back fiercely. 'No I won't be all right. But I'll get over it.'

'I'm sorry.'

Allan had said nothing more. Rupert had watched silently as he made his way out of the bar; for a minute or two he could feel nothing but raw pain. But after two more whiskies he'd felt a little better. He'd gone to meet Ben in the pub as arranged, and had drunk a few pints and a good deal more whisky. Later that night, after having had sex with the prettier of the two girls Ben had procured, he'd lain awake and told himself repeatedly that he was normal; he was back on course; he was happy. And for a while, he'd almost managed to believe himself.

'Tom'll be here in a few minutes.' Francesca's voice interrupted his thoughts. Rupert looked up. She was standing at the door, holding a tray. On it was the cream-coloured teapot they'd chosen for their wedding list, together with cups, saucers and a plate of chocolate biscuits.

'Francesca,' said Rupert wearily. 'We're not holding a bloody tea party.' A look of shocked hurt passed over her face; then she composed herself and nodded.

'Perhaps you're right,' she said. She set the tray down on a chair. 'Perhaps this is a bit inappropriate.' Rupert stood up and walked slowly to the door. 'I'm not talking to Tom about my sexuality.'

'But he wants to help!'

'He doesn't.' Rupert looked at Francesca. 'He wants to channel. Not help.'

'I don't understand,' said Francesca, wrinkling her brow.

Rupert shrugged. For a few moments neither spoke. Then Francesca bit her lip.

'I was wondering,' she said hesitantly, 'if you should maybe see a doctor, as well. We could ask Dr Askew to recommend someone. What do you think?'

Rupert stared at her speechlessly. He felt as though she'd hit him in the face with a hammer.

195

'A doctor?' he echoed eventually, trying to sound calm. 'A *doctor*?'

'I thought—'

'You think there's something medically wrong with me?'

'No! I just meant . . .' Francesca flushed pink. 'Perhaps there's something they could give you.'

'An anti-gay pill?' He couldn't control his voice. Who was this girl he'd married? Who was she? 'Are you serious?'

'It's just an idea!'

For a few silent seconds, Rupert gazed at Francesca. Then, without speaking, he strode past her into the hall and snatched his jacket from the peg.

'Rupert!' she said. 'Where are you going?'

'I've got to get out of here.'

'But where!' cried Francesca. 'Where are you going?'

Rupert looked at his reflection in the hall mirror.

'I'm going,' he said slowly, 'to find Allan.'

TEN

Canon Lytton had asked for all the members of the family to be assembled in the drawing room, as though he were about to unmask a murderer in their midst.

'There are only the two of us,' Isobel had said scornfully. 'Would you like us to assemble? Or do you want to come back later?'

'Indeed no,' Canon Lytton had replied solemnly. 'Let us adjourn.'

Now he sat on the sofa, his cassock falling in dusty folds around him, his face stern and forbidding. I bet he practices that expression in the mirror, thought Isobel. To frighten Sunday school children with.

'I come here on a matter of some gravity,' he began. 'To be brief, I wish to ascertain the truth or otherwise of a piece of information which I have been given.'

'By whom?' said Isobel. Canon Lytton ignored her.

'It is my duty,' he said, raising his voice slightly, 'as

parish priest and official at the intended marriage of Milly and Simon, to check whether Milly, as she stated on the form she filled in, is a spinster of the parish of St Edward the Confessor, or whether – in fact, she is not. I will ask her myself when she returns. In the meantime, I would be grateful if you, as her mother, could answer on her behalf.' He stopped and looked impressively at Olivia, who wrinkled her brow.

'I don't understand,' she said. 'Are you asking if Milly and Simon live together? Because they don't, you know. They're quite old-fashioned like that.'

'That was not my question,' said Canon Lytton. 'My question, more simply, is: has Milly been married before?'

'Married before?' said Olivia. She gave a shocked little laugh. 'What are you talking about?'

'I have been given to believe—'

'What do you mean?' interrupted Olivia. 'Is someone saying Milly's been married before?' Canon Lytton inclined his head slightly. 'Well, they're lying! Of course Milly hasn't been married! How on earth can you believe such a thing?'

'It is my duty to follow up all such accusations.'

'What,' said Isobel, 'even if they come from complete crackpots?'

'I use my discretion,' said Canon Lytton, giving her a hard look. 'The person who told me this was quite insistent – and even claimed to have a copy of a marriage certificate.'

'Who was it?' said Isobel.

'That, I am not at liberty to say,' said Canon Lytton, rearranging his cassock carefully.

You love this, thought Isobel, gazing at him. You just love it.

'Jealousy!' said Olivia suddenly. 'That's what this is. Somebody's jealous of Milly, and they're trying to spoil her wedding. There must be a lot of disappointed girls out there. No wonder they're targeting poor Milly! Really, Canon Lytton, I'm surprised at you. Believing such scurrilous nonsense!'

'Scurrilous nonsense it may be,' said Canon Lytton. 'Nevertheless, I wish to speak to Milly herself on her return. In case there are facts pertaining to this matter with which you' – he nodded at Olivia – 'are not acquainted.'

'Canon Lytton,' said Olivia furiously. 'Are you seriously suggesting that my daughter might have got married without telling me? My daughter tells me everything!'

There was a small movement from the sofa, and both Olivia and Canon Lytton turned to look at Isobel.

'Would you like to say something, Isobel?' said Canon Lytton.

'No,' said Isobel quickly, and coughed. 'Nothing.'

'Who's she supposed to have married, anyway?' demanded Olivia. 'The postman?'

There was a short silence. Isobel glanced up, trying not to look too tense.

'A man named Kepinski,' said Canon Lytton, reading from a piece of paper. 'Allan Kepinski.'

Isobel's heart sank. Milly didn't have a hope.

'Allan Kepinski?' said Olivia incredulously. 'That's a made-up name, if ever I heard one! The whole thing's obviously a hoax. Set up by some poor character, obsessed by Milly's good fortune. You read about this sort of thing all the time. Don't you, Isobel?'

'Yes,' said Isobel weakly. 'All the time.'

'And now,' said Olivia, standing up, 'if you'll excuse me, Canon Lytton, I've a thousand things to do, and they don't include listening to made-up lies about my daughter. We do have a wedding on Saturday, you know!'

'I am aware of that fact,' said Canon Lytton. 'Nevertheless, I will need to speak to Milly about this. Perhaps later this evening will be convenient.'

'You can speak to her all you like,' said Olivia. 'But you're wasting your time!'

'I will return,' said Canon Lytton portentously. 'Permit me to see myself out.'

As the front door slammed behind him, Olivia looked at Isobel.

'Do you know what he's talking about?'

'No!' said Isobel. 'Of course not.'

'Isobel,' said Olivia sharply. 'You may have fooled Canon Lytton, but you don't fool me! You know something about this, don't you? Is something going on?'

'Look, Mummy,' said Isobel, trying to sound calm. 'I think we should just wait until Milly gets back.'

'Wait for what?' Olivia stared at her in dismay.

'Isobel, what are you saying? There's no truth in what Canon Lytton said, is there?'

'I'm not saying anything,' said Isobel stoutly. 'Not until Milly gets back.'

'I won't have you girls keeping secrets from me,' said Olivia angrily. Isobel sighed.

'To be honest, Mummy,' she said, 'it's a bit late for that.'

Milly was trudging back from the station when a car pulled up alongside her.

'Hello, darling,' said James 'Would you like a lift?'

'Oh,' said Milly. 'Thanks.'

Without meeting her father's eye, she got into the car and stared straight ahead at the darkening street, trying desperately to organize her thoughts. She had to decide what she was going to do. She had to come up with a plan. All the way back from London she had tried to think rationally; to form some sensible solution. But now here she was, back in Bath, minutes away from home, and she was still in a state of uncertainty. Could she really force Alexander to keep quiet! Already it was Thursday evening; the wedding was on Saturday. If she could just get through Friday . . .

'Did you have a good time in London?' said James. Milly jumped.

'Yes,' she said. 'Shopping. You know.'

'I do,' said James. 'Did you find anything nice?'

'Yes,' said Milly. There was a pause, and she realized

that she didn't have any shopping bags. 'I bought . . . cuff links for Simon.'

'Very nice. He said he would call for you later, by the way. After work.'

A spasm of nerves hit Milly in the stomach.

'Oh good,' she said, feeling sick. How could she face Simon? How could she even look him in the eye?

As they got out of the car she felt a sudden desire to run away, down the street, and never see anybody ever again. Instead, she followed her father up the steps to the front door.

'She's back!' She heard her mother's voice cry as the door opened. Olivia appeared in the hall. 'Milly,' she said in clipped, furious tones. 'What's all this nonsense?'

'All what nonsense?' said Milly apprehensively.

'All this nonsense about you being married?'

Milly felt a hammer-blow to her heart.

'What do you mean?' she said shakily.

'What's going on?' said James, following Milly into the hall. 'Olivia, are you all right?'

'No, I'm not all right,' said Olivia jerkily. 'Canon Lytton came to see us this afternoon.' She glanced over her shoulder. 'Didn't he, Isobel?'

'Yes,' said Isobel, coming out of the drawing room. 'He came to see us.' She pulled a quick face at Milly, and Milly stared back at her, feeling fear rising inside her like choking gas.

'What did he—'

'He had some ridiculous story about Milly,' said Olivia. 'He said she'd been married before!'

Milly didn't move. Her eyes flickered to Isobel and back again.

'Only Isobel doesn't seem to think it is so ridiculous!' said Olivia.

'Oh, really?' said Milly, looking at Isobel with scorching eyes.

'Mummy!' exclaimed Isobel, scandalized. 'That's not fair! Milly, honestly, I didn't say anything. I said we should wait till you got back.'

'Yes,' said Olivia. 'And now she's back. So one of you had better tell us what this is all about.' Milly looked from face to face.

'All right,' she said shakily. 'Just let me take off my coat.'

There was silence as she unwrapped her scarf, took off her coat, and hung them both up. She turned round and surveyed her audience.

'Maybe we should all have a drink,' she said.

'I don't want a drink!' exclaimed Olivia. 'I want to know what's going on. Milly, is Canon Lytton right? Have you been married before?'

'Just . . . just give me a minute to sit down,' said Milly desperately.

'You don't need a minute!' cried Olivia. 'You don't need a minute! What's the answer? Have you been married before or not? Yes or no, Milly? Yes or no?'

'Yes!' screamed Milly. 'I'm married! I've been married for ten years!'

Her words resonated round the silent hall. Olivia took a small pace back and clutched the stair banister.

'I got married when I was at Oxford,' Milly continued in a trembling voice. 'I was eighteen. It . . . it didn't mean anything. No-one knew. *No-one knew.* And I thought no-one would ever find out. I thought . . .' She broke off. 'Oh, what's the point?'

There was silence. Isobel glanced apprehensively at Olivia. Her face was an ugly scarlet; she seemed to be having trouble breathing.

'Are you serious, Milly?' she said eventually.

'Yes.'

'You really got married when you were eighteen. And you really thought that no-one would ever find out.'

There was a pause – then Milly nodded miserably.

'Then you're a stupid, stupid girl!' shrieked Olivia. Her voice lashed across the room like a whip, and Milly turned pale. 'You're a stupid, selfish girl! How could you have thought that no-one would find out? How could you have been so stupid? You've ruined everything for all of us!'

'Stop it!' said James angrily. 'Stop it, Olivia.'

'I'm sorry,' whispered Milly. 'I really am.'

'It's no good being sorry!' screamed Olivia. 'It's too late for sorry! How could you have done this to me?'

'Olivia!'

'I suppose you thought it was clever, did you? Getting married and keeping it a secret. I suppose you thought you were being frightfully grown-up.'

'No,' said Milly miserably.

'Who was he? A student?'

'A research fellow.'

'Swept you off your feet, did he? Promised you all sorts of things?'

'No!' shouted Milly, suddenly snapping. 'I married him to help him! He needed to stay in the country!'

Olivia stared at Milly, her expression gradually changing as she worked out what Milly was saying.

'You married an illegal immigrant?' she whispered. Her voice rose to a shriek. 'An illegal *immigrant*?'

'Don't say it like that!' said Milly.

'What sort of illegal immigrant?' A note of hysteria entered Olivia's voice. 'Did he threaten you?'

'For God's sake, Mummy!' said Isobel.

'Olivia,' said James. 'Calm down. You're not helping.'

'Helping?' Olivia turned on James. 'Why should I want to help? Do you realize what this means? We'll have to call the wedding off!'

'Postpone it, maybe,' said Isobel. 'Until the divorce comes through.' She pulled a sympathetic face at Milly.

'We can't!' cried Olivia desperately. 'It's all arranged! It's all organized!' She thought for a moment, then whipped round to Milly. 'Does Simon know about this?'

Milly shook her head. Olivia's eyes began to glitter.

'Well, then we can still go through with it,' she said quickly. Her eyes darted urgently from face to face. 'We'll fob Canon Lytton off! If none of us says a word, if we all hold our heads high . . .'

'Mummy!' exclaimed Isobel. 'You're talking about bigamy!'

'So what?'

205

'Olivia, you're mad,' said James in disgust. 'Obviously the wedding must be cancelled. And if you ask me, it's no bad thing.'

'What do you mean?' said Olivia hysterically. 'What do you mean, it's no bad thing? This is the most terrible thing that's ever happened to our family, and you're saying it's no bad thing!'

'Frankly, I think it would be good for us all to get back to normal!' exclaimed James angrily. 'This whole wedding has got out of hand. It's nothing but wedding, wedding, wedding! You talk of nothing else.'

'Well, someone has to organize it!' shrieked Olivia. 'Do you know how many things I've had to sort out?'

'Yes I do!' shouted James in exasperation. 'A thousand! Every day, you've got a thousand bloody things to do! You realize that's seven thousand things a week? What is this, Olivia? An expedition to the moon?'

'You just wouldn't understand,' said Olivia bitterly.

'The whole family's obsessed! I think it would be a very good thing for you, Milly, if you just got your feet back on the ground for a while.'

'What do you mean?' said Milly shakily. 'My feet are on the ground.'

'Milly, your feet are up with the birds! You've gone rushing into this marriage without considering what it means, without considering all the other options. I know Simon's a very attractive young man, I know his father's very rich . . .'

'That's got nothing to do with it!' Milly stared at

James with an ashen face. 'I love Simon! I want to marry him because I love him.'

'You think you do,' said James. 'But perhaps this is a good chance for you to wait for a while. See if you can stand on your own two feet, for a change. Like Isobel.'

'Like Isobel,' echoed Milly, in a disbelieving voice. 'You always want me to be Isobel. Perfect bloody Isobel.'

'Of course I don't,' said James impatiently. 'That's not what I said.'

'You want me to do the things that Isobel does.'

'Maybe,' said James. 'Some of them.'

'Daddy—' began Isobel.

'Well, fine!' screamed Milly, feeling blood rush to her head. 'I'll be like Isobel! I won't get married! I'll get pregnant instead!'

There was a sharp silence.

'Pregnant?' said Olivia incredulously.

'Thanks a lot, Milly,' said Isobel shortly, stalking to the front door.

'Isobel—' began Milly. But Isobel slammed the door behind her without looking back.

'Pregnant,' repeated Olivia. She groped for a chair and sat down.

'I didn't mean to say that,' muttered Milly, appalled at herself. 'Can you just forget I said it?'

'You're married,' said Olivia shakily. 'And Isobel's pregnant.' She looked up. 'Is she really pregnant?'

'That's her business,' said Milly, staring at the floor. 'It's her business. I shouldn't have said anything.'

The doorbell rang, jolting them all.

'That'll be Isobel,' said James, getting up. He opened the door and took a step back.

'Ah,' he said. 'It's you, Simon.'

Isobel strode along the pavement, not stopping, not looking back, not knowing where she was going. Her heart was thumping hard, and her jaw was set and tense. The snow had turned to slush; a cold drizzle was coating her hair and dripping down her neck. But with every step she felt a little better. With every step she was further into anonymity; further away from the shocked faces of her family.

Her whole body still prickled with anger. She felt betrayed, misrepresented, too furious with Milly to speak . . . and yet too sorry for her to blame her. She'd never witnessed such an ugly family scene, with Milly defenceless in the middle of it. No wonder she'd lashed out with the first diversionary tactic she had to hand. It was understandable. But that didn't make it any easier.

Isobel closed her eyes. She felt raw and vulnerable; unready for this. On her return, her parents would surely expect her to talk to them. They would expect her to answer questions, to reassure them and help them digest this piece of startling information. But she had barely digested it herself. Her condition was a nebulous fact floating around her mind, unwanted and unformed, as yet unpresentable to the outside world. She couldn't articulate what she thought about it; could no longer distinguish between emotional and physical sensation. Energy and optimism alternated with tear-fulness and the nausea made everything even worse. What does it feel like? Milly would no doubt ask. What does it feel like, to have a child inside you? But Isobel didn't want to answer that. She didn't want to think of herself as carrying a child.

She stopped at a corner and cautiously laid her hand over her stomach. When she imagined whatever was inside her, it was as a small shellfish, or a snail. Something coiled up and hardly human. Something indeterminate, whose life had not begun. Whose life might, if she chose, progress no further. A wave of strong feeling, half grief, half sickness, swept over her, and she began to tremble. The whole family, she thought, is concerned with whether Milly's wedding should go ahead or not. While I, all alone, am trying to decide whether another human's life should go ahead or not.

The thought transfixed her. She felt almost overcome by her burden, overwhelmed by the decision she was going to have to make, and for a moment she thought she might collapse, sobbing, on the hard pavement. But instead, with a slight impatient shake of the head, she thrust her hands deeper into her pockets and, teeth gritted, began once more to walk.

Simon and Milly sat, facing each other on armchairs in the drawing room, as though appearing on a television chat show.

'So,' said Simon finally. 'What is all this?'

Milly gazed at him silently. Her fingers shook as she pushed a frond of hair back from her face; her lips opened to speak, then closed again.

'You're making me nervous,' said Simon. 'Come on, sweetheart. Nothing's that bad. It's not life-threatening, is it?'

'No.'

'Well then.' He grinned at her, and Milly smiled back, feeling a sudden relief.

'You won't like it,' she said.

'I'll be brave,' said Simon. 'Come on, hit me with it.'

'OK,' said Milly. She took a deep breath. 'The thing is, we can't get married on Saturday. We're going to have to postpone the wedding.'

'Postpone?' said Simon slowly. 'Well, OK. But why?'

'There's something I haven't told you,' said Milly, meshing her hands together, twisting them around until her knuckles felt as though they might break. 'I did something very stupid when I was eighteen. I got married. It was a fake marriage. It didn't mean anything. But the divorce never went through. So I'm – I'm still married.'

She glanced at Simon. He looked bewildered but not angry, and she felt a sudden flood of reassurance. After her mother's hysterics, it was a relief to see Simon taking the news calmly. He wasn't freaking out; he wasn't yelling. But of course he wasn't. After all, this was nothing to do with their relationship, was it? This was nothing but a technical hitch.

'All it means is, I'll have to wait for the decree

absolute before we can get married,' she said. She bit her lip. 'Simon, I'm really sorry.'

There was a long silence.

'I don't get it,' said Simon eventually. 'Is this a joke?'

'No,' said Milly. 'No! God, I wish it was! It's true. I'm married. Simon, I'm married!'

She gazed at him miserably. His dark eyes scanned her face; slowly a look of disbelief crept over his features.

'You're serious.'

'Yes.'

'You're really married.'

'Yes. But it wasn't a proper marriage,' said Milly quickly. She stared down at the floor, trying to keep her voice steady. 'He was gay. The whole thing was fake. To keep him in the country. It honestly meant nothing. Less than nothing! You do understand, don't you? You do understand?'

She looked up at his face. And as she saw his expression she realized, with a thud of dismay, that he didn't.

'It was a mistake,' she said, almost tripping over the words in her haste. 'A big mistake. I see that now. I should never have agreed to do it. But I was very young, and very stupid, and he was a friend. Or at least I thought he was a friend. And he needed my help. That's all it was!'

'That's all it was,' echoed Simon in a strange voice. 'So, what, did this guy pay you?'

'No!' said Milly. 'I just did it as a favour!'

'You got married . . . as a favour?' said Simon incredulously. Milly stared at him in alarm. Somehow this was coming out all wrong.

'It meant nothing,' she said. 'It was ten years ago? I was a child. I know I should have told you about it before. I know I should. But I just . . .' She broke off and looked at him desperately. 'Simon, say something!'

'What am I supposed to say?' said Simon. 'Congratulations?' Milly winced.

'No! Just – I don't know. Tell me what you're thinking.'

'I don't know what to think,' said Simon. 'I don't even know where to start. I can't believe it. You tell me you're married to some other guy. What am I supposed to think? His glance fell on her left hand; on the finger wearing his engagement ring, and she flushed.

'It didn't mean anything,' she said. 'You have to believe that.'

'It doesn't matter what it meant! You're still married, aren't you?' Simon suddenly leapt up and stalked away to the window. 'Christ, Milly!' he exclaimed, his voice shaking slightly. 'Why didn't you tell me?'

'I don't know. I didn't . . .' She swallowed. 'I didn't want to spoil everything.'

'You didn't want to spoil everything,' echoed Simon. 'So you leave it until two days before our wedding to tell me you're married.'

'I thought it wouldn't matter! I thought—'

'You thought you wouldn't bother to tell me at all?' He turned round and gazed at her in sudden comprehension. 'You were never going to tell me! Am I right?'

'I didn't—'

'You were going to keep it a secret from me!' His voice rose. 'From your own husband!'

'No! I *was* intending to tell you!'

'When? On our wedding night? When our first child was born? On our golden anniversary?'

Milly opened her mouth to speak, then closed it again. She felt a hot fear creeping over her. She had never seen Simon angry like this before. She didn't know how to defuse him; which way to move.

'So, what other little secrets are you keeping from me? Any hidden children? Secret lovers?'

'No.'

'And how am I supposed to believe that?' His voice lashed across the room, and Milly flinched. 'How am I supposed to believe anything you say any more?'

'I don't know,' said Milly hopelessly. 'I don't know. You just have to trust me.'

'Trust you!'

'I know I should have told you,' she said desperately. 'I know that! But the fact that I didn't doesn't mean I'm keeping anything else secret from you. Simon—'

'It's not just that,' said Simon, cutting across her. 'It's not just the fact you kept it secret.' Milly's heart began to thump nervously.

'What is it, then?'

Simon sank into a chair and rubbed his face.

'Milly – you've already made the wedding vows to

someone else. You've already promised to love some-one else. Cherish someone else. Do you know what that feels like for me?'

'But I didn't mean a word of it! Not a word!'

'Exactly.' His voice chilled her. 'I thought you took those vows as seriously as I did.'

'I did,' said Milly in horror. 'I do.'

'How can you? You've spoiled them! You've tainted them.'

'Simon, don't look at me like that,' whispered Milly. 'I'm not evil! I made a mistake, but I'm still me. Nothing's changed!'

'Everything's changed,' said Simon flatly. There was a heavy silence. 'To be honest, I feel as if I don't know you any more.'

'Well, I feel as if I don't know *you* any more!' cried Milly in a sudden anguished burst. 'I don't know *you* any more! Simon, I know I've messed the wedding up. I know I've fucked things up completely. But you don't have to be so sanctimonious. You don't have to look at me as if I'm beneath contempt. I'm not a criminal!' She gulped. 'Well, maybe I am, technically. But only because I made a mistake. I made one mistake! And if you loved me, you'd forgive me!' She began to shake with sobs. 'If you really loved me, you would forgive me!'

'And if you really loved me,' shouted Simon, suddenly looking distraught, 'you would have told me you were married! You can say what you like, Milly, but if you'd really loved me, you would have told me!'

Milly stared at him, suddenly feeling unsure of herself.

'Not necessarily,' she faltered.

'Well, we must have different definitions of love,' said Simon. 'Perhaps we've been at cross purposes all along.' He stood up and reached for his coat. Milly stared at him, feeling a horrified disbelief creep over her.

'Are you saying' – she fought a desire to retch – 'are you saying you don't want to marry me any more?'

'As I recall,' said Simon stiffly, 'you've already got a husband. So the question's academic really, isn't it?' He paused at the door. 'I hope the two of you will be very happy.'

'Bastard!' screamed Milly. Tears blurred her eyes as she tugged feverishly at her engagement ring. By the time she managed to throw it at him, the door was closed and he was gone.

ELEVEN

Isobel arrived back to find the house quiet. The lights in the hall were dim; there was no-one in the drawing room. She pushed open the kitchen door and saw Olivia sitting at the table in half-light. A bottle of wine was in front of her, nearly empty; music was playing quietly in the corner. As Olivia heard the sound of the door she looked up with a pale, puffy face.

'Well,' she said flatly. 'It's all over.'

'What do you mean?' said Isobel suspiciously.

'I mean,' said Olivia, 'that the engagement between Milly and Simon is off.'

'What?' said Isobel. She blinked at her mother, aghast. 'Do you mean off completely? Why?'

'They had some sort of row – and Simon called the whole thing off.' Olivia took a slug of wine.

'What about? Her first marriage?'

'I imagine so,' said Olivia. 'She wouldn't say.'

'Where is she?'

'She's gone to Esme's for the night. She said she had to get away from this house. From all of us.'

'I don't blame her,' said Isobel. She sat heavily down on a chair, her coat still on. 'God, poor Milly. I can't believe it! What exactly did Simon say?'

'Milly didn't tell me. She doesn't tell me anything these days.' Olivia took a deep swig of wine. 'Obviously, I'm no longer considered worthy of her confidence.'

Isobel rolled her eyes.

'Mummy, don't start.'

'For ten years she was married to that – that illegal immigrant! Ten years without telling me!'

'She couldn't tell you. How on earth could she tell you?'

'And then, when she was in trouble, she went to Esme.' Olivia raised bloodshot eyes to Isobel. 'To Esme Ormerod!'

'She always goes to Esme,' said Isobel.

'I know she does. She goes running off to that house and comes back thinking she's the Queen of Sheba!'

'Mummy—'

'And then she went to you.' Olivia's voice grew higher. 'Didn't it ever occur to her to come to me? Her own mother?'

'She couldn't!' exclaimed Isobel. 'She knew how you would react. And, frankly, she didn't need that. She needed calm, rational advice.'

'I'm incapable of being rational, am I?'

'When it comes to this wedding,' said Isobel, 'then yes. Yes, you are!'

'Well, there isn't going to be a wedding now,' said Olivia jerkily. 'There isn't going to be a wedding. So perhaps you'll all start to trust me again. Perhaps you'll start to treat me like a human being.'

'Oh, Mummy, stop feeling sorry for yourself!' shouted Isobel, suddenly exasperated. 'This wasn't your wedding. It was Milly's wedding!'

'I know that!' said Olivia indignantly.

'You don't,' said Isobel. 'You're not really thinking about Milly and Simon. You're not thinking about how they must be feeling. You don't even really care if they stay together or not. All you're thinking about is the wedding. The flowers that will have to be cancelled, and your lovely smart outfit that no-one will see, and how you won't get to dance with Harry Pinnacle! Beyond that, you couldn't give a damn!'

'How dare you!' exclaimed Olivia, and two bright spots appeared on her cheeks.

'It's true though, isn't it? No wonder Daddy—'

'No wonder Daddy what?' snapped Olivia.

'Nothing,' said Isobel, aware she had stepped over a boundary. 'I just . . . I can see his point of view. That's all.'

There was a long silence. Isobel blinked a few times in the dim kitchen light. She suddenly felt drained, too tired for argument; too tired even to stand up.

'Right,' she said with an effort. 'Well, I think I'll go to bed.'

'Wait,' said Olivia, looking up. 'You haven't eaten anything.'

'It's all right,' said Isobel. 'I'm not hungry.'

'That's not the point,' said Olivia. 'You need to eat.'

Isobel gave a noncommittal shrug.

'You need to eat,' repeated Olivia. She met Isobel's eyes. 'In your condition.'

'Mummy – not now,' said Isobel wearily.

'We don't have to talk about it,' said Olivia in a voice tinged with hurt. 'You don't have to tell me anything if you don't want to. You can keep all the secret you like.' Isobel looked away uncomfortably. 'Just let me make you some nice scrambled eggs.'

There was a pause.

'OK,' said Isobel at last. 'That would be nice.'

'And I'll pour you a nice glass of wine.'

'I can't,' said Isobel, taken unawares.

'Why not?'

Isobel was silent, trying to sort out the contrary strands of thought in her brain. She couldn't drink, just in case she decided to keep the baby. What kind of a twisted logic was that?

'All that phooey!' Olivia was saying. 'I was on three gins a day when I had you. And you turned out all right, didn't you? More or less?'

A reluctant smile spread over Isobel's face.

'OK,' she said. 'I could do with a drink.'

'So could I,' said Olivia. 'Let's open another bottle.' She closed her eyes. 'I've never known such a dreadful night.'

'Tell me about it.' Isobel sat down at the table. 'I hope Milly's OK.'

'I'm sure Esme will look after her,' said Olivia, and a touch of bitterness edged her voice.

Milly sat in Esme's drawing room, nestling a hot, creamy drink made from Belgian chocolate flakes and a splash of Cointreau. Esme had persuaded her to take a long, hot bath, scented with mysterious potions in unmarked bottles, then lent her a white waffle-weave bathrobe and some snug slippers. Now she was brushing Milly's hair with an old-fashioned bristle hairbrush. Milly stared ahead into the crackling fire, feeling the pull of the brush on her scalp, the heat of the fire on her face, the smoothness of her clean skin inside her robe. She'd arrived at Esme's an hour or so ago; had burst into tears as soon as the door was opened and again in her bath. But now she felt strangely calm. She took another sip of the hot, creamy chocolate and closed her eyes.

'Feeling better?' said Esme in a low voice.

'Yes. A lot better.'

'Good.'

There was a pause. One of the whippets rose from its place by the fire, came over to Milly and nestled its head in her lap.

'You were right,' said Milly, stroking the whippet's head. 'You were right. I don't know Simon. He doesn't know me.' Her voice trembled slightly. 'The whole thing's hopeless.'

Esme said nothing, but continued brushing.

'I know I'm to blame for all of this,' said Milly. 'I know that. It's me that got married, it's me that messed up. But he behaved as though I'd done it all on purpose. He didn't even *try* to see it from my point of view.'

'Such a masculine trait,' said Esme. 'Women twist themselves into loops to accommodate the views of others. Men turn their heads once, then look back and carry on as before.'

'Simon didn't even turn his head,' gulped Milly miserably. 'He didn't even listen.'

'Typical,' said Esme. 'Just another intractable man.'

'I feel so stupid,' said Milly. 'So bloody stupid.' A fresh stream of tears suddenly began to spill over onto her face. 'How could I have wanted to marry him? He said I'd tainted the wedding vows. He said he couldn't believe anything I said any more. He looked at me as if I was some kind of monster!'

'I know,' said Esme soothingly.

'All this time we've been together,' said Milly, wiping her eyes, 'we haven't really got to know each other, have we? Simon doesn't know me at all! And how can you marry someone if you don't know them? How can you? We should never have got engaged. All along, it's just been—' She suddenly broke off, with a new thought. 'Do you remember when he asked me to marry him? He had it all planned, the way he wanted it. He led me to this bench in his father's garden, and he had a diamond ring all ready in his pocket, and he'd even put a bloody bottle of champagne in the tree stump!'

'Darling—'

'But none of that was to do with me, was it? It was all to do with him. He wasn't thinking about me, even then.'

'Just like his father,' said Esme, with a sudden edge to her voice. Milly turned slightly in surprise.

'Do you know Harry, then?'

'I used to,' said Esme, brushing more briskly. 'Not any more.'

'I always thought Harry was quite nice,' gulped Milly. 'But then, what the hell do I know? I was completely wrong about Simon, wasn't I?' Her shoulders began to shake with sobs, and Esme stopped brushing.

'Darling, why don't you go to bed,' she suggested. She gathered Milly's hair into a blond tassle and let it fall. 'You're overwrought, you're tired, you need a good night's sleep. Remember, you were up early; you've been to London and back. It's been quite a day.'

'I won't be able to sleep,' Milly looked up at Esme with tear-stained cheeks, like a child.

'You will,' replied Esme calmly. 'I put a little something into your drink. It should kick in soon.'

'Oh,' said Milly, in surprise. She stared into her mug for a moment, then drained it. 'Do you give drugs to all your guests?'

'Only the very special ones,' said Esme, and gave Milly a serene smile.

* * *

As she finished the last of her scrambled eggs, Isobel sighed and leaned back in her chair.

'That was delicious. Thank you.' There was no response. She looked up. Olivia was drooping forward over her wine glass, her eyes closed. 'Mummy?'

Olivia's eyes flicked open.

'You've finished,' she said in a dazed voice. 'Would you like some more?'

'No thanks,' said Isobel. 'Look, Mummy, why don't you go to bed? We'll have a lot to do in the morning.'

For a moment, Olivia stared at her blankly; then, as though suddenly jolted, she nodded.

'Yes,' she said. 'You're right.' She sighed. 'You know, just for a moment, I'd forgotten.'

'Got to bed,' repeated Isobel. 'I'll clear up.'

'But you—'

'I'm fine,' said Isobel firmly. 'And anyway, I want to make a cup of tea. Go on.'

'Well, goodnight then,' said Olivia.

'Goodnight.'

Isobel watched as her mother left the room, then got up and filled the kettle. She was leaning against the sink, looking out into the dark, silent street, when suddenly there was the sound of a key in the lock.

'Milly?' she said. 'Is that you?'

A moment later, the kitchen door opened and a strange young man came in. He was wearing a denim jacket and carrying a large bag and looked scruffier than most of the bed and breakfasters. Isobel stared at him curiously for an instant. Then, with a sudden start, she realized who he must be. A hot, molten fury began to rise inside her. So this was him. This was Alexander. The cause of it all.

'Well, hello,' he said, dumping his bag on the floor and grinning insouciantly. 'You must be multilingual, multi-talented Isobel.'

'I don't know how you dare come back in here,' said Isobel softly, trying to control her voice. 'I don't know how you have the nerve.'

'I'm brave like that.' Alexander came close to her. 'They didn't tell me you were beautiful, too.'

'Get away from me,' spat Isobel.

'That's not very friendly.'

'Friendly! You expect me to be friendly? After everything you've done to my sister?' Alexander looked up and grinned.

'So you know her little secret, do you?'

'The whole world knows her little secret, thanks to you!'

'What do you mean?' said Alexander innocently. 'Has something happened?'

'Let me think,' said Isobel sarcastically. 'Has something happened? Oh yes. The wedding's been cancelled. But I expect you already knew that.'

Alexander stared at her.

'You're joking.'

'Of course I'm not bloody joking!' cried Isobel. 'The wedding's off. So congratulations, Alexander, you've achieved your aim. You've fucked up Milly's life completely. Not to mention the rest of us.'

'Jesus Christ!' Alexander ran a shaking hand through his hair. 'Look, I never meant—'

'No?' said Isobel furiously. 'No? Well, you should have thought of that before you opened your big mouth. I mean, what did you *think* would happen?'

'Not this! Not this, for Christ's sake! Why the hell did she call off the wedding?'

'She didn't,' said Isobel. 'Simon did.'

'What?' Alexander looked at her. 'Why?'

'I think that's their business, don't you?' said Isobel in a harsh voice. 'Let's just say that if no-one had said anything about her first marriage, everything would still be OK. If you'd just kept quiet . . .' She broke off. 'Oh, what's the point? You're a fucking psychopath.'

'I'm not!' said Alexander. 'Jesus! I never wanted anyone to cancel any wedding. I just wanted to—'

'To what? What did you want?'

'Nothing!' said Alexander. 'I was just . . . stirring things a little.'

'God, you're pathetic!' said Isobel, staring at him. 'You're just a pathetic, inadequate bully!' She looked at his bag. 'You needn't think you're staying here tonight.'

'But my room's booked!'

'And now it's bloody well unbooked,' said Isobel, kicking his bag towards the door. 'Do you know what you've done to my family? My mother's in shock, my sister's in tears . . .'

'Look, I'm sorry, OK!' said Alexander, picking up his bag. 'I'm sorry your sister's wedding's off. But you can't blame me!'

'We can, and we do,' said Isobel, opening the front door. 'Now get out!'

'But I didn't do anything!' exclaimed Alexander angrily, stepping outside. 'I just make a few jokes!'

'You call telling the vicar a fucking *joke*?' said Isobel furiously, and as Alexander opened his mouth to reply, she slammed the door.

Olivia walked up the stairs slowly, feeling a flat, dull sadness creep over her. The adrenalin of the early evening was gone; she felt weary and disappointed and prone to tears. It was all over. The goal to which she'd been working all this time had suddenly been lifted away, leaving nothing in its place.

No-one else would ever understand quite how much of herself she'd put into Milly's wedding. Perhaps that had been her mistake. Perhaps she should have stood back, let Harry's people take over with their cool efficiency, and merely turned up on the day, groomed and politely interested. Olivia sighed. She couldn't have done it. She couldn't have watched as someone else put together her daughter's wedding. So she'd gathered herself up and taken the job on and spent many hours planning and thinking and organizing. And now she would never see the fruits of all her labour.

Isobel's accusing voice rang in her ears and she winced. Somewhere along the line she had become at cross purposes with the rest of the family. Somehow she had become vilified for wanting everything to be just so. Perhaps James was right; perhaps it had become an obsession. But she had only wanted everything to be perfect for Milly. For all of them. And now no-one would ever realize that. They wouldn't see the results. They wouldn't experience the joyous, lavish day she'd planned. They would just remember all the fuss.

She stopped at Milly's bedroom door, which was slightly ajar, and found herself walking in. Milly's wedding dress was still hanging up in its cotton cover on the wardrobe door. When she closed her eyes, Olivia could still see Milly's face as she tried it on for the first time. It had been the seventh dress she'd tried; both of them had known immediately that this was the one. They'd stared silently in the mirror, then, meeting Milly's eye, Olivia had said slowly, 'I think we'll have to have it. Don't you?'

Milly's measurements had been taken and somewhere in Nottingham the dress had carefully been made up again. Over the last few weeks it had been fitted again and again to Milly's figure. And now she would never wear it. Unable to stop herself, Olivia unzipped the wrapper, pulled out a little of the heavy satin and stared at it. From inside the cotton cover, a tiny iridescent pearl glinted at her. It was a truly beautiful dress. Olivia sighed, and before she could descend into maudlin grief, reached for the zip to close the wrapper again.

James, walking past the door, saw Olivia gazing mournfully at Milly's wedding dress and felt a stab of irritation. He stalked into Milly's room without pausing.

'For God's sake, Olivia,' he said brutally. 'The wedding's off! It's off! Haven't you got that into your head yet?'

Olivia's head jerked up in shock and her hands began to tremble as she stuffed the dress back into its cover.

'Of course I have,' she said. 'I was just—'

'Just wallowing in self-pity,' said James sarcastically. 'Just thinking about your perfectly organized wedding, which is now never going to happen.'

Olivia zipped up the cover and turned round.

'James, why are you behaving as though all this is my fault?' she said shakily. 'Why am I suddenly the villain? I didn't push Milly into marriage. I didn't force her to have a wedding! She wanted one! All I did was to organize it for her as best I could.'

'Organize it for yourself, you mean!'

'Maybe,' said Olivia. 'Partly. But what's so wrong with that?'

'Oh, I give up,' said James, his face white with anger. 'I can't get through to you!' Olivia stared at him.

'I don't understand you, James,' she said. 'I just don't understand. Weren't you ever happy that Milly was getting married?'

'I don't know,' said James. He walked stiffly over to the window. 'Marriage. What the hell has marriage got to offer a young girl like Milly?'

'Happiness,' said Olivia after a pause. 'A happy life with Simon.' James turned round and gave her a curious expression.

'You think marriage brings happiness, do you?'

'Of course I do!'

'Well, you must be a bigger optimist than I am.' He leaned back against the radiator, hunched his shoulders, and surveyed her with unreadable eyes.

'What do you mean?' said Olivia in a trembling voice. 'James, what are you talking about?'

'What do you think I'm talking about?' said James.

The room seemed to ring with a still silence.

'Just look at us, Olivia,' said James at last. 'An old married couple. Do we give each other happiness? Do we support each other? We haven't grown together over the years. We've grown apart.'

'No we haven't!' said Olivia in alarm. 'We've been very happy together!'

James shook his head.

'We've been happy separately. You have your life and I have mine. You have your friends and I have mine. That's not what marriage is about.'

'We don't have separate lives,' said Olivia, a throb of panic in her voice.

'Oh come on, Olivia!' exclaimed James. 'Admit it. You're more interested in your bed and breakfast guests than you are in me!'

'No I'm not,' said Olivia, flushing.

'Yes you are. They come first, I come second. Along with the rest of the family.'

'That's not fair!' cried Olivia at once. 'I run the bed and breakfast *for* our family! To give us holidays. Little luxuries. You know that!'

'Well, perhaps other things are more important,' said James. Olivia looked at him uncertainly.

'Are you saying you want me to give up the bed and breakfast?'

'No!' said James impatiently. 'I just . . .'

'What?'

There was a long pause. Eventually James sighed. 'I suppose,' he said slowly, 'I just want you to need me.'

'I do need you,' said Olivia in a small voice.

'Do you?' A half-smile came to James's lips. 'Olivia, when was the last time you confided in me? When was the last time you asked my advice?'

'You wouldn't be interested in anything I've got to say!' cried Olivia defensively. 'Whenever I tell you anything, you get bored. You start to look out of the window. Or you read the paper. You behave as though nothing I've got to say is of any importance. And anyway, what about you? You never confide in me, either!'

'I try to!' said James angrily. 'But you never bloody listen! You're always rabbiting on about the wedding. The wedding this, the wedding that. And before the wedding there was always something else. Rabbit, rabbit, rabbit! It drives me mad.'

There was silence.

'I know I run on a bit,' said Olivia at last. 'My friends tell me. They say "Pipe down, Olivia, let someone else speak." And I pipe down.' She gulped. 'But you've never said anything. You never seem to care one way or the other.'

James rubbed his face wearily. 'Perhaps I don't,' he

said. 'Perhaps I've got beyond caring. All I know is . . .'
He paused. 'I can't go on like this.'

The words resounded round the tiny room like gas from a canister. Olivia felt the colour drain from her cheeks and a slow, frightening thud begin like a death-knell in her stomach.

'James,' she said, before he could continue. 'Please. Not tonight.'

James looked up and felt a jolt as he saw Olivia. Her cheeks were ashen, her lips were trembling, and her eyes were full of a deep dread.

'Olivia—' he began.

'If you have something you want to say to me –' Olivia swallowed '– then please don't say it tonight.' She began to back jerkily away, not looking him in the eye. 'Not tonight,' she whispered, and groped behind her for the door handle. 'I just . . . I just couldn't bear anything more tonight.'

Rupert sat at his desk in chambers, staring out of the window at the dark, silent night. On the desk in front of him was a list of phone numbers, some now crossed out or amended; some newly scribbled down. He'd spent the last two hours on the phone, talking to people he'd thought he would never speak to again. An old friend of Allan's from Keble, now at Christ Church. An old tutorial partner of his, now working in Birmingham. Half-remembered acquaintances, friends of friends, names he couldn't even put to faces. No-one knew where Allan was.

But this last phone call had given him hope. He'd spoken to an English professor at Leeds, who had known Allan at Manchester.

'He left Manchester suddenly,' he'd said.

'So I gather,' said Rupert, who had already jotted this information down three or four times. 'Do you have any idea where he went?' There was a pause.

'Exeter,' the professor said eventually. 'That's right. Exeter. I know, because around a year later, he wrote to me and asked me to send him a book. The address was Exeter. I may even have typed it into my electronic organizer.'

'Could you . . .' Rupert had said, hardly daring to hope. 'Do you think . . .'

'Here we are,' the professor had said. 'St David's House.'

'What's that?' said Rupert, staring at the address. 'A college?'

'I haven't heard of it,' the professor had replied. 'Perhaps it's a new hall of residence.'

Rupert had put the phone down and immediately called Directory Enquiries. Now he looked at the telephone number written in front of him. slowly he picked up the phone and tapped it in. Perhaps Allan would still be there. Perhaps he would answer the phone himself. A strong pounding began in Rupert's chest; his fingers felt slippery around the telephone receiver. He felt almost sick with apprehension.

'Hello?' A young male voice answered. 'St David's House.'

'Hello,' said Rupert, gripping the receiver tightly. 'I'd like to speak to Allan Kepinski, please.'

'Just a second, please.'

There was a long silence, then another young male voice came on the line.

'You wanted to speak to Allan.'

'Yes.'

'May I ask who's calling?'

'My name's Rupert.'

'Rupert Carr?'

'Yes,' said Rupert. His hand gripped the receiver tightly. 'Is Allan there?'

'Allan left St David's House five years ago,' said the young man. 'He went back to the States.'

'Oh,' said Rupert. 'Oh.' He gazed blankly at the phone. It had never even occurred to him that Allan would go back to the States.

'Rupert, are you in London?' the young man was saying. 'Could we meet up tomorrow by any chance? Allan left a letter for you.'

'Really?' said Rupert. 'For me?' His heart began to pound in sudden exhilaration. It wasn't too late. Allan still wanted him. He would call him up; he would fly to the States if need be. And then—

Suddenly his attention was distracted by a sound at the door, and his head jerked up. Standing in the doorway, watching him, was Tom. Rupert's cheeks began to flush red.

'Mangetout on Drury Lane. At twelve,' the young man

was saying. 'I'll be wearing black jeans. My name's Martin, by the way.'

'OK,' said Rupert hurriedly. 'Bye, Martin.'

He put the phone down and looked at Tom. Humiliation began to creep slowly through him.

'Who's Martin?' said Tom pleasantly? 'A friend of yours?'

'Go away,' said Rupert. 'Leave me alone.'

'I've been with Francesca,' said Tom. 'She's very upset. As you can imagine.' He sat down casually on Rupert's desk and picked up a brass paperweight. 'This little outburst of yours has quite thrown her.'

'But it hasn't thrown you,' said Rupert aggressively.

'As a matter of fact,' said Tom, 'it hasn't. I've come across this kind of confusion before.' He smiled at Rupert. 'You're not alone. I'm with you. Francesca's willing to stand by you. We'll all help you.'

'Help me with what? Repent? Confess in public?'

'I understand your anger,' said Tom. 'It's a form of shame.'

'It's not! I'm not ashamed!'

'Whatever you've done in the past can be wiped clean,' said Tom. 'You can start again.'

Rupert stared at Tom. Into his mind came his house; his life with Francesca, his comfortable, happy existence. Everything he could have once more if he lied about just one thing.

'I can't,' he said. 'I just can't. I'm not who you all think I am. I was in love with a man. Not misguided, not led astray. In love.'

234

'Platonic love—'

'Not platonic love!' cried Rupert. 'Sexual love! Can't you understand that, Tom? I loved a man sexually.'

'You committed acts with him.'

'Yes.'

'Acts which you know to be abhorrent to the Lord.'

'We didn't do anybody any harm!' cried Rupert desperately. 'We did nothing wrong!'

'Rupert!' exclaimed Tom, standing up. 'Can you hear yourself? Of course you did yourself harm. You did yourself the gravest harm. You committed perhaps the most odious sin known to mankind! You can wipe it clean – but only if you repent. Only if you acknowledge the evil which you've done.'

'It wasn't evil,' said Rupert in a shaking voice. 'It was beautiful.'

'In the eyes of the Lord,' said Tom coldly, 'it was repugnant. Repugnant!'

'It was love!' cried Rupert. He stood up, so that his eyes were level with Tom's. 'Can't you understand that?'

'No,' snapped Tom. 'I'm afraid I can't.'

'You can't understand how two men could possibly love each other.'

'No!'

Slowly Rupert leaned forward. Fronds of his hair touched Tom's forehead.

'Are you really repulsed by the idea?' he whispered. 'Or just afraid of it?'

Like a cat, Tom leapt backwards.

'Get away from me!' he shouted, his face contorted with disgust. 'Get away!'

'Don't worry,' said Rupert. 'I'm going.'

'Where?'

'Do you care, Tom? Do you really care?'

There was silence. With trembling hands, Rupert picked up his papers and thrust them into his briefcase. Tom watched him without moving.

'You know you're damned,' he said, as Rupert picked up his coat. 'Damned to hell.'

'I know,' said Rupert. And without looking back he opened the door and walked out.

TWELVE

Isobel woke to a thumping headache and grey-green nausea. She lay perfectly still, trying to keep calm; trying to exercise mind over matter – until a sudden urge to throw up propelled her from her bed, out of her bedroom door and across the hall to the bathroom.

'It's a hangover,' she told the bathroom mirror. But her reflection looked unconvinced. She rinsed out her mouth, sat down on the side of the bath and rested her head on her hand. Another day older. Another day more developed. Perhaps it had features by now. Perhaps it had little hands, little toes. It was a boy. Or a girl. A little person. Growing inside her; looking forward to life.

Another wave of sickness swept through her and she clamped her hand to her mouth. She felt ill with indecision. She couldn't come to a conclusion, couldn't even shape the arguments within her mind. Rationality battled with urges she'd never known she had; with every day her mind seemed to weaken a little. The obvious decision now seemed less obvious; the logical views she'd once readily espoused seemed to be crumbling under a sea of foolish emotion.

She stood up, tottering slightly, and walked slowly back onto the landing. There were sounds coming from the kitchen and she decided to go down and make herself a cup of tea. James was standing by the Aga as she walked in, dressed in his work suit and reading the paper.

'Morning,' he said. 'Cup of tea?'

'I'd love one,' said Isobel. She sat down at the table and studied her fingers. James put a mug of tea in front of her and she took a sip, then frowned. 'I think I'll have some sugar in this.'

'You don't normally take sugar,' said James in surprise.

'No,' said Isobel. 'Well. Maybe I do now.' She heaped two spoons of sugar into her mug, then sipped pleasurably, feeling the hot sweetness seep slowly through her body.

'So,' said James. 'Milly was right.'

'Yes.' Isobel stared down into the milky browness of her tea. 'Milly was right.'

'And the father?'

Isobel said nothing.

'I see.' James cleared his throat. 'Have you decided what you're going to do? I suppose it's early days, still.'

'Yes, it is early days. And no, I haven't decided.' Isobel

looked up. 'I suppose you think I should get rid of it, don't you? Forget it ever happened and resume my glittering career.'

'Not necessarily,' said James, after a pause. 'Not unless—'

'My exciting career,' said Isobel bitterly. 'My wonderful life of aeroplanes and hotel rooms and foreign businessmen trying to chat me up because I'm always on my own.' James stared at her.

'Don't you enjoy your work? I thought – we all thought – you enjoyed it.'

'I do,' said Isobel, 'most of the time. But sometimes I get lonely and sometimes I get tired and sometimes I feel like giving up for ever. Just like most people.' She took a sip of tea. 'Sometimes I wish I'd just got married and had three kids and lived in divorced bliss.'

'I had no idea, darling,' said James, frowning. 'I thought you liked being a career girl.'

'I'm not a career girl,' said Isobel, putting down her mug loudly. 'I'm a person. With a career.'

'I didn't mean—'

'You did!' said Isobel exasperatedly. 'That's all you think I am, isn't it? My career and nothing else. You've forgotten all about the rest of me.'

'No!' said James. 'I wouldn't forget about the rest of you.'

'Yes you would,' said Isobel. 'Because I do. Frequently.'

There was a pause. Isobel reached for a packet of cornflakes, looked inside, sighed and put it down.

James took a final sip of tea then reached for his briefcase.

'I must go, I'm afraid.'

'You're really going to work today?'

'I don't have much choice. There's a lot going on at the moment. If I don't show my face, I may find my job gone tomorrow.'

'Really?' Isobel looked up, shocked.

'Not really.' James gave her a half-grin. 'Nevertheless, I do have to go in.'

'I'm sorry,' said Isobel. 'I had no idea.'

'No,' said James. 'Well.' He paused. 'You weren't to know. I haven't been exactly forthcoming about it.'

'I suppose there's been enough going on at home.'

'You could say that,' said James. Isobel grinned at him.

'I bet you're glad to get away from it all, really.'

'I'm not getting away from anything,' said James. 'Harry Pinnacle's already been on the phone to me this morning, requesting a meeting at lunchtime. No doubt to talk about the costs of this whole fiasco.' He pulled a face. 'Harry Pinnacle snaps his fingers and the rest of the world has to jump.'

'Oh well,' said Isobel. 'Good luck.'

By the door, James paused.

'Who would you have married, anyway?' he said. 'And had your three kids with?'

'I dunno,' said Isobel. 'Who was I going out with? Dan Williams, I suppose.' James groaned.

'Darling, I think you made the right choice.' He

suddenly stopped himself. 'I mean – the baby isn't . . .'

'No,' said Isobel, giggling in spite of herself. 'Don't worry. It's not his.'

Simon woke feeling shattered. His head ached, his eyes were sore, his chest felt heavy with misery. From behind the curtains was coming a sparkling shaft of winter sunlight; from downstairs wafted the mingled smells of the wood fire burning in the hall and freshly ground coffee in the breakfast room. But nothing could soothe his grief, his disappointment and, above all, his sharp sense of failure.

The angry words he had spat at Milly the night before still circled his mind with as much clarity as though he had uttered them only five minutes ago. Like a scene learned from a play. A scene which, it now seemed, he should in some way have predicted. A stab of mortified pain hit him in the chest, and he turned over, burying his head under the pillow. Why hadn't he seen this coming? Why had he ever let himself believe he could achieve a happy marriage? Why couldn't he just accept the fact that he was an all-round failure? He'd failed dismally at business and now he'd failed at marriage, too. At least, thought Simon bitterly, his father had actually made it to the altar. At least his father hadn't been let down, two nights before his bloody wedding day.

An image came to him of Milly's face the night before: red, tear-stained, desperate with unhappiness. And for a moment he felt himself weakening. For a moment he felt like calling her up. Telling her he still loved her, that he still wanted to marry her. He would kiss her poor swollen lips; take her to bed; try to forget all that was past. The temptation was there. If he was honest with himself, the temptation was huge.

But he couldn't do it. How could he marry Milly now? How could he listen to her making promises she'd made before to someone else; spend the rest of his life wondering what other secrets she might be concealing? This was no small rift that might be patched up and healed. This was a gaping, jagged chasm which changed the whole order of things; turned their relationship into something he no longer recognized.

Without meaning to, he recalled the summer evening when he'd asked her to marry him. She'd behaved impeccably: crying a little, laughing a little, exclaiming over the ring he'd given her. But what had she really been thinking? Had she been laughing at him? Had she ever taken their intended marriage seriously? Did she share any of his ideals at all?

For a few minutes he lay miserably still, tormenting himself with images of Milly, trying to reconcile what he now knew about her with his memories of her as his fiancée. She was beautiful, sweet, charming. She was untrustworthy, secretive, dishonest. The worst thing was, she hadn't even seemed to realize what she'd done. She'd dismissed it, as though being married to another man were a trifling matter, to be brushed over and ignored.

An angry hurt began to throb inside him, and he sat

up, trying to clear his mind; trying to think of other things. He pulled open the curtains and, without seeing the beautiful view before him, quickly began to get dressed. He would throw himself into work, he told himself. He would start again, and he would get over this. It might take time, but he would get over it.

Briskly, he walked downstairs, and into the breakfast room. Harry was sitting at the table, hidden behind a newspaper.

'Morning,' he said.

'Morning,' said Simon. He looked up suspiciously, ready to detect a note of mocking or ridicule in his father's voice. But his father was looking up at him with what seemed genuine concern.

'So,' he said, as Simon sat down. 'Are you going to tell me what this is all about?'

'The wedding's off.'

'So I gather. But why? Or don't you want to tell me?'

Simon said nothing, but reached for the coffee pot. He had stormed in the night before, too angry and humiliated to talk to anyone. He was still humiliated; still angry; still inclined to keep Milly's betrayal to himself. On the other hand, misery was a lonely emotion.

'She's already married,' he said abruptly. There was a crackling sound as Harry thrust down his paper.

'Already married? To who, for God's sake?'

'Some gay American. She met him ten years ago. He wanted to stay in the country, so she married him as a favour. As a favour!'

'Well, thank God for that,' said Harry. 'I thought you

meant really married.' He took a sip of coffee. 'So what's the problem can't she get a divorce?'

'The problem?' said Simon, gazing at his father incredulously. 'The problem is that she lied to me!' The problem is that I can't trust anything else she says! I thought she was one person – and now I've discovered she's someone else. She's not the Milly I know.'

Harry stared at him in silence.

'Is that it?' he said at last. 'Is that the only reason it's all off? The fact that Milly married some dodgy guy, ten years ago?'

'Isn't that enough?'

'Of course it's not enough!' said Harry furiously. 'It's not nearly enough! I thought there was something really wrong between you.'

'There is! She lied to me!'

'I'm not surprised if this is the way you're reacting.'

'How do you expect me to react?' said Simon. 'We had a relationship built on trust. Now I can't trust her any more.' He closed his eyes. 'It's finished.'

'Simon, just who the fuck do you think you are?' exclaimed Harry. 'The Archbishop of Canterbury? Why does it matter if she lied to you? She's told you the truth now, hasn't she?'

'Only because she had to.'

'So what?'

'So it was perfect before this happened!' shouted Simon desperately. 'Everything was perfect! And now it's ruined!'

'Oh grow up!' thundered Harry. Simon's chin jerked

up in shock. 'Just grow up, Simon! And for once in your life stop behaving like a self-indulgent, spoilt brat. So your perfect relationship isn't as perfect as you thought. So what? Does that mean you have to chuck it away?'

'You don't understand.'

'I understand perfectly. You want to bask in your perfect marriage, with your perfect wife and kids, and gloat at the rest of the world! Don't you? And now you've found a flaw, you can't stand it. Well, stand it. Simon! Stand it! Because the world is full of flaws. And Frankly, what you had with Milly was about as good as it gets.'

'And what the hell would you know about it?' said Simon savagely. He stood up. 'What the hell would you know about successful relationships? Why should I respect a single word you say?'

'Because I'm your fucking father!'

'Yes,' said Simon bitterly. 'And don't I know it.' He kicked back his chair, turned on his heel and stalked out of the room, leaving Harry staring after him, cursing under his breath.

At nine o'clock, there was a ring at the doorbell. Isobel, who had just come down into the kitchen, screwed up her face. She padded out into the hall and opened the front door. A large white van was parked outside the house and a man was standing on the doorstep, surrounded by white boxes.

'Wedding cake delivery,' he said. 'Name of Havill.'

'Oh God,' said Isobel, staring at the boxes. 'Oh God.'

She bent down, lifted one of the cardboard lids, and caught a glimpse of smooth white icing; the edge of a sugar rose. 'Look,' she said, standing up again. 'Thank you very much. But there's been a slight change of plan.'

'Is this the wrong address?' said the man. He squinted at his piece of paper. 'One! Bertram Street.'

'No, it's the right address,' said Isobel. 'It's the right address.'

She gazed past him at the van, feeling suddenly depressed. Today should have been a happy day, full of excitement and anticipation and bustling, last-minute preparations. Not this.

'The thing is,' she said, 'we don't need a wedding cake any more. Can you take it away again?'

The man gave a sarcastic laugh.

'Carry this lot around in my van all day? I don't think so!'

'But we don't need it.'

'I'm afraid, my dear, that's not my problem. You ordered it – if you want to return it, that's between you and the company. Now, if you could just sign here' – he thrust a pen at her – 'I'll get the rest of the boxes.'

Isobel's head jerked up.

'The rest? How many are there, for God's sake?'

'Ten in all,' said the man, consulting his piece of paper. 'Including pillars and accessories.'

'Ten,' echoed Isobel disbelievingly.

'It's a lot of cake,' said the man.

'Yes,' said Isobel, as he disappeared back to the van. 'Especially between four of us.'

* * *

By the time Olivia appeared on the stairs, the white boxes had been neatly piled in a corner of the hall.

'I didn't know what else to do with them,' said Isobel, coming out of the kitchen.

She glanced at her mother and blanched. Olivia's face was a savage mix of bright paint and deathly white skin. She was clinging tightly to the banisters and looked as though she might keel over at any moment.

'Are you OK, Mummy?' she said.

'I'll be fine,' said Olivia with a strange brightness. 'I didn't get much sleep.'

'I shouldn't think any of us did,' said Isobel. 'We should all go back to bed.'

'Yes, well. We can't, can we?' said Olivia. She smiled tautly at Isobel. 'We've got a wedding to cancel. We've got phone calls to make. I've made a list!'

Isobel winced.

'Mummy, I know this is really hard for you,' she said.

'It's no harder for me than anyone else,' said Olivia, lifting her chin. 'Why should it be harder for me? After all, it's not the end of the world, is it? After all, it was just a wedding!'

'Just a wedding,' said Isobel. 'To be honest, I don't think such a thing exists.'

Mid-morning, there was a knock on Milly's door.

'Are you awake?' said Esme. 'Isobel's on the phone.'

'Oh,' said Milly dazedly, sitting up and pushing her hair back off her face. Her head felt heavy; her voice

247

sounded like a stranger's. she looked at Esme and tried to smile. But her face felt dry and old and her brain felt as though it was missing a cog. What was going on, anyway? Why was she at Esme's house?

'I'll get the cordless phone,' said Esme, and disappeared.

Milly sank back on her pillow and stared at Esme's pistachio ceiling, wondering why she felt so light-headed, so unreal. And then, with a dart of shock, she remembered. The wedding was off.

The wedding was off. She ran the idea experimentally round her head, waiting for a stab of grief, a renewed rush of tears. But this morning her eyes were dry. Her mind was calm; the sharp emotions of the night before had been rounded over by sleep. She felt more startled than upset; more disquieted than grief-stricken. She could scarcely believe it. The wedding – her huge, immovable wedding – wasn't going to happen. How could it not happen? How could the centre of her life simply disappear? She felt as though the peak to which she'd been climbing had suddenly vanished, and she'd been left, clinging to the rocks and peering disorientedly over the edge.

'Here you are,' said Esme, suddenly appearing by her bed. 'Would you like some coffee?'

Milly nodded, and took the phone.

'Hi,' she said in a scratchy voice.

'Hi,' came Isobel's voice down the line. 'Are you OK?'

'Yes,' said Milly. 'I suppose so.'

'You haven't heard from Simon?'

'No.' Milly's voice quickened. 'Why? Has he—'

'No,' said Isobel hurriedly. 'No, he hasn't. I just wondered. In case.'

'Oh,' said Milly. 'Well, no. I've been asleep. I haven't spoken to anyone.'

There was a pause. Milly watched as Esme pulled back the curtains and fastened them with thick braided tie-backs. The day was bright, sparkling with frost. Esme smiled at Milly, then walked softly out of the room.

'Isobel, I'm really sorry,' said Milly slowly. 'For landing you in it like that.'

'Oh, that,' said Isobel. 'Don't worry. That doesn't matter.'

'I just got rattled. I just— Well. You know what it was like.'

'Of course I do. I would have done exactly the same.'

'No you wouldn't,' said Milly, grinning faintly. 'You've got a zillion times more self-control than me.'

'Well, anyway, don't worry,' said Isobel. 'It hasn't been a problem.'

'Really? Hasn't Mummy been lecturing you all day?'

'She hasn't had time,' said Isobel. 'We're all too busy.'

'Oh,' said Milly, wrinkling her brow. 'Doing what!'

There was silence.

'Cancelling the wedding,' said Isobel eventually, her voice full of distress.

'Oh,' said Milly again. Something heavy sank inside her stomach. 'Oh, I see. Of course.'

'Oh God, Milly, I'm sorry,' said Isobel. 'I thought you would realize.'

'I did,' said Milly. 'I do. Of course you have to cancel it.'

'That's partly why I phoned,' said Isobel. 'I know this is a dreadful time to ask. But is there anyone else I need to call? Anyone who isn't in the red book?'

'I don't know,' said Milly. She swallowed. 'Who have you told already?'

'About half our guests,' said Isobel. 'Up to the Madisons. Harry's people are doing his lot.'

'Wow,' said Milly, feeling stupid, irrational tears coming to her eyes. 'You didn't hang about, did you?'

'We couldn't!' said Isobel. 'Some people would have been setting off already. We had to put them off.'

'I know,' said Milly. She took a deep breath. 'I know. I'm just being stupid. So. How are you doing it?'

'We're going down the list in the red book. Everybody – everybody's being really nice about it.'

'What are you telling them?' said Milly, winding the sheet round her fingers.

'We've said you're ill,' said Isobel. 'We didn't know what else to say.'

'Do they believe you?'

'I don't know. Some of them.'

There was silence.

'OK,' said Milly at last. 'Well, if I think of anyone I'll call you.'

'When are you coming back home?'

'I don't know,' said Milly. She closed her eyes and thought of her room at home. Presents and cards every-where; her honeymoon case open on the floor; her

250

wedding dress hanging up in the corner, shrouded like a ghost. 'Not yet,' she said. 'Not until—'

'No,' said Isobel after a pause. 'Fair enough. Well, look. I'll come round and see you. When I've finished.'

'Isobel – thanks. For doing all this.'

'No problem,' said Isobel. 'I expect you'll do the same for me one day.'

'Yes.' Milly managed a wan smile. 'I expect so.'

She put the phone down. When she looked up, she saw Esme at the door. She was holding a tray and looking thoughtfully at Milly.

'Coffee,' she said, putting the tray down. 'To celebrate.'

'Celebrate?' said Milly disbelievingly.

'Your escape.' Esme came forward, holding two porcelain mugs. 'Your escape from matrimony.'

'It doesn't feel like an escape,' said Milly.

'Of course it doesn't,' exclaimed Esme. 'Not yet. But it will. Just think, Milly – you're no longer tied down. You can do anything you choose. You're an independent woman!'

'I suppose,' said Milly. She stared miserably into her coffee. 'I suppose.'

'Don't brood, darling!' said Esme. 'Don't think about it. Drink your coffee and watch some nice television. And then we're going out for lunch.'

The restaurant was large and empty, save for a few single men, reading newspapers over their coffee. Rupert gazed about awkwardly, wondering which one was Martin. Black jeans, he'd said. But most of them were wearing black jeans. He felt over-smart in his own suit and expensive shirt.

After he'd left chambers the night before, he'd walked mindlessly for a while. Then, as morning began to approach, he had checked into a seedy Bayswater hotel. He had lain awake, staring up at the stained ceiling. After breakfast at a café he'd taken a taxi home and crept into the house, praying that Francesca would already have left. Feeling like a burglar, he'd taken a shower, shaved and changed his clothes. He'd made a cup of coffee and drunk it in the kitchen, staring out into the garden, then had put the mug in the dish-washer, looked at the clock and picked up his briefcase. Familiar actions; an automatic routine. He had felt, for an instant, almost as though his life were carrying on as before.

But his life was not the same as before. It would never be the same as before. His soul had been wrenched open and the truth had been pulled out, and now he had to decide what to do with it.

'Rupert?' A voice interrupted his thoughts and he looked up. Standing at a nearby table was a young man dressed in black jeans. He had close cropped hair and a single ear-ring and looked very obviously homosexual. In spite of himself, a shiver of dismay went through Rupert as he cautiously advanced.

'Hello,' he said, aware that he sounded pompous. 'How do you do.'

'We spoke on the phone,' said the young man. His voice was soft and singsong. 'I'm Martin.'

'Yes,' said Rupert, clutching his briefcase tight. He felt suddenly petrified. Here was homosexuality. Here was his own hidden, unspoken side, duplicated in front of him for all to see.

He sat down, and shifted his chair slightly away from the table.

'It was good of you to come up to London,' he said stiffly.

'Not at all,' said Martin. 'I'm up at least once a week. And if it's important . . .' He spread his hands.

'Yes,' said Rupert. He began to study the menu intently. He would take the letter and if possible a telephone number for Allan, then leave, as soon as possible.

'I think I'll have a cup of coffee,' he said, not looking up. 'A double espresso.'

'I've been waiting for your call,' Martin said. 'Allan told me a great deal about you. I always hoped that one day you might start to look for him.'

'What did he tell you?' Rupert raised his head slowly. Martin shrugged.

'Everything.'

A fiery red came to Rupert's cheeks and he put the menu down on the table. He looked at Martin, ready for a surge of humiliation. But Martin's eyes were kind; he looked as though he wanted to understand. Rupert cleared his throat.

'When did you meet him?'

'Six years ago,' said Martin.

'Did you . . . have a relationship with him?'

253

'Yes,' said Martin. 'We had a very close relationship.'

'I see.'

'I don't think you do,' Martin paused. 'We weren't lovers. I was his counsellor.'

'Oh,' said Rupert confusedly. 'Was he—'

'He was ill,' said Martin, and looked straight at Rupert.

A flash of deadly understanding passed through Rupert and he lowered his eyes. So here it was, without warning. His sentence; the end of the cycle. He had sinned, and now he was being punished. He had committed unspeakable acts. Now he was to suffer an unspeakable disease.

'AIDS,' he said calmly.

'No,' said Martin, the tiniest note of scorn creeping into his voice. 'Not AIDS. Leukaemia. He had leukaemia.'

Rupert's eyes jerked up, to see Martin staring sadly at him. he felt suddenly sick, as though he'd entered a nightmare. White stars began to dance around his field of vision.

'I'm afraid so,' said Martin. 'Allan died, four years ago.'

THIRTEEN

For a while there was silence. A waiter came up and Martin discreetly ordered, while Rupert stared ahead with glassy eyes, trying to contain his pain. He felt as though something inside him was splitting apart; as though his whole body was filling up with grief and guilt. Allan was dead. Allan was gone. He was too late.

'Are you OK?' said Martin in a low voice.

Rupert nodded, unable to speak.

'I can't tell you much about his death. I'm afraid. It happened in the States. His parents came over and took him home. I understand it was quite peaceful at the end.'

'His parents,' said Rupert in a cracked voice. 'He hated his parents.'

'They came to an understanding. Everything changed, of course, when Allan became ill. I met them when they came over. They were decent, compassionate people.'

He looked up at Rupert. 'Did you ever meet them?'

'No,' said Rupert. 'I never met them.'

He closed his eyes and imagined the two elderly people Allan had described to him; imagined Allan being carted back to a town he'd always hated, in order to die. A fresh pain swept over him and suddenly he felt as though he might break down.

'Don't think it,' said Martin.

'What?' Rupert opened his eyes.

'What you're thinking. What everybody thinks. If only I'd known he was going to die. Of course you would have done things differently. Of course you would. But you didn't know. You couldn't have known.'

'What . . .' Rupert licked his lips. 'What did he say about me?'

'He said he loved you. He said he thought you loved him. But he wasn't angry any more.' Martin leaned forward and took Rupert's hand. 'It's important you understand that, Rupert,' he said earnestly. 'He wasn't angry with you.'

A waiter suddenly appeared at the table, carrying two cups of coffee.

'Thank you,' said Martin, without taking his hand from Rupert's. Rupert saw the waiter's gaze run over the pair of them, and, in spite of it all, stiffened slightly.

'Will there be anything else?' said the waiter.

'No thank you,' said Rupert. He met the waiter's friendly eye and a painful embarrassment flooded him like hot water. He felt like running for cover; denying everything. But instead he forced himself to leave his hand calmly in Martin's. As though it were normal.

'I know this is hard for you,' said Martin as the waiter left. 'On all levels.'

'I'm married,' said Rupert roughly. 'That's how hard it is.' Martin nodded slowly.

'Allan thought you might be.'

'I suppose he despised me,' said Rupert, gazing into his cup of coffee. 'I suppose you despise me, too.'

'No,' said Martin. 'You don't understand. Allan *hoped* you were married. He hoped you were with a woman, rather than—' Rupert looked up.

'Rather than a man?' Martin nodded.

'He agonized over whether to contact you. He didn't want to rock the boat if you were happy with a woman. But equally, he couldn't face discovering that you were with some other man. What he wanted to believe was that if you had ever changed your mind, you would have come back to him first.'

'Of course I would,' said Rupert, his voice trembling slightly. 'He knew I would. He knew me like no other human being has ever known me.'

Martin shrugged diplomatically.

'Your wife—'

'My wife!' exclaimed Rupert. He looked at Martin with pained eyes. 'My wife doesn't know me! We met, we went out to dinner a few times, we took a holiday together, we got married. I see her for about an hour every day, if that. With Allan if was—'

'More intense.'

'It was all day and all night,' said Rupert. He closed

257

his eyes. 'It was every hour and every minute and every single thought and fear and hope.'

There was silence. When Rupert opened his eyes, Martin was pulling a letter out of his bag.

'Allan left you this,' he said. 'In case you ever came looking.'

'Thank you,' said Rupert. He took the envelope and looked at it silently for a few moments. There was his name, written beautifully in Allan's handwriting. He could almost hear Allan's voice, speaking to him. he blinked a few times, then tucked the letter away in his jacket. 'Do you have a mobile phone?' he said.

'Sure,' said Martin, reaching into his pocket.

'There's someone else who needs to know about this,' said Rupert. He tapped in a number, listened for a moment, then switched the phone off. 'Busy,' he said.

'Who is it you're going to tell?' asked Martin.

'Milly,' said Rupert. 'The girl he married to stay in Britain.'

Martin frowned.

'Allan told me about Milly,' he said. 'But she ought to know. He wrote to her.'

'Well if he did, she never got the letter,' said Rupert. 'Because she doesn't know.' He tapped in the number again. 'And she needs to.'

Isobel put down the telephone and ran a hand through her hair. 'That was Aunt Jean,' she said. 'She wanted to know what we're going to do with the present she sent.'

She leaned back in her chair and surveyed the

cluttered kitchen table. Lists of names, address books and telephone books were spread over the surface, each covered in a pattern of brown coffee cup rings and sandwich crumbs. Shoe boxes filled with wedding bumf, brochures and catalogues were stacked high on a kitchen chair: from one box protruded a glossy black and white print; from another had spilled a length of lace. Open in front of her was a sample bag of pastel-coloured sugared almonds.

'It takes so long to put a wedding together,' she said, reaching out for a handful. 'Months and months of time and effort. And then it takes about five seconds to dismantle it all. Like jumping on a sandcastle.' She crunched on the sugar almonds, and pulled a face. 'God, these things are disgusting. I'm going to break my teeth.'

'I'm very sorry, Andrea.' Olivia was saying into her mobile phone. 'Yes, I do realize that Derek bought a morning suit especially. Please give him my apologies . . . Yes, perhaps you're right. Perhaps a lounge suit would have done just as well.' There was a pause and her hand tensed around the phone. 'No, they haven't set a new date as yet. Yes, I'll let you know . . . Well, if he wants to take it back to the shop, then that's really up to him. Yes, dear, goodbye.'

She turned the phone off with a trembling hand, ticked off a name and reached for the red book. 'Right,' she said. 'Now, who's next?'

'Why don't you take a break?' said Isobel. 'You look whacked.'

'No, darling,' said Olivia. 'I'd rather carry on. After all, it's got to be done, hasn't it?' She smiled brightly at Isobel. 'We can't all just sit around feeling sorry for ourselves, can we?'

'No,' said Isobel. 'I suppose not.' She stretched her arms into the air. 'God, my neck's aching from all this phoning.'

As she spoke, the phone rang again. She pulled a face at Olivia and picked it up.

'Hello?' she said. 'Oh, hello. Yes, it is true, I'm afraid. Yes, I'll give her your best wishes. OK then. Bye.' She slammed the phone down, then took it off the hook.

'Everyone has to ring back and gloat,' she said irritably. 'They all know she isn't ill.'

'Perhaps we should have given some other excuse,' said Olivia, rubbing her brow.

'It doesn't matter what excuse we give,' said Isobel. 'They'll all guess. Horrible people.' She pulled a face. 'Bloody Aunt Jean wants us to send her present back straight away. She's going to another wedding in two weeks' time and she wants to use it. I'm going to tell her we thought it was so hideous we threw it away.'

'No,' said Olivia. She closed her eyes. 'We must try to act with dignity and poise.'

'Must we?' Isobel peered at Olivia. 'Mummy, are you OK? You're acting very weirdly.'

'I'm fine,' whispered Olivia.

'Well, OK,' said Isobel doubtfully. She looked down at her list. 'I also had a call from the florist. She suggested that as Milly's bouquet is already made up, we might like to have it pressed and dried. As a memento.'

'A memento?'

'I know,' said Isobel, beginning to shake with giggles in spite of herself. 'Who are these people?'

'A memento! As if we'll ever forget! As if we'll ever forget today!'

Isobel glanced up sharply. Olivia's eyes were open and glittering with tears.

'Mummy!'

'I'm sorry, darling,' said Olivia. A tear landed on her nose and she smiled brightly. 'I don't mean to be silly.'

'I know how much you wanted this wedding,' said Isobel. She reached over and took her mother's hand. 'But there'll be another one. Honestly, there will.'

'It's not the wedding,' whispered Olivia. 'If it were just the wedding . . .' She broke off as the doorbell rang. They both looked up.

'Who the hell can that be?' said Isobel impatiently. 'Don't people realize we're not in the mood for visitors?' She put down her list. 'Don't worry, I'll go.'

'No, I'll go,' said Olivia.

'Let's both go.'

The couple on the front doorstep were strangers, dressed in shiny green Barbours and carrying matching Mulberry holdalls.

'Hello,' said the woman brightly. 'We'd like a room, please.'

'A what?' said Olivia blankly.

'A room,' said the woman. 'A bed and breakfast room.'

She waved a copy of the *Heritage City* guidebook at Olivia.

'I'm afraid we're full at the moment,' said Isobel. 'Perhaps if you try the Tourist Board . . .'

'I was told we would be able to have a room,' said the woman.

'You can't have been,' said Isobel patiently, 'because there aren't any rooms.'

'I spoke to someone on the phone!' The woman's voice rose crossly. 'I specifically checked that we would be able to stay here! And I might add, you were recommended to us by our friends the Rendles.' She looked impressively at Isobel.

'What an honour,' said Isobel.

'Don't take that tone with me, young woman!' snapped the woman. 'Is this the way you usually conduct business? The customer comes first, you know! Now, we were told we could have a room. You can't just turn people away at the door with no explanation.'

'Oh, for God's sake,' said Isobel.

'You want an explanation?' said Olivia in a trembling voice.

'Mummy, don't bother. Just—'

'You want an explanation?' Olivia took a deep breath. 'Well, where shall I start? Shall I start with my daughter's wedding the wedding that was supposed to be taking place tomorrow?'

'Oh, a family wedding!' said the woman, disconcerted. 'Well that's different.'

'Or shall I start with her first wedding, ten years ago?'

said Olivia, ignoring the woman. 'The wedding we didn't even know about?' Her voice began to rise dangerously. 'Or shall I start with the fact we're having to call the whole thing off, and that our entire family and all our friends are mocking us behind our backs?'

'Really, I didn't—' began the woman.

'But come in anyway!' cried Olivia, pulling the door open wide. 'We'll find you a room! Somewhere among all the wedding presents we're going to have send back, and the wedding cake we're going to have to eat, and the clothes that will never be worn, and that beautiful wedding dress . . .'

'Come on, Rosemary,' said the man awkwardly, tugging his wife's sleeve. 'Very sorry to have disturbed you,' he said to Isobel. 'I always said we should have gone to Cheltenham.'

As the pair backed away, Isobel looked at Olivia. She was still gripping the door, her face streaked with tears.

'I really think you should have a break, Mummy,' she said. 'Keep the phone off the hook. Watch the telly. Or go to bed for a bit.'

'I can't,' said Olivia. 'We need to keep telephoning.'

'Rubbish,' said Isobel. 'Everyone I've spoken to has already heard. Gossip travels fast, you know. We've called the most important people. All the others will keep.'

'Well,' said Olivia after a pause. 'I do feel a little bit weary. Maybe I'll lie down for a bit.' She closed the front door and looked at Isobel. 'Are you going to have a rest, too?'

'No,' said Isobel. She reached for her coat. 'I'm going to go out. I'm going to go and see Milly.'

'That's a good idea,' said Olivia slowly. 'She'll be pleased to see you.' She paused. 'Be sure . . .'

'Yes?'

'Be sure to give her my love,' said Olivia. She looked down. 'That's all. Give her my love.'

Esme's drawing room was warm and tranquil; a haven of quiet civlization. As Isobel sat down on a pale, elegant sofa she looked about her pleasurably, admiring the collection of silver boxes heaped casually on a side table; the applewood dish filled with smooth grey pebbles.

'So,' said Milly, sitting down opposite her. 'Is Mummy still furious?'

'Not really,' said Isobel, screwing up her face. 'She's weird.'

'That probably means she's furious.'

'She isn't, honestly. She said to give you her love.'

'Really?' said Milly. She curled her feet underneath her and sipped at her coffee. Her hair was tied up in a dishevelled pony-tail and, under her jeans, she was wearing a pair of ancient ski socks.

'Here you are,' said Esme, handing a mug of coffee to Isobel. 'But I'm afraid I'll have to steal Milly in a little while. We're going out to lunch.'

'Good idea,' said Isobel. 'Where are you going?'

'A little place I know,' said Esme, smiling at them both. 'About ten minutes, Milly?'

'Fine,' said Milly. They both waited for Esme to close the door.

'So,' said Isobel, when she'd gone. 'How are you really?'

'I don't know,' said Milly slowly. 'Sometimes I feel fine – and sometimes I just want to burst into tears.' She took a shuddery breath. 'I keep thinking, what would I have been doing now?' She closed her eyes. 'I don't know how I'm going to get through tomorrow.'

'Get drunk.'

'I'm doing that tonight.' A flicker of a smile passed over Milly's face. 'Care to join me?'

'Maybe,' said Isobel. She sipped at her coffee. 'And Simon hasn't been in touch?'

'No.' Milly's face closed up.

'Is it really all over between you two?'

'Yes.'

'I can't believe it.' Isobel shook her head. 'Just because . . .'

'Because I deceived him about one thing,' said Milly in sharp, sarcastic tones. 'So obviously I'm a patho-logical liar. Obviously, no-one can trust anything I say ever again.'

'Bastard. You're better off without him.'

'I know.' Milly looked up and gave the tight smile of someone battling with pain. 'It's for the best, really.' Isobel looked at her and suddenly felt like crying.

'Oh Milly,' she said. 'It's such a shame.'

'It doesn't matter,' said Milly lightly. 'Come on. It's not as if I was pregnant. Now, that really would be a

265

disaster.' She took a sip of coffee and gave Isobel a half-grin.

Isobel met her eyes and gave an unwilling smile. For a while there was silence.

'Do you know what you're going to do?' said Milly at last.

'No.'

'What about the father?'

'He doesn't want a baby. He's made that very plain.'

'Couldn't you persuade him?'

'No. And I don't want to! I don't want to push someone into fatherhood. What chance would our relationship have then?'

'Maybe the baby would bring you together.'

'Babies aren't glue,' said Isobel. She pushed her hands through her hair. 'If I had the baby, I would be on my own.'

'I would help you!' said Milly. 'And so would Mummy.'

'I know.' Isobel's shoulders twitched in a shrug. Milly stared at her.

'Isobel, you wouldn't really get rid of it.'

'I don't know!' Isobel's voice rose in distress. 'I'm only thirty, Milly! I could meet some fantastic guy tomorrow. I could be swept off my feet. But if I've already got a kid . . .'

'It wouldn't make any difference,' said Milly stoutly.

'It would! And you know, having a baby is no picnic. I've seen friends do it. They turn into zombies. And they're not even doing it on their own.'

'Well, I don't know,' said Milly, after a pause. 'It's your decision.'

'I know it is,' said Isobel. 'That's exactly the problem.'

The door opened and they looked up. Esme smiled at them from under a huge fur hat.

'Ready to go, Milly? Isobel, sweetheart, do you want to come too?'

'No thanks,' said Isobel, getting up. 'I'd better get back home.'

She watched as Milly got into Esme's red Daimler and suddenly wished that her own godmother might suddenly appear and whisk her away, too. But Mavis Hindhead was a colourless woman living in the north of Scotland who had not acknowledged Isobel's existence since the eve of her confirmation, when she'd sent her a knobby, ill-fitting jersey and a spidery, hand-written card of which Isobel had never managed to make sense. Not many godmothers, thought Isobel, were like Esme Ormerod.

When they'd roared off round the corner she began to walk away from Esme's house, telling herself to go straight home. But she couldn't quite face returning to the claustrophobic, sad atmosphere of the kitchen; couldn't face sitting down and making yet more awkward phone calls to curious strangers. Now that she was out in the fresh air, she wanted to stay out and stretch her legs and enjoy the sensation of not having a telephone clamped to her ear.

She began to walk briskly back towards town, feeling

a mild sense of irresponsibility, as though she were bunking off school. At first she strode without considering where she was heading, merely enjoying the feel of her legs stretching out with every stride, the lightness of her arms swinging at her sides. Then, as a sudden thought struck her, she paused and, propelled by a curiosity she recognized as ghoulish, she turned off the main road, towards St Edward's Church.

As she stepped into the porch, she almost expected to hear bridal music playing on the organ. The church was filled with flowers; the pews were empty and waiting; the altar was shining brightly. Slowly she walked up the aisle, imagining the church filled with happy, expectant faces; imagining what it would have been like, parading behind Milly in a bridesmaid's dress, watching as her sister made the ancient vows that everyone knew and loved.

As she reached the front she stopped, and noticed a pile of white, redundant orders of service stacked at the end of a pew. With a stab of sadness, she reached for one – then, as she saw the two names printed on the cover, blinked in surprise. *Eleanor and Giles*. Printed in nasty, loopy silver lettering. Who the hell were Eleanor and Giles? How had they muscled in on the act?

'Bloody parasites!' she said aloud.

'I beg your pardon?' A man's voice came from behind her, and she whipped round. Walking up the aisle towards her was a young man in a cassock.

'Do you work here?' said Isobel.

'Yes,' said the young man.

'Well, hello,' said Isobel. 'I'm Milly Havill's sister.'

'Ah yes,' said the priest embarrassedly. 'What a shame. We were all very sorry to hear about that.'

'Were you?' said Isobel. 'So what happened? Did you think you might as well put Milly's expensive flowers to good use?'

'What do you mean?' Isobel gestured to the orders of service.

'Who's this bloody Eleanor and Giles? How come they've been given Milly's wedding day?'

'They haven't,' said the curate nervously. 'They're getting married in the afternoon. They booked it a year ago.'

'Oh,' said Isobel. She looked at the order of service, then put it down again. 'Well, all right then. I hope they have a happy day.'

'I'm really very sorry,' said the curate awkwardly. 'Maybe your sister will be able to get married at some time in the future. When she's straightened everything out.'

'It would be nice,' said Isobel. 'But I doubt it.' She glanced once more round the church, then turned on her heel to leave.

'Actually, I was about to lock up,' said the curate, hurrying after her. 'It's a precaution we often take when there are flower arrangements in the church. You'd be surprised what people steal these days.'

'I'm sure,' said Isobel. She stopped by a pillar, plucked a single white lily from a twining arrangement, and breathed in the sweet aroma. 'It really would have been a beautiful wedding,' she said sadly. 'And now it's all destroyed. You people don't know what you've done.' The young curate bridled slightly.

'As I understand it,' he began, 'this was a case of attempted bigamy.'

'Yes,' said Isobel. 'But no-one would have known. If your Canon Lytton had just turned a blind eye, and hadn't said anything—'

'The couple would have known!' said the curate. 'God would have known!'

'Yes, well,' said Isobel tersely. 'Maybe God wouldn't have minded.'

She strode out of the church with her head down, and walked straight into someone.

'Sorry,' she said, and looked up, then stiffened. Harry Pinnacle was standing in front of her, wearing a navy blue cashmere overcoat and a bright red scarf.

'Hello, Isobel,' he said. He glanced over her shoulder at the curate, who had followed her out. 'Terrible business, all this.'

'Yes,' said Isobel. 'Terrible.'

'I'm on my way to meet your father for lunch.'

'Yes,' said Isobel. 'He mentioned it.'

There was a clanking sound as the curate pulled the church door closed, suddenly they were alone.

'Well, I must be off,' muttered Isobel. 'Nice to see you.'

'Wait a minute,' said Harry.

'I'm in a bit of a hurry,' said Isobel, and she began to walk away.

'I don't care.' Harry grabbed her arm and pulled her round to face him. 'Isobel, why have you been ignoring all my messages?'

'Leave me alone,' said Isobel, twisting her head away.

'Isobel! I want to talk to you!'

'I can't,' said Isobel, her face closing up. 'Harry, I just . . . can't.'

There was a long silence. Then Harry dropped her arm.

'Fine,' he said. 'If that's what you want.'

'Whatever,' said Isobel in a dead voice. And without meeting his gaze, she thrust her hands in her pockets and strode off down the street.

FOURTEEN

Harry was sitting by the bar, beer in hand, when James arrived at the Pear and Goose. It was a small pub in the centre of Bath, packed with cheerful, anonymous tourists.

'Good to see you, James,' he said, standing up to shake hands. 'Let me get you one of these.'

'Thanks,' said James. They both watched silently as the barman filled a pint glass with beer, and it occurred to James that this was the first time the two of them had ever met alone.

'Cheers,' said Harry, raising his glass.

'Cheers.'

'Let's sit down,' said Harry, gesturing to a table in the corner. 'It's more private over there.'

'Yes,' said James. He cleared his throat. 'I imagine you want to talk about the practicalities of the wedding.'

'Why?' said Harry, looking surprised. 'Is there a

problem? I thought my people were sorting it all out with Olivia.'

'I meant the financial aspect,' said James stiffly. 'Milly's little revelation has cost you a small fortune.' Harry waved a hand.

'That's not important.'

'It is important,' said James. 'I'm afraid it's not within my means to pay you back fully. But if we can come to some arrangement—'

'James,' interrupted Harry. 'I didn't ask you here so we could talk about money. I just thought you might like a drink, OK?'

'Oh,' said James, taken aback. 'Yes. Of course.'

'So let's sit down and have a fucking drink.'

They sat down at the corner table. Harry opened a packet of crisps and offered it to James.

'How is Milly?' he said. 'Is she OK?'

'I'm not sure, to be honest,' said James. 'She's with her godmother. How's Simon?'

'Stupid kid,' said Harry, crunching on crisps. 'I told him he was a spoilt brat this morning.'

'Oh,' said James, unsure what to say.

'The first sign of trouble, he runs away. The first hitch, he gives up. No wonder his business failed.'

'Aren't you being a little harsh?' protested James. 'He's had a huge shock. We all have. It's hard enough for us to deal with, so what Simon must be feeling . . .' He shook his head.

'So you really had no idea she was married,' said Harry.

'None whatsoever.'

'She lied to you all.'

'Every single one of us,' said James soberly. He looked up, to see Harry half grinning. 'What? You think it's funny?'

'Oh come on,' said Harry. 'You've got to admire the girl's chutzpah! It takes a lot of guts to walk up the aisle knowing you've got a husband out there just waiting to trip you up.'

'That's one way of looking at it,' said James.

'But not your way.'

'No.' James shook his head. 'The way I see it, Milly's thoughtlessness has caused a lot of trouble and distress to a lot of people. Frankly, I'm ashamed to think she's my daughter.'

'Give the girl a break!'

'Then give Simon a break!' retorted James. 'He's the innocent one, remember. He's the wronged one.'

'He's a high-handed, moralistic little dictator. Life has to go a certain way, otherwise he's not interested.' Harry took a slug of beer. 'He's had it far too easy for far too long, that's his trouble.'

'You know, I'd say just the opposite,' said James. 'It can't be easy, walking in your shadow. I'm not sure I'd be able to do it myself.'

Harry shrugged silently. For a while neither of them spoke. Harry took a large gulp of beer, paused for a second, then looked up.

'How about Isobel?' he said casually. 'How's she reacted to all of this?'

'As usual,' said James. 'Gave very little away.' He drained his glass. 'Poor old Isobel's got enough on her plate as it is.'

'Work problems?' Harry leaned forward.

'Not just work.'

'Something else, then? Is she in some kind of trouble?' A flicker of a smile passed over James's face.

'You've hit the nail on the head,' he said.

'What do you mean?'

James stared into his empty beer glass.

'I don't suppose it's any secret,' he said after a pause, and looked at Harry's frowning face. 'She's pregnant.'

'Pregnant?' A look of utter shock came over Harry's face. 'Isobel's pregnant?'

'I know,' said James. 'I can't quite believe it myself.'

'Are you sure about this?' said Harry. His hand gripped his beer glass tightly. 'Could it be a mistake?'

James smiled at him, touched by his concern.

'Don't worry,' he said. 'She'll be OK.'

'Has she spoken to you about it?'

'She's keeping her cards pretty close to her chest,' said James. 'We don't even know who the father is.'

'Ah,' said Harry, and finished his beer.

'All we can do is support her in whatever decision she makes.'

'Decision?' Harry looked up.

'Whether to keep the baby or . . . not.' James shrugged awkwardly and looked away. A strange expression passed over Harry's face.

'Oh, I see,' he said slowly. 'I see. Of course that

would be an option.' He closed his eyes. 'Stupid of me.'

'What?'

'Nothing,' said Harry, opening his eyes again. 'Nothing.'

'Anyway,' said James. 'It isn't your problem.' He looked at Harry's empty glass. 'Let me get you another.'

'No,' said Harry. 'Let me get you one.'

'But you've already—'

'Please, James,' said Harry. He sounded suddenly dejected, James thought. Almost sad. 'Please, James. Let me.'

Isobel had walked as far as the Garden for the Blind. Now she sat on an iron bench, watching the fountain trickle endlessly into the little pond and trying to think calmly. Inside her mind, like a circular film, she saw Harry's expression as she'd left him; heard his voice again and again. The continuous repetition should, she thought, have dulled the pain inside her, should have left her numb and free to analyse her situation logically. But the pain would not be dulled; her mind would not still itself. She felt physically torn apart.

They had met for the first time only a few months before, at the party to celebrate Simon and Milly's engagement. As they'd shaken hands, a startled recognition had passed between them; both their voices had trembled slightly, and, like mirror images, they had each turned away quickly to talk to other people. But Harry's eyes had been on her every time she turned, and she had felt her entire body responding to his attention.

The next week, they had met surreptitiously for dinner. He had smuggled her back into the house; the next morning, from his bedroom window, she had seen Milly in the drive waving goodbye to Simon. The month after that they had travelled to Paris on separate planes. Each encounter had been exquisite; a fleeting, hidden gem of experience. They had decided to tell no-one; to keep things light and casual. Two adults enjoying themselves, nothing more.

But now nothing could be light; nothing could be casual. There was no longer any neutral. Whichever way she turned, she would be taking an action with huge consequences. One tiny, unwitnessed biological event meant that, whatever she chose to do, neither of their lives would be the same again.

Harry didn't want a baby. He'd made that perfectly clear to her. If she went ahead and had the child, she would be on her own. She would lose Harry. She would lose her freedom. She would be forced to rely on the help of her mother. Life would become an unbearable round of drudgery and coffee mornings and mind-numbing baby babble.

If, on the other hand, she got rid of the baby . . .

A slow pain rose through Isobel's chest. Who was she kidding? What was this so-called choice? Yes, she had a choice. Every modern woman had a choice. But the truth was, she had no choice. She was enslaved to herself – to the maternal emotions which she'd never known she possessed; to the tiny self growing within her; to the primal, overpowering desire for life.

* * *

Rupert sat on a bench in the National Portrait Gallery, staring at a picture of Philip II of Spain. It was a good two hours since Martin had said goodbye, clasping Rupert's hand and exhorting him to call whenever he felt like it. Since then, Rupert had wandered mindlessly, not noticing where he was going, not noticing the crowds of shoppers and tourists who kept bumping into him; unaware of anything except his own thoughts. From time to time he had stopped at a public phone and dialled Milly's number. But each time the line had been busy, and a secret relief had crept through him: he didn't want to share Allan's death with anyone else. Not yet.

The letter was still in his briefcase, unopened. He hadn't yet dared to read it. He had been too afraid – both that it wouldn't live up to his expectations and that it would. But now, under Philip's stern, uncompromising stare, he reached down, fumbled with the clasps of his briefcase and brought the envelope out. A stab of grief hit him as, again, he saw his name written in Allan's handwriting. This was the last communication that would ever exist between them. Part of him wanted to bury the letter unopened; keep Allan's last words unread and unsullied. But even as the thought passed through his mind, his shaking hands were ripping at the paper, and he was pulling out the thick, creamy sheets, each covered on one side only with a black, even script.

Dear Rupert,

Fear not. Fear not, said the angel. I'm not writing to you just so that you'll feel bad. At least not consciously. Not much.

In truth, I'm not sure why I'm writing at all. Will you ever read this letter? Probably not. Probably you've forgotten who I am; probably you're happily married with triplets. My occasional fantasy is that any moment you'll appear through the door and sweep me into your arms while all the other terminally ill patients cheer and bang their walking sticks. In reality, this letter will probably end up, like so many other once-meaningful pieces of the world's fabric, in a garbage truck, to be recycled into somebody's breakfast. I rather like that idea. Allan flakes. With added optimism and a tinge of bitterness.

And yet I keep writing – as though I'm sure that one day you'll trace a path back towards me and read these words. Perhaps you will, perhaps you won't. Has my addled mind got it wrong? Have I elevated what we had to a significance it doesn't deserve? The proportions of my life have been curtailed so dramatically, I know my view of events has become somewhat skewed. And yet – against all the odds – I keep writing. The truth is, Rupert, I cannot leave this country, let alone this world, without somewhere recording a farewell to you.

When I close my eyes and think of you, it's as you were at Oxford – though you must have changed since then. Five years on, who and what is Rupert? I have my own ideas, but am unwilling to reveal them. I don't want to be the asshole who thought he knew you better than you know yourself. That was my mistake at Oxford. I confused anger with insight. I mistook my own desires for yours. What right did I have to be angry with you? Life is a far more complicated picture than either of us realized back then.

What I hope is that you're happy. What I fear is that if you're reading this letter you're probably not. Happy people don't trawl through the past looking for answers. What is the answer? I don't know. Perhaps we would have been happy if we'd stayed together. Perhaps life would have been sweet. But you can't count on it.

As it turns out, what we had might have been as good as it was ever going to get. So we broke up. But at least one of us had a choice about that, even if it wasn't me. If we'd left it until now, neither of us would have had a choice. Breaking up is one thing; dying is something else. Frankly, I'm not sure I could cope with both at once. It's going to take me long enough to get over my death as it is.

But I promised myself I wouldn't talk about dying. That's not what this is about. This isn't a guilt letter. It's a love letter. Just that. I still love you, Rupert. I still miss you. That's really all I wanted to say. I still love you. I still miss you. If I don't see you again then . . . I guess that's just life. But somehow I'm hoping I will.

Yours always
Allan

Some time later, a young teacher arrived at the door of the gallery, surrounded by her swarming class of cheerful children. They had intended to spend the afternoon sketching the portrait of Elizabeth I. But as she saw the young man sitting in the middle of the room, she swiftly turned the children round and shepherded them towards another painting.

Rupert, lost in silent tears, didn't even see them.

Harry arrived back that afternoon to find Simon's car parked in its usual place outside the house. He went straight up to Simon's room and knocked. When there was no answer, he pushed the door open slightly. The first thing he saw was Simon's morning suit, still hanging up on the door of the wardrobe. In the waste-paper basket was a copy of the wedding invitation. Harry winced, and pushed the door shut again. He paused for a moment, then retraced his steps down the stairs and along the corridor to the leisure complex.

The swimming pool was gleaming with underwater lighting, music was softly playing, but no-one was swimming. In the far corner, the steam room door was misted up. Without pausing, Harry strode to the steam room and opened the door. Simon looked up, his face reddened and vulnerable with surprise.

'Dad?' he said, peering through the thick steam. 'What are you—'

'I need to talk to you,' said Harry, sitting down on the moulded plastic bench opposite Simon. 'I need to apologize.'

'Apologize?' said Simon in disbelief.

'I shouldn't have yelled at you this morning. I'm sorry.'

'Oh,' said Simon, looking away. 'Well. It doesn't matter.'

'It does matter,' said Harry. 'You've had a big shock. And I should have understood that. I'm your father.'

'I know you are,' said Simon without moving. Harry gazed at him steadily for a moment.

'Do you wish I weren't?'

Simon said nothing.

'I wouldn't blame you,' said Harry. 'Some fucking father I've been.' Simon shifted awkwardly on his seat.

'You—'

'Don't feel you have to be polite,' interrupted Harry. 'I know I screwed up with you. For sixteen years you never see me, then suddenly bam! I'm in your face all the time. No wonder things have been a bit tricky. If we were a married couple, we'd be divorced by now. Sorry,' he added after a pause. 'Sensitive subject.'

'It's OK.' Simon turned and gave him an unwilling grin, then, for the first time, registered his father's appearance. 'Dad, you know you're meant to take your clothes off?'

'That's for a steam bath,' said Harry. 'I came in here for a conversation.' He frowned. 'OK, so I've said my piece. Now you're supposed to tell me I've been a wonderful father, and I can rest easy.'

There was a long pause.

'I just wish . . .' began Simon at last, then stopped.

'What?'

'I just wish I didn't always feel like a failure,' said Simon in a rush. 'Everything I do goes wrong. And you . . . By the time you were my age, you were a millionaire!'

'No I wasn't.'

'It said in your biography . . .'

'That piece of shit. Simon, by the time I was your age, I owed a million. Fortunately, I found a way of paying it back.'

'And I didn't,' said Simon bitterly. 'I went bust.'

'OK,' said Harry, 'so you went bust. But at least you never sold out. At least you never came crying to me to bail you out. You stayed independent. Fiercely independent. And I'm proud of you for that.' He paused. 'I'm even proud you gave me back the keys to that flat. Pissed off – but proud.'

There was a long pause, punctuated only by the two of them breathing in the steamy air, and the odd spatter as a shower of warm drops fell to the floor.

'And if you have a go at working things out with Milly,' continued Harry slow, 'instead of walking away – then I'll be even prouder. Because that's something I never did. and I should have done.'

There was a silence for a while. Harry leaned back, stretched his legs out and winced. 'I have to say,' he said, 'this is not a nice experience. My underpants are sticking to my skin.'

'I told you,' said Simon.

'I know you did.' harry looked at him through the steam. 'So, are you going to give Milly another chance?' Simon exhaled sharply.

'Of course I am. If she'll give me another chance.' He shook his head. 'I don't know what I was thinking of last night. I was stupid. I was unfair. I was just a . . .' He broke off. 'I tried calling her this afternoon.'

'And?'

'She must have gone out with Esme.'

'Esme?' said Harry.

'Her godmother. Esme Ormerod.'

Harry looked up with raised eyebrows.

'That's Milly's godmother? Esme Ormerod?'

'Yes,' said Simon. 'Why?' Harry pulled a face.

'Strange woman.'

'I didn't know you knew her.'

'Took her out to dinner a few times,' said Harry. 'Big mistake.'

'Why?' Harry shook his head.

'It doesn't matter. It was a long time ago.' He leaned back and closed his eyes. 'So she's Milly's godmother. That surprises me.'

'She's some cousin or something.'

'And they seemed such a nice family,' said Harry in half-jesting tones. Then he frowned. 'I'm serious, you know. They are a nice family. Milly's a lovely girl. James seems a very decent guy. I'd like to get to know him better. And Olivia . . .' He opened his eyes. 'Well, what can I say? She's a fine woman.'

'You said it.' Simon grinned at his father.

'I just wouldn't like to meet her on a dark night.'

'Or any night.'

There was a short silence. Water dripped onto Harry's head and he winced.

'The only one I'm not sure about,' said Simon thoughtfully, 'is Isobel. She's a bit of an enigma. I never know what she's thinking.'

'No,' said Harry after a pause. 'Neither do I.'

'She's nothing like Milly. But I still like her.'

'So do I,' said Harry in a low voice. 'I like her a lot.' He stared silently at the floor for a few moments, then stood up. I've had enough of this hell. I'm going to take a shower.'

'Try taking your clothes off this time,' said Simon.

'Yes,' said Harry. 'Clever.' And he gave Simon a friendly nod before closing the door.

By the time Rupert rose stiffly to his feet, put Allan's letter away and made his way out of the gallery, it was late afternoon. He stood in Trafalgar Square for a bit, watching the tourists and taxis and pigeons, then turned and began to walk slowly to the tube. Every step felt unsure and shaky; he seemed to have lost some vital part of himself that kept him balanced.

All he knew was that the one certainty he'd had in life was gone. The grounding force, to which his life had been nothing but counterpoint, had vanished. It now seemed to him that everything he'd done over the last ten years had been part of an internal battle against Allan. And now the battle was over and neither of them had won.

As he rode in the train back to Fulham he stared blankly ahead at his reflection in the dark glass, wondering with an almost academic curiosity what he might do next. He felt tired, ragged and washed up, as though a storm had deposited him on a strange shore with no clear way back. On the one hand there was his wife. There was his home and his old life and the compromises he'd come to take as second nature. Not quite happiness, but not quite misery either. On the other hand, there was honesty. Raw, painful honesty. And all the consequences that honesty brought.

Rupert passed a weary hand over his face and gazed at his blurred, uncertain features in the window. He didn't want to be honest. He didn't want to be dishonest. He wanted to be nothing. A person on a train, with nothing to decide, nothing to do but listen to its trundling sound and watch the unconcerned faces of other passengers reading books and magazines. Postponing life for as long as possible.

But eventually the train reached his stop. And, like an automaton, he reached for his briefcase, stood up, and stepped onto the platform. He followed all the other commuters up the steps and into the dark winter evening. A familiar procession moved down the main road, decreasing in size as people peeled off down side streets, and Rupert followed them, slowing down as he neared his street. When he reached his own corner he stopped altogether, and for a moment considered turning back. But where would he go? There was nowhere else for him to go.

The lights were off in his house, and he felt a tiny relief as he opened the gate. He would take a bath and have a couple of drinks and perhaps by the time Francesca arrived home, his mind would be clearer. Perhaps he would show her Allan's letter. Or perhaps not. He reached in his pocket for his key and put it in the lock, then stopped. It didn't fit. He took it out, looked at it, and tried again. But the lock was impervious, and when he looked more closely, he could see signs of handiwork around the keyhole. Francesca had changed the lock. She'd shut him out.

For a few seconds he could not move. He stared at the door, shaking with fury and a sharp humiliation. 'Bitch,' he heard himself saying in a strangled voice. 'Bitch.' A sudden stab of longing for Allan hit him in the chest and he started to back away from the door, his eyes clouding with tears.

'Are you OK?' A cheerful girl's voice came from across the road. 'Are you locked out? You can phone from here, if you like!'

'No thanks,' muttered Rupert. He glanced at the girl. She was young and attractive and looked sympathetic – and for a moment he felt like falling onto her shoulder and telling her everything. Then it occurred to him that Francesca might be watching him from inside the house, and he felt a shaft of panic. Quickly, clumsily, he began to walk away, down the street. He reached the corner and hailed a taxi without knowing where he was going.

'Yes?' said the driver as he got in. 'Where to?'

'To . . . to . . .' Rupert closed his eyes for a few moments, then opened them and looked at his watch. 'To Paddington station.'

At six o'clock there was a ring at the front door. Isobel opened it, to see Simon standing on the doorstep holding a large bunch of flowers.

'Oh it's you,' she said in unfriendly tones. 'What do you want?'

'To see Milly.'

'She isn't here.'

'I know,' said Simon. He looked anxious and strangely well scrubbed, thought Isobel, like an old-fashioned suitor. The sight almost made her want to smile. 'I wanted to check her godmother's address.'

'You could have telephoned,' said Isobel uncompromisingly. 'You didn't need to drag me to the door.'

'Your phone was engaged.'

'Oh,' said Isobel. She folded her arms and leaned against the door frame, unwilling to let him off. 'So. Have you come down off your mountainous horse yet?'

'Just shut up, Isobel, and give me the address,' said Simon irritably.

'I don't know,' said Isobel. 'Does Milly want to talk to you?'

'Oh, forget it,' said Simon, turning and going back down the steps. 'I'll find her myself.'

Isobel stared at him for a few seconds, then called, 'It's Walden Street. Number 10.' Simon stopped walking and turned to look at her.

'Thanks,' he said. Isobel shrugged.

'That's OK. I hope . . .' She paused. 'You know.'

'Yup,' said Simon 'So do I.'

The door was answered by Esme, wearing a long white bathrobe.

'Oh,' said Simon awkwardly. 'Sorry to disturb you. I

wanted to speak to Milly.' Esme scanned his face, then said, 'She's asleep, I'm afraid. She drank quite a lot at lunchtime. I won't be able to wake her.'

'Oh,' said Simon. He shifted from one foot to the other. 'Well . . . just tell her I called round, would you? And give her these.' He handed the flowers to Esme and she looked at them with faint horror.

'I'll tell her,' she said. 'Goodbye.'

'Perhaps she could give me a ring. When she's up.'

'Perhaps,' said Esme. 'It's up to her.'

'Of course,' said Simon, flushing slightly. 'Well, thanks.'

'Goodbye,' said Esme, and closed the door. She looked at the flowers for a moment, then went into the kitchen and put them into the rubbish bin. She went upstairs and tapped on Milly's door.

'Who was that?' said Milly, looking up. She was lying on a massage table and Esme's beautician was rubbing a facial oil into her cheeks.

'A salesman,' said Esme smoothly. 'He tried to sell me some dusters.'

'Oh, we get those people, too,' said Milly, relaxing back onto the table. 'They always come at the worst time.' Esme smiled at her.

'How was your massage?'

'Wonderful,' said Milly.

'Good,' said Esme. She wandered over to the window, tapped her teeth for a few moments, then turned round.

'You know, I think we should go away,' she said. 'I should have thought of it before. You don't want to be in Bath tomorrow, do you?'

'Not really,' said Milly. 'But then . . . I don't really want to be anywhere.' Her face suddenly crumpled and tears began to ooze out of the sides of her eyes. 'I'm sorry,' she said huskily to the beautician.

'We'll drive into Wales,' said Esme. 'I know a little place in the mountains. Fabulous views and Welsh lamb every night. How does that sound?'

Milly was silent. The beautician dabbed tenderly at her tear stains with a yellow liquid from a gold embossed bottle.

'Tomorrow will be difficult,' said Esme gently. 'But we'll get through it. And after that . . .' She came forward and took Milly's hand. 'Just think, Milly. You've been given a chance which hardly any woman is given. You can start again. You can remould your life into whatever you want.'

'You're right,' said Milly, staring up at the ceiling. 'Anything I want.'

'The world is yours to reclaim! And to think you were about to settle for becoming a Mrs Pinnacle.' A note of scorn entered Esme's voice. 'Darling, you've had such a narrow escape. When you look back on all of this, you'll be grateful to me, Milly. You really will!'

'I already am grateful,' said Milly, turning her head to look at Esme. 'I don't know what I would have done without you.'

'That's my girl!' said Esme. She patted Milly's hand. 'Now you just lie back and enjoy the rest of your facial – and I'll go and pack the car.'

FIFTEEN

As James arrived home that evening the lights were low and the house silent. He hung up his coat and grimaced at his reflection in the mirror, then noiselessly pushed open the door to the kitchen. The table was covered in forlorn wedding debris and coffee cups, and Olivia was sitting in the dim stillness, her head bent forward, her shoulders hunched and defeated.

For a few moments she didn't see him. Then, as though he'd spoken, she raised her head. Her eyes met his apprehensively and flickered quickly away; her hands rose defensively to her face. James stepped forward awkwardly, feeling like a schoolroom bully.

'So,' he said, putting his briefcase down on a chair. 'It's all done.' He looked around. 'You must have had a hell of a day, putting the world and his wife off.'

'Not so bad,' said Olivia huskily. 'Isobel was a great help. We both . . .' She broke off. 'What about *your* day?

Isobel told me you've been having trouble at work. I . . . I didn't realize. I'm sorry.'

'You couldn't have realized,' said James. 'I didn't tell you.'

'Tell me now.'

'Not now,' said James wearily. 'Maybe later.'

'Yes, later,' said Olivia, her voice unsteady. 'Of course.' James raised his gaze to hers and felt a dart of shock as he saw the fear in her eyes. 'Let me make you some tea,' she said.

'Thank you,' said James. 'Olivia—'

'I won't be a moment!' She stood up hurriedly, catching her sleeve on the corner of the table, then wrenched it free as though desperate to turn away from him, towards the sink, the kettle; familiar inanimate objects. James sat down at the table and picked up the red book in front of him. He began to leaf idly through it. Page after page of lists, of ideas, self-reminders, even small sketches. The blueprint, he realized, for something quite spectacular.

'Swans,' he said, stopping at a starred item. 'You weren't really going to hire live swans for the occasion?'

'Swans made of ice,' said Olivia, brightening a little. 'They were going to full of . . .' She halted. 'It doesn't matter.'

'Full of what?' said James. There was a pause.

'Oysters,' said Olivia.

'I like oysters,' said James.

'I know,' said Olivia. She picked up the teapot with fumbling hands, turned to put it on the table and slipped. The teapot crashed loudly onto the quarry tiles and Olivia gave a small cry of distress.

'Olivia!' exclaimed James, leaping to his feet. 'Are you all right?' Pieces of broken china lay on the floor amid a puddle of hot tea; rivulets were running between the tiles towards his feet. The yellow-rimmed eye of a duck stared up at him reproachfully.

'It's broken!' said Olivia in anguish. 'We've had that teapot for thirty-two years!' She bent down, picked up a piece of the handle and stared at it disbelievingly.

'We'll get another one,' said James.

'I don't want another one,' said Olivia shakily. 'I want the old one. I want . . .' She suddenly broke off and turned round to face James. 'You're going to leave me, aren't you, James?'

'What?' James stared at her in shock.

'You're going to leave me,' repeated Olivia calmly. She looked down at the jagged piece of teapot and her hand tightened around it. 'For a new life. A new, exciting life.'

There was a still pause, then James exhaled in sudden comprehension.

'You heard me,' he said, trying to gather his thoughts. 'You *heard* me. I hadn't realized . . .'

'Yes, I heard you,' said Olivia, not looking up. 'Isn't that what you wanted?'

'Olivia. I didn't mean—'

'I assume you've been waiting until the wedding was over,' broke in Olivia, turning the piece of teapot over and over in her fingers. 'You probably didn't want to ruin the happy event. Well, the happy event's been ruined anyway. So you don't have to wait any longer. You can go.' James looked at her.

'You want me to go?'

'That's not what I said.' Olivia's voice roughened slightly; her head remained bowed. For a long while there was silence. On the other side of the room, the last brown rivulet of spilled tea slowly came to a standstill.

'The trouble at work,' said James suddenly, walking to the window. 'The trouble that Isobel was talking about. It's a restructuring of the company. They're relocating three departments to Edinburgh. They asked me if I'd like to move. And I said . . .' He turned round. 'I said I'd think about it.' Olivia looked up.

'You didn't mention it to me.'

'No,' said James defensively. 'I didn't. I knew what your answer would be.'

'Did you?' said Olivia. 'How clever of you.'

'You're rooted here, Olivia. You've got your business and your friends. I knew you wouldn't want to leave all of that. But I just felt as though I needed something new!' Pain flashed across James's face. 'Can you understand that? Have you never wanted to escape and start again? I felt trapped and guilty. I thought maybe a new city would be the answer to my malaise. A fresh view every morning. Different air to breathe.'

The kitchen was silent.

'I see,' said Olivia, eventually, her voice clipped and brittle. 'Well then, off you go. Don't let me hold you up. I'll help you pack, shall I?'

'Olivia—'

'Make sure you send us a postcard.'

'Olivia, don't be like this!'

'Like what? How else do you expect me to react? You've been planning to leave me!'

'Well, what was I supposed to do?' said James furiously. 'Just say no on the spot? Settle down to another twenty years in Bath?'

'No!' cried Olivia, her eyes suddenly glittering with tears. 'You were supposed to ask me to come with you. I'm your wife, James. You were supposed to ask me.'

'What was the point? You would have said—'

'You don't know what I would have said!' Olivia's voice trembled and she lifted her chin high. 'You don't know what I would have said, James. And you couldn't even be bothered to find out.'

'I . . .' James stopped.

'You couldn't even be bothered to find out,' repeated Olivia, and a slight note of scorn entered her voice.

There was a long silence.

'What would you have said?' asked James finally. 'If I had asked you?' He tried to meet Olivia's eye, but she was staring down at the piece of teapot which she still held in her hands, and her face was unreadable.

The doorbell rang. Neither of them moved.

'What would you have said, Olivia?' said James.

'I don't know,' said Olivia at last. She put the piece of teapot down on the table and looked up. 'I probably would have ask you if you were really so unhappy with the life you have here. I would have asked if you really thought a new city would solve all your problems. And if you'd said yes—' The doorbell rang again, loud and insistent, and she broke off. 'You'd better get that,' she said. James gazed at her for a few seconds, then got to his feet.

He strode into the hall, opened the door and took a step back in surprise. Alexander was standing on the doorstep. His face was unshaven, he was surrounded by bags and his eyes were wary.

'Look,' he said, as soon as he saw James. 'I'm sorry, I really am. You've got to believe me. I didn't mean to set all this off.'

'It hardly matters any more, does it?' said James wearily. 'The damage is done. If I were you, I'd just turn around and go.'

'It matters to me,' said Alexander. 'Plus . . .' He paused. 'Plus, I've still got some stuff here. In my room. Your daughter chucked me out before I could get it.'

'I see,' said James. 'Well, you'd better come in, then.'

Cautiously, Alexander entered the house. He glanced at the wedding cake boxes and grimaced.

'Is Milly here?' he asked.

'No. She's with her godmother.'

'Is she all right?'

'What do you think?' said James, folding his arms. Alexander flinched.

'Look, it wasn't my fault!' he said.

'What do you mean, it wasn't your fault?' Olivia appeared at the kitchen door, her face indignant. 'Milly told us how you teased her. How you threatened her. You're nothing but a nasty little bully!'

'Give me a break,' said Alexander. 'She's hardly a saint herself!'

'Perhaps, Alexander, you thought you were doing the world a service by exposing her,' said James. 'Perhaps you thought you were doing your duty. But you could have come to us first, or Simon, before informing the vicar.'

'I didn't want to expose her, for God's sake,' said Alexander impatiently. 'I just wanted to wind her up.'

'Wind her up?'

'Tease her a bit. You know. And that's all I did. I didn't tell the vicar! Why should I tell the vicar?'

'Who knows how your nasty little mind might work,' said Olivia.

'I don't know why I'm bothering,' said Alexander. 'You're never going to believe me. But I didn't do it. OK! Why should I wreck Milly's wedding? You were paying me to photograph the fucking thing! Why should I want to ruin it?'

There was silence. James glanced at Olivia.

'I don't even know the vicar's name,' said Alexander. He sighed. 'Listen, I tried to tell Isobel and she wouldn't listen, and now I'm trying to tell you, and you won't listen. But it's true. I didn't tell anyone about Milly. I really didn't. Jesus, she could have six husband for all I care!'

'All right,' said James, exhaling sharply. 'All right. Well, if you didn't say anything, who did?'

'God knows. Who else knew about it?'

'No-one,' said Olivia. 'She hadn't told anyone.'

There was silence.

'She told Esme,' said James eventually. He met Olivia's eyes. 'She told Esme.'

Isobel sat in a remote corner of the drive to Pinnacle Hall, looking through her car windscreen at Milly's marquee, just visible behind the corner of the house. She had been sitting there for half an hour, quietly composing her thoughts; honing her concentration as though for an exam. She would say what she had to say to Harry, brook as little objection as possible, then leave. She would be friendly, but businesslike. If he refused her proposal, she would . . . Isobel's thoughts faltered. He couldn't refuse such a reasonable plan. He simply couldn't.

She stared at her hands – already swollen, it seemed, with pregnancy. The very word sent teenage shivers down her back. Pregnancy, they had been instructed at school, was akin to a nuclear missile – destroying everything in its path and leaving its victims to struggle through a subsequent life hardly worth living. It destroyed careers, relationships, happiness. The risk was simply not worth it, the mistresses had opined, and at the back the lower sixth had sniggered and passed the telephone numbers of abortion clinics along the rows. Now Isobel closed her eyes. Perhaps the teachers had been right all along. Had this pregnancy not occurred, her relationship with Harry might have flowered into something more than occasional meetings. She had already begun to feel a longing to be with him more often; to share moments of pleasure and pain; to hear his voice when she woke up. She had wanted to tell him she loved him.

But now there was a baby. There was a new element, a new pace: a new pressure on both of them. To keep the baby would be to trample across Harry's wishes, to force their relationship into a new climate where, already, she knew it would not survive. To keep the baby would destroy their relationship. And yet to do anything else would destroy her.

Her heart aching a little, she reached inside her bag and gave her hair one final comb, then opened the car door and got out. The air was surprisingly mild and breezy, like a spring evening. Calmly she walked across the gravel towards the big front door, for once unafraid of observation by suspicious eyes. Today she had every reason to be at Pinnacle Hall.

She rang at the door and smiled at the red-haired girl who answered.

'I'd like to see Harry Pinnacle, please. It's Isobel Havill. The sister of Milly Havill.'

'I know who you are,' said the girl in less than friendly tones. I suppose it's about the wedding? Or the non-wedding, I should say.' She stared with bulging eyes at Isobel as though it were all her fault, and for the first time, Isobel wondered what people might be saying and thinking about Milly.

'That's right,' she said, 'if you could just say I'm here.'

'I'm not sure he's available,' said the girl.

'Perhaps you could ask,' said Isobel politely.

'Wait here.'

After a few minutes the girl returned.

'He can see you,' she said, as though bestowing a huge favour. 'But not for long.'

'Did he say that?' The girl was aggressively silent and Isobel found herself smiling inwardly.

They arrived at the door of Harry's study and the girl knocked.

'Yes!' came Harry's voice at once. The girl pushed open the door and Harry looked up from his desk.

'Isobel Havill,' she announced.

'Yes,' said Harry, meeting Isobel's eyes. 'I know.'

As the door closed behind the girl he put his pen down and looked at Isobel without saying anything. Isobel didn't move. She stood, trembling slightly, feeling his gaze on her skin like sunshine, then closed her eyes, trying to gather her thoughts. She heard him rise; heard him come towards her. His hand had grasped hers; his lips were pressed against the tender skin of her inner wrist, before she opened her eyes and said 'No.'

He looked up, her hand still in his, and she gazed desperately into his face, trying to convey all that she had to say in a single look. But there were too many conflicting desires and thoughts for him to read. A flash of something like disappointment passed over his face and he dropped her hand abruptly.

'A drink,' he said.

'I've got something to say to you,' said Isobel.

'I see,' said Harry. 'Do you want to sit down?'

'No,' said Isobel. 'I just want to say it.'

'OK, then say it!'

'Fine!' said Isobel. 'Here it is.' She paused, steeling herself to utter the words. 'I'm pregnant,' she said, then stopped, and the guilty word seemed to echo round the room. 'With your baby,' she added. Harry made a slight start. 'What?' said Isobel defensively. 'Don't you believe me?'

'Of course I fucking *believe* you,' said Harry. 'I was going to say . . .' He broke off. 'It doesn't matter. Carry on.'

'You don't seem surprised,' said Isobel.

'Is that part of your little speech?'

'Oh, shut up?' She took a deep breath and fixed her eyes on the corner of the mantelpiece, willing her voice to remain steady. 'I've thought about it very hard,' she said. 'I've considered all the options, and I've decided to keep it.' She paused. 'I've taken this decision knowing you don't want a child. So she'll have my name and I'll be responsible for her.'

'You know it's a girl?' interrupted Harry.

'No,' said Isobel shakily, put off her stride. 'I . . . I tend to use the feminine pronoun if the gender is unspecific.'

'I see,' said Harry. 'Carry on.'

'I'll be responsible for her,' said Isobel, speaking more quickly. 'Financially, as well as everything else. But I think every child needs a father if at all possible. I know you didn't choose for things to be this way – but neither did I, and neither did the baby.' She paused and clenched her fists tightly by her sides. 'And so I'd like to ask that you carry some parental responsibility and involvement. What I propose is a regular meeting, perhaps once a month, so that this child grows up knowing who her father is. I'm not asking any more than that. But any child deserves that minimum. I'm just trying to be reasonable.' She looked up, with sudden tears in her eyes. 'I'm just trying to be reasonable, Harry!'

'Once a month,' said Harry, frowning.

'Yes!' said Isobel angrily. 'You can't expect a child to bond on twice-yearly meetings.'

'I suppose not.' Harry stalked to the window and Isobel watched him apprehensively. Suddenly he turned round.

'What about twice a month? Would that do?'

Isobel stared at him.

'Yes,' she said. 'Of course—'

'Or twice a week?'

'Yes. But . . .' Harry began to walk slowly towards her, his warm eyes locked onto hers.

'How about twice a day?'

'Harry—'

'How about every morning and every afternoon and all through the night?' He gently took hold of her hands; she made no effort to resist.

'I don't understand,' she said, trying to retain control of herself. 'I don't—'

'How about I love you?' said Harry. 'How about I want to be with you all the time? And be a better father to our child than I ever was with Simon.'

Isobel gazed up at him. Emotions were pushing up to the surface in an uncontrollable surge.

'But you can't! You said you didn't want a baby!' The words came rushing out of her in a hurt, accusatory roar; tears suddenly spilled onto her cheeks and she pulled her hands away. 'You said—'

'When did I say that?' interrupted Harry. 'I never said that.'

'You didn't exactly say it,' said Isobel after a pause. 'But you pulled a face.'

'I did what?'

'A few months ago. I said a friend of mine was pregnant and you pulled this ... this face.' Isobel swallowed. 'And I said, Oh don't you like babies? And you changed the subject.' She looked up, to see Harry staring at her incredulously.

'That's it?'

'Isn't it enough? I knew what you meant.'

'You nearly got rid of our baby because of that?'

'I didn't know what to do!' cried Isobel defensively. 'I thought—'

Harry shook his head.

'You think too much,' he said. 'That's your problem.'

'I don't!'

'You reckon I don't like babies. Have you ever seen me with a baby?'

'No,' gulped Isobel.

'No. Exactly.'

He put his arms firmly round her and she closed her eyes. After a while, she felt the tension start to sag out of her. A thousand questions were racing around her mind, but, for the moment, she let them race.

'I like babies,' Harry said comfortably. 'As long as they don't squawk.' Isobel tensed and her head jerked up.

'All babies squawk!' she said. 'You can't expect—' She broke off, seeing his face. 'You're joking.'

'Of course I'm joking,' said Harry. He raised his eyebrows. 'Are you this good at interpreting your foreign diplomats? No wonder the world's at war – Isobel Havill's been conducting the negotiations. She thought you didn't want peace because you pulled a nasty face.'

Isobel gave a shaky half-giggle half-sob, and nestled into his chest.

'You really want to have this baby?' she said. 'Seriously?'

'I seriously do,' said Harry. He paused, stroking her hair. 'And even if I didn't,' he added in a deadpan voice, 'you shouldn't get rid of it. You never know, this might be your only chance.'

'Thanks a lot.'

'You're welcome.'

They stood for a while saying nothing, then Isobel pulled reluctantly away.

'I've got to go,' she said.

'Why?'

'They might need me at home.'

'They don't need you,' said Harry. 'I need you. Stay here tonight.'

'Really?' Isobel tensed. 'But what if someone sees me?' Harry began to laugh.

'Isobel, haven't you got it into your head yet?' he said. 'I *want* everyone to see you! I love you! I want to—' He broke off and looked at her with a different expression. 'Try this for size. What would you think about . . . about giving the baby my name?'

'You don't mean . . .' Isobel stared up at him, feeling her skin begin to tingle.

'I don't know,' said Harry. 'It depends. Do you already have a husband I should know about?'

'Bastard!' said Isobel, kicking his shins.

'Is that a yes?' said Harry, starting to laugh. 'Or a no?'

'Bastard!'

James and Alexander sat at the kitchen table, drinking brandy and waiting for Olivia to come off the phone.

'I got these developed, by the way,' said Alexander suddenly, pulling out a stiff brown envelope from his bag. 'On the house.'

'What are they?' said James.

'Have a look.'

James put down his drink, opened the envelope and pulled out a sheaf of glossy black and white photographs. He stared at the top one silently, then leafed through slowly to the bottom. Milly stared up at him again and again, her eyes wide and luminous, the curves of her face falling into soft shadows, her engagement ring sparkling discreetly in the corner of the frame.

'These are incredible,' he said at last. 'Absolutely extraordinary.'

'Thanks,' said Alexander offhandedly. 'I was pleased with them.'

'She looks beautiful, of course,' said James. 'She always looks beautiful. But it's not just that.' He gazed again at the top print. 'You've captured a depth to Milly in these pictures I've never seen before. She suddenly looks . . . intriguing.'

'She looks like a woman with a secret,' said Alexander. He took a swig of brandy. 'Which is exactly what she was.'

James looked up at him.

'Is that why you teased her? To get these pictures?'

'Partly,' said Alexander. 'And partly because . . .' he shrugged. '. . . I'm an evil bastard, and that kind of thing gives me kicks.'

'And never mind the consequences?' said James.

'I didn't know there would be any consequences,' said Alexander. 'I certainly didn't realize she would panic. She seemed so . . .' He paused. 'On top of herself.'

'She may look strong,' said James, 'but she's fragile underneath.' He paused. 'Just like her mother.'

They both looked up as Olivia appeared in the kitchen.

'So,' said James grimly. 'Did you speak to Canon Lytton? Was it Esme who told him?'

'That silly young curate wouldn't tell me!' said Olivia, with a spark of her old vigour. 'Can you believe it? He said it wasn't up to him to break a confidence, and Canon Lytton was too busy to come to the phone. Too busy!'

'What's he doing?' asked James.

Olivia exhaled sharply and a curious flicker passed across her face.

Conducting a wedding rehearsal,' she said. 'For the other couple getting married tomorrow.' There was a subdued little pause. 'I don't suppose there's much we can do about it,' she added, pouring herself a glass of brandy.

'Yes there is,' said James. 'We can go round there and we can get an answer.'

'What, and interrupt the wedding rehearsal?' Olivia stared at him. 'James are you serious?'

'Yes,' said James. 'I am. If my cousin has betrayed Milly's confidence and deliberately ruined her wedding, then I want to know about it.' He put down his drink. 'Come on, Olivia! Where's your fighting spirit?'

'Are you serious?' repeated Olivia.

'Yes,' said James. 'And besides –' he glanced at Alexander '– it might be fun.'

Simon was sitting by the window of his bedroom, trying to read a book, as the doorbell rang. A spasm of nerves went through him and he quickly got to his feet, discarding the book. It was Milly. It had to be Milly.

He had driven back to Pinnacle Hall from Esme's house with a hopeful happiness bubbling through him like spring water. After the wounding shock and anger of last night, he felt as though life was once again on course. He'd made the first move towards a reconciliation with Milly; as soon as she responded, he would renew his apologies and try to heal the wound between them as best he could. They would wait patiently for her divorce to come through; organize another wedding; start life again.

And now here she was. He descended the wide stairs, a foolish grin spreading over his face, and briskly crossed the hall. But before he was halfway across, his father's study door opened and Harry appeared. He was laughing and gesturing to someone in his room; a whisky glass was in his hand.

'It's all right,' said Simon quickly. 'I'll get it.' Harry turned round in surprise.

'Oh, hello,' he said. 'Are you expecting someone?'

'I don't know,' said Simon awkwardly. 'Milly maybe.'

'Ah,' said Harry. 'I'll get out of your way, then.'

Simon grinned at his father and, without thinking, allowed his eyes to roam inside the open door study. To his surprise he caught a glimpse of female leg by the fire. A mild curiosity began to rise through him and he glanced questioningly at his father. Harry seemed to think for a couple of seconds, then he flung the study door open.

Isobel Havill was sitting by the fire. Her head shot up, a shocked expression on her face, and Simon stared back at her in surprise.

'You know Isobel, don't you, Simon?' said Harry cheerfully.

'Yes, of course,' said Simon. 'Hi, Isobel. What are you doing here?'

'I'm here to talk about the wedding,' she said after a pause.

'No you're not,' said Harry. 'Don't lie to the boy.'

'Oh,' said Simon confusedly. 'Well, it doesn't—'

'We have something to tell you, Simon,' said Harry. 'Although this may not be quite the best time . . .'

'No, it's not,' interrupted Isobel firmly. 'Why doesn't one of you answer the door?'

'What have you got to tell me?' said Simon. His heart began to thud. 'Is it about Milly?'

Isobel sighed. 'No,' she said.

'Not directly,' said Harry.

'Harry!' said Isobel, a note of irritation entering her voice. 'Simon doesn't want to hear this now!'

'Hear what?' said Simon as the doorbell rang again. He looked from one to the other. Isobel was giving his father a private little grown; Harry was grinning back at her teasingly. Simon stared at the two of them, communicating in a silent, intimate language, and suddenly, with a lurch, he understood.

'Get the door,' said Isobel. 'Somebody.'

'I'll go,' said Simon in a strangled voice. Isobel shot his father an angry look.

'Simon, are you OK?' said Harry apologetically. 'Listen, I didn't mean to—'

'It's OK,' said Simon, not looking back. 'It's OK.'

He strode up to the front door and yanked it open with a shaking, clumsy hand. On the doorstep was a stranger. A tall, well-built man, with blond hair that shone under the lantern like a halo, and bloodshot blue eyes full of a miserable wariness.

Simon stared back at the stranger in disappointment,

too nonplussed by events to speak. Thoughts were skittering round his mind like mad bowling balls, as his brain tried to link this new information to all the evidence that had been before him over the last few months. How many times had he seen his father and Isobel together? Hardly ever. But maybe that fact should have been a sign in itself. If he'd paid more attention, might he have noticed something? How long had their affair been going on, anyway? And where the hell was Milly?

'I'm looking for Simon Pinnacle,' said the stranger at last. His eyes shone entreatingly at Simon and there was a curious, pre-emptive defensiveness to his voice. 'Are you him, by any chance?'

'Yes,' said Simon, forcing himself to focus; to pull himself together. 'I am. How can I help you?'

'You won't know who I am,' said the man.

'I think I do,' interrupted Isobel, from behind Simon. 'I think I know exactly who you are.' An incredulous note entered her voice as she gazed up at him. 'You're Rupert, aren't you?'

Giles Claybrook and Eleanor Smith were standing at the altar of St Edward's, gazing silently at one another.

'Now,' said Canon Lytton, smiling benevolently at the pair of them. 'Is it to be one ring or two?'

'One,' said Giles, looking up.

'Giles won't wear a wedding ring,' said Eleanor, a slight flush of annoyance coming to her features. 'I've tried to persuade him.'

'Ellie, love,' said Eleanor's uncle, filming behind on a video camera. 'Could you move slightly to the right. Lovely.'

'One ring,' said Canon Lytton, making a note on his service sheet. 'Well, in that case . . .'

There was a rattle at the doors at the back of the church, and he looked up in surprise. The door swung open, to reveal James, Olivia and Alexander.

'Forgive us,' said James, walking briskly up the aisle. 'We just need a moment with Canon Lytton.'

'We won't be long,' said Olivia.

'Sorry to interrupt,' added Alexander cheerfully.

'What's going on?' said Giles, peering down the aisle.

'Mrs Havill, I am busy!' thundered Canon Lytton. 'Kindly wait at the back!'

'It won't take a second,' said James. 'We just need to know – who told you about Milly's first wedding?'

'If you are trying to convince me, at this late stage, that the information is false . . .' began Canon Lytton.

'We're not!' said James impatiently. 'We just need to know.'

'Was it him?' demanded Olivia, pointing to Alexander.

'No,' said Canon Lytton, 'it wasn't. And now if you would kindly—'

'Was it my cousin, Esme Ormerod?' asked James.

There was silence.

'I was told in confidence,' said Canon Lytton at last, a slight stiffness entering his confirmation. 'And I'm afraid that—'

'I'll take that as confirmation that it was,' said James. He sank down onto a pew. 'I just don't believe it. How could she? She's supposed to be Milly's godmother! She's supposed to help and protect her!'

'Indeed,' said Canon Lytton sternly. 'And would it be helping your daughter to stand back as she deliberately entered a marriage based on lies and falseness?'

'What are you saying?' said Olivia incredulously. 'That Esme was trying to act in Milly's best interests?'

Canon Lytton made a small gesture of assent.

'Well then you're mad!' cried Olivia. 'She was acting out of spite and you know it! She's a spiteful, malicious troublemaker! You know, I never liked that woman. I saw through her, right from the start.' She nodded at James. 'Right from the start.'

Canon Lytton had turned to Giles and Eleanor.

'My apologies for this unseemingly interruption,' he said. 'Now let us resume. The giving and receiving of the ring.'

'Hold on,' said Eleanor's uncle. 'I'll rewind the video, shall I? Or do you want me to keep all this?' He gestured to James and Olivia. 'We could send it in to a TV show.'

'No we bloody couldn't,' snapped Eleanor. 'Carry on, Canon Lytton.' She shot a malevolent look at Olivia. 'We'll ignore these rude people.'

'Very well,' said Canon Lytton. 'Now, Giles, you will place the ring on Eleanor's finger, and repeat after me.' He raised his voice. 'With this ring, I thee wed.'

There was a pause, then Giles said self-consciously. 'With this ring, I thee wed.'

'With my body, I thee worship.'

'With my body I thee worship.'

As the ancient words rose into the empty space of the church, everyone seemed to relax. Olivia raised her eyes to the vaulted ceiling, then looked down at James. A wistful look came over her face and she sat down next to him. they both watched Alexander as he crept forward and took a discreet picture of Canon Lytton trying to ignore the video camera.

'Do you remember our wedding?' she said quietly.

'Yes,' said James. He met her eyes cautiously. 'What about it?'

'Nothing,' said Olivia. 'I was just . . . remembering it. How nervous I was.'

'You nervous?' said James, half smiling.

'Yes,' said Olivia. 'Nervous.' There was a long pause, then she said, without meeting his eyes. 'Perhaps next week – if you felt like it – we could go up to Edinburgh. Just for a break. We could have a look around. Stay in a hotel. And . . . and talk about things.'

There was silence.

'I'd like that,' said James eventually. 'I'd like that very much.' He paused. 'What about the bed and breakfast?'

'I could close it for a bit,' said Olivia. She flushed slightly. 'It's not the most important thing in my life, you know.'

James stared at her silently. Cautiously, he moved his hand across towards hers. Olivia remained motionless. Then there was a sudden rattling at the door, and they jumped apart like scalded cats. The young curate of the church was striding up the aisle, cordless phone in hand.

'Canon Lytton,' he said, a note of excitement in his voice. 'You have a very urgent telephone call from Miss Havill. I wouldn't interrupt, normally, but—'

'From Milly?' said Olivia in surprise. 'Let me speak to her!'

'From Isobel Havill,' said the curate, ignoring Olivia. 'Speaking from Pinnacle Hall.' He handed the phone to Canon Lytton, his eyes gleaming. 'Apparently there's been a rather startling development.'

Isobel put down the telephone and looked at the others.

'I just spoke to Mummy at the church,' she said. 'You know, it wasn't Alexander who told the vicar about Milly.'

'Who was it?' said Simon.

'You won't believe this,' said Isobel. She paused for effect. 'It was Esme.'

'That doesn't surprise me,' said Harry.

'Do you know her?' said Isobel, staring at him in surprise.

'I used to,' said Harry. 'Not any more. Not for a long time,' he added hastily. Isobel gave him a briefly suspicious look, then frowned, tapping her nails on the phone.

'And Milly doesn't even realize! I must call her.'

'No wonder she wouldn't let me in the house,' said

Simon, as Isobel picked up the phone again. 'The woman's a bloody weirdo!'

There was a tense silence as Isobel waited to be connected. Suddenly her face changed expression, and she motioned for the others to be quiet.

'Hi, Esme,' she said, her voice airily casual. 'Is Milly there by any chance? Oh, right. Could you maybe wake her up?' She pulled a face at Simon, who grimaced back. 'Oh, I see. OK, well, not to worry. Just give her my love!'

She put down the phone and looked at the others.

'You know, I really don't trust that woman,' she said. 'I'm going round there.'

SIXTEEN

As she reached the bottom of the stairs, Milly stopped and put her case down on the floor.

'I'm not sure,' she said.

'What do you mean, you're not sure?' said Esme briskly, coming into the hall. She was wearing her fur hat and holding a pair of black leather gloves and a road map. 'Come on! It's getting late.'

'I'm not sure about going away,' said Milly. She sat down on the stairs. 'I feel as if I'm running away from everything. Maybe it would be better to stay and be brave and face it out.' Esme shook her head.

'Darling, you're not running away – you're being sensible. If we stay here, you'll spend all of tomorrow with your face pressed against the window, brooding. If we go away, at least you'll have a different view to distract you.'

'But I should talk to my parents, at least.'

'They'll still be here on Monday. And they'll be too busy to talk at the moment.'

'Well, then, maybe I should help them.'

'Milly,' said Esme impatiently, 'you're being ridiculous. The best place for you at the moment is somewhere far away, tranquil and discreet, where you can think about life properly for once. Take some time out, rebalance yourself, work out your priorities.'

Milly stared at the floor for a while.

'It's true,' she said at last. 'I do need a chance to think.'

'Of course you do!' said Esme. 'You need some unhurried peace and solitude. If you go home, you'll be surrounded by mayhem and distraction and emotional pressure. From your mother especially.'

'She was very upset,' said Milly. 'Mummy. She really wanted the wedding to happen.'

'Of course she did,' said Esme. 'We all did. but now that it's not going to happen, you're going to have to think about life in a different way. Aren't you?'

Milly sighed and stood up.

'Yes,' she said. 'You're right. A weekend in the countryside is exactly what I need.'

'You won't regret it,' said Esme, and smiled at her. 'Come on. Let's get on the road.'

Esme's Daimler was parked on the street outside, underneath a street light. As they got in, Milly turned round in her seat and peered curiously through the back window.

'That looks like Isobel's car,' she said.

'There are lots of these little Peugeots around the

place,' murmured Esme. She turned on the ignition and a blast of Mozart filled the car.

'It *is* Isobel's car!' said Milly, peering harder. 'What's Isobel doing here?'

'Well, I'm afraid we can't hang around,' said Esme, swiftly putting the car into gear. 'You can give her a ring when we get there.'

'No, wait!' protested Milly. 'She's getting out. She's coming towards us. Esme, stop!' Esme put the car into gear and began to drive off, and Milly stared at her in astonishment. 'Esme, stop!' she said. 'Stop the car!'

Hurrying along the street, Isobel saw Esme's car pulling away from the kerb and felt a thrust of panic. She began to run after the car, panting in the winter air, desperate not to let Milly out of her sight. She could just see Milly's blond head incarcerated behind Esme's expensive Daimler windows; as she ran, she saw Milly turn and see her, then say something to Esme. But the car didn't stop. A surge of fury went through Isobel as she saw it disappearing away from her towards the end of the road. Who did this bitch think she was? Where the hell was she taking Milly? A furious adrenalin began to pump round her body and, with an almighty effort, she upped her pace to a sprint. She careered along the pavement, keeping the rear lights of the Daimler in sight, unsure what she would do when Esme turned the corner and zipped off down the main road.

But the traffic lights at the end of the road were red, and as Esme's car approached them it was forced to slow down. Feeling like a triumphant Olympic athlete, Isobel caught up with the car and began to bang on Milly's window. Inside, she could see Milly shouting animatedly at Esme, then struggling with the handbrake. Suddenly Milly's door opened and she spilled out, half falling, onto the pavement.

'What do you want?' she gasped to Isobel. 'I thought it must be important.'

'Too right it's important!' managed Isobel, red in the face and panting hard, almost unable to speak for anger. 'Too right it's important! My God!' She pushed her hair out of her eyes and forced herself to take a couple of deep breaths. 'For a start, you might like to know, it was this bitch who shopped you to the vicar.' She gestured scornfully at Esme, who stared back at her from the driver's seat with furious, glinting eyes.

'What do you mean?' said Milly. 'It was Alexander.'

'It wasn't Alexander, it was Esme! Wasn't it?' snapped Isobel at Esme.

'Really?' said Milly, looking at Esme with wide eyes. '*Really?*'

'Of course not!' said Esme tartly. 'Why would I do such a thing?'

'To get back at Harry, perhaps,' said Isobel, a new, scathing note entering her voice.

'You're talking nonsense!'

'I'm not,' said Isobel. 'He's told me all about you. Everything.'

'Has he now?' said Esme mockingly.

'Yes,' said Isobel coldly. 'He has.'

There was silence. Esme's glinting eyes ranged sharply over Isobel's face, then suddenly flickered in comprehension.

'I see,' she said slowly. 'So that's how it is.' She gave Isobel a tiny, contemptuous smile. 'I might have guessed as much. You Havill girls do have a penchant for money, don't you?'

'You're a bitch, Esme,' said Isobel.

'I don't understand,' said Milly, looking from Isobel to Esme. 'What are you talking about? Esme, did you really tell Canon Lytton about me being married?'

'Yes I did,' said Esme. 'And it was for your own good. You didn't want to marry that immature, sanctimonious little prig!'

'You betrayed me!' cried Milly. 'You're supposed to be my godmother! You're supposed to be on my side!'

'I am on your side,' retorted Esme.

Behind them, a line of cars was beginning to mount up. One of them sounded its horn and Isobel gestured impatiently back.

'Milly, listen,' said Esme. 'You're far too good for marriage to Simon Pinnacle! Your life hasn't begun yet. Don't you understand? I saved you from a life of tedium and mediocrity.'

'Is that what you think?' said Milly, her voice rising in disbelief. 'That you saved me?'

Several more cars began to sound their horns. Towards the back of the queue, a driver got out of his car and began to walk along the pavement.

'Darling, I know you very well,' began Esme. 'And I know that—'

'You don't!' interrupted Milly. 'You don't know me very well. You don't know me at all! All of you think you know me – and none of you do! You haven't got any idea what I'm really like, underneath . . .'

'Underneath what?' challenged Esme.

Milly gazed silently at Esme, panting slightly, her face bathed green in the glow of the traffic light above, then looked away.

'Excuse me.' A truculent male voice interrupted them. 'Have you seen the light?'

'Yes,' said Milly dazedly. 'I think I probably have.'

'The lady was just leaving,' said Isobel, and slammed the passenger door of Esme's car viciously. 'Come on, Milly,' she said, taking her sister's arm. 'Let's go.'

As they sped away in Isobel's car, Milly sank bank into her seat and massaged her brow with her fingertips. Isobel drove quickly and efficiently, glancing at Milly every so often but saying nothing. After a while, Milly sat up and smoothed back her hair.

'Thanks, Isobel,' she said.

'Any time.'

'How did you guess it was Esme?'

'It had to be,' said Isobel. 'No-one else knew. If Alexander hadn't told anyone, it had to be her. And . . .' She paused. 'There were other things.'

'What things?' Milly swivelled her head towards Isobel. 'What was all that about getting back at Harry?'

'They had a liaison,' said Isobel shortly. 'Let's just say it didn't work.'

'How do you know?'

'He told Simon. And me. I was over there just now.' A tinge of pink came to Isobel's cheeks and she put her foot down rather hard on the accelerator. Milly stared at her sister.

'Is something wrong?'

'No,' said Isobel. But the pink in her cheeks was deepening to a red and she wouldn't look round. Milly's heart began to thump.

'Isobel, what's going on? What did Esme mean, you've got a penchant for money?'

Isobel said nothing, but changed gear with a crunch. She signalled to turn left and turned the windscreen wipers on by mistake.

'Damn,' she said. 'This bloody car.'

'There's something you're not telling me, Isobel,' said Milly. 'You're hiding something.'

'I'm not,' said Isobel.

'What were you doing at Pinnacle Hall?' Milly's voice suddenly sharpened. 'Who were you seeing?'

'No-one.'

'Don't play games with me! Have you and Simon been seeing each other behind my back?'

'No!' said Isobel, laughing. 'Don't be ridiculous.'

'How do I know? If my godmother can betray me, then why can't my own sister?'

Isobel glanced at Milly. Her face was white and tense and her hands were tightly gripping the seat.

'For God's sake, Milly,' she said quickly. 'We're not all Esme Ormerod! Of course I haven't been seeing Simon.'

'Well, what is it, then?' Milly's voice rose higher. 'Isobel, tell me what's going on!'

'OK!' Isobel said. 'OK. I'll tell you. I was going to break it to you gently but since you're so bloody suspicious . . .' She glanced at Milly and took a deep breath. 'It's Harry.'

'What's Harry?' said Milly.

'Who I was seeing. He's . . .' Isobel swallowed. 'The father,' she glanced at Milly's face, still blank and uncomprehending. 'Of my child, Milly! He's . . . he's the one I've been seeing.'

'What?' Milly's voice ripped through the car like the cry of a bird. 'You've been seeing Harry Pinnacle?'

'Yes.'

'He's the father of your child?'

'Yes.'

'You've been having an affair with Simon's *dad*?' Milly's voice was becoming higher and higher.

'Yes!' said Isobel defensively. 'But—' She stopped at the sound of Milly bursting into sobs. 'Milly, what's wrong?' She shot a quick look at Milly, who was doubled over in her seat, clasping her face in her hands. Tears suddenly sprang to her own eyes, blurring her view of the road. 'Milly, I'm really sorry,' she said. 'I know this is a terrible time to tell you. Oh Milly, don't cry!'

'I'm not crying,' managed Milly. 'I'm not crying!'

'What do you—'

'I'm laughing!' Milly gasped for breath, looked at Isobel, then erupted into hysterical giggles again. 'You and Harry! But he's so old!'

'He's not old!' said Isobel.

'He is! He's ancient! He's got grey hair!'

'Well I don't care. I love him. and I'm going to have his baby!'

Milly raised her head and looked at Isobel. She was staring ahead defiantly but her lips were trembling and tears had spilled onto her cheeks.

'Oh Isobel, I'm sorry!' Milly said in distress. 'I didn't mean it! He's not old really.' She paused. 'I'm sure you'll make a lovely couple.'

'Of fogies,' said Isobel, signalling to turn right.

'Don't!' said Milly. A tiny giggle erupted from her and she clamped her mouth shut. 'I can't believe it. My sister, having a secret affair with Harry Pinnacle. I knew you were up to something. But I never would have guessed in a million years.' She looked up. 'Does anyone else know?'

'Simon.'

'You told Simon before me?' said Milly, hurt. Isobel rolled her eyes exasperatedly.

'Milly, you sound just like Mummy!' she said. 'And no, I didn't. He came across us.'

'What, in bed?'

'No, not in bed!'

Milly giggled.

'Well, I don't know, do I? You might have been.' She glanced at Isobel's profile. 'You're very good at keeping secrets, you know.'

'Speak for yourself!' said Isobel.

'Yes, I suppose so,' said Milly, after a pause. 'I suppose so. But you know . . .' She stretched out her legs and put her feet up on the dashboard. 'I never thought of my marriage to Allan as a secret, exactly.'

'What was it, then?'

'I don't know,' said Milly vaguely. She thought for a moment. 'A secret is something which you have to keep hidden. But that was more like . . . something in a different world. Something which never really existed in this world.' She gazed out of the window, watching as the inky black hedgerow sped by. 'I still think of it a bit like that. If no-one had found out about it, it wouldn't have existed.'

'You're mad,' said Isobel, signalling left.

'I'm not!' Milly pointed her feet, encased in pink suede, against the glass. 'Do you like my new shoes, by the way?'

'Very nice.'

'Twenty quid. Simon would *hate* them.' A tiny satisfaction entered her voice. 'I thought I might cut my hair too.'

'Good idea,' said Isobel absently.

'Bleach it. And get a nose-ring.' She met Isobel's horrified eye and grinned. 'Or something.'

As they approached Pinnacle Hall, Milly's eyes suddenly focused on her surroundings, and she stiffened.

'Isobel, what's going on?' she said.

'We're going to Pinnacle Hall,' said Isobel.

'I can see that,' said Milly. 'But why?'

Isobel didn't reply for a while.

'I think we should wait until we get there,' she said at last.

'I don't want to see Simon,' said Milly, 'if that's your idea. If you've set up some meeting, you can forget it. I'm not going to see him.'

'You know, he came to apologize to you this afternoon,' said Isobel. 'He brought you flowers. But Esme wouldn't let him in.' She turned towards Milly. 'Now do you want to see him?'

'No,' said Milly after a pause. 'It's too late. He can't undo the things he said.'

'I think he's genuinely sorry,' said Isobel, as they approached the gates of Pinnacle Hall, 'for what that's worth.'

'I don't care,' said Milly. As the car crackled on the drive, she shrank down in her seat. 'I don't mind seeing Harry,' she said. 'But not Simon. I'm just not going to see him.'

'Fine,' said Isobel calmly. 'It's not him I've brought you to see, anyway. There's someone else who's come to see you.' She switched off the engine and looked at Milly. 'Brace yourself for a shock,' she added.

'What?' But Isobel was already out of the car and walking towards the house. Hesitantly, Milly got out and began to follow her, crunching on the gravel. Automatically her eyes rose to Simon's bedroom window, in the far left corner of the house. The curtains were drawn but she could see a chink of light. Perhaps he was behind the curtains, watching her. A dart of apprehension went through her and she began to walk more quickly, wondering what Isobel had been talking about. As she neared the front door, it suddenly opened and a tall figure appeared in the shadows.

'Simon!' said Milly, without thinking.

'No.' Rupert's subdued voice travelled easily through the evening air; as he moved forward his blond hair was visible under the light. 'Milly, it's me.' Milly stopped in astonishment.

'Rupert?' she said incredulously. 'What are you doing here? You were in London.'

'I came down by train,' said Rupert. 'I had to see you. There was no-one at your house, so I came here.'

'I suppose you've heard, then,' said Milly, shifting her feet on the gravel. 'It all came out. The wedding's off.'

'I know. That's why I'm here.' He rubbed his face, then looked up. 'Milly, I tracked down Allan for you.'

'You've found him? Already?' Milly's voice rose in excitement. 'Where is he? Is he here?'

'No,' said Rupert. He walked slowly towards her across the gravel and took her hands. 'Milly, I've got some bad news. Allan's . . . Allan's dead. He died four years ago.'

Milly stared at him in stunned silence, feeling as though a bucket of icy cold water had hit her in the face. Allan dead. The idea circled her mind like some sort of foreign body, impossible to digest. It couldn't be true. Allan couldn't be dead. People his age didn't *die*. It was ludicrous.

As she gazed at Rupert, a sudden desire rose within her to giggle; to turn this into the joke it must surely be. But Rupert wasn't smiling or laughing. He was gazing at her with a strange desperation, as though waiting for a reaction; an answer. Milly blinked a few times, and swallowed, her throat suddenly dry like sandpaper.

'What . . . how?' she managed. Visions of car crashes ran through her mind. Aeroplane disasters; mangled wreckage on the television.

'Leukaemia,' said Rupert.

A fresh jolt hit Milly and the base of her spine began to tingle unpleasantly.

'He was ill?' she said, and licked her dry lips. 'All that time, he was ill?'

'Not while we knew him,' said Rupert. 'It was afterwards.'

'Did he . . . suffer much?'

'Apparently not,' said Rupert, a low, suppressed anguish in his voice. 'But I don't know. I wasn't there.'

Milly gazed at him for a few silent seconds.

'It's all wrong,' she said eventually. 'He shouldn't . . .' Something was constricting her throat. 'He shouldn't have died.' She shook her head violently. 'Allan didn't deserve to die.'

'No,' said Rupert in a trembling voice. 'He didn't.'

She stared at him for a moment and a thousand shared memories seemed to pass between them. Then, in a moment of pure instinct, she reached out her arms.

Rupert half fell against her, stumbling on the gravel, and buried his head in her shoulder. Milly held on tightly to him and looked up at the inky sky, tears blurring her view of the stars. And as a cloud passed over the moon it occurred to her for the first time that she was a widow.

As Isobel entered the kitchen, Simon looked up warily from his seat at the huge refectory table. He was cradling a glass of wine and in front of him was the *Financial Times*, open but – Isobel suspected – unread.

'Hi,' he said.

'Hi,' said Isobel. She sat down opposite him and reached for the wine bottle. For a while there was silence. Isobel looked curiously at Simon. He was staring down, avoiding her eye, as though experiencing some kind of internal struggle.

'So,' he said at last. 'I gather you're pregnant. Congratulations.'

'Thanks,' said Isobel. She gave him a little smile. 'I'm really happy about it.'

'Good,' said Simon. 'That's great.' He reached for his glass of wine and took a deep swig.

'It'll be your half-brother,' added Isobel. 'Or sister.'

'I know,' said Simon shortly. Isobel looked at him sympathetically.

'Are you finding this difficult to deal with?'

'Well, to be honest, just a tad!' said Simon, putting down his glass. 'One minute you're going to be my sister-in-law. The next minute you're not going to be my sister-in-law. Then all of a sudden, you're going to be my stepmother, and you're having a baby!'

'I know,' said Isobel. 'It is all a bit sudden. I'm sorry. Truly.' She took a thoughtful sip of wine. 'What do you want to call me, by the way? "Stepmother" seems a bit of a mouthful. How about "Mum"?'

'Very funny,' said Simon irritably. He took a swig of wine, picked up the newspaper and put it down again. 'Where the hell's Milly? They're taking a long time, aren't they?'

'Oh come on,' said Isobel. 'Give the girl a chance. She's just found out that her husband's dead.'

'I know,' said Simon, 'I know. But even so . . .' He stood up and walked to the window, then turned round. 'So – what do you think of this Rupert, then?'

'I don't know,' said Isobel. 'I have to say, I was expecting a complete bastard. But this guy just seems . . .' She thought for a moment. 'Very sad. He just seems very sad.'

'The truth is,' said Rupert, 'I should never have married her.' He was leaning forward, his head resting wearily on his knuckles. Next to him, Milly wrapped her arms more tightly around her knees. They were sitting on a low wall behind the office wing; above them, like a second moon, was the old stable clock. 'I knew what I was. I knew I was living a lie. But, you know, I thought I could do it.' He looked up miserably. 'I really thought I could do it!'

'Do what?' said Milly.

330

'Be a good husband! Be a normal, decent husband. Do all the things everybody else does. Have dinner parties and go to church and watch our children in a nativity play . . .' He broke off, staring into the darkness. 'We were trying for a baby, you know. Francesca was pregnant last year. It would have been due in March. But she lost it. Now everyone will be thanking God that she had that miscarriage, won't they?'

'No,' said Milly uncertainly.

'Of course they will. They'll be calling it a blessing.' He looked up with bloodshot blue eyes. 'Maybe I'm being selfish. But I wanted that baby. I desperately wanted that baby. And I—' He faltered slightly. 'I would have been a good father to it.'

'It would have been lucky to have you,' said Milly stoutly.

'That's sweet,' said Rupert, a faint smile coming to his face. 'Thanks.'

'But a baby isn't glue, is it?' said Milly. 'A baby doesn't keep a marriage together.'

'No,' said Rupert. 'It doesn't.' He thought for a moment. 'The odd thing is, I don't think we ever had a marriage. Not what I would call a marriage. We were like two trains, running side by side, barely aware of each other's existence. We never argued; we never clashed. To be honest, we hardly knew each other. It was all very civil and pleasant – but it wasn't real.'

'Were you happy?'

'I don't know,' said Rupert. 'I pretended to be. Some of the time I even fooled myself.'

There was silence. Somewhere in the distance a fox barked. Rupert sighed and stretched out his legs in front of him.

'Shall we go in?' he said.

'OK,' said Milly vaguely. Rupert looked at her curiously for a while.

'How about you?' he said at last.

'What about me?'

'You know Allan's death changes everything.'

'I know,' said Milly. She examined her hands intently for a moment, then stood up. 'Come on. I'm getting cold.'

At the sound of the front door opening, Simon stood up, as abruptly as though a small electric current had been passed through his body. He smoothed back his hair and began to make awkwardly for the kitchen door, checking his appearance as he passed the un-curtained window. Isobel looked at him with raised eyebrows.

'She probably won't want to talk to you,' she said. 'You really hurt her, you know.'

'I know,' said Simon, halting at the door. 'I know. But . . .' He reached for the door knob, hesitated for a few seconds, then pushed the door open.

'Good luck,' called Isobel after him.

Milly was standing just inside the front door, her hands deep in her pockets. At the sound of Simon's tread, she looked up. Simon stopped, and stared at her. She seemed suddenly different; as though the events of the last two days had remoulded her face, her entire person.

'Milly,' he said shakily. She gave a faint acknowledgement. 'Milly, I'm sorry, I'm so sorry. I didn't mean any of the things I said.' His words came tumbling out like apples from a tree. 'I had no right to speak to you like that. I had no right to say those things.'

'No,' said Milly in a low voice. 'You didn't.'

'I was hurt, and I was shocked. And I lashed out without thinking. But if you give me another chance, I'll . . . I'll make it up to you.' Simon's eyes suddenly shone with tears. 'Milly, I don't care if you've been married before. I don't care if you've got six children. I just want to be with you.' He took a step towards her. 'And so I'm asking you to forgive me and give me another chance.'

There was a long pause.

'I forgive you,' said Milly at last, staring at the floor. 'I forgive you, Simon.'

'Really?' Simon stared at her. 'Really?' She gave a tiny shrug.

'It was understandable, the way you reacted. I should have told you about Allan in the first place.'

There was an uncertain silence. Simon moved forward and tried to take Milly's hands but she flinched. He dropped his hands and cleared his throat.

'I heard what happened to him,' he said. 'I'm really sorry.'

'Yes, said Milly.

'You must be—'

'Yes.'

'But . . .' He hesitated. 'You know what it means for us?' Milly looked at him as though he were speaking a foreign language.

'What?' she said.

'Well,' said Simon. 'It means we can get married.'

'No, Simon,' said Milly. Simon paled slightly.

'What do you mean?' he said, keeping his voice light. Milly met his eyes briefly, then looked away.

'I mean, we can't get married.' And as he watched her in disbelief, she turned on her heel and walked out of the front door.

SEVENTEEN

Milly didn't stop walking until she reached Isobel's car. Then she leaned against the passenger door and scrabbled in her pocket for a cigarette, trying to ignore the burning ache in her chest; trying not to think of Simon's startled face. She had done the right thing, she told herself. She had been honest. Finally, she had been honest.

With shaky hands she put the cigarette in her mouth and flicked repeatedly at her lighter, but the evening breeze blew the flame out every time. Eventually, with a little cry of frustration, she threw the cigarette on the ground and stamped on it. She felt suddenly powerless and marooned. She couldn't go back into the house. She couldn't drive off without a car key. She didn't even have a mobile phone. Perhaps Isobel would come and find her in a moment.

There was a sudden crunching on the gravel and she

looked up, then jumped as she saw Simon striding towards her, a look of serious intent on his face.

'Look, Simon, don't even bother,' she said, turning away. 'It's over, OK?'

'No, it's not OK!' exclaimed Simon. He reached the car, panting slightly. 'What do you mean, we can't get married? Is it because of the things I said? Milly, I'm just so sorry. I'll do anything I can to make it up. But don't give up on us just because of that!'

'It's not about that!' said Milly. 'Yes, you hurt me. But I told you, I forgive you.' Simon stared at her.

'Well, what, then?'

'It's more basic than that. It's . . . us. You and me as a couple, full stop.' She gave a small shrug and began to walk off.

'What's wrong with you and me as a couple?' said Simon, starting to follow her. 'Milly, talk to me! Don't just run away!'

'I'm not running away!' said Milly, wheeling round to face him. 'But there's no point talking about it. Take it from me, it just wouldn't work. So let's act with a little dignity, shall we? Goodbye, Simon.'

She paused, then began to walk quickly off again.

'Fuck dignity!' exclaimed Simon, hurrying after her. 'I'm not going to just let you walk out of my life like that! Milly, I love you. I want to marry you. Don't you love me? Have you stopped loving me? If you have, just tell me!'

'It's not that!' said Milly.

'Then what's wrong!' His voice jabbed at the back of her head. 'What's wrong?'

'OK!' said Milly, suddenly stopping. 'OK!' She closed her eyes, then opened them and looked straight at him. 'What's wrong is that . . . I haven't been honest with you. Ever.'

'I told you, I don't care about that,' said Simon. 'You can have ten husbands for all I care!'

'I'm not talking about Allan,' said Milly desperately. 'I'm talking about all the other lies I've told you.' Her words rose into the evening air like birds escaping. 'Lies, lies, lies!'

Simon stared at her in discomposure. He swallowed, and pushed his hair back.

'What lies?'

'You see?' cried Milly. 'You have no idea! You have no idea who I really am! You don't know the real Milly Havill.'

'Kepinski,' said Simon.

Milly's eyes narrowed; she turned round and began to stride away.

'I'm sorry,' said Simon at once. 'I didn't mean it! Milly, come back!'

'It's no good!' said Milly, shaking her head. 'It won't work. I can't do it any more.'

'What are you talking about?' exclaimed Simon, hurrying after her.

'I can't be what you think I am! I can't be your perfect Barbie doll.'

'I don't treat you like a fucking Barbie doll!' said Simon in outrage. 'Jesus! I treat you like an intelligent, mature woman!'

'Yes!' cried Milly, turning with a spatter of gravel. 'And that's the trouble! You treat me like some thinking man's version of a Barbie doll. You want an attractive intelligent woman who wears expensive shoes and thinks soap operas are trivial and knows all about the effect of the exchange rate on European imports. Well, I can't be her! I thought I could turn into her, but I can't! I just can't!'

'What?' said Simon, staring at her in astonishment. 'What the hell are you talking about?'

'Simon, I can't live up to your expectations any more.' Tears sprang to Milly's eyes and she brushed them away impatiently. 'I can't play a part all my life. I can't be something I'm not. Rupert tried to do that, and look where it got him!'

'Milly, I don't want you to be something you're not. I want you to be you.'

'You can't want that. You don't even know me.'

'Of course I know you!'

'You don't,' said Milly despairingly. 'Simon, I keep trying to tell you. I've been lying to you ever since we first met.'

'About what?'

'About everything!'

'You've been lying to me about *everything*?'

'Yes.'

'Like what, for Christ's sake?'

'Everything!'

'Name one thing.'

'OK.' Milly paused, and ran a shaky hand through her hair. 'I don't like sushi.'

There was a stupefied silence.

'Is that it?' said Simon eventually. 'You don't like sushi?'

'Of course that's not it,' said Milly quickly. 'Bad example. I . . . I never read the newspapers. I only pretend to.'

'So what?' said Simon.

'And I don't understand modern art. And I watch terrible TV.'

'Like what?' said Simon, laughing.

'Things you've never heard of! Like . . . like *Family Fortunes*!'

'Milly—' Simon began to walk towards her.

'And I . . . I buy cheap shoes and don't show you them.'

'So what?'

'What do you mean, so what?' Angry tears started to Milly's eyes. 'All this time, I've been pretending to be something that I'm not. At that party, where we first met, I didn't really know about vivisection! I saw it on *Blue Peter*!'

Simon stopped still. There was a long silence.

'You saw it on *Blue Peter*,' he said at last.

'Yes,' said Milly tearfully. 'A *Blue Peter* special.'

With a sudden roar, Simon threw back his head, and began to laugh.

'It's not funny!' said Milly indignantly.

'Yes it is!' said Simon through his laughter. 'It's very funny!'

'No it's not!' cried Milly. 'All this time, I've been feeling guilty about it. Don't you understand? I've been pretending to be mature and intelligent. And I fooled you. But I'm not intelligent. I'm just not!'

Simon abruptly stopped laughing.

'Milly, are you serious?'

'Of course I am,' said Milly, in tears. 'I'm not clever! I'm not bright!'

'Yes you are.'

'No I'm not! Not like Isobel.'

'Like *Isobel*?' echoed Simon incredulously. 'You think Isobel's bright? How bright is it to get knocked up by your boyfriend?' He raised his eyebrows at Milly and suddenly she gave a little giggle.

'Isobel may be intellectual,' said Simon. 'But you're the brightest star of your family.'

'Really?' said Milly in a little voice.

'Really. And even if you weren't – even if you had only one brain cell to call your own – I'd still love you. I love *you*, Milly. Not your IQ.'

'You can't possibly love me,' said Milly jerkily. 'You don't . . .'

'Know you?' said Simon. 'Of course I know you.' He sighed. 'Milly, knowing a person isn't like knowing a string of facts. It's more like . . . a feeling.' He lifted his hand and gently pushed back a strand of her hair. 'I can feel when you're going to laugh and when you're going to cry. I can feel your kindness and your warmth and your sense of humour. I feel all that inside me. And that's what matters. Not sushi. Not modern art. Not *Family Fortunes*.' He paused, then said in a deadpan voice, ' "Our survey said . . ." '

Milly gaped at him.

'Do you *watch* it?'

'I catch it occasionally.' He grinned. 'Come on, Milly, I'm allowed to be human, too. Aren't I?'

There was silence. In the distance a clock chimed. Milly exhaled shakily and said, almost to herself, 'I could do with—'

'A cigarette?' interrupted Simon, Milly raised her head to look at him, then gave a tiny shrug.

'Maybe,' she said.

'Come on,' said Simon, grinning. 'Did I get that right? Doesn't that prove I know you?'

'Maybe.'

'Admit it! I know you! I know when you want a cigarette. That's got to be true love. Hasn't it?'

There was a pause, then Milly said again, 'Maybe.' She reached in her pocket for her cigarette packet and allowed Simon to cradle the flame of her lighter from the wind.

'So,' he said, as she inhaled her first drag.

'So,' said Milly.

There was a still, tense silence. Milly took another drag, not meeting Simon's eyes.

'I was thinking,' said Simon.

'What?'

'If you'd like to, we could go and get some pizza. And maybe . . .' He paused. 'You could tell me a little bit about yourself.'

'OK,' said Milly. She blew out a cloud of smoke and gave him half a smile. 'That would be nice.'

'You do like pizza,' added Simon.

'Yes,' said Milly. 'I do.'

'You're not just pretending, to impress me.'

'Simon,' said Milly. 'Shut up.'

'I'll go and get the car,' he said, feeling in his pocket for his keys.

'No, wait,' said Milly, waving her cigarette at him. 'Let's walk. I feel like walking. And . . . talking.' Simon stared at her.

'All the way into Bath?'

'Why not?'

'It's three miles!'

'You see, that just shows,' said Milly. 'You don't know me. I can walk three miles. At school I was in the cross-country team.'

'But it's bloody freezing!'

'We'll warm up as we walk. Come on, Simon.' She put her hand on his arm. 'I really want to.'

'OK,' said Simon, putting away his car keys. 'Fine. Let's walk.'

'They're going into the garden,' said Isobel. 'Together.' She turned back from the window. 'But they haven't kissed yet.'

'Maybe they don't want an audience,' said Harry. 'Especially a nosy older sister.'

'They don't know I'm watching!' retorted Isobel. 'I've been very careful. Oh. They've gone now.' She bit her lip and sat back on the window-seat. 'I hope . . . you know.'

'Relax,' said Harry from his seat by the fire.

'Everything will be fine.' Isobel looked at him. He had a piece of paper in his hand and a pen.

'What are you doing?' she asked. Harry glanced up and saw her gazing at him.

'Nothing,' he said, and quickly folded the piece of paper in two.

'Show me!' said Isobel.

'It's nothing important,' said Harry, and began to put the paper in his pocket. But Isobel was across the room in a moment, and whipped it out of his grasp.

'It's just a few names that sprang to mind,' said Harry stiffly, as she uncrumpled it. 'I thought I'd jot them down.'

Isobel stared down at the page and started to laugh.

'Harry, you're mad!' she said. 'We've got seven months to think about it!' She looked down the list, smiling at some of the names and pulling faces at others. Then she turned over the paper. 'And what's all this?'

'Oh that,' said Harry. A slightly shamefaced look came to his face. 'That was just in case we have twins.'

Milly and Simon were walking slowly through the gardens of Pinnacle Hall, towards a wrought-iron gate which opened onto the main road.

'This isn't at all what I was supposed to be doing tonight,' said Milly, gazing up into the starry sky. 'Tonight, I was supposed to be having a quiet supper at home and packing my honeymoon case.'

'I was supposed to be smoking a cigar with Dad and having second thoughts,' said Simon.

'And are you?' said Milly. 'Having second thoughts?'

'Are you?' rejoined Simon.

Milly said nothing, but continued to stare at the sky. They carried on walking silently, past the rose garden, past the frozen fountain and into the orchard.

'There it is,' said Simon, suddenly stopping. 'The bench. Where I proposed to you.' He glanced at her. 'Remember?' Milly stiffened slightly.

'Yes,' she said. 'Of course I remember. You had the ring in your pocket. And the champagne ready in the tree stump.'

'I spent days planning it,' said Simon reminiscently. He went over and patted the stump. 'I wanted it to be perfect.'

Milly stared at him, clenching her fists by her sides. Honesty, she told herself furiously. Be honest.

'It was too perfect,' she said bluntly.

'What?' Simon's head jerked up in shock and Milly felt a stab of guilt.

'Simon, I'm sorry,' she said at once. 'I didn't mean it.' She walked a little way away from him and looked into the trees. 'It was lovely.'

'Milly, don't pretend,' said Simon, his voice stiff with hurt. 'Tell me the truth. What did you really think?'

There was a pause.

'Well, OK,' said Milly at last. 'If I'm really going to be honest, it was beautiful – but . . .' She turned round to face him. 'Just a bit too planned. You had the ring on my finger before I could take a breath. The next minute, you're cracking open the champagne and we're officially engaged. I never . . .' She broke off and rubbed her face. 'I never had time to think about it.'

There was silence.

'I see,' said Simon at last. 'And if you'd had time to think, what would you have said?' Milly looked at him for a few long seconds, then turned away.

'Come on,' she said. 'Let's go and get that pizza.'

'OK,' said Simon, his voice tinged with disappointment. 'OK.' He took a few steps, then stopped. 'And you're quite sure you want to walk.'

'Yes,' said Milly. 'Walking always clears my head.' She held out her hand. 'Come on.'

Half an hour later, in the middle of the dark road, Milly stopped.

'Simon?' she said in a little voice. 'I'm cold.'

'Well, let's walk more quickly then.'

'And my feet hurt. My shoes are giving me blisters.'

Simon stopped, and looked at her. She had wrapped her hands in the ends of her jersey sleeves and buried them under her armpits; her lips were trembling and her teeth were chattering.

'Is your head clear?' he asked.

'No,' said Milly miserably. 'It's not. All I can think about is a nice hot bath.'

'Well, it's not long now,' said Simon cheerfully. Milly peered ahead at the black, unlit road.

'I can't go on any more. Are there any taxis?'

'I don't think so,' said Simon. 'But you can have my jacket.' He took it off and Milly grabbed it, snuggling into the warm lining. 'Won't you be cold?' she said vaguely

'I'll be all right,' said Simon. 'Shall we go on?'

'OK,' said Milly, and began to hobble forward again. Simon stopped, and looked at her.

'Is that the best you can do?'

'My feet are *bleeding*,' wailed Milly. Simon's eyes fell on her feet.

'Are those new shoes?'

'Yes,' said Milly dolefully. 'And they were very cheap. And now I hate them.' She took another step forward and winced. Simon sighed.

'Come here,' he said. 'Put your feet on my feet. I'll walk you for a bit.'

'Really?'

'Come here. Put your shoes in your pocket.'

He grasped Milly firmly round the waist and began to stride awkwardly forward into the night, carrying her feet on his own.

'This is nice,' said Milly after a while.

'Yes,' grunted Simon. 'It's great.'

'You walk very quickly, don't you?'

'I do when I'm hungry.'

'I'm sorry about this,' said Milly in a subdued voice. 'It was a nice idea though, wasn't it?' There was a pause, and she turned round, nearly throwing Simon off balance altogether. 'Wasn't it, Simon?'

Simon began to laugh, his voice hoarse from the evening air.

'Yes, Milly,' he said at last, almost gasping with the effort of speaking. 'One of your best.'

When they finally arrived at the pizza restaurant, they were both nearly speechless with cold and effort. As they opened the door, the warmth of the air and the garlic-laden smell of food hit them in the face in an intoxicating blast. The place was full, buzzing with people and music; the cold dark road suddenly seemed a million miles away.

'A table for two, please,' said Simon, depositing Milly on the floor. 'And two large brandies.'

Milly smiled at him, rubbing her cold, reddened cheeks.

'You know, my feet feel a bit better now,' she said, trying them out experimentally on the marble floor. 'I think I'll be able to walk to the table.'

'Good,' said Simon, stretching his back. 'That's great.'

They were shown to a booth by a red-dressed waiter, who immediately returned with the two brandies.

'Cheers,' said Milly. She met Simon's eyes hesitantly. 'I don't quite know what we're toasting. Here's to . . . the wedding we never had?'

'Let's toast us,' said Simon, looking at her suddenly seriously. 'Let's toast us. Milly—'

'What?'

There was silence. Milly's heart began to thump. Nervously, she began to shred her paper napkin.

'I haven't planned this,' said Simon. 'God knows I haven't planned this. But I can't wait any longer.'

He put down his menu and sank to one knee on the floor beside the booth. There was a slight flurry around the restaurant as people looked over and began to nudge each other.

'Milly, please,' said Simon. 'I'm asking you again. And I . . . I hope beyond hope that you'll say yes. Will you marry me?'

There was a long silence. At last Milly looked up. Her cheeks were tinged a rosy pink; her napkin was a red papery mess in her fingers.

'Simon, I don't know,' she said. 'I . . . I need to think about it.'

As they came to the end of their pizzas, Milly cleared her throat and looked nervously at Simon.

'How was your pizza?' she said in a dry voice.

'Fine,' said Simon. 'Yours?'

'Fine.' Their eyes met very briefly; then Simon looked away.

'Do you . . .' he began. 'Have you . . .'

'Yes,' said Milly, biting her lip. 'I've finished thinking.'

Her gaze ran over him – still kneeling on the floor beside the table, as he had been throughout the meal, his food spread around him like a picnic. A tiny smile came to her face.

'Would you like to get up now?' she said.

'Whatever for?' said Simon, taking a swig from his glass of wine. 'I'm very comfortable down here.'

'I'm sure you are,' said Milly, her lips trembling. 'I'm sure you are. I just thought . . . you might want to kiss me.'

There was a tense silence.

'Might I?' said Simon eventually. Slowly he put down his wine glass and raised his eyes to hers. For a few moments they just gazed at each other, unaware of the waiters nudging one another and calling into the kitchen; oblivious of anything but themselves. 'Might I really?'

'Yes,' said Milly, trying to control her shaking voice. 'You might.' She put down her napkin, slid down off her seat beside him onto the marble floor and wrapped her arms around his neck. As her lips met his there was a small ripple of applause from around the restaurant. Tears began to stream down Milly's cheeks, onto Simon's neck and into their mingled mouths. She closed her eyes and leaned against his broad chest, inhaling the scent of his skin, suddenly too weak to move a muscle. She felt drained of all energy, emptied of all emotion; unable to cope with anything more.

'Just one question,' said Simon into her ear. 'Who's going to tell your mother?'

EIGHTEEN

At nine o'clock the next morning the air was bright and crisp. As Milly's little car pulled up outside 1 Bertram Street, the postman was about to push a bundle of letters through the letterbox.

'Morning!' he said, turning round. 'How's the bride?'

'Fine,' said Milly, giving him a tight little smile. She took the letters from him, reached inside her pocket for her key then paused. Her heart was beating in a mixture of anticipation and dread, and a thousand introductory phrases whirled around her mind. She stared for a few seconds at the shiny gloss of the front door, then put her key into the lock.

'Mummy?' she called as she entered, her voice high with nerves. 'Mummy?' She put the letters down on the hall stand and took off her coat, trying to stay calm. But suddenly excitement was bubbling through her like soda, and she could feel a wide grin licking across her face. She felt like laughing and singing and jumping up and down like a little girl. 'Mummy, guess what?'

She threw open the door of the kitchen joyfully and felt a sudden jerk of astonishment. Her mother and father were sitting companionably together at the kitchen table, both still in their dressing gowns, as though they were on holiday.

'Oh,' she said, not quite sure why she felt so surprised.

'Milly!' exclaimed Olivia, putting down her paper. 'Are you all right?'

'We assumed you stayed the night at Harry's,' said James.

'Have you had breakfast?' said Olivia. 'Let me get you some coffee – and how about some nice toast?'

'Yes,' said Milly. 'I mean, no. Look, listen!' She pushed a hand through her hair, and the smile returned to her face. 'I need to tell you some good news. Simon and I are going to get married!'

'Oh, darling!' cried Olivia. 'That's wonderful!'

'So you made up with him,' said James. 'I'm very glad to hear it. He's a good chap.'

'I know he is,' said Milly. A smile spread across her face. 'And I love him. And he loves me. And it's all lovely again.'

'This is simply marvellous!' said Olivia. She picked up her mug and took a sip of coffee. 'When were you thinking of having the wedding?'

'In two hours' time,' said Milly happily.

'What?' exclaimed Olivia, dropping her mug down on the table with a little crash.

'Milly, are you serious?' said James. 'This morning?'

'Yes! This morning!' said Milly. 'Why not?'

'Why not?' said Olivia, her voice rising in panic. 'Because nothing's arranged! Because we've cancelled everything! I'm very sorry, darling, but there isn't a wedding to have any more!'

'Mummy, we've got everything we need for a wedding,' said Milly. 'A bride and a groom. Someone to give me away' – she looked at James – 'and someone to wear a big hat and cry. We've even got the wedding cake. We don't need any more than that.'

'But Canon Lytton—'

'We told him last night,' said Milly. 'In fact, it's all arranged. So come on!' She gestured to the pair of them. 'Get dressed! Get ready!'

'Wait!' called Olivia, as Milly disappeared out of the kitchen door. 'What about Simon? He hasn't got a best man!' The door opened and Milly's face appeared again.

'Yes he has,' she said. 'He's got a jolly fine best man.'

'It's all very easy,' said Simon, taking a gulp of coffee. 'Here are the rings. When the vicar asks you for them, you just hand them over. And that's it!'

'Right,' said Harry heavily. He took the two gold bands from Simon and stared at them for a couple of seconds as though trying to commit their form to memory. 'The vicar asks me for the rings, and I hand them over. Do I hold them out on the palm of my hand, or in my fingers, or what?'

'I don't know,' said Simon. 'Does it matter?'

'I don't know!' said Harry. 'You tell me! Jesus!'

'Dad, you're not nervous, are you?' said Simon.

'Of course I'm not fucking nervous!' said Harry. 'Now go on. Go and shine your shoes.'

'See you later,' said Simon at the kitchen door, and grinned back at Harry.

'*Are* you nervous? Said Isobel, from the window-seat, when Simon had gone.

'No,' said Harry, then looked up. 'Maybe a bit.' He pushed back his chair abruptly and strode over to the window. 'It's ridiculous. I shouldn't be Simon's best man, for Christ's sake!'

'Yes you should,' said Isobel. 'He wants you.'

'He hasn't got anyone else, you mean. So he asks his old dad.'

'No, that's not what I mean,' said Isobel patiently. 'He could easily phone up a friend from work. You know he could. But he wants you. You *are* his best man. And mine.' She reached for his hand and after a moment he squeezed hers. Then she glanced at her watch and pulled a face. 'And now I really must go. Mummy will be having kittens.'

'I'll see you there, then,' said Harry.

'See you there,' said Isobel. At the door, she turned back.

'Of course, you know what the perk of being the best man is.'

'What's that?'

'You get to sleep with the chief bridesmaid.'

'Is that so?' said Harry, brightening.

'It's in all the rule books,' said Isobel. 'Ask the vicar. He'll tell you.'

As she went into the hall, she saw Rupert coming down the stairs. Unaware that he was being watched, his face was full of an unformed grief; a raw misery that made Isobel's spine prickle unpleasantly. For a few moments she stood silently, saying nothing. Then, suddenly feeling like a voyeur, she forced herself to make a sound with her foot and pause for a moment before walking forward, giving him a chance to gather his thoughts before he saw her.

'Hello,' she said. 'We were wondering if you were all right. Did you sleep well?'

'Great, thanks,' said Rupert, nodding. 'Very kind of Harry to put me up.'

'Oh my God,' said Isobel. 'That was nothing! It was very kind of you to come all this way to tell Milly about . . .' She tailed off awkwardly. 'You know the wedding's back on?'

'No,' said Rupert. He gave her a strained smile. 'That's great news. Really great.' Isobel stared at him in compassion, wanting somehow to make everything right for him.

'You know, I'm sure Milly would want you to come,' she said. 'It isn't going to be a big, smart wedding any more. Just the six of us, in fact. But if you'd like to, we'd all be delighted if you could come.'

'That's very kind,' said Rupert after a pause. 'Very kind

354

indeed. But . . . I think I might go home instead. If you don't mind.'

'Of course not,' said Isobel. 'Absolutely. Whatever you want.' She looked around the empty hall. 'I'll find someone to drive you to the station. There's a fast London train every hour.'

'I'm not going to London,' said Rupert. A distant, almost peaceful expression came to his face. 'I'm going home. To Cornwall.'

By ten-thirty, Olivia was fully dressed and made up. She peered at her reflection in the mirror and gave a satisfied smile. Her bright pink suit fitted perfectly and the matching wide-brimmed hat cast a rosy glow over her face. Her blond hair shone brightly in the winter sunshine as she turned her face this way and that, checking for make-up imperfections and fluff on the black velvet collar of her jacket. Finally she turned away and picked up her bag, noticing with pleasure the handmade pink silk bows now decorating her patent leather shoes.

'You look stupendous!' said James, coming in.

'And you look very handsome,' said Olivia, running her eyes over his morning coat. 'Very distinguished. Father of the bride.'

'Mother of the bride,' rejoined James, grinning at her. 'Speaking of which, where I she?'

'Still getting ready,' said Olivia. 'Isobel's helping her.'

'Well then,' said James, 'I suggest we go and partake of a little pre-wedding champagne. Shall we?' He held out his arm and, after a moment's hesitation, Olivia took it. As they descended the stairs into the hall, a voice stopped them.

'Hold it. Just for a second. Don't look at me.'

They paused, smiling at each other while Alexander snapped away for a few seconds.

'OK,' he said. 'You can carry on now.' As Olivia passed him, he winked at her. 'Great hat, Olivia. Very sexy.'

'Thank you, Alexander,' said Olivia, a slight blush coming to her cheeks. James squeezed her arm and her blush deepened.

'Come on,' she said quickly. 'Let's have the champagne.'

They went into the drawing room, where a fire was crackling and James had laid out a champagne bottle and glasses. He handed her a glass and raised his own.

'Here's to the wedding,' he said.

'The wedding,' said Olivia. She sipped at her champagne, then sat down gingerly on the edge of a chair, being careful not to crease her skirt. 'Are we having speeches at the reception?'

'I don't know,' said James humorously. 'Are we having a reception?' Olivia shrugged and took a sip of champagne.

'Who knows? It's up to Milly. This is her day now.' A flicker of emotion passed over her face. 'I'm just another guest.' James met her eyes compassionately.

'Do you mind?' he said. 'Do you mind that we aren't having the big lavish wedding that you planned? The ice swans and the organist flown in from Geneva and the five thousand VIPs?'

'No,' said Olivia after a pause. 'I don't mind.' She smiled brightly at James. 'They're getting married. That's the important thing, isn't it? They're getting married.'

'Yes,' said James. 'That's the important thing.'

There was a pause. Olivia stared into the fire, cradling her drink.

'And you know,' she said suddenly, 'in many ways, it's more *original* to have a tiny, private wedding. Big weddings can become rather vulgar if one isn't careful. Don't you think?'

'Absolutely,' said James, smiling.

'One might almost have planned this all along!' said Olivia, happiness starting to edge her voice. 'After all, we don't want the world and all its riff-raff at the wedding of our daughter, do we? We want an intimate, exclusive wedding.'

'Well, it'll certain be intimate,' said James, draining his glass. 'I'm not sure about exclusive.'

There was a sound at the door and he looked up. Isobel was standing in the doorway, dressed in a long flowing column of pale pink silk. Her hair was wreathed in flowers and her cheeks were self-consciously flushed.

'I've come to announce the bride,' she said. 'She's ready.'

'You look wonderful, darling!' exclaimed James.

'Absolutely beautiful!' said Olivia. Isobel shrugged.

'I look all right,' she said. 'You should see Milly. Come and watch her walking down the stairs. Alexander is taking pictures.'

357

'Darling,' said Olivia sharply, as Isobel turned to go. 'What happened to the roses?'

'What roses?'

'The silk roses that were on your dress!'

'Oh, those,' said Isobel after a pause. 'They . . . fell off.'

'Fell off?'

'Yes,' said Isobel. 'You can't have sewn them on very well.' She looked at Olivia's perplexed face and grinned. 'Come on, Mummy. The roses don't matter. Come and see Milly. She's the main attraction.'

They all filed into the hall and looked up the stairs. Coming slowly down, smiling shyly through her veil, was Milly, wearing a starkly cut dress of ivory satin. The stiff, embroidered bodice was laced tightly around her figure; the long sleeves were edged at the wrist with fur; in her hair sparkled a diamond tiara.

'Milly!' said Olivia shakily. 'You look perfect. A perfect bride.' Tears suddenly filled her eyes and she turned away.

'What do you think?' said Milly tremulously, looking around at them all. 'Will I do?'

'Darling, you look exquisite,' said James. 'Simon Pinnacle can count himself a very lucky young man.'

'I can't believe it's really happening,' said Olivia, holding a tiny hanky to her eyes. 'Little Milly. Getting married.'

'How are we all going to get there?' said Alexander, taking a final picture. 'I want to take my tripod with me.'

'Milly?' said James, looking up at her. 'It's your show.'

'I don't know,' said Milly, a perturbed expression

coming over her face. She descended a few steps, her train falling behind her. 'I hadn't thought about it.'

'Let's walk!' said Isobel, grinning at her.

'Shut up, Isobel,' said Milly. 'Oh God. What are we going to do?'

'If we take both cars,' said James, looking at Olivia, 'you could drive Alexander and Isobel, and I could come on with Milly . . .'

He was interrupted by a ring at the front door and they all looked up.

'Who on earth—' said James. He looked around, then silently went to open it. A man holding a peaked cap under his arm was standing on the steps. He bowed, stiffly.

'Wedding cars for Havill,' he said.

'What?' James peered past him onto the street. 'But these were cancelled!'

'No they weren't,' said the man. James turned back.

'Olivia,' he said. 'Didn't you cancel the wedding cars?'

'Of course I did,' said Olivia crisply.

'Not according to my information,' said the man.

'Not according to your information,' echoed Olivia, shaking her head in exasperation. 'Does it ever occur to you people that your information might be wrong? I spoke to a young woman at your company only yesterday and she assured me that everything would be cancelled. So what I suggest is that you get back in your car, and speak to whoever mans the telephone, and sure enough, you will find—'

'Mummy!' interrupted Milly in agonized tones.

'Mummy!' She pulled a meaningful face at Olivia, who suddenly realized what she was saying.

'However,' she said, pulling herself up straight. 'By very good fortune, the situation has changed once again.'

'So you do want the cars,' said the man.

'We do,' said Olivia haughtily.

'Very good, madam,' said the man, and disappeared down the steps. As he reached the bottom, the words 'fucking nutter' travelled audibly back towards them.

'Right,' said James. 'Well, you lot go off . . . and Milly and I will follow. Isn't that the protocol?'

'See you there,' said Isobel, grinning at Milly. 'Good luck!'

As they descended the steps to the waiting cars, Alexander drew Isobel back slightly.

'You know, I'd really like to take some shots of you on your own some time,' he said. 'You've got fantastic cheekbones.'

'Oh really?' said Isobel, raising her eyebrows. 'Is that what you say to all the girls?'

'No,' said Alexander. 'Only the stunning ones.' He looked at her. 'I'm serious.'

Isobel stared at him.

'Alexander—'

'I don't know if this is out of order,' he said, hoisting his tripod on his shoulder. 'But maybe, when all this wedding business is over . . . you and I could go for a drink?'

'You've got a nerve!' said Isobel.

'I know,' said Alexander. 'Do you want to?'

Isobel began to laugh.

'I'm very flattered,' she said. 'I'm also pregnant.'

'Oh.' He shrugged. 'That doesn't matter.'

'And . . .' she added, a faint tinge coming to her cheeks, '. . . I'm going to get married.'

'What?' Ten yards ahead of them, Olivia wheeled round on the pavement, her eyes bright. 'Isobel! Are you serious?'

Isobel rolled her eyes at Alexander.

'It's just an idea, Mummy,' she said in a louder voice. 'It isn't definite.'

'But who is he, darling? Have I met him? Do I know his name?'

Isobel gazed dumbly at Olivia. She opened her mouth to speak, closed it again, looked away and shifted on the ground.

'He's . . . he's someone I'll introduce you to later,' she said at last. 'After the wedding's finished. Let's just get that over first. All right?'

'Whatever you say, darling,' said Olivia. 'Oh, I'm so thrilled!'

'Good!' said Isobel, smiling weakly. 'That's good.'

Harry and Simon arrived at the church at ten to eleven. They pushed open the door and looked silently around the huge, empty, decorated space. Simon glanced at his father, then walked a few paces up the broad aisle, his shoes echoing on the stones.

'Aha!' said Canon Lytton, appearing out of a side

door. 'The bridegroom and his best man! Welcome!' He hurried down the aisle towards them, past the gleaming rows of empty mahogany pews, each adorned with flowers.

'Where do we sit?' said Harry, looking around. 'All the best seats are taken.'

'Very droll,' said Canon Lytton, beaming at him. 'The places for the groom and his best man are at the front, on the right-hand side.'

'This is very good of you,' said Simon, as they followed him towards the front of the church. 'To reinstate the service at such short notice. And with such small numbers. We're very grateful.'

'Numbers are immaterial,' said Canon Lytton. 'As our Lord said Himself, "Where two or three have met together in my name, I am there among them"' He paused. 'Of course, the collection plate may suffer a little as a result . . .' He broke off delicately, and Harry cleared his throat.

'Naturally, I'll make up the shortfall,' he said. 'If you give me some kind of estimate.'

'So kind,' murmured Canon Lytton. 'Ah, here comes Mrs Blenkins, our organist. You were very fortunate that she was free this morning!'

An elderly woman in a brown anorak was walking up the aisle towards them.

'I haven't practised anything up,' she said as soon as she reached them. 'There hasn't been the time, you see.'

'Of course not,' said Simon at once. 'We completely—'

'Will "Here Comes the Bride" do you?'

'Absolutely,' said Simon, glancing at Harry. 'Whatever. Thanks very much. We're very grateful.' The woman nodded, and marched off, and Canon Lytton disappeared in a rustle of linen.

Simon sat down on the front pew and stretched his legs out in front of him.

'I'm terrified,' he said.

'So am I,' said Harry, giving a little shudder. 'That priest gives me the creeps.'

'Will I be a good husband?' Simon threw back his head and looked into the cavernous space of the church. 'Will I make Milly happy?'

'You already do make her happy,' said Harry. 'Just don't change anything. Don't think you have to act differently because you're married.' He met Simon's eye. 'You love her. That's enough for anyone.'

There was a noise at the back of the church and Olivia appeared, a vision in bright pink. She walked up the aisle, her heels clacking lightly on the floor.

'They'll be here in a minute,' she whispered.

'Come and sit beside me,' said Harry, patting the pew. For an instant, Olivia wavered.

'No,' she said regretfully. 'It wouldn't be right. I have to sit on the other side.' She lifted her chin slightly. 'Since I am the mother of the bride.'

She sat down, and there was a few minutes' silence. From out of nowhere the organ began to play quietly. Simon stretched out his fingers and stared hard at them. Harry looked at his watch. Olivia brought out a compact and checked her reflection.

Suddenly there was a rattling at the back of the church and they all jumped.

Simon took a deep breath, trying to steady his nerves. But his heart was pounding and his palms felt damp.

'Do you think we should stand up?' he whispered to his father.

'I don't know!' hissed back Harry. He looked equally agitated. 'How the fuck do I know?'

Olivia turned and peered towards the back of the church.

'I can see her!' she whispered. 'She's here!'

The organ music slowed down, then stopped altogether. Looking hesitantly at each other, the three of them stood up. There was an agonized silence; no-one seemed to be breathing.

Then the familiar chords of Wagner's Wedding March swelled into the air. Simon felt a lump coming to his throat. Not daring to look round, he stared ahead, blinking furiously, until he felt Harry tugging his sleeve. Very slowly he swivelled his head round until he was looking down the aisle, and felt his heart stop. There was Milly on her father's arm, looking more beautiful than he'd ever seen her. Her lips were parted in a tremulous smile; her eyes were sparkling behind her veil; her skin glowed against the pale creaminess of her dress.

As she reached his side she stopped. She hesitated, then, with trembling hands, slowly lifted the gauzy veil from her face. As she did so, her fingers brushed the necklace of freshwater pearls she was wearing. She paused, holding one of the tiny pearls, and for a few moments her eyes dimmed.

Then she let go of it, took a deep breath and looked up.

'Ready?' said Simon.

'Yes,' said Milly, and smiled at him. 'I'm ready.'

As Rupert arrived at the little cottage perched on the cliffs, it was nearly midday. He glanced at his watch as he walked up the path, and thought to himself that Milly would be married by now. She and Simon would be drinking champagne, as happy as two people could ever be.

The door opened before he reached it, and his father looked out.

'Hello, my boy,' he said kindly. 'I've been expecting you.'

'Hello, Father,' said Rupert, and put down his briefcase to give his father a hug. As he met the older man's mild, unquestioning gaze, he felt his defences crumble completely, as though he might suddenly burst into unstoppable sobs. But his emotions were run dry; he was beyond tears now.

'Come and have a nice cup of tea,' said his father, leading the way into the tiny sitting room, overlooking the sea. He paused. 'Your wife called today, wondered if you were here. She said to tell you she was sorry. And she sends you her love and prayers.'

Rupert said nothing. He sat down by the window and looked out at the empty blue sea. It occurred to him that he'd almost completely forgotten about Francesca.

'You also had a call from another young woman a few days ago,' called his father from the tiny kitchen. There was a clatter of crockery. 'Milly, I think her name was. Did she manage to track you down?'

The flicker of something like a smile passed across Rupert's face.

'Yes,' he said. 'She tracked me down.'

'I hadn't heard of her before,' said his father, coming in with a teapot. 'Is she an old friend of yours?'

'Not really,' said Rupert. 'Just . . .' He paused. 'Just the wife of a friend of mine.'

And he leaned back in his chair and stared out of the window at the waves breaking on the rocks below.

THE END

Sleeping Arrangements

SOPHIE KINSELLA
writing as **MADELEINE WICKHAM**

Chloe needs a holiday. She's sick of making wedding dresses and her partner is having trouble at work. Her wealthy friend Gerard has offered the loan of his luxury villa in Spain – perfect.

Hugh is not a happy man. His immaculate wife seems more interested in the granite for the new kitchen than in him, and he works so hard to pay for it all, he barely has time to see their children. But his old schoolfriend Gerard has lent them a luxury villa in Spain – perfect.

Both families arrive at the villa and get a shock: Gerard has double-booked. An uneasy week of sharing begins, and tensions soon mount in the soaring heat. But there's also a secret history between the families – and as tempers fray, an old passion begins to resurface...

'Lightness of touch and witty observation make this a perfect holiday read'
Sunday Mirror

Visit

www.sophiekinsella.co.uk

The official website of

SOPHIE KINSELLA

for more on all the Sophie Kinsella and Madeleine Wickham novels.
You'll find updates from Sophie, news, videos, audio clips,
downloads and some great prizes up for grabs.

Plus keep up to date with all the latest news on Sophie's books,
events and more with Sophie's official e-mail newsletter.